About the A

Sarah Darmody is the author of *Fil*
employment excursions have been
film production, the depths of Middle Eastern toilet cleaning,
and the big-grin thrill of working full-time with firefighters.
Raised in Sydney but at home in the world, she now lives in
Melbourne, where her cravings for long stories, good coffee, the
affections of stray cats and the Boy can all be satisfied.

★ TICKET TO RIDE ★

Sarah Darmody

BANTAM
SYDNEY • AUCKLAND • TORONTO • NEW YORK • LONDON

TICKET TO RIDE
A BANTAM BOOK

First published in Australia and New Zealand in 2005
by Bantam

National Library of Australia
Cataloguing-in-Publication Entry

Darmody, Sarah Jane.
Ticket to ride.

ISBN 1 86325 525 7.

1. Darmody, Sarah Jane – Journeys – United States. 2. Bus
travel – United States. 3. United States – Description and
travel. I. Title.

917.304

Transworld Publishers,
a division of Random House Australia Pty Ltd
20 Alfred Street, Milsons Point, NSW 2061
http://www.randomhouse.com.au

Random House New Zealand Limited
18 Poland Road, Glenfield, Auckland

Transworld Publishers,
a division of The Random House Group Ltd
61-63 Uxbridge Road, Ealing, London W5 5SA

Random House Inc
1745 Broadway, New York, New York 10036

Cover design by Christabella Designs
Cover photographs courtesy Getty Images
Internal design by Darian Causby/Highway 51 Design Works
Map by Andrew Buchanan
Typeset by Midland Typesetters, Maryborough, Victoria
Printed and bound by Griffin Press, Netley, South Australia

10 9 8 7 6 5 4 3 2 1

'Do I contradict myself?
Very well, then, I contradict myself;
I am large – I contain multitudes.'

Walt Whitman
Song of Myself

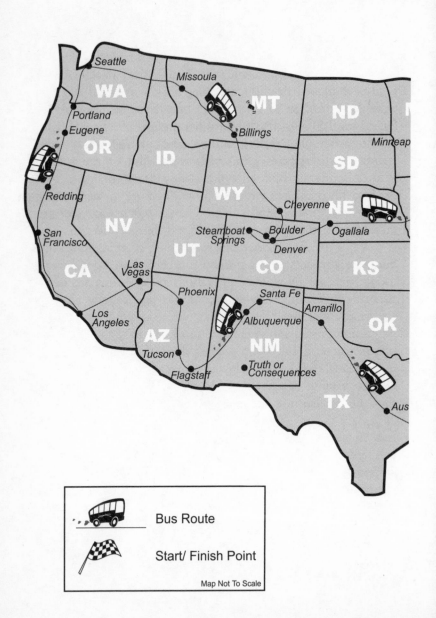

Bus Route

Start/ Finish Point

Map Not To Scale

Continental USA

Contents

Chapter 1

Winning isn't everything

They say a story that begins on a Greyhound bus can only end in the Big House, the poorhouse, or the outhouse. I've decided to start mine a bit further back.

Historically, I don't win things. Not three-legged races, lucky door prizes, instant scratchies or drunken snooker. It has just been confirmed that Dad rigged the triumphant treasure hunt at my sixth birthday party, and I won't count my 'bronze star' for a supermarket art competition in which there were only three entrants. It reeks of pity. I am never the sixteenth caller. I never find five bucks down the back of the couch. I'm not a loser or anything, don't get me wrong. I do okay. I'm even kind of hip. I just never win.

There's a difference.

I hope.

So you can imagine my total, complete, knee-trembling surprise when I won an entire nation. Correct. An actual, factual, rocks and soil, flag and anthem *country*. And not just any country, mind you. Not tiny Kiribati, or one of those European nations with half a train station and two cows. Not some distant camel-tethering post like Kyrgyzstan, and not some fake-country tax haven either. I won a big country. A fat country. A country with states as big as other people's countries (50 of them, in fact). I won America.

*

On 23 April 2002, my evening date with *Buffy the Vampire Slayer* and a cup of Irish Breakfast is interrupted by a letter from the US Immigration and Naturalization Service. It informs me that after a lifetime of prize-winning ineptitude, my name has been pulled out of the hat for something other than designated driver. My name has been pulled out of a hat the size of a suburb, from a pool of over 6.5 million entries. 'Congratulations!' the letter reads. 'You are among those randomly selected and registered for further consideration in the DV-2003!' This sounds very much like a sports car, and I am intrigued, reading on to learn how being selected for the less sexy-sounding 'diversity immigrant program for fiscal year 2003' is indeed very much like winning a sports car. Dealer statutes and delivery charges apply, limit one per customer, colour and size may vary from actual country pictured, not to be used in conjunction with any other Nation Sweepstakes offer and further charges may be added.

It's a strange thing, winning America. Nothing quite prepares you for it. A lot travels through your mind very quickly. Krispy Kreme donuts for one, stars and stripes, skyscrapers, desert palms, baseball and yellow cabs. Old episodes of *Seinfeld*. My impatient brain launches past all the practical concerns brought about by the letter and starts to conjure up exciting American futures for me. It doesn't pause to consider that the fact I'm not already the head of a large cookie-making corporation has very little to do with geography, nor that my Australian residency is not the only reason I don't currently own a sunny loft apartment. My poor old brain doesn't care. All it knows is that we've finally won something, something very big, and it's still leaping around by the time the Boy comes in to investigate the uncharacteristic silence during *Buffy*.

I flaggle the letter around in triumph. 'I. Just. Won. *America*.'

He blinks. 'That's not from those time-share people again is it?'

The Boy is not the only sceptic. Many people have similar questions ('You won a *what*? Is that like conscription?') and

I find myself on the receiving end of the same kind of looks you might give a neighbour who's convinced he's about to become an Amway millionaire. But my prize, however dubious it may seem, is very real. Every year, just after Thanksgiving, the US State Department conducts a literal hand-in-bag lottery at 5005 Visa Crest, Migrate, Kentucky. The good people of the INS spend over a month pulling envelopes with exotic postmarks from a barrel the size of Tasmania, until they reach 55,000, just in time for the office Christmas party. This year, they pulled out mine. I have won a Green Card; the right to live and work in the United States of America.

While still coming to terms with the fact that my prize actually works, I now have to figure out how to use it, and from the moment the magic envelope is opened, the pressure is on. My winning ticket reads, 'In order to help ensure all available visas are used each year, more people are randomly selected than there are visas; thus visa issuance to you cannot be guaranteed, even if you meet all the qualifications. You must complete and return the forms below as quickly as possible.' I am reminded at every paragraph and sub-sub-heading that my vital, critical, essential, total adherence to their strict instructions is necessary in order to process me, and it's one-more-peep-out-of-you-young-lady and I'll be hit with 'failure to comply'.

There is little question that I will follow their directives. I am at the long end of 23, stumbling and stagnant for the first time after more than a few years of adventuring and good fortune. I might not be a winner, but I have been lucky; a lucky girl in a lucky country. It is surprising what a stumbling block being brought up lucky can be. I blame my parents (frankly, this is very easy to do and I recommend anyone try it when confronted with their own bone-laziness) who, as two youngsters from rural Australia, set out to see the world past the Bega Valley and the dry plains of Cooma Monaro, taking my brother and me with them before we were old enough to remember leaving. We lived in Egypt, America and Borneo before returning home to Australia with our heads full of wonders. Realising my Australian identity later in life than my primary school pals, I nevertheless to it with all the zeal of the newly converted. Mum and Dad still persisted in taking us on long-haul trips to see the world outside our own Aussie patch of paradise. They worked hard to help me head off to the United States as a university exchange student, and later to spend six months in New York as a recent film studies graduate with big career dreams. Those jerks.

Because now that I'm in charge, I realise the bar might have been set a bit high. I am barely subsisting in expensive Sydney. Working in bars, hawking denim and learning how to make the perfect chicken and mayo on white under pressure, I find myself squinting at the weekly help wanted ads with no idea what will come next – except, perhaps, insolvency. It's been a while since uni, and a longer while since I remember much about what I went there for.

The lovely Boy I'm living with is younger than me, and too young, really, to be living with his girlfriend, although too old to be living with his mama. After a whirlwind romance, the Boy had run off with me to experience that heady time in New York where it had felt like the real world was finally beginning. Back at home, we are stalled. We have joined our friends still lurking in the shadows of adulthood, wincing at the thought of being one, sullen because we can't quite get there when we want to.

So it's not quite out of the blue when the Boy tells me that sure, it's great we have an apartment together and yes, he still adores my pre-menstrual ramblings, faded sushi-print jammies and annexation of all available cupboard space, but he's thinking of heading off to school in Chile for a while, or maybe living with the lads for a bit. I beg and wail, but mostly out of envy for his surplus of plans. I have none. Correction, I am scared to make any, experiencing the oddly terrifying glut of choices available to an educated twenty-something in the land of plenty. It seems it's never too late to become a lawyer, director, composer, designer, master chef or mother of six home-schooled geniuses. Having long craved the freedom to decide things for myself, I find myself sneakily desperate for someone else to choose the right things for me. Now, with the opening of a single slender envelope, I have a *masterplan*. When my friends get together over cheap drinks and stutter about their fledging careers or final uni assignments, my contributions will be simple and confident.

'I'm heading to the US,' I can say. 'I have a Green Card to process. This is very serious and important stuff, and I'd better have another pint.' At this stage, such a clear and obvious objective is the best prize of all. The relief is staggering.

I quickly arrange to be fired from my latest job (being newly self-employed this is relatively painless) in order to devote myself full-time to translating documents in Officialese and Bureaucratian. My room begins to resemble those prison movies where formerly illiterate death-rowers sit surrounded by legal texts, mumbling and cross-referencing deep into the night. I become expert at sub-section 12, paragraph 49 (trans. 'You are never allowed to call us or ask questions.') and special clause E-19 (trans. 'Never. We mean it.')

Through outright lies, some shifty accounting practices and the suddenly convenient fact that Dad is living and working a gazillion miles away in the USA already, I fulfil many of the criteria and can move on to the medical.

There is only one doctor in Sydney who can perform a medical exam to satisfy the US Consul. When I hand this exalted medical practitioner my little yellow 'Baby's Health' card to prove my inoculations, his reaction suggests he doesn't find a hand-written piece of paper from the seventies to be the watertight evidence I had hoped for.

After giving blood in such quantities it has to be measured in cats and ponies, I am jabbed in the bum three times before learning I'm two inches shorter and two kilos heavier than I imagine. I leave off rubbing my bum just long enough to get naked and be x-rayed. Barely dressed again, the doctor asks me to open wide while he checks my mouth like a dairy cow, and then briefs me on how many ways my life will be destroyed should my HIV test be positive. I stumble out onto the streets of my home town feeling poxy and communicable. Under one sore arm is my mandatory x-ray, which I've just learnt will have to travel with me to America so that the INS can have immediate access to the inside of my bosom in order to be certain my lungs are free of some nameless contagion.

*

My farewells are brief and strange. Nobody knows quite what to expect from my solo jaunt to become an American resident, least of all me. My brother, Simon, inherits my aged VCR and seems happy enough, and my best friend Renee asks me to bring her back 'genuine cheerleading merchandise', reminding me not to take my corners too wide while driving on the wrong side of the road. Mum, who lives in Melbourne, discovers that it's cheaper to call the US for an hour than Sydney, so she reassures me that my temporary relocation just means longer chats.

The Boy drops me at the airport and rolls my luggage past the luxe lighting of the duty free shops to a long, lumpy line like a stuffed stocking. Halfway through the wait, while the Boy is dusting the back of my neck with my ponytail and whispering bad jokes about shoe bombs, I'm suddenly overcome. We hug for a long time and I'm acutely aware of his large body over mine. A canopy. A shield. When he leaves I feel like a squinting field mouse after the harvest. I buy six kinds of chockie for the plane.

At Los Angeles airport some fifteen hours later, I can pick my fellow Green Card recipients by their monstrous yellow envelopes carried upright under one arm. X-rays don't fold. We all walk with one stiff arm like Lurch and the darting eyes of sixteen-year-olds waiting for their first formal dates. This morning there are only three of us from Australasia. Herded into a special area, it dawns on me that the next time I come into a US airport I'll be using the 'residents' line at immigration just like I do at home in Oz. I still can't believe it's possible to just randomly win something of this magnitude.

Waiting for my turn at the luminous and imposing counter, I am handed a packet of papers to go over. Pulling the top one out, my flesh prickles with déjà vu. I am greeted like an old friend by a small, slug-like oval of grease left by a stray blob of cream cheese. I know that's what it is because I put it there. Right beside my photo and personal details is the tiny remnant of a snack I ate over a year ago, half a world away. This lone smear of Philly is a sudden portal back to that time, conjuring up the New York offices of my film internship. If you could get below the bottom of the totem pole you would have found me there, answering phones through the lunch hour, learning how to talk around chewy bagel stuffed into one cheek. It was in the time between calls that I typed up these particulars, and it gives me a shiver now to remember just how close this piece of paper was to not being sent at all. Twelve dollars, that's how close. Twelve New York dollars. A movie ticket and a smuggled-in bottle of Arizona iced tea. Twelve dollars. Two 40-ounce beers, a bad video and half a Snickers. Twelve dollars for a photo-booth string of shiny paper with my face on it to mail off for the Green Card lotto.

I can so easily see myself at that tiny office desk, bored with the intern's lot, suffering from having long blown my savings in one of the world's most glorious but spendiest cities, and hesitating over parting with $12 for what I was convinced would be a fruitless endeavour. And if I did win, I'd asked myself, what then? Come back here to this city for more of the same? Despite the small daily thrills of life in the Big Apple, I remember my homesickness and confusion. Thankfully I wasn't jaded enough to snuff out the chance of returning for the sake of a ten- and two one-dollar bills. Dear reader, I spent it. I look around me now, out to the haze on the tarmac and the wide horizon beyond it, giddy with the realisation that I have just bought an entire country for 12 schmackers.

An Aussie guy goes first in the line, and I hear him tell the huge black INS officer about his swish marketing job with the Nike head office up in Oregon. 'Man, that must be *somethin*'!' the officer says, and the Aussie agrees. He is grinning as widely as the Kiwi guy who goes next. He's off to Texas to work on fighter jets. 'Man, what an op-or-*toon*-itee!' the officer says, stamping his papers, and Mr Kiwi actually punches the air on his way out.

I step up to the counter. I clear my throat. 'I'm, um, I'm going to Florida to live with my dad.'

The officer leans right over. 'Well, welcome,' he says. 'This is your country too now, how 'bout that?' He shakes his head with wonder and rests one cheek on his palm. 'You can go wherever you want in it and stay wherever you like for as long as you like. It's a beautiful country, Sarah, I hope you'll like it. Now stay outta trouble and say hi to your dad for me.'

I walk away with my wobbling x-ray, feeling more than a little shell-shocked from such sweetness, and surprisingly stirred. This is not what I expected at all, and certainly not what I've experienced from US immigration as a tourist or student. I feel strangely legitimate and terribly important. I sleep all the way to Miami, the kind of indulgent, self-righteous, three-economy-seat sleep of a winner.

Chapter 2

Alien Nation

When I win America, it is the cause of much celebration for Dad. An Australian working for an American company, he has recently moved himself and his American wife to a barrier island off the Florida coastline. Drifting at an insurance-unfriendly four feet above sea level in the Gulf of Mexico, Sanibel Island is a resort town with a stable population of a few thousand people that swells to theme-park proportions in high season. The island is populated largely by wealthy retirees, dot-com millionaires working from home and a few island business owners. The median age is sixty.

Dad fits into none of these categories. The poor man must feel like a permanent exchange student. He works off-island as a water treatment engineer in a nearby city which resembles one of those Queensland waterfront sub-sub-divisions that is spreading as wide and fast as good gossip.

Dad loves working in the States, but this hasn't stopped him from turning his office into what is practically an Australian consulate. His workmates stream in Triple J from the web, have lively discussions concerning pavlova, meat pies and rugby, and I'm pretty sure they offer political asylum. Through a cunning office recruitment program, Dad has single-handedly doubled the Australian population of southwest Florida, and is now inter-marrying them with the American staff in a bid to create a master race.

Less than three weeks after I arrive in Sanibel, my Green Card appears in the mail. I am very excited but also hopping mad. Mad because, after being firmly directed to remain in the US for the entirety of the 'six months processing time', I have sold my stuff in Oz, fired myself twice and the Boy has moved into a new house with friends. I'm not quite sure I like the idea of six months in limbo, but I console myself with the inspection of my prize.

The Green Card is actually a white card, and, dare I say, very cool. True, it features an image that rates with my colposcopy exam as the most unflattering and unnatural angle I've been photographed from, but it also displays my fingerprint amongst the fanciest of holograms, as well as a great deal of digits, arrows and a strip of what appears to be film negative covering the back. It looks like it would open security-access doors on Mir. Like every fabulous high-end accessory, it comes with a special protective carry-case, which is going to be necessary considering the card has to be kept on my person at all times as proof of my status as a 'legal alien'. I consider sending it to ASIO to scan for tracking devices.

The letter accompanying my new card is addressed 'To all immigrants and refugees' and says 'We are pleased to welcome you to the United States.' It goes on to tell me that if I want to work, open a bank account, get a driver's licence, buy a hamster or have a haircut in the US, I had better get myself a Social Security number pretty damn quick. A Social Security number seems like a funny thing for anyone outside of a Hollywood movie to have and the reality of my second identity begins to sink in.

I am now a legal, permanent resident of the United States of America. I can work here at anything I choose to do. Well, almost anything. Turns out that I can never be Special Agent Darmody of the FBI, CIA or any other so-called intelligence agency, and because I wasn't born on American soil, I can never be President. It was probably a long shot anyway, seeing as I can't reliably place more than two or three of the fifty states on the map, but I'm still a bit deflated.

I can live in America for as long as I want, for the rest of my life actually, and it seems as if my second nation would quite like me to. In fact, they make it bloody hard to leave. Unsure of my rights and fast making up some dodgy foreign policy on my own, Dad intervenes and buys me an hour with a fast talking immigration attorney from the Bronx.

'Guilia's great,' he enthuses. 'She's the one I went to before I married Caroline. We walked in together, she looked us up and down like we were dirt and said, "Gimme one good reason why I shouldn't throw ya outta my awfice right now!"' Dad chuckles, 'She's the best all right.'

'Oh. Yeah. That's just what you want in a lawyer, Dad. Bare-faced hostility.'

'Nah, she was just getting us ready for the INS. They're the real toughies.'

Fantastic.

'So, I have to check in once a year, right?' I confirm with Guilia, Dad's immigration wunderkind. 'Does that mean a week? Two weeks? The airport in Hawaii?'

Guilia's smile of greeting turns rigid. 'You're kiddin' me,' she says. 'You really have no idea, do you?' She sits back in her chair and regards me with obvious distaste. 'Why do you want a Green Card if you don't want to stay in the US?' she asks, with distinct trick-question tone.

'Well, I won it, I mean –'

'WHY did you enter the lottery if you didn't want to live here?'

'Well, because I could, I mean, it was free, and I thought –'

'You thought WHAT?'

'Maybe I could live here for a bit, y'know, work in New York one summer, or maybe –'

'Maybe WHAT?'

'I don't know.'

Jeez, where's that big scary guy from LAX? I had expected congratulations from this woman. A wink and a handshake perhaps, maybe a 'Good for you' or 'Lucky girl'. Doesn't she know I *won* something? I repeat my answer.

'No,' Guilia confirms. 'You don't know. You don't know anything. But I DO, so I'm gonna tell you.' She swivels in her chair and inhales deeply, lacing her fingers and pursing her lips. I'm in trouble, this much is clear.

'Do you know what people would give to have what you've got? People would kill, they would *kill*, to get a Green Card.' She snaps her fingers. 'Just like that. And you come in here, sit down and tell me, "Oh, Guilia, wah wah wah, when can I go home please?"'

My mouth drops open and I look to Dad, but he just smiles an isn't-she-great and I see that I'm to be tortured alone.

'PEOPLE,' she continues, 'People from India, Pakistan, and Bangladesh who applied for Green Cards in 1984 are only just now having their cases presented for CONSIDERATION. Do you understand this? Do you know how LONG this is? Do you see how LONG this is?'

Holy immigration, Batman! I can barely stand having two people in front of me at the ATM. Guilia is right. I'd kill someone too. I was six years old when those people applied.

'Okay,' I concede, 'but people need to leave Bangladesh right? Basic services are bad, inadequate sanitation, no beaches, lousy coffee, and I've heard the selection of latest release DVDs is very poor.'

'What's your point?' she says.

'I don't think there's a big rush to leave Australia,' I say. 'It's a great place. After all, we've got quite a lot going on down there. Marsupials even. Healthcare, sometimes, and Dick Smith crunchy peanut butter.'

Guilia is not impressed.

'So go home,' she says, and shrugs, with a look that tells me any minute now she might spit at my feet. 'Go home and just fogeddaboudit. If you're not serious, just go home, because this is not a little girly birthday party you been invited to, understand?'

I nod, but I don't. The hard facts start rolling in and they aren't good. If this were a cash prize I think the Lottery and Gaming spooks would be onto the INS in a flash. The fine print on my winning ticket could fill a book. Oh look.

It has. A shelf of them. Right behind Guilia.

'Okay, you stay out for more than a year, poof, gone, see you – *never*. Understand? But that doesn't mean you just come in for a holiday, oh no. See this word?' she says, thumping a photocopied document the size of a NASA in-flight entertainment guide. 'It spells *discretionary*. Do you know what that means?'

I nod.

'Good,' she says, 'so do the INS, and they like to use it a LOT. Okay? So if you think you can just come in and out, in and out like tag-you're-it, fogeddaboudit. They don't think you look serious, they take it away. *Discretionary*.'

I'm having trouble understanding why the US government would want me to stay so badly when it seems like America has such a hard time keeping people out, but I'm too scared to ask. I feel so guilty and miserable for all those other Green Card hopefuls that I begin to wish my prize was transferable. I don't come from Bangladesh. Being born in Australia makes me part of a very small club of exceptionally lucky people already.

'Okay,' she sighs, the dealing-with-morons sigh, 'another big word. *Citizenship*. You know what that means.'

I nod again. Don't need to worry about that one, I think, took care of it in '78. First job on the planet. Name, date, place of birth. Did it all before breakfast.

'Okay. You can expect to get it in about, mmmm, five years, maybe a little more since 9/11, who can tell. But you gotta work for it, none of this tag-you're-it stuff. You gotta be here five years in a row, and then –'

'Oh no,' I say, smiling at last, exhaling mightily over the misunderstanding, 'no, I don't want citizenship, I just want to keep my Green Card.'

This time I think she will spit on the floor. She puts her hands behind her head instead. 'Oh yeah? That's very interesting.'

'I mean, I need to go home soon,' I say. 'My Boy lives there and I need to get a real job, stop firing myself and, you know, start a career? And I don't think you can have a career for just a few months of the year –'

'Work here!' Guilia screams. 'Whatever you can do in Australia you can do in the US twice as big for three times the cash! Don't you get it?' – to Dad – 'Doesn't she get it?' She puts her head in her hands, then her head on the table, then her hands are in the air, closed fingertips making please-please-oh-please gestures. 'They love Ossies here, people will CLIMB over each other to hire you and they will THROW money at you. We got everything here you could get at home but more. It's a beeeutiful country. You want deserts, we got deserts, you want coral, we got coral, mountains, lakes, big cities, small cities, crazy cities, quiet cities, friggin' islands and forests. Heck, we own half the Caribbean! Don't just think mainland! Any industry you like, wherever you wanna work, we got it.'

'But my Boy –'

'Eh. You're young, you'll get a new one.' That smarts. The Boy is really quite precious to me, and not negotiable. It has been hard enough to find someone who puts up with all my crap and doesn't feature on my birth certificate, and our crazy adventuring (him as an exchange student to Norway, me on a semi-confused trek through the Middle East) has forced us apart for long periods of time already.

'No,' I say, finding a squeak of courage. 'I like this one.'

Guilia looks to my Dad for confirmation and he shrugs what-are-you-gonna-do?

I think it's over then, but no. This bitch is good.

'Wanna get married?' she asks me.

'Well, I'm flattered, but we've only just met –' I quip.

'DO YOU WANT TO MARRY THIS PERSON?'

Hmm, I think. I don't know. I mean, he's still at uni, we share a teddy bear called Goofa, and we can't even afford the kind of cheese we like. Second-tier, no-name cheese. A wise man would probably call that not quite ready.

'Well . . .'

Guilia sighs and leans back in her chair.

'Look. This is the way it works for Green Card holders. If you were to marry this person, he would NOT get your rights, understand? Worse, he wouldn't just be able to come and stay with you and not work. Oh no. In fact, they wouldn't let him in the country at all. This is because as the SPOUSE of a permanent resident, the INS would assume he was here for more than a holiday. They would assume he was here to be as close to his wife for as long as possible.'

'But of course he would be, I mean, if we were married.'

'Ah ha! You see? And if you had married him before you won the lottery, sure, fine, no problems, he gets the same rights, and any kids too. But even one day, even ONE DAY later, the INS don't want to know this person you married. They want to keep them out.'

Hmm, this is a new angle. More like a schlumpy, ill-made curve than an angle. The assumption upon winning this thing was that if I could convince the Boy to sign the dotted line for a year or two of a marriage of convenience, he could share my prize. The realisation dawns that I never really plan on using this Green Card alone for any significant amount of time, and Guilia is making it sound as though I have to or I'll lose it.

'What are my options then?'

'There are four. No, five. First one: go home, stay home, come back sometimes as a tourist to visit Daddy. Throw the card away.'

Okay.

'Second: marry this Australian person, leave him, and come to the US. It will take about five years for him to get a Green Card processed to match yours, during which time he cannot visit the US. You can go home, but for no longer than about three months of the year.'

What?

'Third: don't marry him, and stay in the US. Have short trips to Australia for you, and for him, short trips to the US. If you stay here for about five years without a real break, you can get citizenship. As a citizen, you can marry him and give him your rights. Fourth,' she sighs, 'you can keep playing in and out, tag-you're-it by yourself and hope the INS don't take your card away before you figure out what you wanna do.'

I look at the wobbly world globe on her desk, digesting. My Green Card is burning a smug hole in my pocket. All these options sound emotionally wrenching and, most importantly, very expensive. Emotional resources I have.

If the only way I can keep this prize, keep my country and my Boy too is to try to become a US citizen, then I need to take vintage parental advice: go back to my room, have a long, hard look at myself and think about what I've done. At this stage, the idea of working towards an American passport is not an option. It would be like telling the world I was now a boy instead of a girl, or that I liked girls instead of boys, or that my name was Mabel Jennings. Nothing that objectionable, just completely false.

'What's five?' I ask.

Guilia brightens.

'Marry a nice American boy.'

Deciding I'll probably never get to use my prize again, I endeavour to make the most out of this trip. I settle into Sanibel for six uneventful months, a girl alone on an island filled with honeymooners and retirees. Back under the parental roof for the first time since leaving the nest, I wallow in the comforts of an industrial-sized washing machine, endless supplies of groceries with attractive packaging and 8-ply toilet paper. I share my role as wastrel and malingerer with a cranky little Amazon parrot called Gringo, and get a job as a hostess in a piano bar for old rich folks.

To say I'm missing my peer group here would be quite something of an understatement. My best friend on the island has a dinner party one night, and her grandkids come. After enduring a long discussion involving bond traders and mutual funds, I excuse myself and go home, where I diagnose a peculiar longing for pizza and drunken debate over dodging HECS repayments. The closest I get to commonality with my new friends and neighbours is through my recently opened account at the local Bank of the Islands, into which I deposit my pay-slips from the Offshore Trading Company Pty. Ltd. The semantics of my banking makes me feel all Ricky Big-Time. I actually spend a lot of time hanging out at the bank. They have fresh hot cookies every two hours, cable TV and a nice deep couch. It more closely resembles a frequent flyer club than a financial institution. Sometimes the teller and I get together to laugh at my Australian credit card statements, which, due to the state of the Australian rouble, read something like 'QUIK-E-MART: pack of gum, bottle of water – $158.93 AUD.' I think I'm both their best and worst customer.

With the Oz dollar at 49 cents to the US dollar, I figure I'll keep my mindless job as long as I can to earn some greenbacks and cart them home. The Boy and I are already making plans for Asian travel and name-brand cheese. Sometimes, lonely and bored, I find myself wondering why I entered the lottery and why I'm here at all. I can barely remember my instinctive pull towards America, my joy at coming to this country as a visitor and student.

As a tweenager, I recall developing a general fascination with all things American, much to the horror of my best friend Michelle. She understood quite early that Australia was heaven, and had once travelled to Disneyland with her family on a trip she best remembered as a catalogue of the gastronomic transgressions of overly large American people. I turned to our best friend Zoe (it was a trio, high school is often thus) for sympathy, because she had an equal crush on the country. We were young enough then to idolise Johnny Depp playing an undercover cop on 21 Jump Street and to sigh over the endless stream of teen movies and TV shows like Beverly Hills 90210, where kids wore outrageous clothes to school and drove cars at about thirteen.

These kids were always off to summer camps for months on end, where they got lost hiking the Appalachian Trail and had their first kiss with a blue-eyed, chisel-jawed boy called Chip. The States rocked, was our pubescent conclusion, and we longed for that same kind of drama and mufti at our laid-back, school-uniformed, suburban Australian high school. American music, style, products and entertainment were hot property then, and it seemed that the USA had the cultural monopoly on what it meant to be a teenager.

As high school progressed so did our tastes. We grew out of the fascination with teen-cool and forgot about America. We didn't want to be cheerleaders anymore. We wanted to travel through Asia with our friends, drink lots of Arak and smoke clove cigarettes in Bali and Thailand.

This rejection culminated when an American film company (for reasons shadily related to local-content-in-advertising laws) came and shot a Coke commercial at our school. Despite some stargazing and general excitement, we largely made fun of them. 'Bloody Yanks!' we said. 'They're so up themselves.' We mocked the starlet's vacuous speech – 'Oh, like, cool, like, totally,' – and knew that despite his fame, actor Jared Leto would have had the ultra-white smile thumped out of him pretty quickly if the American show pony dressed in our school uniform had really been a student. It cured me. Like, totally. I forgot about the US and moved on to the rest of the world.

Some years later I found myself in a tiny storeroom that was the student exchange department at my Australian university, sitting on scratchy government carpet and scanning an upended box of promotional material, fanned out on all sides. After a few months of studying film, I'd figured out that 'The Industry' existed over the sea in Hollywood and New York City, where it seemed that everyone was a cinematographer with a screenplay in one hand and a lucky break in the other. I bought books about the film schools Scorcese and George Lucas went to, I dreamt of the editing facilities at USC and NYU, of schools that had their own camera cranes and wardrobe departments. Alas, the fledgling Australian exchange office hadn't kept in step with my dreams.

They had offered me a choice of three universities in Wisconsin, a business school in Boston or the University of Southern Mississippi. I wondered if any of those were near LA. A quick look at a photocopied map from someone's *Explaining Geography* textbook and I was immediately disappointed. It didn't take much longer to discover that the state of Wisconsin was known predominantly for cheese and freezing weather, that I didn't want to study business in any city, and that Mississippi was nowhere near Hollywood. But it was near the mythical New Orleans.

I'm trying to remember why and how a Sydney girl could have fallen in love, sight unseen, with a swampy city in Louisiana, but that's what happened. All the rock songs about Delta blues and bayous seemed to creep up on the radio, poor beautiful Jeff Buckley went and drowned in the Mississippi River, and that part of the planet suddenly seemed like a ghostly, other-worldly place of dreams and sweltering, voodoo-black nights.

I became obsessed with the Deep South and certain I had to see it. So it wasn't UCLA; I announced to my mother that I was going to make my name as a documentarian, and convinced her to sponsor a video camera to record my adventures in the land of Cajun food, Zydeco bands and historic racial tension. After many mix-ups on the Australian end, I received my student visa for the US with great surprise about ten days before I had to be on the other side of the world. I think the staff at 'Southern Miss' were equally surprised when the first Australian exchange student the school had ever hosted actually turned up.

I spent the next few months recording every detail of Homecoming games, tasty alligator meat and fried green tomatoes, blues festivals and Mardi Gras madness, jugs of American beer, fraternity parties, campus beauty pageants and the Gothic splendour of plantation homes. As part of a slightly bewildered tribe made up of other exchange students, I saw Savannah and Washington DC, Tahoe and Texas, New Orleans and New York, Las Vegas and Los Angeles, Santa Barbara and Santa Cruz, Tallahassee and Tupelo (that's where Elvis was born, y'all). I tumbled down sand dunes in Death Valley, and our dormitory stairs after illegal drinking jags involving Everclear, a 90-per-cent-proof grain alcohol capable of turning a can of Pepsi into a mind bomb. In between, I went to school for what amounted to about eleven days, where I caught up on my sleep and dreamed of never leaving. I ate, talked and lived Southern, and became incredibly fond of the region, despite and because of its traditions and peculiarities.

The more I schemed to return, the more I had realised that it would be impossible to survive in the US without working, and I saw my fantastical film career slipping away. Then, like now, it was punishing to travel in the US because the dollar was so strong. Everything cost twice as much in America, and I figured out quickly that the reason Australians go on working holidays to England and Canada instead is because, duh, they let you work. American exchange students in Australia are allowed to work to support their drinking and education, but here in the US, there was no reciprocation. It seemed hopeless. I hardened my heart and left New Orleans and my Hollywood dreams without a backwards glance. I was certain that, short of marrying an American or winning a Nobel prize, the only chance I had at ever being able to spend any time in the US with food and shelter would be if I won a Green Card out of thin air. And then, one day, I did. Fancy that.

But now, since arriving, all I've really thought about is leaving, and how I'll have to give up my lousy lotto win. I'm not convinced anything could be worth all this hassle; worth talking to the Boy in the middle of the night as months without him drag by and my friends all go off on holidays together. Would I really choose a country over a relationship, I wonder, a prize over a person? Because on paper, at least, it certainly doesn't appear that I can keep them both.

There's also a war going on and, while I'm just as unhappy with the government at home, patriotism is running high in the US and it's shutting me out. Is this lottery win really a prize? Or have I come to the land of too many choices – where buying peanut butter can take 40 minutes because there's an aisle full of it – to find what many Americans know already: that choice can be crippling? (Not to mention fattening, by the way, in the case of peanut butter with chocolate and marshmallow swirled through it.)

At the same time, I can't help being depressed by the corpse-heavy certainty that if I go home now, I know exactly what kind of post-uni first base I'll be stuck at. I have little idea of what to do next coupled with a clammy dread that in ten years' time my casual rejection of the grand and mighty USA might seem like a scandalous waste. My semester here as an exchange student and the subsequent roller-coaster ride of living in New York exist in my memory among the most interesting and sharply-felt times of my life. At the moment, though, this grand America consists of a job that relies too heavily on the muscles in my napkin-folding arm, and the regression to a life spent largely in a teenage bedroom on the phone. Something has to change.

With my time in Sanibel rolling to an end, the head waiter at the piano bar asks me when I'll be back. Unexpectedly, I find myself pouring out the convoluted story of my Green Card prize to a gathering crowd. Over the coffee machine and maraschino cherries, wiping crystal glasses and mahogany tabletops, I tell them I'm probably going home for good. It was great to be a winner, I say, but this kind of America is just not very *me* after all.

J.R., bartender extraordinaire and a former truck detailer from Idaho, finds this completely ridiculous. 'But you haven't even seen America,' he says. 'Florida's not the *real* America, no one's even from Florida, it's just like a permanent vacation. They don't call it God's Waiting Room for nothing, kiddo. You haven't seen America.'

'Well,' I say, 'I've spent time in New York too.'

This is not the deciding argument I'd hoped for. There are guffaws all round. 'Man, they don't even want to be part of America. They've gone past America in that town, you can't count it.' Shaking heads concur.

'Okay, how about LA?' I counter. 'I even lived there for a while when I was little.'

'La-La land? No way, doesn't count.' J.R. is clearly appalled at my ignorance. 'That's Hollywood, that's like hyper-America, like, crazy America – can't count it.'

'Las Vegas?'

'You're kidding.'

'All right, New Orleans. I've been there too.'

'Man, they don't even have the same laws as the rest of the country! Heck, they're barely even *attached*: Lake Pontchartrain Bridge is over 24 miles long! Different food, different language, local government, music, buildings – that's not America. Should be, but s'not.'

'Mississippi?' I try. 'Texas?'

But by now everyone is rolling around with the hilarity of my positively un-American list of places I've seen in America. Savannah. DC. San Fran. My workmates have ten good reasons why these places don't properly represent the quintessential American experience.

'Heck, I could live in New Orleans, though,' says Jerri, my waitress pal. 'That's my kind of town. Couldn't you just move there instead, hon? Try it out for a while?'

Maybe I could. With a bit of money under my starchy apron, I certainly could move to New Orleans or . . . somewhere.

I suddenly realise I don't know that much about the US, and that my not-much is still a lot more than most people know. If I go home now, I'll be missing out on something I don't even properly understand.

Over the next few days I catch myself thinking about all those Stephen King books set in faraway Maine, and the quiet golden prairies that captured my imagination when I saw *Dances with Wolves* in the Manly Twin Cinema, age 14. I resurrect fractured memories of the huge sequoia trees in California where I experienced snow for the first time as a kindergartener. I remember the delights of the Deep South and my college roommate's pictures of her life in lush, green Oregon. I become quietly seduced by possibility. I need to have a look, I'm thinking, a big long look at what I'm really saying no to if I choose not to play this half-on, half-off game with two nations for the rest of my life.

I withdraw some of my savings from the Bank of the Islands, precious US dollars meant to be converted to other currencies for maximum value, and decide to use them to travel here instead. 'Are you *mental*?' an Aussie friend accuses. 'You could travel for a year in Asia instead of two months in the US. Bring that money home! You've already seen America.'

Well, no, apparently I haven't. Apparently it's huge. I try unsuccessfully to convince several people to come with me, but there are no takers. Renee is keen, but the greenback is so strong that her Aussie savings won't buy the taxi to the airport, let alone the airfare. So I get out the map, turn it the right way up, turn it the other right way up, and conclude that I'll have to go and find America for myself.

There is nothing quite like the sight of an empty backpack, recently pulled from the linen cupboard and given a vigorous kicking, adjacent to a ridiculously large map covering half the floor, to inspire fierce, adventuresome feelings in my small pale breast. Add to map and bag a crisp letter of resignation from the menial job, a bold 'To Bring!' list covered in pin-stripes of biro and some fluorescent Post-it notes to get my toes twitching.

'Can't talk!' I shout down the hall, decisive, Amundsen-like. 'Planning trip!'

I'm going off to see the USA, off to find what the future might look like in the vast, creased and brightly coloured continent spread out before me. Two already dog-eared guidebooks wait smug and paternal in the front waterproof pocket of my bag, ready to stage-whisper the goods on improbable places like Badlands, South Dakota, promising with palms out and eyebrows raised they can find me food and lodging just about anywhere I care to go. That's right, I think, I can go anywhere, ha HA! All this – sweeping over the out-folded Rand McNally – can be *mine*.

I've decided to take the bus for this expedition and now Mum is scared for me. She's haunted by my Greyhound bus stories from my university days in America, when I set off with some fellow exchange students on an ill-fated voyage from Mississippi to Las Vegas. It was one of those hideously miscalculated scenarios you stumble into, with ominous music overplaying a happy scene that turns immediately to disaster. Roughly four days after boarding that bus we had crawled into Las Vegas, filthy, starving and utterly wretched. Across miles of desert and through countless eerie bus stations we had been forced into the literal laps of people and lifestyles that our gentle, middle-class existences had kept us innocent from. Each of us finished that journey closer to Jesus and an understanding of Brando at the end of *Apocolypse Now*.

Because there were four of us together for safety and support, our hair-raising bus stories quickly became bar-stool favourites rather than painful recountings. Mum loved those tall tales, but she doesn't think it's very funny now that I'm proposing to do it alone. Across the entire nation. She can't believe I would take the infamous bus again by choice, but I tell her it's the only way I can see all of this massive country unless I become an overnight pop sensation.

I try to get her involved. 'Do you want to come too? See the US?'

She seems genuinely surprised, as if this has never occurred to her. Dad's job took us to live in Los Angeles for two unremarkable years when I was very little, after four lovely years in Egypt that Mum rates as among the best in her life. I don't think she's forgiven the City of Angels or its people for not being the Mediterranean coastline of Alexandria, and I can't say I really blame her. Still, Mum has always been adventurous, and so I press her to see the merit in my bold plan. After vaguely implying that the USA might be devoid of both culture and interest, she reminds me to be careful for the hundredth time.

'Neeni,' she says, because that's what she calls me (it was the cat's nickname first, but he declined), 'just keep your eyes open. There's lots of creeps and weirdos in America, especially on those buses.'

'There's lots of everyone in America, Mum,' I point out, consulting my printed material. 'Almost 300 million people live here. They can't all be the same.'

My room turns slowly into a command post, where maps and printouts of Greyhound bus routes fight for space with scrawled A4 warnings like 'Fast-drying towel!' and 'WHERE is cunning multi-tool?!' I begin recalibrating my scribbled charts to include the hard data from the Greyhound website. Greyhound offers an 'Ameripass' that includes unlimited, continuous bus travel for different periods of time. Hopping on and off with only a few days in each city is all I can afford at this stage, as a week in any city here seems likely to cost me a bomb for accommodation. I am armed with a good hostel guidebook, but when I call to make reservations, its quoted prices of '$16 a night' keep turning into '$37.50 plus tax, pillow and shower surcharge, sanitation levy, sleep not included'. The costs on my piece of ruled paper start to mount and I'm leaning towards the 45-day Ameripass as a consequence. I'm not sure how much of the US I can see in that time, but it's all I can realistically keep myself mobile and alive for.

My next problem is one of spatial relations. There are just too many cities in America. I start to wish I'd won Belgium.

Miami seems the logical city to start in – only three hours from Sanibel it's the steamy, tropical city way at the bottom of the map that people refer to as the 'Capital of the Caribbean', implying that it's only barely the beginning of mainland USA.

I head outside to visit my neighbours with questions and then email a few of my American friends, conscious of the fact that if one of them turned up in Australia for a month and had decided on two weeks touring Brisbane, I would be forced to intervene.

Gently inebriated from sniffing the lotions without labels in my ancient travel kit, I sprawl amongst the Post-it rainbows on the floor, engaging in delicious pre-travel daydreams. There's me hauling lobster pots onto a boat off the coast of Maine. The air is sweet and clean, the ocean spray refreshing, and my buff fisher-boy shipmates nod approvingly at how well I'm holding my own for a skinny girl. It's kind of like *The Perfect Storm* starring me and minus the scary bits. I drift to a dude ranch in New Mexico. I've stolen Madonna's cowboy hat and I'm decked out in fringed double-suede, accented by my very own pearl-handled gun. Cowboys with stubble exist in this scenario, and they are definitely checking me out. 'Bring the little Palomino 'round for me, Jose,' I drawl, 'I'm goin' to town for victuals.' Once I've ridden Hollywood-style to town, however, my brain won't override jerky and refried beans as the only supplies on offer, and I'm forced back to reality.

There are now a lot of pins on my map, but it still looks very patchy. I'm frowning as I wave the flag of a map around, pointing out to Dad that only 16 states out of a possible 50 doesn't seem like much of an effort. 'Well,' says Dad, scribbling metric conversions, 'it's over 17,000 kilometres of travel. That's a pretty good start.' Horrified at this number, I draw the line at any further destinations when he calculates I will be on the bus for 255 hours. WHAT? My brain goes into a quiet corner to deduce that for ten and a half full days and nights I won't be anywhere except on my bum on a freeway. I'm in shock. I can't imagine doing anything I *like* for that long. But I'm committed now, newly jobless, friendless and forced into making immigration-type decisions.

I want to go home, but I don't want to let go of this chance at a totally different life. If I don't go and have a look now, I might as well just throw my Green Card away. I'm already homesick for Australia and eager to start my adult life, preferably with any job that allows me to use my university degree rather than my napkin-folding arm. It's time to figure things out.

Chapter 3

Bienvenido Miami

When the morning of the grand adventure arrives, I wake spectacularly underwhelmed. I can't even manage whelmed, let alone excited. Outside my window it's grey and raining the kind of sluggish, here-to-stay rain that turns up like your jobless friend in tracksuit pants with a six-pack under each arm. I'm already weary and I haven't even left my bed. Out of the corner of my eye I can see my swollen backpack, bright red like some kind of obese tomato, my new white sneakers standing to attention beside a pair of folded jeans and a white T-shirt on the floor. This will be my uniform for the next two months. Last night that was tickling. This morning, after four hours of sleep, dreaming of general misadventure, it seems pathetic and intolerable.

I scooch back down under the covers, deciding I can find America on the Internet. I'm not going out in the wet to sit on buses for weeks, spending all the tips I earned in the last six months on having my bum bitten by bugs in low-rent motels. I'll go to Europe with the money instead, where you still pay for the bugs but get a breakfast croissant thrown in free. And you can cross national borders quicker than states. On a train. With your friends. Or your Boy.

I can hear Dad padding to my door across the polished wooden floor in his open-planned Floridian dream-house, and

I'm squashing my face into the pillow, exhaling mightily. Just let me stay here, close to the spa tub and the ice-making fridge. I still have the receipt for the backpack, we need never speak of it again. There's a little knock. 'Someone's off to Miami today!' He's using the same voice that announced Christmas to my brother and me in the years before Santa was presented with shortlists asking for 2-litre bottles of Absolut and health insurance. I am going to Miami.

After two cups of Caroline's teeth-grinding, face-slap coffee and a teary *auf Wiedersehen* to the uncaring parrot, we hit the road, heading over the Sanibel Causeway and entering mainland USA. The Causeway, a series of bridges connected by man-made islands of white sand and chubby palms, is only two miles long, but locals love to joke about needing your passport to cross it, and they'll remind you, winking, to 'be careful out there!'.

Rifling through the ugly tomato-bag in the back seat, I become aware of some provision shortfalls and order a screeching stop at a Wal-Mart just before the Interstate. Wal-Mart is a 24-hour mega-mart, an institution that can only be supported by a population fifteen times as big as Australia's, and one that I already know I'll miss like oxygen as soon as I leave the US. As an exchange student my letters home were often filled with rambling testimonials to the luxury of replacing a dud pillow at 2 am while I bought hot chocolate, sunglasses and had my film developed.

Even regular stores have generous trading hours in America. Arriving in Florida with only one pair of underpants due to some farewell party confusion, I had asked Dad as a matter of some urgency which day late-night trading was in the US. He just smiled and patted my shoulder, one shopping aficionado to another, and said, 'Nine to nine every day but Sunday, when the doors close at six.'

The national Wal-Mart chain is cheap, fat and one of the unfriendliest places in the otherwise professionally friendly USA. This is despite enormous cheery name-tags and those computerised checkout screens issuing directives such as 'SMILE at the customer!' or 'GREET the customer!', which are woefully ignored. Being faced with such jubilant instructions in letters as tall as your hand produces an itch to be a smart-arse and point out that a dull glare does not constitute smiling-at-customer, and that 'Hiwelumooalart' does not count as a greeting.

We do some smash-and-grab-style shopping down the massive aisles, picking up locks for my bag, wet wipes, a small umbrella and army-tent-grade deodorant. In the personal electrical aisle, I select a travel hairdryer that claims to condition hair using ionic power. Thanks to new technology, it tells me, a cloud of negative ions can now envelop my hair as I dry. I nearly take Caroline's eye out waving it around in my excitement as I explain this groundbreaking advance in personal grooming. Dad picks up a regular model at half the price and compares the boxes. '1875 wattage, folding handle, dual control, elemental heating . . . there's no reason they should work any differently.' The regular dryer goes in the double-sized shopping trolley (called 'carts' in America, where a trolley is a tram, unless you're in New Orleans, where a tram is a streetcar and Trolli is a brand of gummi bears) and I wander behind, sulking at having had my purchasing power thwarted by a thinking consumer.

On the way out I look for a tiny wallet to hide in my bra. None of the hostels around the US take credit cards, so I'm stuck with a wad of theft-inviting cash. It soon becomes apparent that even the smallest coin purse is going to cause a startling imbalance in my less than ample bosom, but I finally find a small fabric sunglasses bag with a drawstring: black, $1.97. Forget $5000 worth of surgery, $500 in folded bills brings me up two cup-sizes with minimal discomfort and side effects limited to the occasional crunkling noise.

It's still raining as we leave Wal-Mart and head for the stretch of highway known so universally by its nickname, Alligator Alley, that it even appears in parentheses on all the maps. This is the east to west portion of I-75, dead flat for hours and separated by a wide, soggy, green median strip. There is an astounding array of wildlife in Florida and in the dry season the dense vegetation on both sides of Alligator Alley is overrun with deceptively lounging alligators as they flock to the water along with thousands of birds. Part of the freeway cuts through the Big Cypress National Preserve, home to some of the endangered Florida panthers, beautiful big golden cats that occasionally munch on neighbourhood kitties for hors d'oeuvres.

Since my arrival in the US, I've driven Alligator Alley a few times in previous attempts to find Miami. It doesn't look that hard on paper: Sanibel to Miami. It's a straight shot down the Interstate, no problems there, but when it reaches the outskirts of the city, it does what Dad calls 'the noodle', where massive spaghetti strands of concreted steel twist and loop over each other up high into the sky, peeling off in directions that are completely oppositional to their exit signs.

These exits are free from reasonable, human-friendly names, and are marked like surveyor's maps with 'P288 Nth, 76#8*q' instead of 'Flamingo St', or 'South Beach', or wherever the hell it was people told you to head for three hours ago. Driving on the wrong side of the road, squinting at the map in your lap at over a hundred kilometres an hour, is now the only option, and the ensuing panic causes tears and vicious swearing that result in my inevitable experience of Miami thus far. The dizzying loops around exits, the pulling in at dodgy gas stations for the purchase and consumption of calming chocolate treats and the predictable drive back out to the first and easiest exit, 'Sawgrass Mills', home to one of the largest outlet malls on earth. There I would get lost in the miles of outdoor carpark for an hour or so (Dolphin P288 Nth, Seashell 76#8*q) before purchasing a new summer wardrobe and three pairs of shoes for forty bucks in total, and driving home wondering if I'll ever get to see Miami. Now I'm finally on my way.

Today the straight road is open-mouth boring, apart from the occasional vulture on top of a tall tree, balanced oddly on one foot like the Karate Kid, stretching out its wings to dry during breaks in the rain. We pass little more than the halfway point, where a motel-sized super-toilet is tacked on to the side of the Everglades, and a few trucks towing airboats, one with a bumper sticker that proclaims its owner to be a 'Smart-Ass Whiteboy'. I think there must have been a rule once that every movie filmed in Florida should involve at least one of those fabulous airboats at some point, preferably in a chase scenario. With 'gators.

The road yawns on without interruption, prompting me to ask, 'Why is it so flat in the Everglades, Dad?'

'Well, because it's part of an old . . . flat . . . bit.'

Good thing I brought the *Lonely Planet*. I consult it now to learn it will take me about ten hours on a bus to go from one end of Florida to the other. That's not even counting the Florida Keys, which I will have to miss on this trip. The Keys are small consecutive island towns strung like beads along highway A1A, the massive two lane bridge which runs for about 200 miles connecting the tiny islands with the rest of the country. It will take me ten hours from Miami just to leave the state, and it says here that Florida is only the twenty-second-largest state in the US. I'm further surprised to learn that over 16 million people live in Florida, not counting the hordes of seasonal visitors. That's only, say, the city of Sydney less than the entire population of Australia, and yet it doesn't feel crowded at all. It feels positively sprawling and empty.

When the radio stations change abruptly to Spanish, it signals the beginning of greater Miami. Shakira and the junior Iglesias belt out their hits in both languages, Gloria Estefan is always on some station feelin' hot, hot, hot, and every commercial shouts over a background of salsa and merengue. Caroline fiddles with the controls and the digital display flickers, hiccuping every split second on a new station. Out of each ten possible stations in Miami, five will be Spanish, four will be high-energy dance music of the type favoured by 14-year-old girls and gay men, along with a single lonely station of regular top-40 tunes for the 28 straight white people who must live in Miami.

A little wooden road sign on the outskirts of Miami reads 'Indian Crafts, Gas, Lodging' in faded, fifties style writing. I finally feel a twinge of excitement about joining the great tradition of American road-trips, never mind that mine won't be with a cool chum in sunnies and a headscarf in a vintage car. I begin to hum the tune to the Griswald's family vacation. Dad ploughs ahead, negotiating the noodle-bowl of freeways with deceptive ease, and we are now officially in Miami-Dade, a county best known as the butt of jokes associated with those infamous butterfly ballots and the hanging chads on voting cards in the 2000 presidential election, the county whose confused electoral practices held the country to ransom for a few weeks before delivering an uncertain victor to the White House.

We zip past Miami Airport where airbuses from Cayman Airways and the West Indies are painted brightly with citrus shapes and colours that punctuate the grey sky. This is where I'll return tomorrow to the Greyhound bus terminal, which must be slumming it somewhere in the industrial wasteland surrounding the tarmac. All along the Miami River are houses like Disneyfied Spanish castles, with massive pleasure boats moored in front like in *Lifestyles of the Rich and Famous*. The wealth and beauty of these dwellings is stupefying and casual, one after the other after the other. Even in gloom it's gorgeous. With the sun on the water and the tropical colours it must be really spectacular to wake up in Miami.

Affected by all the glamour, I'm feeling pleased with myself for doing a bit of research on the hotel. We pull up in South Beach at a hotel on Collins Street that is part of a group of old Art Deco hotels refitted by very cool people to cater to very cool people, and to people like me who walk into glass doors and hope that cool is somehow transferable.

A smartly-uniformed valet approaches the car, but I've stopped being impressed with this kind of service long ago. In a country that runs on gratuity, every restaurant, motel, and supermarket in America has a valet service, four porters, and a guy to carry your keys to the car. I half expect to be valet parked at McDonald's. Ronnie, the valet, is somewhat overly helpful on a rainy day when the guest and street traffic is minimal. I'm no stranger to cajoling tips, but his material is a little thin. 'Yes, that's rain all right. Don't walk in it unprotected, you'll get wet. Wet from the moisture. In the air. That's rain, that's what we call sky juice round these parts, don't stand in it, just get inside under my protection.' Inside, our room is all steel and blonde wood, with a space-age coat stand offering two lilac hooded dressing gowns that resemble Jedi nightware. I put one on immediately and prance. I can feel the cool.

Outside, the rain is slowly drying up and we find ourselves wandering through an explosion of youth, energy, art and trashy beauty. I am gleeful. Everything feels impossibly young and frivolous after so many months spent being the only person born after Watergate, and I'm lapping it up without any reservations. Miami is a revelation to me. Like Chinese circus panda Pinky meeting Jeronimo from the Bronx Zoo, I see my own kind and want to groom and mate. Set loose in a city filled with pop-cool and the music of my peers, I am suddenly desperate to assert my twenty-something status. The whisper of pre-cellulite thighs in denim and the smell of scents other than denture-mint and Old Spice is intoxicating me. I must be strong. It's been half a year of cultural exile, I tell myself. I can't let this sway my judgement on Miami – I'm on a mission after all.

But so far the news is good for Miami. People lounge on banquettes outside bars in the sultry afternoon air, listening to deep grooves being mixed by open-air DJs, sipping at beverages of impossible hues. Miami is a big drug haven, as its Caribbean port makes it a prime point of entry for class-A party fun. Cocaine is definitely the drug of choice in this town. Two beautiful girls walk past us, arm in arm; one wearing a T-shirt parodying the popular America-wide Dairy Council 'Got milk?' ad, asking boldly 'Got Blow?'; the other in tiny pink shorts with 'Party Girl' written across her mango-sized buttocks. Girls everywhere are dressed like Britney Spears' backup dancers, while willowy young men with rouged cheeks wander about dressed like a cross between Beck and Little Miss Muffet, and over it all is *musica*! *Musica*! It's Saturday night and I trip along behind the parental units, wishing my mates weren't thousands of miles away.

A huge dreadlocked guy with a parrot on his shoulder cruises past, in keeping with the Caribbean feel of this town. Barefoot rocker Jimmy Buffet made the laid-back Key-island lifestyle famous through his music, which is still very popular with baby boomers and US college kids alike. Parrots and margaritas are de rigueur here, and Buffet's Margaritaville concept has been turned into an empire of theme restaurants and Bahaman-style clothing. South Beach is a bit more sophisticated than Buffet tunes and sloppy T-shirts with Macaws, though. It's making me reverse my opinions on this city already and I've only been here for half an hour.

After declaring with typical Aussie charm that he's so hungry he could eat the crotch out of a low-flying bird, Dad has now gone into a kind of caloric swoon. In search of sustenance we walk a street over to Ocean Drive, the beachfront strip filled with Art Deco cafés and the houses of a limited number of the genuinely fabulous.

Crowds of tourists stop to gawk and whisper outside the Versace manor, where Gianni was shot dead after buying the morning paper. America certainly can be a dangerous place. His manor is right on the main drag opposite the sea, and this place puts the prime in prime real estate.

We find a colourful Cuban café for dinner, and, upon being seated, a large woman dressed entirely in purple pushes a baby carriage past us with an iguana in it. The iguana is dressed smartly in denim, with an American flag pin in his lapel. 'Wanna pet him?' the beast's mother growls. 'He's *real* frenerly.' Before I have time to politely decline, all eyes are drawn to the shining Miami-Dade Police cruiser that has just pulled into the strip, piloted with studied casualness by a cop sporting a cigar the size of a juvenile coconut palm.

He parks at an angle inconsistent with legality and swings out to reveal two ham-steak thighs crammed into government-issue blue shorts which are in the process of being gobbled whole by his generous bum cheeks. It looks like some kind of joke, or perhaps a movie set – *Miami Vice Live: The Reunion*. Sucking mightily on the dangling cigar, Miami's finest steps out with a jaunty little stride to seek out crimes and misdemeanours. I imagine his bulky bullet-proof vest is a good idea. The Armani Exchange crowd along Ocean Drive are clearly appalled and, according to our waiter, everyone in Miami owns an Uzi. The cop makes his way through the Saturday afternoon throng, passing the beautiful Latino girls who line the Drive selling roses and cigars (some assumed to be Cuban contraband) from discretely covered boxes slung around their necks. Many of these boxes also contain the kind of wearable neon gee-gaws sold to crowds on New Year's Eve. They seem to be doing a roaring trade in these dance-party favours, because the little devices glow and pinwheel through the crowd all night.

When the sun has gone completely, the same girls collect together on the corners – the rose girls, glow girls and cigar girls – gossiping in torrents of husky Spanish, smoking and posturing in jeans that barely make it to their hip bones. There must be huge money to be made in Brazilian bikini waxes in this town. I don't see a single pair of pants with a rise over two inches.

Settling the bill, Dad notices a large proclamation taped to the counter, which declares it 'illegal in Miami-Dade County for any business to condone, in any manner, tipping based on race, colour, religion, ancestry, national origin, age, sex, sexual orientation, pregnancy, disability, marital or financial status of a person or persons giving or receiving a tip'.

'Well,' says Dad, 'that just about covers it. Maybe you should move to Miami. Even the bloody iguana could get a job in here.'

Back at the hotel, ensconced in my full Jedi regalia, I fall asleep in the heart of Miami to the constant vibration of Latino drumbeats and the hum of tropical-strength air conditioning.

The next morning is Father's Day in the US. I decide to celebrate the occasion by forcing the old man out of bed to buy me a good hot breakfast before my solo mission begins. There is already a DJ in the foyer and his mixed-up reggae samples Marley singing, 'Sun is shining, weather is sweeet . . .' Imitating art, the sun does just about whiplash my eyes as we leave the hotel. Now this is more like it. Sunshine appears wholly necessary in order to understand South Beach.

We breakfast around the corner at an agreeable café, where we watch sunnies and swimsuits go by on everything with two legs and some with four, enjoying the haze of steam ribboning out from the cooling water-misters around shops and restaurants. Despite the ambiance, American breakfasts are generally disappointing if you are Australian, European, or just someone who enjoys coffee, bacon, sausages or toast. Pancakes and hash browns are generally safe, but coffee in the US is invariably drip-filtered McDonald's-style, and sausages – when included – are either in patties, or, as now, tiny and lumpy, like the oily leftovers of a rich woman's dog.

The bacon on my breakfast plate this morning is also true to form and could double as page dividers; wafer-thin and stiff like salty parchment. Thick-cut bacon is a rarity in US cafés and restaurants, where if it exists at all it is referred to on the menu as 'Canadian' bacon. I need to teach those pigs to leap the border in Seattle. The disturbing lack of tastily prepared breakfast pork in this country has been under the 'cons' heading of my 'Why am I here again?' list since the first week off the plane.

Just like Sydney, the Sunday morning latte scene here seems to be dominated by women gazing at beautiful men gazing at each other. Gay culture in Miami is very loud and very proud. Unlike Sydney, though, it doesn't take long to see how gender has all but been exploded in South Beach. A cursory examination of street traffic reveals conservatively dressed middle-aged women who turn out to have five o'clock shadows underneath that Chanel concealer, and the throngs of men built like Dreamdate Ken are just as likely to be strolling with women dressed like Hoochie Pole-Dancing Barbie as with androgynous-looking teenage boys with camel's eyelashes and low-riding jeans.

Tough-looking guys in biker boots turn out to be girls, and tough-looking guys with handlebar moustaches carry designer handbags and check their nails. It is an absolute theme park of sexuality. Add to this street-wide mating dance hordes of hormonal, alcohol-fuelled college kids on holidays like the Spring Break vacation and it's a shock after spending so long on Sanibel. I'm already beginning to see how much more there is to the US and I've only travelled three hours in the car.

Continuing to slander my foodstuffs, light breakfast chatter turns insolently to the homogeneity of American culture, but I'm struck in the middle of my lofty arguments with the realisation that these people walking around me are Americans too; this Spanish-speaking, tattooed sexual rainbow of Miami. And if Miami can be dismissed as too Caribbean, or too heavily subcultured to be considered American, then what is? I suppose I have 45 days to find out.

On the perfect white sand of South Beach, I manage to get

sunburned through my allegedly 30-plus Burstin' Cherry Scent Hawaiian Tropic Stick, which the thinking-consumer failed to notice in the Wal-Mart cart, and I lie painfully in the shallows. All around me are glistening, perfect bodies cavorting against a backdrop of charming Art Deco buildings and a carefree, tropical vibe. It's hard to imagine actually living in South Beach, though, and the rest of Miami offers little more than vast tracts of semi-tropical suburbia.

Despite my initial enthusiasm for the energy here, I'm not rich, gay or plastic enough to exist happily in this place, where there is more than a hint of freak-show riding alongside its beauty. To make a life in South Beach I would need a parrot or iguana on my shoulder, a profound disconnection from reality and an exclusive mode of transportation. The streets are lined with nothing but Hummers, vintage roadsters and precious little Vespas. SoBe, as the locals call it, is a figment of its own imagination, a place to visit and make merry, or to see and be seen. Hardened plastic mammaries like demi-basketballs mosey down the streets, seemingly independent of their tanned and bleached owners. The hundredth pair prompts an incredulous snort from Caroline.

'All these tiny, tiny waists and huge ... It's not natural, it can't be.'

'No,' agrees Dad, surveying the territory. 'Sure are a lot of augmented waists down here.'

Chapter 4

Ain't nothin' but a
hound dog

Walking into the Greyhound bus station in Miami feels much like those westerns where the luckless hero stands in the entrance of a saloon, the swinging doors creaking behind him and the rough crowd snickering at his britches pulled up too high. I swagger on over to the counter and lay my money down. 'I'd like an Ameripass, please.' My accent seems to fill the little room, to ricochet off the walls and bounce back to me, thin and strange and reedy. The uniformed woman stops, mid-gum-chew, and then resumes, slower this time. She looks me up and down. 'Choo want to see America, ah?' She pulls out a sheaf of forms and starts scribbling without even looking down. 'Choo go to New York, ah? Maybe DC?' Before I can answer she leans as far forward as her impressive bust can take her and pumps a finger in my face. 'Choo be careful girl! Dis bus go places that are no good! Choo don't talk to no one but the driver, ah?' She starts muttering to herself in Spanish through her chewing, pausing to flick her tongue at her fingers while she whips through the papers.

For $499 I am presented with a hand-sized oblong of paper. Under the clear plastic covering the front, my printed particulars are recorded in grey along with instructions to keep my non-refundable, non-replaceable bus pass safe at all times. For a period of 45 days (starting two minutes ago) I can hop on and off any Greyhound bus in the continental USA. My initial smugness begins to evaporate as I look around and remember what I'm getting for my money. With cheap cars, cheaper fuel, and the absence of convenient pedestrian life anywhere but Manhattan, if you don't drive in America you are swinging precariously off the bottom rung of society. Which, of course, now officially places me on those very same monkey bars.

Standing there with my luggage and pass, I'm all keyed up to go, when I make the discovery it's going to be at least five hours before the first bus leaves Miami. This is my cue to pinch myself cruelly for sticking to my guns when Dad offered to drive me back home for dinner and a rest before picking up the bus nearby in Fort Myers. Insistent that I start my American Odyssey at the right spot on the map, my sense of the dramatic has been satiated at the expense of comfort, something I'm already in short supply of. My skin feels like it's suddenly a half-size too small for the rest of me. Even my eyeballs feel sunburned. Damn that useless Burstin' Cherry sunscreen and the cunning applicator pack it rode in on.

From my wire bucket seat I see that the marketing team at Greyhound (who I imagine, with their budget, to be a single day-release patient from a special care facility) have taken their canine theme and run with it a little too cheerfully. All over the Miami terminal there are posters depicting an ugly cartoon dog dressed in clothes, dapper luggage in hand or swung jauntily over his mangy shoulder, announcing his 'super friendly fares' to be a traveller's best friend. A cardboard mobile swings overhead with picture cards hanging from a little paper bus with signs in Spanish and English. There's Señor Greyhound in white and rhinestones, smiling a tad too suggestively with his shades tipped down outside Graceland. 'Ain't Nothing but a Greyhound', the card declares, and several of my fellow travellers have already commented on the wit. A Spanish speaker points it out to his silent group of buddies, making sure each of them get the joke in turn, singing 'Nothing but a Hound Dawg' and slapping his thigh each time.

The dog, who bears an uncanny resemblance to the Simpsons' pet, Santa's Little Helper, appears again with a fluffy dice collar in the bright lights of Vegas. 'Talk About a Lucky Dog!' he says, and waving an American flag outside the White House he further declares himself 'Doggone Proud to be American'. After an hour or so with nothing else to look at, I begin to get disturbingly involved with these images, which I take to be serving suggestions for my Greyhound Pass. There he is under the Hollywood sign, and there he is snuggling up to a flamingo in Florida, and over there, begging me to meet him in St Louis (what state is that in again?) and at some point I actually feel a small thrill. Sure thing, my furry friend! Meet you there, I say, and inside my wallet the Ameripass silently confirms these possibilities and more.

Using the facilities in here appears to involve a key as big as two clipboards, and one man has made this usually brief interlude his personal time filler, requesting the oven-tray-sized device to go in and out every few minutes. The counter lady finally says something cranky in Spanish but the man just points to his depleted Big Gulp by way of explanation. This little game goes on for nearly two hours, until the attendant takes the key, planting it under one generous armpit, and shakes her tiny braids in a firm no. The offender scratches his head, burps loudly and leaves for good through the besmeared doors. I wonder what he was doing in here all this time if he wasn't waiting for a bus. We are absolutely nowhere. Looking around, I soon figure out this false passenger isn't the only one.

It's easy to separate us actual ticket holders from the non-coms. We get up every forty minutes or so, walk around, read bits and pieces of useful info about our impending motorised travel and peruse the unsettling number of Miami-Dade Crimestopper posters stuck to the four grimy walls. Eventually I itch to call 305-471-TIPS and whisper, 'Well, it's just a feeling I have, y'know, a hunch, about some of the people at the Greyhound bus station on 43rd?' The ticket holders doze, but we wake often, usually when someone opens the door to our cool-box, inviting in the noises of the six jumbos landing next door at Miami International Airport every two minutes. Huge planes rumble overhead in a giant extra-terrestrial traffic jam, getting closer and closer until it seems that 747s are buzzing the windows of our fibro shelter on purpose. After a while, as the jet-fuel-to-oxygen ratio becomes consistent with hallucination, I feel certain I spy Salman Rushdie in economy class near the wing and I begin to drop in and out from the fumes.

The non-coms, however, do not sleep. They just stare. In fact, if they shift at all it is imperceptible. Is their bus tomorrow? Next week? And if there is no bus, why on earth would you camp out here when you could join the legions in SoBe dragging baby-stroller-loaded castles of junk around to the next five-star foraging point before sleeping under palm trees? Why stare at this buckling grey linoleum when you can have golden sand?

As the hours roll on, all arrivals are met with grateful interest. A woman enters with a cut-off sleeved shirt that reads 'G_ F_CK Y__RS_LF. Pick a vowel, Cancun, Mexico.' Her pre-pubescent daughter, probably gorgeous underneath thick brown layers of puppy fat, is dressed to kill in a pink shirt, with the waist tied just bellow her collarbone, and tight jeans that barely cover her cha-cha. It is evident that this poor creature's vowel-less mother has been late-night shopping and has purchased a Bedazzler – 'Courtney' is spelled out on her drum-tight jeans in gems of radioactive fluorescence.

They take seats next to a largely unconscious man wearing a pink T-shirt that reads 'Welcome to Strawberry Country!'. He is sleeping with his head thrown back on the metal mesh of the chairs, his six-foot frame spreading itself like a rubber chicken. He moves around, finding sleep and losing it within the same ten-minute cycles, until at last he comes to rest kneeling on the floor, his hip and stomach lying diagonally across the waffle pattern of the seat, chest straighter against its back, neck laid out over the inclining headrest. Poor bastard, I think, chuckling with the fragile superiority of one who is declining to think about the kind of sleep deprivation she will experience for the next six weeks of bus travel.

Standing up to use the ironing-board-sized key, I discover with alarm that I have to pull my jeans out of some 80 grooves as deep as my pinky finger is wide, along my buttocks and thighs. I check my watch. Only three hours down and it's already intolerable. I look around for new seating options. One row of seats are moulded black plastic attached to what look like oversized versions of the radar guns police use to check speed. They proclaimed themselves to be 'TeeVee Viewing Chairs'. Coin-op TVs! Trés cool. Despite dire warnings from their manufacturers that they are for paying viewers only, no one is using these devices, but they are the first seats taken because they lack the dangerous waffle-iron bottom. They are completely filled by the non-coms too, damn them.

There isn't much to play with in the Greyhound terminal, but after a few more hours, I decide to give it a big Aussie try. I fish for a quarter and throw it into an ancient machine that asks me boldly, like an eager English-as-a-Second-Language student 'What is your weight?' in fifties amusement park scrawl. I hop on. The counter whirrs and blinks. The room looks on expectantly. I learn I weigh 116 pounds and my lucky number is 328. Cool. I check my watch. That's two minutes sewn up right there. If I play my cards right, it might be another thirty seconds before I sit back down, too. After a few more turns at the weight machine – with bag, without shoes, bag by itself, one foot off – I go in search of my next favourite pastime. Treats.

Dear old Dad, bless him, has foreseen an early snack-crisis and packed me off with some small bills to play the chip machines, but I'll be damned if the team from Tropic Food Machines haven't last visited the Miami terminal sometime before the Cuban missile crisis. The only packets swinging like the last teeth in a trailer-park smile are filled with Snyder's Diet Pretzels, Zoo Crackers and TGI Friday's Cheddar and Bacon Potato Shakes. Feeling decidedly snacky despite the meagre offerings, I settled for the dubious sounding Potato Shakes. As soon as I pop one in it melts and adheres to the top of my mouth, causing me to curl my tongue upwards and flick it forward in a scraping motion. They are tasty enough that I persist, eating my dinner much as I imagine a tamarin monkey might eat his.

When the bus finally arrives, the packed station seats are filled with people so bored they're taking off their shirts to read the washing instructions. The few children trapped here with us have been through all seven screaming stages that lead to comatose and now there is only one left to torment us. He has been singing without respite or audience response for forty minutes now, and I make an important cultural note that 'Old McDonald' is even more annoying in Spanish.

Now, I love children. I used to be one, after all, and I love animals and dolls, kids being a hybrid form of these interests. However, one hour of 'Ay eye, AY EYE ooooOOOOH!' later, I itch to lift the warbling child up by his feet and shake his spleen out through his nose. His wee brother finally takes care of it for all of us, finding the strength to lift himself from his grubby stroller hell and bop his sibling right in the kisser. Grim sounds of satisfaction rise from the crowd. That kid has E-I-Oed his last.

We line up loosely outside, and my head becomes one of many reflected and elongated in the windscreen of the bus. Stepping aboard, up onto the rumbling plate before the steps begin, I feel a warm buzz. I am going to see America. To search out my prize, to briefly give myself over to this foreign land, to experiment with my future.

An old man shuffles over and takes the seat next to mine. 'You on vay-cay-shun?' he asks. 'No,' I tell him, 'I live here.' And I do. From a cosmic sleight of hand so quick and daring I didn't quite catch it, I am now a Permanent Resident of the United States of America, the behemoth nation at the head of the twenty-first century.

The old man leans closer, furrowing his brow. His teeth clack. 'You live on the *Greyhound*?'

No.

But I'm about to.

As we pull away from the Miami terminal at last, the driver lurches the bus around like a stolen car and I worry I'll throw up my Potato Shakes and Vanilla Coke before we even leave the block.

We make a pick-up in Fort Lauderdale and just when I think I'm in control of my tum, the driver slams on the brakes. 'Anyone need to be in Fort Lauderdale? Think hard, people! Because ah DON' do u-turns! Okay. Lights out till Jacksonville,

5.15 am.' We set off properly then, on the freeway at zooming speed, heading towards Savannah, Georgia, the first stop on my grand excursion. Outside it's black and hazy, the city lights streaking against the sky. Sharing a puppy's affinity with being up high and moving fast, I start to feel better. We pass a giant billboard featuring a porcelain device half a mile high, which, with the bowl tilted towards my face, announces 'Mr Bidet – For A Healthy Clean Tush!' The Potato Shakes lurch again.

My old blow-up airline pillow continues to deflate around my neck with the smell and consistency of a cheap cask-wine bladder. Despite the frustration and dubious odour, I am forced to retain it as a plastic neck warmer as the temperature on the bus continues to fall below the spring average of Reykjavic. Pushed away from the window by the cold air shooting in a continuous jet up my nose and behind my ear, I become creative in my discomfort and sleep bum in the sky and head facing ground for two twisted, freezing hours, trapped in a nightmare that has something to do with ice and evisceration.

Eventually, I peel dried-out contact lenses from my eyes and sway up the front of our thundering vehicle. In the cosy booth behind the windscreen, the handsome driver is warm as toast. He is gently illuminated by a small overhead light, until his features shine as if carved from caramel butter. 'Excuse me? Sir?' I bleat, 'It's so very cold back there . . .' My thin little accent and my pale, shivering hands make this plea particularly Dickensian. The driver chuckles and puts his hand on the mighty control benevolently. 'I'll see what I can do, hon. You jes' go on back now.'

It's still dark when the bus arrives in Jacksonville, an east Florida town of about 700,000 people and miles of beaches. I've seen beautiful holiday snaps from Jacksonville, with perfect white sand dunes beside water the colour of kids' marble collections.

The Greyhound station is marked only by a grim and depressing poverty and sameness. Nothing advertises the world outside it enough to make me want to wander out and explore. With an hour to kill and nowhere free of blinding fluorescence to sleep, I figure I might as well wake up.

The dingy food service area has been set up to look like a popular fast-food chain, with 'combo deals' advertised alongside vaguely familiar logos. The overall effect is not unlike what might happen if a Burger King was looted and left abandoned to crack-addicted squatters, then reopened four months later without a refit. I feel absurdly thankful I'm not hungry. What I'm really after is a bottle of water, but there's none to be had. Apart from Dodgy Brothers Cola, there's nothing to drink but three flavours of Hi-C Punch. A treacly, vibrant-coloured concoction, Hi-C Punch seems to be the fizzy-drink alternative at fast-food outlets in the US and it's strong enough to set my teeth on edge just thinking about it. I'm surprised how much I miss lemon-squash drinks from home like Lift and Solo. There are so many treats I had expected the global might of Coca-Cola and Cadbury Schweppes to distribute in the US that just don't exist here.

At the front of the shuffling queue, the groggy attendant offers me a tall cup of water for 64 cents, and then tells me that it's free when I ask her to hold the ice. I wander around sucking at my bendy paper cup, the tomato-pack punishing sunburned shoulders, trying to wake myself up. On a wobbly card table beside the dodgy food concession a bizarre collection of goods have been arranged. Behind a sign declaring 'Now reduced' there's everything the discerning Greyhound bus traveller could want. Fake snakeskin luggage in an unnatural shade of yellow. His 'n' hers rain ponchos in pink and blue, as well as six metal eggbeaters, some bags of Sherman's Cows – 'the hard candy made from real dairy cream' – and heart-framed sunnies in thick green plastic from Guatemala beside a load of plastic US flags labelled 70 per cent off.

There are surprising numbers of soldiers scattered around the terminal, young and fit and much too alert for this time of the morning. Their sharp, handsome uniforms and quiet banter seem out of step with the general slumlord atmosphere of the station. These men are going off to join Dubya's War on *Trr* (that's 'Terror' for those not schooled in Texan President) and it makes me nervous to look at them, the visual equivalent of hearing a long squeal of brakes late at night. An old man brings in what must be his reservist son, soft around the middle and well past

35, both men looking nervous and excited. The man stoops along with a cane, his uniformed son matching his slow speed, jaw set, staring ahead as if readying himself for combat, his old man sabotaging the drama of the moment with a series of noisy farts at every step.

After circling for a while I finally secure a 'Strictly for TeeVee viewers!' quarter-slot TV chair, to avoid waffle-bum. There are two rows of us, all surreptitiously engaged in investigating the odd-looking boxes. One guy decides to commit, produces a coin and fires up his TV. There is a crunching noise, followed by a great deal of black and white fuzz. We all strain for a look. He's under pressure. Twirling the dial, he eventually finds one channel, which is blurred and crackling. He settles back, and we all feel ripped off together.

From the toilets, a young guy with a straggly moustache emerges and flops into a plastic chair. He chucks in a quarter and his TV jumps to life with perfect picture and sound. In colour. With a four-station selection. The first guy pretends not to notice.

Two huge, uniformed cops enter and make me feel twitchy and nervous. Police have the ability to make a room full of people certain they're guilty in the same way that the suggestion of head lice can cause a class of ten-year-olds to become instantly itchy. My face is now four colours of blotch from the South Beach sun and without my lenses I have no way of telling if they're looking right at me, attempting full contact only to be met by a glazed, burnt eye-lid roll. The cops ask for tickets from young single black men, until I start to be embarrassed by my pink girl's face. Teacher's pet.

I reach for new contact lenses. With salty, dirty fingers and the drying air conditioning, contact lenses are a foolish choice for the bus, but I left my only pair of glasses on the flight over here six months ago. I called LA airport the next day to inquire whether anyone had seen a pair of black spectacles left in the seat pocket of a jumbo and the attendant was surprisingly helpful. 'Sure!' he said, 'whaddoo they look like?' I answered him with the detail and precision of a forensic scientist. 'Um, they're black, with glass, well, that plastic glass stuff that's not really glass, but it looks like glass, well, not like window glass or anything, but lighter, like ... anyway, they're, um, oval-y, roundish near the eyes with, ah, two, mm, sticks for behind the ears. So they don't fall off. Black. Sticks.' There was silence before he said, 'Sure! I think we got another seven hundred of them yesterday, so whyonchoo come on back to LA and have a look.'

I rub my sore eyes and sigh. Maybe I'll leave the lenses out for awhile. I have a feeling that 20/20 might not be a blessing in a Greyhound terminal after all.

Chapter 5

Old Glory

The nearly empty bus pulls in to the Savannah station in quiet morning sunshine. Stumbling off onto the street, my nose and fingertips begin to thaw as I de-cement my eyes with my palm. The relief I feel to be off the bus fades quickly when I consult my map and see that I've barely made it inches along the continent. The state of Georgia is just over the northern border of Florida, so I haven't come nearly as far as it feels. Shit. This doesn't bode well. My back thinks we've clocked at least a thousand miles and my immersion in Greyhound culture cannot so far be rated as particularly successful or interesting.

The hostel guidebook advises me to call the Savannah International Hostel for pick-up information, and a pick-up sounds like just the thing after such a buckled sleep. Unfortunately, the pick-up information consists of, 'Well, you could always walk, but we close up in a half an hour, so I'd get a cab if I were you.'

I hang up and head for the busiest road I can see, hoping with all of my sinking heart that the hostel manager knows something I don't about cabs in America. Cabs are a strange phenomenon in the US. There are some cities – many cities – where I'm certain people live their whole lives without so much as glimpsing a cab, believing them to be some kind of quaint historical article like those horse-drawn carriages for tourists. As a student in the town of Hattiesburg, Mississippi, no one I knew had ever ridden in a cab, let alone called one, and so it was left to the international students (always desperate to get to Turtle Creek Shopping Mall and buy pretzels with dipping sauce and other American products) to figure out the protocol.

We learned quickly that a spontaneous outing was a hilarious impossibility. Instead, we would call both of Hattiesburg's cab companies – Vinyl and Rust, I think they were – roughly three hours before we needed to be anywhere, and then settle down beside the pay-phone in our dorm. We called in shifts every twenty minutes to check the status of our cab, which was always five minutes away. We played both companies to improve our odds. Only one ever turned up, and when it did we whooped and ran out to the street, flinging the doors open and piling in behind a driver who inevitably looked surprised to see passengers. (You wanna go where? In *my* car? Well, I guess I can take ya.) Several times we had drivers who were legally drunk enough to be dead, but we cared not for such things, only pretzels. Only once did I fear for my safety, when a toothless driver turned around to spit, 'You're from Os-trayl-yuh? Mah cousin died in Os-trayl-yuh. In fact, I think they *keeled* 'im.'

It is just past peak hour in Savannah, though, 9.30 in the morning near the only bus station in town, so I figure my chances of finding one here are much better. Ten minutes later an old blue Ford crests the hill, dragging its bumper, and it looks sufficiently cab-like for me to take a run at it. The driver shares that same look of surprise to be hailed, but agrees to take me where I want to go as soon as he figures out how to turn the ancient meter on.

The hostel is only a few minutes away, right in the heart of the historic district and opposite what must be the only big supermarket downtown. I clap my hands at the prospect of cheap supplies and check-out treats. The building itself is a creepy old mansion, 'restored' in real-estate speak, but decrepit in a university housing kind of way that means inch-thick dust and greasy spots covering an eclectic motley of fabrics. The proprietor, a friendly chap with a lovely old dog he introduces as

Tyrone, beckons me in sleepily. He is making strange noises with his sinuses, and I am instantly reminded of the Southern forgiveness for what my American friend Cheyenna calls 'snotsuckin' – the loud, internal clearing of one's nasal passages, culminating in a throaty swallow.

Playing with your phlegm before ingesting it during polite conversation quite horrifies me, but in the South this practice seems to provoke the same disinterest as a light, mouth-covered cough might in my neck of the woods. Just as most Americans would no doubt be outraged by public nose-picking in China, I suppose it's all relative. And so I am greeted. Snort, snorrrrt. 'Hi. Come on in.' Snorrrt. SnOOOOORRRT. Gulp.

There is a list of rules written on a large whiteboard. The owner scratches his head, yawning. 'So. Read the sign and tell me what you think.' We stand together in respectful silence of his felt-tipped commandments. Lockout, 10–5. I check my watch. 9.45. Bugger. 'Great!' I tell him, my legs pointing towards his shower facilities unbidden. Snort. Snoooort. Swallow.

Upstairs, two girls from New York are abandoning the room. On a road trip for a wedding they have veered down south, as wide-eyed and genuinely hungry as I am to see their vast country. They seem nice. They wish me well. But when I hop into the bathroom I am met by half a foot of water in the shower tub, with matted hair and soap scum congealing as it cools on the surface and nary a bubble of drainage to be seen. What? Those sweet-faced girls left me this? A knock on the door. Snoorrrt. 'Lockin' up the place in five minutes. Just ta let you know.'

Sporting natty dreads from the deflated pillow and still reeking of the ineffectual Burstin' Cherry Scent, I fall to my knees and reach inside for the drain-hole, searching my brief memories of the girls for any signs of mange or leprosy. Gagging as my fingers explore an impenetrable thicket left from all the travellers who have gone before me, I realise that there is no unplugging this baby. Well, not unless its owner can teach it how to snort Southern-style. I leap in, breaking the surface into individual islands of filth, scorching and freezing my skin in turn for the next three minutes as the water trickles and then shatters down from above. I am trying to ignore the queries my feet are sending me. 'Hey, Sarah, what do you think this is? Big Toe says it's squishy, but the three little piggies think it's furry ... Can you see anything from up there?'

Out of a shower that is already filling me with dread and sanitation-panic about the weeks ahead, it is time to test the gadget towel I have supplied myself with. Stiff as board and dry as biscuit base, you wet the 'body-chamois' to bring it to life, which invites an odour somewhere between wet dog, old washing and low tide. Tasty. Somehow I had remembered backpacking as a state of being with rather more fun and less stinky humiliation than the past 48 hours have offered. We're having an adventure, dammit, I tell myself.

I fall out the door at ten sharp, still wet, bedraggled, and carrying all the wrong heavy things, clutching the hostel door-code on a piece of sodden newspaper. Outside the air is sultry and humid in the extreme, but it feels wonderful after being snap-frozen with swollen vertebrae for the past twelve hours. I set off lighthearted to rediscover Savannah, a city with a global siren song powerful enough that it called me all the way from Australia at 19, just to see this tiny corner of Georgia and its big sister (thematically, anyway), New Orleans.

I don't have to walk far to see that the houses, squares, parks and foliage are as rich with old-world beauty as I remember. I quickly snap off an entire roll of film even though I know it will resemble a real estate primer as soon as it's developed. It's very hard to capture how lovely Savannah is without taking pictures of people's homes. Each house seems more intriguing than the next, and I click away, leaning over flower beds, crouching beside stone stairs and hiding around cornices and behind fountains like *Better Homes and Gardens* paparazzi. I keep walking straight until I hit the river, revisiting the same cobblestoned waterfront where I unwittingly stumbled into Savannah's biggest annual party some years before.

On a fairly sedate Spring Break vacation with some American girlfriends, we had wandered down here to the edge of the Mississippi River to take some photos before completing a brief visit to this historic town. It was St Patrick's Day and, unbeknownst to us, Savannah was in a positive froth about it.

Outside of Dublin and Boston, there is no greater hoo-ha made over St Patrick's Day than by the citizens of Savannah. By the majestic paddle-boats and the massive gulf of water, we found a party in progress like nothing imagined outside of Mardi Gras in New Orleans. Charter buses of fraternity boys were pulling in and discharging their handsome, drunken cargo into old stone bars jumping with six kinds of music and seven kinds of revelry. Girls leaned from wrought-iron balconies, their necks draped in green beads, with shamrocks painted suggestively on cleavage and flushed cheekbones. People flooded in, the sun went down, and before we knew it, we had massive commemorative plastic pints of ale in our underage hands, beads and painted shamrocks of our own, and a bevy of attractive Southern gentlemen to woo us. I have a deep affection for this place.

Empty of people on a weekday morning out of season, the waterfront today is more Mark Twain than Mardi Gras. Big stone buildings speak of the country's earliest history and the nostalgic white paddleboats complete the picture. The old stone warehouses are now shops and taverns which are very touristy, most failing the 'Would locals buy this stuff?' test, but still gorgeous, much like The Rocks at home in Sydney. There is a huge, old-fashioned candy store making fresh pralines, a Southern delicacy consisting largely of nuts, melted butter and sugar, and the aroma they produce while cooking makes it easy to decide that a pound of these will make the perfect breakfast. I eat them lying on a riverfront bench in the sun, gazing up at my little chunks of caramelised heaven before devouring them with Homer Simpson noises of pure satisfaction. I am pretty sure the term 'comfort food' originates in the South.

Savannah is a completely gorgeous city, it's impossible to overstate it. The city is an unusual mix of European lifestyle and Gothic Old-South architecture, of *Gone With The Wind* meets *Roman Holiday*. It appears at once to be an immensely livable city, a city built for pedestrians and free fun rather than consumers and vehicles like so many modern American towns. Everybody is walking on the old ballast streets, strolling through the parks and riding bicycles. I find myself so completely flushed with pleasure at the sight of people outside, out of their cars and using their downtowns, that I vow immediately to never live in a place where this doesn't happen. Even from my limited experience of the US so far, I'm fast predicting this means that Savannah just moved way up the top of a very short list of potential addresses.

Walking around town, my camera knocking against my wrist and my head turning like a cat in an aviary, it is clear that someone here once had a few great ideas about town planning. That someone turns out to be a British general called Oglethorpe, who sailed up 270 years ago and was a real clever-clogs in this very lasting way. From a series of tasteful plaques and some big-ears-ing of tour groups, I learn that the creation of Savannah's 22 city squares was the brainchild of this man, who arrived to set up Savannah as the thirteenth American colony.

The squares are wonderful devices that act like miniature parks, around which hundreds of historic homes and buildings settle quietly under huge trees. Savannah made a tremendous amount of good old-fashioned cash in the early nineteenth century, when cotton was king and the South was springy with it. The bust came quickly, though, and although Savannah's economy was never hot again, the good news was that no one could afford to update all the opulent mansions and public buildings. No one ever had the dough to tear down crumbling antebellums and build sixties apartment blocks. A little sign points out that another key factor in the preservation of these delightful buildings is that Savannah was spared the torching many other graceful Southern cities endured in the Civil War. All that burning-of-Atlanta cinema drama finally impacts on me. I can't imagine the spiteful, shitty wastefulness of destroying five or six other Savannahs. What a terrible shame. I have to have a bit of a sit-down and eat another bag of pralines to lessen the melancholy.

I wander around looking for an Internet café so I can check the Greyhound departure times. When nothing jumps out, I poke my head into a video store to ask for directions. A young guy behind the counter watching Taiwanese movies nods vigorously and tells me, in what I believe to be English, 'Puh-lick Lie-tally.' By the time I translate this to 'Public Library,' my new friend is crawling under the counter with embarrassment and we are both volleying apologies.

'Solly, so solly, my Engrish no good, no good,' he says, despairing.

'No!' I insist, horrified my request has caused him so much distress. 'My . . . I don't speak anything else!'

'No!' he says, shaking his head again, pounding at his heart. 'No good, wery poor, no good, solly, so solly.'

'But I'm ignorant!' I say. 'I only speak English! *I'm* sorry!'

'No,' he says, inconsolable. 'No. Solly.'

He draws me a quick map to get to the library, blushing and continuing his sollys under his breath. I thank him profusely and when I turn to go he says, 'Ah! Wait! You go tidy?' I look down. He's right. I'm a grub. 'They have a dress code?' I ask. 'No sneakers?' I say, indicating my footwear.

'No, no,' he tries again, clutching his throat, tears sprouting, 'YOU GO TIDY?'

After another round of bowing and apologies on both sides he says, 'Pick-lah! Pick-lah tidy?' I am no closer, so we play an interesting miming game which he obviously finds excruciating until I finally get it. 'Oh, I see! ID, yes, with my picture.' He is actually sweating when I leave.

After a brief walk, I present my pick-lah tidy at the library and enjoy free Internet access and the use of their sparkling clean toilet for the rest of the day. I want to go back and thank my helpful friend but I worry it might hurt him.

I check the Greyhound times online and then send a group email home detailing my grand plan to discover my Green Card lotto prize. No sooner have I hit 'send' than I get a rather curt email in response. It's from the Savannah Puh-lick Lie-tally. They regret to inform me that, as this is a public Internet service, my email is deemed unsendable due to racy content. They have names for people like me, they imply, but they're too polite to say them. Now it's my turn to blush. I pore over the text, trying to decipher what was dodgy enough for this local government facility to refuse to send. I look past references to naked sunburn and shower filth to discover that my three small kisses at the end – xxx – have deemed my correspondence terminally offensive.

I have to minus a kiss, and tell my nan I'm sorry the censors wouldn't allow hers through.

After walking for an hour, taking more lifeless house photos designated to never be seen again, I head away from the river and through some squares to Forsyth Park. This park is huge, some seven city blocks in size, in a small city already filled with parks. There are strange little buildings in the middle that look like forts and, as I get closer, a sign tells me they are just that. Practice forts, built for training during World War I. Today the incongruous forts are kid-magnets, drawing them from their mothers' picnic rugs all over the park.

The two main groups of tourists in Savannah are still in evidence everywhere: those who have read John Berendt's charming *Midnight in the Garden of Good and Evil,* a book based on the author's years as an outsider amongst the colourful characters of this town, and those who are Girl Guides. Girl Guides founder Harriet Beecher Stowe was born here and bits and bobs commemorating her life are everywhere in Savannah, prompting troupes of nice little girls to travel here all year round. If you happened to be a Guide and a *Midnight* reader, I imagine Savannah would be roughly equivalent to Mecca.

Forsyth Park is a lovely, tranquil place to hang out and people-watch, but I can't seem to escape the tiny black flies that swarm to my hair and mouth if I sit still for longer than three minutes. Running with my hands batting at my face, I'm saved when I spy a coffee shop at the far end of the park and realise that it's well past caffeine o'clock.

The Sentient Bean is an establishment purveyed and serviced by the terribly sensitive students of Savannah's lovely Art and Design School. These hemp-clad angels charge about $7 for a cup of Joe that is as weak as Alpine tap water, but promises to be organically shade-grown and friendly to ethnically persecuted one-armed lesbians of colour abroad. Bob Marley provides the soundtrack (he's following me from SoBe), which at first seems out of kilter with the time-frozen white Southern gentility outside. After awhile, I see how it actually fits the already mellow vibe of the city, which is warm, youthful, and reggae-paced. The softly dangling Spanish moss, the fecund gravity of the old houses, the ancient iron street lamps and the lush gardens that seem to whisper, 'Hush, child, hush now, sit down, sleep a while, shugah, sleep in the sun . . .' Savannah is wonderfully hypnotic.

Colourful ads posted at the Bean announce that housemates are wanted for houses in some of the most beautiful park-lined streets. The going share-rate is between $200 and $350 a month. I wonder idly what kind of job I might find here. This is certainly a lottery prize worth winning, I think, and I picture what life might be like for me in Savannah, Georgia, USA.

There are no jobs in my future-casting, just an old creeper-covered house, with creaking polished boards and a big claw-footed tub. The Boy is a shaggy haired student still (I'll stick his Green Card-less self in the Design College) and we ride matching low-riders about town, with big grocery baskets in the front to pile up the treats. We have a couple of lazy house cats who lie in the afternoon sun on the antebellum porch and twitch whiskers in their sleep, as well as a big dog who accompanies us on impromptu picnics in the parks or down by the river. We go to the Bean in the mornings for breakfast and then out to Tybee Island to fish. We see movies at the tiny local cinema and get fat on pralines after dinner. Each year we put up decorations for St Patrick's Day and get mightily drunk at O'Connell's old stone pub.

I walk around for a while with my eyes wide open and really consider it. Eyes wide open, but nostrils soon closed. There is a particularly bad smell hanging over Savannah, way out of step with the scenery, like excessive bovine farting. It wafts in from the couple of paper mills churning out stink on the edges of town. It's such a terrible thing to do to a place, a paper mill. People should know better. My high school was near evacuated the year our art teacher attempted papier-mâché; even kids know that rotting cellulose smells like liquid ass.

But apart from the smell and those sticky little flies, Savannah is indeed something special. Courteous citizens, devastating beauty, a genuine downtown where people actually live, walk, work and play, and the final ingredient – squirrels. Okay, these aren't unique to Savannah, but Americans don't know how lucky they are to live in such close proximity to such divine little creatures, all silky fur, graceful leaping and nut-filled cheeks. I could watch them for hours and now I do, spending the rest of my afternoon trying to catch the big fat ones for a bit of a cuddle.

As soon as the hostel reopens I'm already there by the door, making asphalt angels with the toe of my shoe, eager to dump the backpack full of junk that I've been carting around all day. The owner asks how my day was with genuine interest, and tells me that there are a few others coming back if I want to meet up for a drink. 'There's only a few of ya here tonight,' he says. 'Two guys come in on their own and ah, a French couple. They're out to dinner though an' I think they want to be by themselves.' He winks. I go back upstairs and put on my drinking pants, pleased that I won't have to resort to carting a book with me to one of the convivial pubs by the river.

I always envy people with penises their ability to walk into any bar in any town and enjoy a quiet beer by themselves. Not owning one myself, I find I have to borrow a penis to take along with me unless I want to end up fielding dodgy conversation from a whole lot of random, univited ones. When the boys come back, I can tell they're glad to see me too. It's a universal truth that three people with nothing in common except for location is leagues more fun than two.

'I'm Sarah,' I tell them, while the manager looks on benevolently like he's seating us together at the kids' table.

'I'm Jason,' says a short, tea-coloured man with a nervous smile and curly hair. A towering giant with Viking-like dread-locks regards us carefully before announcing, 'I am The Swede.' Jason and I look at each other.

'Oh, okay.' Before I can ask if that's *Mr* The Swede, the Viking explains in a deep, serious voice reminiscent of the Terminator, 'It's my party name.'

'Oh,' we say again, 'okay.'

'You should get one,' The Swede says, pointing in my face, 'for the Good Times.' I don't know about Jason, but the notion of a party name has me feeling a bit pressured. It's a Monday night, after all, and we are currently the only people we know.

I flirt briefly with Farrah, Charlie and Minx, before settling on Pixie. Jason, after much deliberation, chooses Jase. The Swede, snorting, is clearly unimpressed and Jase looks like he's in danger of sulking, so we set off rather hastily to the ale district.

It doesn't take long to get back down to the river, where the old English and Irish-run pubs have great views and giant mugs. All of us are smiling as the first round arrives and Jase is talking a mile a minute about his life in the Peace Corps in Africa. 'I've worked for a lot of non-profits, y'know, all over the world, and as soon as people know I'm from the US, they always have a pile of questions. Finally I realised I'm, like, 27, and I've never even seen anything of the US outside of Philly. So now I'm driving around for a while just to see what I can see, you know?' This leads me to confess the aim of my own journey, and I tell them about my Green Card win and my plans to discover what's really on offer for me in this massive land.

The Swede has been quiet for much of the first hour, putting away three or four beers to our one. My revelation prompts him to belch sombrely and announce, 'Yah, I have a Green Card too. But I hate the US, so I would never use it.' It turns out that The Swede is only half Swedish: his Dad's from New Jersey so he's always had US residency. His old man doesn't want him to let it expire, so he comes here each year to drink and party ('No one parties like Americans, do you understand? No one!' he tells us, using that pointing finger again), working his way up the coast from Miami to New York for a month, before leaving.

Jase sympathises, 'After so many years abroad, I can understand your anger towards America, Swede. Our foreign policy sure has a lot to answer for.' The Swede looks confused. Then he pounds the table with sudden vigour. 'I hate America because they have mostly no care for the fashions of the world. They will never understand European styling.' The Swede drains his tankard and belches again. 'Also, they think I like ABBA. Everywhere I go here. This is all they know of Sweden and it makes me feel aggressive.' He considers this statement. 'Yah, hurtful, and aggressive.'

'Yeah?' I pipe up, 'Have you seen *The Crocodile Hunter*?' But the Swede ignores me, still thinking. 'Also, their food is too sweet,' he says, ordering another beer, 'and did I mention of ABBA?'

Jase is nodding. 'Here I was thinking you might be P.O.'d about Kyoto or our idiot cowboy President blowin' up the world. It's nice to see we're being more creative lately.'

'Hey!' shouts The Swede, banging down his new beer, 'Cowboy? Bush is not a real cowboy! He is like a crying girl compared with real cowboys!' He leans in, sloshing his beer, 'Have you guys ever watched *Young Guns*?' The Swede proceeds to give us the synopsis and blow-by-blow highlights of every crap cowboy series ever shown on TV and any eighties movie featuring a few stetsons and a faithful horse. For another five beers all we hear about are *real* cowboys and their inherent coolness. When The Swede starts singing 'Blaze of Glory', we decide to call it a night.

It's pretty dark outside and each of us might have been adequately intoxicated with a few rounds less. We walk too far down Lincoln and get quite convincingly lost. It soon penetrates my sloshing skull that somehow we've wandered into a bad part of town, the only one the guidebook cautions against. The stately homes are still here, but they are decrepit, with a distinct haunted-mansion seediness. 'Scooby Dooby Doo, where are you?' Jase giggles, stumbling, and I agree. At one am on a Tuesday, none of these creepy bare-gardened houses are asleep. Naked bulbs swing in windows where TV lights flicker. A low-slung car rumbles along behind us for a while. Jase loses the giggles and starts up a nervous mantra of 'Ohshitohshitohshitohshit' while I begin to wonder how many people The Swede could take in a fight.

The car accelerates a little and then stops in front of us. The interior light comes on and the rear window rolls down. At first I think the car must be on fire, but then I realise it's only the ''erb' as the H-less Americans like to say. A woman with a gold front tooth leans out and rasps, 'Y'all wanna party or what?'

The Swede stops and considers it drunkenly. 'But do you have a Party Name?' he inquires.

'A fuckin' *what*?' she asks, struggling to keep her head from wobbling.

'It's Scandinavian for "map", I tell her. 'Which way is downtown?'

'Oh, y'all wanna turn left, hon, and go back maybe . . . seven blocks.' We stumble off in the direction alluded to by a long acrylic nail and a hash pipe, and Jase keeps reliving the moment all the way home: 'Man, that was so intense!'

After fumbling with the door code for what feels like an hour, we bang up the stairs and fall into our beds. I am the only one in my room, which makes me pathetically grateful. I brush my teeth with my eyes closed and plan to leave the next day. Savannah is a small town, revisited with ease in 24 hours, and I have much of the US left to see.

At 4 am I wake to find Veronique, one half of the doe-eyed French couple who arrived quietly just before we went to the bar, exiting the bathroom wearing nought but a tiny travel towel over her tanned skin. Glowing, tousled and wide awake, she looks sheepish as she glides away like a whisper back to her man and her bed. My heart constricts. I feel a deep, drunken melancholy. The trip ahead seems to be less of an adventure and more of a lonesome time delay in the wake of this love-gilded night creature. I will only be travelling further away from the Boy with every mile across this land, with every inch along my ambitious map, with each traitorous fantasy of a new life in a different city. I could cash in my chips and go home tomorrow, so why am I sleeping alone in Georgia? Because someone picked my name out of a barrel? I fall back to sleep with bad dreams.

Chapter 6

Oh Carolina

In the morning, aided by a plunger, a plastic bag, and five bucks for pastries, I manage a real shower and tasty breakfast, which improves my mood. Hungover, I try for a cuppa in the kitchen, but The Swede still hasn't washed up the forty kitchen implements he used last night, despite signs in six languages and dramatic pictures of rodents and roaches carrying travellers from their narrow bunks at night. Using disposable chopsticks to extract a mug at the bottom of the sink, I can hear an Aussie voice at the bottom of the stairs and run down two at a time in my excitement to make that person speak some more. It's been half a year since I saw an Aussie who wasn't my dad. I had taken to cranking up the car stereo every time there was an ad for Outback Steakhouse and they dragged their Australian voice talent in.

It turns out this Aussie is just as pleased to see me. She's an exchange student who has been living in North Carolina for a year and we squawk at full volume to each other while our accents readjust. Somehow I let it slip that I have a small jar of Vegemite in my backpack. She gasps, hand flying to her mouth. 'Ohmygod. No way!' Her eyes actually fill when she sees it and I'm very proud of myself. My fellow countryman's name is Kate and we ponder our cultural fondness for black salty yeast reduction as I join her in a second breakfast.

Dabbing on the spread with reverence, Kate takes a big bite and announces, 'There's no place like home!' Neither of us has really questioned it before, but between us we can't come up with a single Australian we know who doesn't eat Vegemite. Or a single American who has ever professed anything other than terrified disgust after its ingestion. It's a happy moment, crunching our crusts, feet swinging under the grimy kitchen table. Suddenly I'm just really ready to go home to Oz. This is the easiest conversation I've had with a stranger in months.

Kate follows me out onto the street to wish me luck for the trip. Hefting the tomato-pack onto still sunburned shoulders, I set off for the bus stop on foot this time, swinging an apple and some bread and cheese in a plastic bag from the supermarket. The bag keeps breaking and by the time I get two blocks away, the handles are a series of complicated knots biting into my sweaty hand. I have already lost my hostel guidebook, too, missing since I pulled it out at the Greyhound stop yesterday to make the 'pick-up' call. When I arrive at the bright little terminal I go straight up to the counter to ask if it was handed in, but no one has seen it. Grumpy, I sit down to wait for the bus. That book was my secret weapon and now it's gone before I've even left my first destination. I put a new copy on my list of immediate priorities in next-stop New York City, right up there with Krispy Kreme donuts and fake Gucci sunnies.

I have a long way to go today and I've timed my entrance to the bus stop so that I only have about a half-hour wait this time, vowing there will be no repeats of the Miami terminal experience if it can ever be helped. I will be travelling up the South Atlantic coast, through South Carolina and then her Northern sister, through Virginia and then Maryland, which is beside America's only district (fifty states *and* a district, my prize just keeps growing!), the District of Columbia. Halfway up the eastern seaboard, Washington DC does seem like another logical place to stop, but I've been there twice, summer and winter, and straining to see the President's dog make ka-ka on the White House lawn is a strictly one-time kind of thrill. I've seen the museums, the public buildings, memorials and parks, the conspiracy theorists with their sandwich boards proclaiming doom and the huge stately neighbourhoods with trees that rise up high like pictures of Switzerland. It was great, but it was done.

This trip I'll just ride on through, on past the state of New Jersey until, finally, New York. I pull out the map again. My destinations are still flexible and I'm making a shortlist of attractive and improbable places. Tracing a lazy line with my pencil, I toy with Waco and Roswell for obvious reasons, and then I see it. Truth or Consequences, New Mexico. Now we're talking. Straight to the top of the list.

There are only a handful of people in the station this morning. A European couple sits a few rows away wearing matching white sneakers and tight acid-wash jeans. They are bopping to Kenny G piped in as vibrating muzak, exalting, in some language filled with consonants, over their limp Hardee's burgers. Through my early morning hangover I deem them way too cheery to be normal.

Another abnormally cheery woman, noisome and bulky in her wide Bermuda shorts, is pointing to a small plastic sign thanking us for visiting Georgia and exclaiming to her husband, 'Isn't that just the sweetest thang!' over and over again. With her tight peroxide perm and her butterfly glasses, she resembles a character from Gary Larson's *The Far Side* cartoons. Eventually, quite overcome by the sign, she stands up and waddles over to the counter, bailing up the unsuspecting bus staff. 'Well, thank *you* so much for having us! We all really enjoyed your state!' A young girl in uniform with huge hoop earrings looks around for a way out. 'Uh huh . . .' she says. The woman stands on the tips of her puffy-painted Keds and leans over the counter, whispering just loud enough for all of us to hear her charity. 'I just think we should all try to get along, y'know? All the states? And my momma always said to say something nice when you go visiting.' The Greyhound attendant is nodding slowly, trying to look busy despite the obvious lack of competition for her attention. The woman sticks a hand out anyway. 'I'm Betty. I'm from North Carolina, do you know where that is? What's your name, hon?' Jeezus, is she for real? My head throbs and I want to smack her, and the Kenny-G-loving Euro duo, who are now jostling me in a line of precisely three people to get a spot on a half-empty bus.

Our driver's name is Frankie and he immediately forbids us from making any contact with him except for in a dire emergency. Clearly he has driven a Betty or five before. Sweaty from the walk and waiting in the sun by the bus, my damp skin is now drying under the AC and I'm chilled. I discipline myself against putting my jumper on this early in the game and thus, as Renee always says, having 'nowhere to go' later on.

Comforting myself with thoughts of my favourite American fast food, Krispy Kreme Donuts and Popeye's Chicken, which await me at the other end of this bus trip, I snuggle down into myself and dream of treats. With my head lolling dangerously from lack of a workable blow-up pillow, we drive out of Savannah and into sparse forests of black-trunked trees with dappled leafy tops. If I can manage to stay awake, I can tell it's going to be much more fun on these buses in the daytime with a bit of scenery.

The road stretches on out of town, and the world outside the windows becomes increasingly green and lovely. The bus slows past the Lemon Island Marina, a quaint wooden building with hand-painted signs promising live fish and crabs. The marina sits on a headland about a foot above the water, which stretches out wide and still, dotted with scores of low, grassy islands and marshes. There's a lot of water as we drive, and lots of long, slender bridges too. There's nothing remotely Australian about it, but nevertheless, it all looks very familiar. I realise it's because this landscape appears so often on screen. There are many movies and television shows I can think of that must have been set around these parts, including the nineties teen melodrama *Dawson's Creek*, shot somewhere out here in the Carolinas. I half expect to see the whiny cast delivering monologues amongst the lush tall grasses with those fluffy, feathered ends. Even on the bus it always feels like you've stumbled into a film in America. I've seen this very Greyhound bus trip so many times before on the big and small screen, I think, with all these same characters and props.

It is a big, beautiful expanse of country, and I'm sure I could spend all day out there on the water in a little boat with a fishing rod and some snacks. Billboards advertising the evidently popular radio station 104.9 'Gator Country – 'Nothin' but Country and NASCAR!' – begin to interrupt my reverie, and I start to rethink my swamp-livin' fantasies when lots of tumble-down houses appear looking much the one belonging to Jen-ay's poppa in *Forrest Gump*, and I remember that NASCAR motor racing is America's most-watched sport. Hmm, these are not my people.

Our first major stop is at the Beaufort National Cemetery. Briefly confusing Beaufort (*Bew*fort), South Carolina for Beaufort (*Bo*fort), North Carolina, I slump glum and achy when I realise that we are not, in fact, in the North and thus much, much closer to getting off the bus. Having two Carolinas is confusing enough; you'd think they'd have the decency to mix the other names up a little. Out the window as far as the eye can see there are lines of identical white headstones, with wilting flowers and wilting old men scattered in between. The bus comes to a full, engine-off halt and it becomes apparent that some people have made this trip just to visit these ghostly rocks. I feel sorry for them as they shuffle off. War cemeteries the world over leave you feeling like grief has ambushed and beaten the tar out of you.

A few minutes later we pull in at a tiny blue bus station covered in vines, where a strange group of guys are waiting on the little platform. They are all impossibly young, with no hair, and clothes which are a little too carefully creased to be normal. I think we must be picking up kids for some kind of cancer-support camp, then I see the camouflage-covered packs these boys carry and start to get the feeling that Beee-you-fort might be a military town. Armed Forces get a heavy discount on Grey-hound, apparently, as do senior citizens, which explains the high ratio of both types of passengers so far.

The bus door opens, and the boys are full of high spirits as their commanding officer sends them off. They hop in, grinning, and address us all. 'Morning ladies! Morning gentlemen!' They are wearing caps to try to cover their lack of hair, which I find surprisingly endearing despite my general distrust of all things bang-bang-kaboom. These caps get fiddled with and their walks get jaunty when they pass my seat, and I realise I'm the only single female on the bus. My hangover groans for me. A little girl called Molly (all little girls in America are called Molly, it must be a tax-break or something) sits up the front with a T-shirt that announces 'My brother is a Proud US Marine'. A quick flick through the *Lonely Planet* reveals we are about three miles from the Marine Corps Recruit Depot, a US Army boot camp that has trained over a million marines.

It occurs to me now that such a huge war cemetery next to a base of new recruits might fairly be construed as a little odd. It's certainly a constant reminder of the negative job consequences attached to professional warmongering. I wonder if it ever freaks them out when the Greyhound rumbles past it on the way into town.

The military is huge in the US, and a massive part of life in this nation. Looking at these gawky boys I remember the students in the ROTC program at my exchange university in Mississippi. One day out of each week, the kids enrolled under military contracts would have to come to class in full uniform. Well, they might have warned the gentle foreigners is all I'm saying. The first time it happened only Muhammad the Iranian and Viktor the Serb were left standing as the rest of the exchange students hit the ground. Pulling on my jumper and rubbing sleepy eyes, I was flattened on my way to class when a hundred marines suddenly jogged past screaming commands at each other. Confused and utterly petrified, I searched for cover but there was none. Campus lawns were taken up by fields of jack-booted kids pushing themselves up off the ground with one arm, while flocks of suited-up Air Force cadets compared their spit shines. The library was so filled with people in uniforms inspecting shelves that it looked like an anthrax scare.

It makes me uncomfortable to remember it now. Even without the current international strife, this strong military image is a big part of how the rest of the world perceives the US, thanks in large part to Hollywood and the icon of the smiling, liberating GI, the Stallone lone warrior, *M*A*S*H*, *JAG*, the endless Vietnam sagas and World War II epics. These days that image is simply sinister to many and I have mixed feelings when confronted by the reality of these friendly, dedicated young men on the bus and my current fury and amazement over US foreign policy.

It's a tough call to make, though, when I realise that I love Australia and its people just fine despite a disgusted rejection of my own government and their policies on just about everything. Australia is currently sending men and women off to war with the same shameful lack of hesitation. Hmm. I wonder why I never give the American people that same right of separation from their leaders. After all, this is also the country that made Michael Moore's reactionary books and documentaries the bonanza best-sellers that they are. I doze off for a bit, with troubling dreams of cemeteries where headstones are covered by empty baseball caps.

When I wake, it's because someone's eating an overripe banana and this noxious fruit is poisoning the air of the entire bus. The oh-so-cunningly-packaged banana has long been my travel nemesis. It always comes out on buses and planes, boats and trains, just when my lifelong battle with motion sickness reaches its peristaltic peak. Everyone insists I shouldn't blame the wonderful banana when it's obviously an associative thing, like my aversion to Sprite after years of being forced to drink 'flat lemonade' after hwarking all over the place. We have also stopped again to let three women get on with Big Gulps the size of their heads. There is a national obsession with beverages in the US, in particular with the size of them. In a country where the right to free refills of soda and coffee is regarded as constitutional, it puzzles me why people still buy bucket-sized drinks, but maybe it's just to make room for the ice. Americans love ice. It's practically a food group.

Molly the Marine's Proud Sister and I soon become entranced with the nails gripping these Big Gulps. All of the women sport extravagantly architectured talons inlaid with tiny gemstones, as well as miniature scenes depicting sunsets, waterfalls and even unicorns adorning every one. When they finally abandon their drinks, the women keep time in their conversations with a kind of clacking noise from the tips of these little plastic paintings knocking against each other.

Passing a giant warehouse called Harris Pillow Supply, I feel a full-body tug of longing, certain that the past few days with Greyhound have done irreparable damage to my neck. The air conditioning is still shooting up beside the window where I've tried to plug the long vent with paper napkins. In Savannah, Kate had sympathised with me. She had planned to use her towel or jumper as a pillow on her single bus trip into town, but it was so cold she ended up wrapped in them instead, straining to keep her spinal column intact by other means. Americans love air conditioning. Maybe it's related to the ice thing, I don't know. I have friends in the US who have remote control AC so they can turn it on in their homes or cars before they get there to ensure immediate comfort. Climate control is huge here. I may be travelling into summer, but the next few weeks in the bus will be arctic, I can already tell.

In the outside world everything proclaims itself to be Low Country: Low Country Real Estate, Low Country Dollar Store, Low Country Pak & Ship, Low Country Gas and Bait. America from these grimy windows is a little straggly, but as the Low Country rolls on, superficially rural and poor, I can see there are still spots of beauty as well as a delightful familiarity to these scenes. I look out at each town like a location scout. Magnolias are everywhere, gorgeous plate-sized blooms hanging heavy on the trees. Little white wooden buildings and churches, old Dodge trucks and yellow schoolbuses, dogs lying weary in the dust, and kids eating icy-poles with their hair in cornrows. Lush fields of corn and sunflowers butt up against so many wounded-looking houses, abandoned or being slowly pulled down by vegetation. There are hundreds of Spanish-moss-covered trees you might want to hang a rope swing from, add a lemonade stall and cast kids with freckles.

The downtowns are marked simply by dark convenience stores and bars, as well as odd little gas stations with ancient pumps. Whenever we pick up passengers, Frankie takes the mike and drawls, 'Nosmokinnodrinkinnoboozenolikkerandnobooze, that's agin for the learnin' impaired.' Occasionally he will return to the mike and promise to throw anyone off who 'so much as reaches in thar sleep for a cigga-red'. The bus takes us on back roads and suburban streets. We drive so close to houses that at times I think we'll pull up in someone's backyard. I keep squinting and consulting my home-cooked route map. It becomes woefully apparent that I have taken the non-direct bus to New York City by mistake, but by the time I figure out this error and promise to all known deities to never, ever make it again if they rescue me now, it's far too late.

As the hours drag by I become so well acquainted with these godforsaken suburbs I could probably drop most of Dudsville Elementary's fifth grade home after school and take the rest to band practice. I don't think I ever saw this much of Sanibel in six months and it's a bloody island. I fall into a swoon, staring hopefully for freeway signs as the world outside begins to repeat itself. There are rusted porch swings and inflatable pools, half-hearted treehouses, and lost or abandoned toys keep turning up everywhere like part of an eerie exodus. There's a lot of stoop-sitting in the areas where faces are black, looking fairly relaxed and convivial. It is all very interesting, but not quite the sweeping road-trip vistas I imagined with the map before me on Dad's polished floorboards.

Still, I was looking forward to seeing the rest of the Carolinas, and so when I awake four hours later, hair pasted solid to my cheek with freeze-dried dribble, I curse myself for unforgivable sloth and silently minus one donut from the tray of Krispy Kremes I have promised myself. The reason for the sudden stop – full brakes thrown and a lurch of steel leading to an embrace of industrial carpet – is soon apparent. I can smell this region's main export on the air and I shiver with anticipation. Uh oh, Frankie's gonna getcha! There's a tap on the mike. 'Okay, folks. Whomsoever was stupid enough to light up a cigga-red on mah bus, this is you own special stop you lookin' at.' Frankie turns toward the window and makes as if checking a sign. 'Dead Hoss, South Carolina. Population ten. Population will be eleven when you ugly ass follows you ugly luggage offa mah bus.' Craning around in our seats, we wait, toes curling. While everyone's looking around I realise I'm in a bus full of strangers; only the white-shoed couple still sit up the front, as well as a handful of original weirdos. Frankie is quiet, scanning our faces. He stands and yells, 'If you in the restroom and you need help getting out, just holler 'n' I'll be sure and getcha out. Oh, I'll come and getcha.' Silence. The engine is vibrating on, embarrassed to be the only noise. 'Thar's no one in tha toilet,' comes a small voice from the back. Frankie takes a deep breath and exhales loudly through his nose. The engine shudders back into driving speed and we set off, with everyone sitting up extra straight.

There's a madman I suspect to be the secret smoker, and I can tell from the other furtive glances cast his way that I'm not the only one. A few hours ago he drew attention to himself after he got on by crying out at random, 'I doan remember, Juney, I doan remember!' until Frankie told him to shut up or ship out. He mumbled it to himself viciously instead, interspersed with the hissing of, 'I didn't do it, Juney, I didn't do it.' When the mumbling abruptly ceased, the silence was even more unnerving. I had finally built up the courage to turn around and check the madman wasn't arming himself, when his loony voice filled the bus with 'Tiny Dancer' sung in an ultra-serious, cracked falsetto, and I joined the remaining coherent passengers in smothering our frightened giggles.

Shortly after the cigga-red incident, we pull into Williamsburg, which is small and buckled and poor. I'm not sure which Carolina it's in and I no longer care. It's late afternoon and I'm resigned to the fact that I'm not getting out of here any time soon. There is a dark tavern next to the Greyhound station on one side, and the county's drug and alcohol abuse centre on the other. Everything is in a state of disrepair, except the discount tobacco store, which is bright and buzzing. There are a few beautiful old houses scattered around, shuttered and awkward-looking, as if they'd long ago turned up to the wrong party.

All the signs are ancient and peeling, including a large one proclaiming 'Jesus died for your sins, you'd *better* trust him!'. Across the expressway in the pebbled parking lot of a strip mall, a young black man with a Bible is waving madly, flinging his arms up to the heavens and talking to no one that I can see. At his final fling, he holds his arms where they are and lets himself fall backwards, like you do in those office team-building games where you learn to trust the visual-merchandising manager. He lands – *smack* – arms still wide, on his back in the lot. There is a general groan of sympathetic pain from the bus. 'He goan hurt hisself,' a voice declares from the back, 'but he's goin' straight to heaven, that boy.' What follows is the noise of agreement unique to groups of black women – 'Ummmmmmmmmm *hmmmmmmmmmm*' – while they nod deeply. I love that sound. There's something so exclusive and certain about it. The quartet of black women issuing it have the most fantastic and elaborate hair. They have created towering structures of lacquer, synthetic hair-pieces, heat, chemicals and tension to form wedding cakes of gleaming black which shine like feathers. Keeping these dos intact over days in which you would also like to sleep occasionally is quite an achievement. My friends in Mississippi once explained the torturous processes that must be visited upon their tight black curls in order for them to behave like my own limp locks, and I think there should be some kind of follicular Geneva Convention.

A sign proclaims, 'South Carolina. Smiling faces, beautiful places!' but so far I'm not seeing much of either. I sigh and settle down. The bus has been rolling along for hours now, slowly filling, and it doesn't look like I'll keep my own seat for long. The toilet reeks because it's not flushable, just a great sloshing soup tureen holding everyone's mess a foot away from your bum. I make a note to always sit as far from the back as possible on each trip.

The woman opposite me keeps farting. She farts, giggles, and then the evil odour hits me. It gets to the point where I hear the giggle and hold my breath. Tying my jumper arms around my nose and mouth, trying not to hear the sloshing or giggling, homicidal thoughts regarding my fellow passengers begin to fester. The Euro couple are annoying me irrationally by assuming what they must believe to be correct stopping procedure whenever our bus slows. Arm-rests twisted down, seats in upright position, they sit up straight and smile around at everyone inanely. Only the farting woman smiles back. Then she giggles.

The view improves as we begin passing quaint old businesses like the Sunshine Car Wash and the All-Nite Diner, through a small place where it's somehow still 1964. I realise that I have expensive ironic T-shirts with this kind of retro signage on them, and it tickles me to see the real thing. The old-time diner that is so heavily romanticised seems to barely exist anymore, and all the big chains are doing cracking business in their place. It's sad. America is much more charming wherever it manages to ditch the chain stores. Still, I've fielded enough complaints of a similar nature about Australia, which is so tied to its rugged outback image when it's really one of the most urbanised nations in world.

The bus wheezes to a stop in Florence, where a small crowd has gathered with their lumpy bags, pillows and walking sticks. Much disgruntled mumbling follows as everyone realises together that our bus is about to fill completely. First up the stairs is a massive woman who is holding herself like an Amazonian Queen and her luggage like she's just been evicted. Compared to the other people in here, I am small enough to look less like a passenger than a colourful little smear against the window. My seat is the one this woman heads for. 'Good afternoon, child,' she says to me. 'My name is Virginia. Is there room here for another?' I'm smiling a bit of a pinched, fake smile, but she soon wins me over. Especially when I see the state of the other animals coming in two by two, and then I'm just thankful Virginia got to me first.

Driving out of town we pass the Thunderbird Buffet, prompting Virginia to whistle and say, 'My, my, my,' while she waves a hand at her face as if to cool herself. 'Child, I'll tell you something. If you should ever find yourself in Florence, you head straight for the Thunderbird. The food there will make you believe it's the Second Coming. Ummmmmmmmmm *hmmmmmmmmmm.*' My bread and cheese ran out a long time ago and I'm more than ready to discuss snacks. Like two starving souls in a lifeboat, we spend the next hour lost in a private reverie over food. We argue the merits of sweet corn on the cob (white, yellow, with syrup, with butter and salt), lovingly shape the perfect apple pie and roll our lips together in ecstatic contemplation of Popeye's hot biscuits. 'Child, excuse me for saying so,' says Virginia, 'but you much too skinny and much too milky-coloured to like Popeye's Chicken. That's down-home food, child. Food like a fatty huuug. Brings you comfort like a huuug, but it makes you fatty fat fat!' She starts laughing until she has to wipe her eyes, 'Oh my, oh yes it does.' When she discovers I like Krispy Kreme too, we are off again. Peach cobbler, sweet potatoes, red beans and spicy rice, chicken wings, pork ribs . . . aaaarrrrgh.

We pass the South Florence Mobile Home Park, a vast expanse with just one trailer. It might be the haze, but this whole area feels somehow claustrophobic despite its space. It looks eerily like scenes from the movie *The Gift*, and I'm becoming gradually alarmed by the multitude of billboards featuring a hot stove grill with the earnest message 'A stove should only be a place to cook dinner' followed by the Prevent Child Abuse hotline number. It seems some kind of child-cooking epidemic is afoot. The billboards continue to hold my interest. I count 26 signs asking 'Pregnant and scared?' interspersed with ones that shout 'Every 48 minutes a South Carolina teen falls pregnant!' Dark posters as big as the bus remind us that a young mind is a terrible thing to waste, picturing skinny boys ingesting an astonishing array of drugs. I'm tippin' there are some social issues to work through in the Carolinas.

This is confirmed when, from behind us, a couple of thirty-year-olds begin to discuss the wayward behaviour of their grandchildren. One of the women has her ears pierced six times on each side, but each earring has been ripped out through the now separated strips of lobe except for one pair. I decide I would have stopped after the third at least. This is Jerry Springer country, where the poor have become an unfortunate global joke. 'Lil' Carl?' starts one, 'he only three, but he sooooo baaad, jes' a baaaad kid.'

'Ummmm *hmmm* . . .'

'He Donnell's boy, he jes' baaaad like his daddy.'

'Where his daddy at? Where Donnell?'

'Oh, he too young fo jail, but thas where he should be!'

'Mah Tarisha, she the same,' sighs the other thirty-year-old grandma. 'She been datin' a-holes since she were in grade school! Lord knows what she do if her boys turn out like they daddy.'

Virgina snorts and leans in to me. 'Children,' she says, 'should not be makin' children.' She sits back, taking a deep breath. 'Ill-considered is a word for that. Ill-con-sid-ered. Umm *hmmmmm*.'

We pass a big supermarket chain called Piggly Wiggly. Really. And a small wooden building proclaiming itself to be the 'Church of the God of the Firstborn'. There are lots of blended religions here, with spackled together names like Mother Zion Episcopalian Baptist Church of the Holy Ghost and the Seventh Trinity, and I eventually have to stop pestering Virginia to explain them to me. 'Child,' she says 'it doesn't matter to Him where you look for Him. You can find the Lord in the broom closet and, frequently, I do.'

The bus continues at its wrong-bus-punishment pace to Fayetteville, where men sit outside gas stations and farmhouses wearing baseball caps and overalls. The late afternoon sun is flattering, and these places seem more pleasantly bucolic. We pass through Tatum, South Carolina, home of the giant 'Marlboro Academy', and the whole bus erupts with a series of bad jokes about just what it is they teach in there. 'How 'bout lyin' real good and runnin' fast with yer money!' suggests Frankie in a rare moment of fraternisation, and we all laugh a bit extra just for him. This is definitely tobacco country, where all the gas stations promise a 'Smokers' Express!' and huge fields of the golden leaf can be seen off in the distance.

Out the window looms a strange little development, which turns out to be 'Cape Fear Family Housing', where it is possible to buy a pre-fabricated home for $39,000. It would be cheap to live here, I reason, very cheap. That's as far as I will ever get to acknowledging a Carolina as a potential home address, I think, mentally ticking two states off my list until I suddenly remember a trip to Raleigh a few years ago. I visited some family friends at their enormous home in that North Carolina city, and the memory of the beautiful tree-lined streets and the astounding wealth of the place, with its blue-blood traditions of debutante balls and old boy alliances, makes me realise that even within each of the 50 states themselves there must be an incredible amount of diversity. If I was worried before that I wouldn't see all of America, now I'm just worried that I won't truly see much of it at all.

At a remote stop where a truck full of live chickens is turning in to a towering soup factory, a little old man inches his way off the bus, vacating the two seats across from the driver. Virginia apologises as she moves her bulk gracefully to this seat, telling me she'll continue to keep an eye on me, but we must try to go it alone if we want to sleep tonight. 'I'll miss you, sugah,' she says, waving from a foot away, and I nod bravely, already starting to shiver. Frankie, however, is having none of it.

'That seat only fo' people with a disability ma'am,' he says. 'You can't sit there.' Without missing a beat, Virginia whips out an ADA card, announcing, 'My size and my age entitle me to this card, and this card en-TY-tles me to this seat.' Frankie is tired, bored and looking for a fight. He pulls some lame regulation out and dusts it off to be difficult, telling Virginia she had to call a 1-800 number to advise the ticket clerk of her seating needs. 'Greyhound?' she scoffs. 'They want to discuss my *seating needs*? Now since when can you book a seat on a Greyhound bus, young man?' Then this Southern granny with her grey cornrow bun does the unexpected, pulls out a little Nokia (pronounced 'Noh-kia' here) and calls the number while Frankie drives on, cranky as all hell. Virginia looks at me and winks. 'I'm a Brooklyn girl,' she whispers. 'Carnasie.' Unsurprisingly, she gets little joy from the Greyhound ticket staff and Frankie is now demanding a confirmation code that Virginia doesn't have.

Suddenly, a body is squashed in next to mine. A fussy little Mexican woman of considerable girth has just moved in. She had originally tried to swipe the disabled seating from the antique man some stops ago, and was told in no uncertain terms to back off. My two seats, up the front and far away from the Bog of Eternal Stench, are increasingly popular real estate.

'Ha!' she says loudly, 'no disability card!'

'Madame,' replies Virginia, 'I have the necessary entitlement. You need a disability card for your temperament.'

'Not talkin' to you!' the woman says. 'Talkin to her!' and she gestures toward my head while she shuffles me further against the window. Frankie, enjoying the ruckus, tells Virginia she'll have to leave the disabled seat. The giant black woman sighs and balances the few steps back towards me.

'No!' says the Mexican woman, addressing the bus. 'She move, she lose her seat! She up, she lose! So move it, lady! You down the back now!' Shocked by such rudeness and injustice, Virginia and I trade open-mouthed indignation as I am forced to move my gear to further accommodate the cranky little fatso. She has left her two junior charges down the back alone in order to snake Virginia's seat for herself, and the bus decides to hate her. I sit and seethe quietly, plotting this woman's ungainly and possibly fatal fall from the bus door. She, in turn, sticks her furred chin out to the onlookers and growls, 'Why don't you all hire limousines if you want special seat!'

After a few minutes in limbo, Virginia draws herself up and gathers her things. She towers over Fatso and declares, 'Re-MOVE yourself from my seat. I have re-TURNED to claim it.' Visiting from the back, Fatso's grandkids look nervous. Stared down, the little cranky-guts does move back, pushing one child into the aisle, sandwiched between her bulk and Virginia's while they trade places. There is much harumphing. Virginia and I are ridiculously pleased to be reunited as seatmates and I get a taste of the micro-politics and pettiness of Greyhound bus travel. 'Welcome home, Virginia,' I whisper, and we make our little alliance fast as we continue to swap treats and stories over the next few hours. We are unlikely mates, a 70-year-old, 250-pound black woman and me. 'I have no concept of Australia,' Virginia says. 'Child, how can I? It is simply too far away.' She's done some travelling, though, she tells me. 'I've been where they make the straw hats, you know? Where they have banana trees with real bananas, and water so clear I could see my feet. My, my, that was fine.' She is excited for me on my trip to explore the America I have won and listens to my new fear that every state is too big and complex for me to figure out its real potential.

'Child,' she says, 'you said that Green Ticket will last forever, right? Well, you just take forever and use it! You'll see everything in its time.' I tell Virginia that the INS definition of forever is more *discretionary* than biblical, and means I would have to lead a disrupted emotional and professional life split between two countries unless I give up one nation or the other completely for five straight years. Virginia changes her tune. 'Oh, then yes, you in big trouble, child,' she says. 'You have to look hard and decide soon, else you gonna give your mind over to a state of confusion and maybe lose that boy at home. Umm *hmmmm*.'

'Hey,' I say, skin prickling. 'How do you know about my Boy?' Virginia looks insulted. 'Child, there is always a boy,' she says, and closes her eyes. 'In every story that has ever been, there is a boy. But that's not important. Now, look hard at this country, child, look hard as you go because you are changin' your future. That is exactly what you are doing. Changin'. Your. Future. Umm *hmmmm*.'

The sun goes down without drama, melting away to nothing in the soupy air. Time rolls on, measured out by the groaning bus, which pushes us along minute by minute into the future I'm supposedly changing. We're two miles from Raleigh and there are bad smells all around; mothballs from musty travel gear produced once a year, stained patio pillows put to use as headrests, dodgy snack-food, diabolical farting, gassy burps, and the everpresent squashy banana undertones.

By and by, Virginia produces an ancient Walkman and soon begins to hum and tap along to the hymnal tape whirring along inside it. 'It's going to be awhile before I can sleep,' she says. 'Oh yes it is. Ummm *hmmm*.' Living alone now, Virginia likes to stay up all night because she loves the luxury of sleeping in 'ex-TRAV-agantly late', with no witnesses. She says this has given her jet lag without the jets. 'I just have lag,' she chuckles. 'Just a mean case of lag, yes I do.' I long to climb up into her lap and take up her offer to braid my fine 'hay-uh' like her own grey and white cornrows. The humming gets deeper and I'm soon lulled to sleep. Virginia's expanse blocks the rank chill of the bus, which is much like a stale refrigerator, and her rhythmic lullaby is intoxicating.

I wake up with a dead, dead bum and feel like something must be seriously wrong, wrong in the region of blood clots or sudden paralysis. The bus has stopped somewhere, and I'm forced to drag my legs off awkwardly like a heartwarming girl-learns-to-walk-again piece on *60 Minutes*. I join the rest of my comrades on a dark patch of asphalt between a toilet block and a tiny 24-hour convenience store. I've moved past hunger now and refuse Virginia's offer of a share in her sack of home-packed treats rescued from under the bus: two bags of deep-fried chicken winglets from Wal-Mart and a jumbo sack of onion rings. 'I have a healthy appetite,' she chuckles. 'Oh my, oh yes I do.'

It soon becomes apparent that we're waiting for a new driver, and so we hunker down in the greasy rubble on the good side of the smokers. A skinny, plain-looking girl with deep neck sores and giant blue Big Gulp hovers around us where we sit in amiable silence. 'Where you from, honey?' Virginia asks her. After a series of unintelligible noises, the girl hangs her head. 'Oh, I see, child. You special,' Virginia diagnoses, and the girl replies, 'YES MA'AM, yes ma'am,' her head twisting for the sky, fingers rolling around and around themselves. 'Yes ma'am, yes ma'am,' she yells, and she starts to cry a little, from confusion or exhaustion or the bladder pressure of the Big Gulp, who could tell?

Virginia just smiles with divine benediction. 'Child, beautiful child,' she starts (and the profoundly retarded girl is just so far left of beautiful I have to lean away a bit in case Virginia can see what's in my black little heart), 'child, did you know that the Lord has blessed you amongst the most favoured of his flock?' The girl stops crying, and snivels with a dull curiosity. 'Mmm *hmmm*,' continues Virginia, 'the Good Lord, he said, "That child there? That child shall fear no evil, shall know no loss, and will live in ignorance of the cruelest things in this world." Mmm *hmm*. That child there?' and Virginia points a finger at the girl who guffaws at the recognition. 'YES MA'AM!' 'That child,' Virginia says, lowering her voice to a calming whisper, 'will know only her mother's kindness, so blessed is she, just like the unthinking lamb of the shepherd – of the ONE shepherd, the son of the carpenter, and of the Virgin, too – just like the lamb she will be lead by stronger hands with no worry for all her days.'

'Yes ma'am,' the girl mumbles, 'yesmamamam,' and she sits down quietly. Virginia leans back on her chubby hands, and regards the distant streetlight with the sort of satisfied smile I reserve for tropical sunsets and new handbags. 'The Lord's work is in everything, Sarah, and even though it might not always seem to be, in all things He is wise.'

If ever I have seen a place for Virginia's brand of fatalistic Christianity it is here tonight; in the freak show of the Carolina Cuss-belt, for the extra card religion offers up to people dealt too few. I look around. What am I getting myself into? The Greyhound bus fraternity is certainly a long way from the luxurious America I have been spoiled by for the last half a year. In the soggy air, the crowd forms pockets; smokers, frighteners, marines, and a few couples splitting off from the rest to talk low between themselves or not at all. But the broken and the calamitous, the ugly and the ill, one by one they seem to find Virginia and shuffle over to her huge, radiant form. She is part Buddha, part Uncle Tom, dispensing comfort and down-home wisdom to anyone who comes near.

Just as the humidity and traffic fumes become too much to bear, we pile back on the bus with a new driver, a smiling Jamaican man who will take us through the night to New York City, which from these backwoods seems laughably distant. The driver's name is Tommy Justice and his voice is bright and jangling like the steel drums of his homeland. 'If you be listenin' to music or da radio, please, please use a headset. Not everybody like what you like, not everybody in dis world want to hear what you hear. If you want to sleep, then please, please don't snore, and if you want to snore, then please, please, don't sleep!' A great belly laugh erupts from the bus and we hurtle off into the night.

Chapter 7

So good they named it twice

I am dimly aware that the night has been broken, but I struggle to hang on to sleep as the bus stops and starts and stops in traffic. Amidst the lurching I realise we must be finally coming in to New York. On waking, our buckled group performs an awkward and smelly early morning stretch class together. The bus wheezes in and brakes at last. Tommy Justice is jubilant. 'Big Apple!' he cries. 'Noo Yawk Cit-ay! We are ah-rive-IN! Take yah bag and yah kettle, yah pot and yah pan! Please, please don't leave notin' behind you!'

'Well, child,' says Virginia. 'Here we are and here we be. New York City. Oh, she a strange old lady this town, yes she is.' Virginia treats me to a huuuug that nearly breaks me and sets off with her head held high, a big hand pushing at her immaculate braided bun. Expelled from the sub-level Port Authority station, I'm greeted by smoking subway grates, slow-moving yellow cabs and the muted morning whistle of sirens and horns. The light is filtered through the steam and humidity; a rising glow from no particular direction. I stand still for a minute and let it soak in. This is Gotham City all right. It feels like the capital of the world.

Without the missing hostel book to guide me, I turn a few quick circles, trying to point myself in the direction of a hostel that was last found in the dark some two years ago. It was called the Aladdin, a detail I have thankfully not forgotten due to the fact that it was filled with at least forty thieves. Some of the rooms were used by welfare organisations as emergency housing, and so the place had fostered an interesting relationship between people who had no worldly possessions living next door to people who had all their worldly possessions zippered inside a tempting backpack. The Aladdin was all right, though, cheap and central, just off Times Square.

After a few false positives, I find the right cross-street, and finally have the building in my sights. Once inside, however, I am informed by the persnickety desk manager that the Aladdin hostel has closed. It is now a privately owned hotel. After a quick look around, I express the thought that one would hope it had been upgraded for what they are now asking to accommodate my small personage. I follow his suggestion and travel a few more blocks to the ingeniously named Big Apple, where I'm hit up for 35 bucks a night for a bunk in a crowded dorm. I can't check in until midday, but I can be liberated from the tomato-pack, which I place in a locker to have a little nap by itself. Struggling with slippery contact lenses and grubby hands, I finally get my 20/20 back to go outside and have a good look.

New York, New York. The sensory memories stamped on my brain are so unexpectedly strong that I'm giddy as soon as I emerge. It's like time travelling. I suddenly have no sense that anything has happened in the years since I last arrived in this city. After a cursory examination lasting as long as it takes to buy a daily subway ticket, I find that New Yorkers are even more beautiful, more haughty, more unusual and more interesting than I remembered. There are all accents here, all colours, ages, makes and models (and models) but everyone shares attitood. No matter where they've come from, they're Noo Yawkers now, dammit. They've conquered this city. If you can run closer to the front of the Human Race than that, they'd like to know about it.

Another brief stocktake reminds me that footwear here is serious stuff. Being summer, most New Yorkers are now sporting thongs created in an impossible array of colours, shapes and materials. Whoa, I think, hold up, there I go again with the thongs thing. Flip-flops, I repeat, flip-flops. I am attempting back-brain re-education here. In America, thongs are g-string underpants, and this confusion of terms loads simple sentences with social-death dynamite. 'Dad just bought me the cutest little pink thongs,' once stopped a room. The gentle folk of Florida are still recovering from 'Can I borrow your thongs to wear down to the beach?' and 'My brother wants the same rubber thongs as me but I can't find a bigger size.' Think flip-flops, I discipline, *flip-flops*. Sneakers are everywhere too. The highest-end high-end sneakers in the world. This is a walking city, a pedestrian town. Walk fast or die. New Yorkers are still chic, but out of necessity they take comfort far more seriously than, say, Los Angelenos, who are happy to cripple themselves for froth and bubble, and who spend all their time in cars.

As for the city that never sleeps, well, bullshit. It's 7 am and I have a three-hour wait for everything I care about to open. First a bookstore to replace the hostel guide, then Popeye's for a fried chickie breakfast, and maybe H&M for an un-stinky T-shirt. I kick around looking at the big closed city. Hey, what about Chinatown? I decide to take the subway down to Canal Street, certain the industrious Chinese community will be open earlier and longer than any other merchants in this city. Surely they will be setting up the street stalls with fake handbags, wild accessories, and dodgy tourist paraphernalia.

Not so. Can't get so much as a key chain and a won ton. Grumpy now, I head back uptown to Union Square: the subway station and park that had been the hub of our existence when the Boy and I lived briefly in New York. Living ten minutes away in Brooklyn, Union Square was the first major subway stop in Manhattan, the point of exchange for just about everywhere we wanted to go.

Getting off the train here is so familiar that it makes the one distinct difference all the more arresting. Up the stairs, on the way out into the park and the sunshine, is an impromptu memorial. A sad thing, really, for such a mighty town; a humble little offering, like a school-project version of the Vietnam Wall. It takes me a minute to figure out its significance. I have been so lost in a comforting daze of memories, of the feelings of sameness and confirmation, that I'm truly shocked into remembering there has been an interval, a blight. An event I witnessed at home in Australia, from the safety of thousands of miles away, and not here, where a small home was once made too. The names are printed in the usual random roll-call of horrifying events, and some have pitiful scribbles added beside them, or photos sticky-taped up. 'I miss you,' they say simply. 'You were my friend.'

The event is long past, with many other hideous ones filling the breach on the world's stage, but I still feel a grief I don't know what to do with rise and lodge in my neck and mouth. It's not easy to forget the images of people falling from the sky onto the streets of this town. Forcing myself away from the tiled wall, I decide immediately there will be no excursions anywhere near the so-called Ground Zero while I'm here. This is close enough to feel its truth.

Of course, everything is shut around Union Square too, and I slump back on the subway, frustrated and snarling for a wake-up coffee. When the train stops at Spring and Prince, I jump off, remembering that people in Soho take their coffee – 'Java' – as seriously as they take themselves, and I trudge around looking at the beautiful stores where not a creature is stirring, not even a louse. I settle my aching jumble of bones at the Bari Café, corner of Spring and Broadway. I look and smell like I've just spent 20 hours on a bus with mad, fat, stinky people chugging through swamp. In an area of town where models eat for free if they sit in café windows, I am afforded only a mite more respect than janitorial staff at Yankee Stadium. The $4 spent on a daily subway pass entitling me to unlimited exploration is a much better deal than my $4 latte. It tastes thin and burnt, and is not improved by the fact that I'm drinking it while perched on the edge of a posh, sore-ass-unfriendly seat.

The woman next to me starts up a conversation with a stranger, who is apparently also local to the area and the café. I frown. I don't remember this kind of interaction here before. NYC is the capital of MYOB. It's not that people are as unfriendly as the punch-lines would have it, just that they like to keep themselves to themselves. It's called self-preservation when you live squished next to nine million others. Without so much as a sugar packet to read, I begin to eavesdrop shamelessly for some low-level entertainment.

The woman says she works as a grief counsellor at a hospital here, a vocational change made in the weeks following the World Trade Center attacks. Instantly they're talking about it – who they lost, who escaped and the woman on their subway route who was just never there again, the worst finally confirmed. Scratch the surface here and it seems you'll now find 9/11 just below, waiting to bubble out and be made sense of. I can tell the other patrons have tuned into the same frequency as me now, and we're all listening, all waiting to hear the stories of courage and chaos that stunned the world. The woman delivers. Her daughter's boyfriend was trapped inside the WTC and the girl ran twenty blocks from uptown to the site to find him, only to be shielded from the tower's sudden collapse by an Arab felafel shop owner. Three hours later she found her boyfriend wandering down near the river, screaming her name. A week later they were married. The mother's eyes fill and there is an audible sniffle from the barista.

The woman goes on to talk about the book she's writing on grief and reincarnation. The man she's talking to lost 15 people he knew, most well, and they discover that some of them were common acquaintances. The man is wiping his eyes with the back of his hand. 'It's okay to me,' the woman says. 'It's okay to me now that I believe in reincarnation. I know they'll be back.' The man nods hopefully and they stare out the window with their thoughts. Just then a baby passes by in a luxury stroller pushed by a Soho über-mom. This is hardly an unusual part of the street traffic in this neighbourhood, but the little bundle of rolls gives them a bobbing head, curious cross-eyed regard and the man laughs a little, saying, 'Maybe they're back already.' The two clink their grande latte glasses together and take a swig. 9/11 has really galvanised this town. I can't believe how little I am prepared for this change.

I don't know anyone who died in the attacks on the WTC. Sometimes I worry about the man who worked on the 89th floor, the man we met on a train at Thanksgiving, but the Boy says he remembers the man looking especially strong and fast. I said I thought he looked a bit fat, but the Boy said that it was all the more reason to suspect he was okay, as he was probably downstairs in the food court eating snacks. The Boy is very comforting and wise on such matters.

Suddenly, it occurs to me that we did lose a friend that day. Turning it round in my head until it resembles Osama v. Krispy Kreme, I am filled with fury at the destruction of our favourite hangout. Right at the bottom of those amazingly tall buildings was our 'Best Krisper', the best and most accommodating of the few Krispy Kreme stores in Manhattan. It was, with some competition, our Happiest Place. Now, somewhere a few blocks from here, it's rubble. I think of the bathroom key with the enormous smiley-face keychain (handed over begrudgingly like all bathrooms keys are in this city) and of the plastic booths made warm by our ever-growing arses as we drank the slippery donuts and chewed through our strong coffee, planning Christmas and feeling the flush of treating ourselves. The chipped mint-green counter, those little plastic donut-trucks, the T-shirt display. I wonder fleetingly, stupidly, if they ever did get the grey one in a medium that we were always ordering to no avail. And if they did, I wonder – stirring my second bad latte and going into full-wonder-mode – I wonder if it ended up forgotten. Discarded, abandoned and left to be crushed into fibres, ash, nothingness, along with the huge machines that made those perfect rings of hot nectar-like dough. It actually hurts me to know that it's probably gone.

The keys though, maybe they made it. That silly toilet key so jealously guarded, did someone take it with them when they left? Was it always kept safe in a pocket so that someone might have just run out with it? And did the last person to use it ever think later, ever understand, that their one turn and click was its last? That the tiny jiggle and the half-tug had crossed the line between sacred and hoarded toilet-privilege to utterly worthless object? I wonder if that moment came and if anyone knew it. I wonder if the key was ever pulled from a pocket later, somewhere else in New York City, and regarded for its sudden value shift – like Prada heels dropped into the Gobi desert.

I wonder now too about the poor bastards who flew the planes into the buildings. The miserable dopes who dragged themselves off to Florida flight schools every day knowing it was just so they could learn how to squash and burn themselves amongst the fuselage. Arming themselves with stationary products and stabbing at surprised people they'd never met with their little plastic box-cutters.

I wonder if they had ever in their short lives had that feeling I used to get there in that place before they blew it up. The equivalent of a sticky, absentminded kiss in a Krispy Kreme booth while swapping parts of the *New York Times*, toes wiggling to be inside and out of the cold, hearts weighed down with nothing more sinister than the prospect of being bitch-slapped by the night air when the donut box was empty and it was time to leave. It wasn't perfect. Even in my fantasies the 300-pound attendant is squat and mean and smells alarmingly of thawing chicken. The couple behind us are hissing about their in-laws, and a pug-faced four-year-old is busy figuring out how to suffocate his sister when Dad's not looking. But it's also safety in here, warmth and love, and the sharing of sugary treats. I wonder finally if anyone could have given those blank-eyed young men a taste of that enough to remind them why any of us bother to live at all. Hell, at $4.86 a dozen, I would have gladly shouted them.

Back out on the streets, slightly wired from breakfasting purely on caffeine, New York is a madhouse. She is waking up and beginning her crazy chatter, banging things around and throwing open doors. She is everything and everyone all at once. I am overwhelmed. How did I ever find myself immune to her charms? She's a bitch goddess and a fruitcake mama. Virgina is right: she's definitely a woman, this town. My senses get a whip-lashing, especially my nose, which I'll have to toughen up if I want to ride that ponky bus again.

New York smells of sugary pastries, urine in the hot sun, cut flowers, fried chicken, Asian grocers and turning fish, of incense and of subway air (which does not actually belong to her, but is a plagiarised approximation of that train smell – warm and dry and faintly peppery – common to all underground railways.) She smells of leather and top-notch Duty Free counters, of chewing gum and electricity, of sauerkraut and mustard, of acrylic nails and bendy pizza, of alcoholic vomit and gasoline, of glitter gel and suncreamed shoulders, of every kind of smokable plant, of every kind of artificial fragrance. She is primped and tanned and pale and pierced and tattooed and coifed and suited and in bags. Like me, she's a glutton for accessories. She loves to wear sunglasses and hats from all eras, in all shapes and sizes and price tags. She is in costume, in drag, in uniform and in swaddling clothes. Above all, she is triumphant, and far too busy to talk to you.

Outside the Soho subway entrance, one smell overpowers the others. A heavenly, wafting smell of vanilla and warm sugar, like cartoon-fingers of irresistible scent that float you along by the nostrils. It comes from the roasted, coated nuts I had forgotten all about. Abruptly, my nose is smacked by those same cartoon fingers – another sensory memory lost was just how bad a burning pretzel smells. Just a bite-sized piece left to scorch is more effective than tear gas at clearing a city block. Acrid and utterly caustic, it doesn't smell like burning dough or, in fact, burning anything from the natural world. If evil alien spacecraft had exhaust systems, I am certain they would expel fumes of similar composition.

A man walks past me with a big golden dog shaved like a lion, its fluffy mane and tufted tail causing people to jump quickly out of the way. Ooh, I think, I want one. With a lion dog in one hand and some burny pretzel in the other I could walk these crowded streets like Moses. New York is a very doggy town. There is almost nothing here that people have and dogs don't. The list of pooch services is astounding. For a city with the smallest dwelling sizes of anywhere in the US, small even by international standards, the obsession with big pooping animals who want to run around outside all day is puzzling. New Yorkers are very fastidious about cleaning up after them, though, which is a relief after other doggy cities like Paris, where visitors can be forgiven for thinking that the locals worship canine faeces, there are so many impromptu shrines erected and left undisturbed every minute of the day.

From the massive Barnes and Noble now open back at Union Square, I purchase another hostel book and am delighted to find that the cheapest digs are in Chelsea, which will be a good base to explore this city all over again. I allow myself a little skip out the doors, feeling a bit better after being hit over the head with the aftermath of international terrorism. After a second mission to grab the tomato-pack from the Big Apple locker, I trek to West 20th Street, eager to get settled so I can run off into the fast advancing day.

The Chelsea Hostel shares a grand allusion to the rock-legend Chelsea Hotel and little else. The rooms are small and stuffy, and the toilets are pretty grim. I rid myself of everything back-packy and dress for New York from the pitiful supplies I have apportioned myself. Shades, denim, ghetto-hoop earrings and a floaty thrift store top. Special bag. Th . . . *flip-flops*. I feel New York again, and when I walk out, it's into the past, into the year 2000.

In that year Bill Clinton was President. I lived with the Boy in an old walk-up on the Hudson, all the way up at 181st Street near the George Washington Bridge. We sub-let from an actress going on tour. She left us a bottle of salad dressing and cable TV. The apartment was furnished when the Boy found a king-sized mattress out the front of a Baskin and Robbins ice-cream store in the middle of the night. He dragged the mattress back and it completely filled our one-roomed apartment, turning our life here into a kind of John and Yoko album cover. With no money, no work visas, and no winter clothes, we spent the chilly months in our bed-room watching *Iron Chef* on Food Network television and cooking increasingly elaborate meals in the one-person kitchen. Working in our kitchen was a bit like playing Twister and Monkeys in a Barrel at the same time, and when we sat on our Manhattan toilet, our knees and thighs fitted under the hand-basin. One night this made us laugh so hard I pulled a muscle in my jaw. This was my New York.

I keep walking. In this year 2000 reality, the Boy would be right here buying corn from the Farmer's Market in Union Square with the silly big grin he reserves for fresh produce. Moving his head in time with the busker's tune from the subway station. Pretending to be interested in whatever junk I've just bought. Making me giggle with some bad footpath dancing.

It starts to come back in a flood now and I feel like I'm choking. I'm more sentimental than a Hallmark greeting writer with a basket of puppies. I must find treats, and fast. But I keep getting lost. I aim my body in the right direction but I'm never really sure. Does Canal follow Prince? Is that the park over there? How am I already at the Empire State? I see myself in a polished window and rapidly deflate. I've got the outfit, the attitude, and the correct pedestrian etiquette down, but my darting-eyed wonderment gives it away. *Turista*! I adopt a haughtier expression. When real tourists start asking me for directions I bubble with pride. This is still my town. Live here again? Hell yeah, I think, in a heartbeat, sure. Now get outta my way.

It only takes a few hours in this city for me to remember why I entered the Green Card lottery, and what it actually means to have one now. The New York of 2000 – that illegal, impoverished, toe-hold New York – is slowly being erased, block by block, by the little plastic card in my pocket.

The Boy and I had arrived here with big plans and no idea, with fabulous apprenticeships and no salaries. The lengths we went to in order to scrounge enough money for rent, a monthly subway ticket and some meals consisting mainly of starches, was the reason I had put my name in that massive barrel; the reason I'm smiling now. Of course I've won something, I think, imagining how thrilling it would have been to be handed this Green Card during that time.

With our unpaid internships set up before we entered the country, the Boy and I had wondered if it was possible – as it is in the UK and Canada – to get a limited working visa for the USA. It is not possible. When you call to ask, there is a moment's silence before the INS laughs at you and adds your name to the 'suspicious entrants' list. There is no such thing as a working holiday and getting a company to financially sponsor you from the other side of the world when they've never laid eyes on you is really the definition of optimistic.

We applied for extended tourist visas, valid for six months each, reasoning that once we were in we'd just get unpaid jobs on the side – waitressing, washing dishes, whatever – you always hear about the tons of people working illegally in the US, right? Right. After weeks of considerable despair, we found that securing even the most menial cash-in-hand jobs was impossible without cracking some kind of migrant network, and we knew not a single soul. It was suggested to us that if we spoke Spanish and looked a little less white, people might be more willing to pay us $4 an hour to scour pans, but then again . . .

I had never in my life wished so hard to be a dishwasher. For people with the magic card I hold now, there were wonderful jobs in the paper each week. Truly amazing vocations. Think of something – no really, go on – the best possible something you would want to do each day for money, and someone is currently advertising it in New York City. Reading descriptions of the dream jobs I would never be entitled to, I had sighed big sighs and worried into the small hours. What had we been thinking? Without Social Security numbers, our names were mud. Worse than mud; people were paying for mud at beauty parlours on Fifth Avenue. The Boy made up a little song on his guitar when our intern lifestyle grew difficult. 'It's not easy, being free,' he sang, channelling the voice of Kermit the Frog, 'spending your whole life, never making any green . . .' New stanzas on poverty were being added every day.

One Cheeto away from living off packets of coffee creamer stolen from the office I was interning in, there came a break-through. We finally found illegal work in New York City. It was not with our unskilled hands after all – oh no, those dishwashing cartels are hard to crack. It was not through our cunning, our determination, our networking or our talent either, but through my chronic dermatitis and the Boy's healthy skepticism. We found our vocations lurking at the back of the *Village Voice*, where two advertisements caught our attention. The first read, 'Are you a woman who suffers from eczema, psoriasis, or rosacea? Who is between the ages of 18 and 35 and has already seen a doctor for this condition? Call this number now to be part of our paying survey.'

'That's me!' I cried to the Boy, scritch-scratching at my palms and elbows for confirmation, 'Look! I practically have all three!'

'Well done, baby,' he said, and he meant it. We were pretty broke. The Boy scanned the rest of the page and read aloud the same ad he had returned to week after week. It read simply, 'Smoke Pot, Get Paid.' He rolled the paper up and tapped the back of his hand with slow purpose. 'Now obviously,' he reasoned, 'there's a big catch, but I think my mission is to find it.'

A week later I found myself in uptown Manhattan, sitting at a conference table with a group of itchy women, while we answered simple questions and ate from a bountiful array of free snacks. In between mouthfuls and filling my pockets, I chatted and performed, eager to have an audience again after having all but worn out my repertoire with the Boy, my only companion in this town. At the end of the 90-minute feast, I was presented with $100 in cash. Even I can do that math. This was the best job I'd ever had. I stumbled out onto the street holding the bill in front of my eyes, counting zeros again and again to be sure.

'Do you think they'll have more of these?' I asked a kindly woman who'd giggled at my flaky skin jokes, 'Other eczema-type paydays?'

'Hmm? Oh, I don't know,' she said, and looked around. 'Look, I don't even have eczema, hon. I have a birthday present to buy this weekend and my rent's due.' I opened my mouth as wide as my eyes, and I suppose she could tell I was innocent. With her finger to her lips she took me around the corner and explained the facts of life as they are in a big hungry city. A few days later my new Fairy Godmother sent me an email containing some of the most jealously guarded material in all of Manhattan. A list of fourteen phone numbers along with extremely detailed instructions on how to play focus groups for fun and profit.

The information came with the caveat that under no circumstances was I ever, EVER, to pass this along to anyone else. She was only imparting it to me because I was leaving the country soon, right? And I was illegal and desperate, right? Right. After a few false starts and rejections, the Boy and I became experts. We learnt all the right answers to 'How did you get this number?', used different accents, details, and basically just lied as hard as we could.

'How old are you ma'am?'

'Twenty-two.'

'Children?'

'No.'

'How many times a week do you wash your hair?'

'Mmm, seven.'

'Do you enjoy alcoholic beverages?'

'Yes.'

'Do you eat fish?'

'Yes.'

'Is your mother still alive?'

'Yes.'

'Okay, and do you have a college degree?'

'Yes.'

'Oh. Well, I'm afraid we can't use you at this time, I'm sorry.'

'That's okay. Oh, hey, my sister doesn't have a degree yet, can she try out?'

'Sure, put her on.'

After a respectable pause, I would begin the questioning again. Or get my brother, or husband, or neighbour or visiting Hungarian cousin. All over America consumers are still enjoying products influenced by the lies of two hungry Australian kids alone in a big city. We would frequently get the same jobs, too, and have to pretend not to know each other, let alone let it slip that we lived together.

'I very much enjoy the taste of Mango Snapple,' the Boy would say, munching from the platter of ham and Swiss sandwiches in front of us, 'and I would love to see a cranberry version, certainly.'

'Cranberry!' I would scoff, 'You don't . . . *look* like the sort of person who would like cranberry.'

Our jobs grew bigger and ever more elaborate. I was served a three-course meal on Madison Avenue over a two hour pow-wow on the merits of Pantene shampoo and was paid 150 bucks. That was just over 300 Australian dollars at the time. I test drove the New York Lotteries website in a silent cubicle where I spoke aloud to myself for twenty minutes for $100. I was flying. For years I had been babbling on about things I had no knowledge of for free, and now my true talent was being recognised with cold hard cash.

I gave impassioned speeches about the necessity of sanitary pads to continue growing wings and suggested that they make panty liners in black; an evolutionary event that has since occurred and for which I take quiet credit. One night the Boy and I hit jackpot. We had both been selected, or should I say, two of our many alter egos had been selected (probably the ones who were entertainment lawyers and investment bankers) to test and discuss Guinness at the coolest hotel in New York, the Soho Grand. Standing outside on the frozen street after the main event (at which I had voted in favour of beer with chocolate and vitamins, the Boy for a double-strength brew), I licked the icing from one of the three cakes I had smuggled away and sighed with deep satisfaction. The Boy gnawed at one of the oversized turkey legs that had lined his deep pockets on the way out, and said thoughtfully, 'Pretty good we couldn't get jobs as dishwashers.'

Eventually, I was getting far more gigs than the Boy. There were always more of these jobs for women than men (apparently women actually buy all the little stuff; we are overly represented in the everyday-consumers-of-useless-crap market). We were down to being a single-income household again, when one day I came home to find an unusually smug looking Boy lying prone on the mattress.

'Guess where I've been all morning,' he said, giggling to himself with red-rimmed eyes.

'No!' I breathed.

'But yes!' he replied, triumphant.

Though America had made it next to impossible for the hugely talented and intelligent Boy to gain the most poorly paid and undesirable work, the US government was growing fields of high-grade marijuana plants which it was – via the middleman of Columbia University – *paying* the Boy to smoke. We found this hilarious for quite some time, and tears of mirth were shed as the Boy described his new vocation (well, what he could remember of it). He filled in questionnaires, kindly doctors tested his vital signs, a delicious hot meal was served and then he repaired to his 'office': a little room overlooking the Hudson River with a two-way mirror. There he was instructed via intercom to spark it up and play a computer game of limited complexity, inhaling and exhaling at the command of his new employers. I have friends who have been in training for this position for years. After whiling away an hour or so in this manner, he was given another (now very necessary) snack, and a subway token to ride home. He had elected to be paid in a lump sum when his tenure at the University was complete. The Boy said he rather enjoyed his new job and didn't think he'd be taking any sick days.

We tried to enrol me in the same program, which sounded too good to be true. I took a day off from my internship and we travelled uptown on the train together, where I was poked and prodded and peed-out, but discovered after all the preliminaries that I was somehow ineligible. Still, after ascertaining that I wasn't pregnant, they offered me a go at some alcohol testing. The Boy got the shits then and said he was calling his union. He viewed it as an unfair promotion, immediately requesting overtime so he too could participate in Get Drunk, Get Paid, but the good doctors were having none of it.

It turned out that the alcohol program involved ingesting five standard drinks and a handful of over the counter flu medication, which I knew from personal experience just made you feel like someone backed a Land Cruiser over your head. I decided I was unwilling to spend a full day feeling poorly when there was still money to be made swindling toothpaste and deodorant surveyors. Also, the Boy and I were putting in serious time at our internships.

I was working four nine-hour days a week for one of the largest film production companies in the world. On the 57th floor of a skyscraper on Seventh Avenue near Radio City Music Hall and the Russian Tearoom, I faxed and filed and photocopied screenplays all day, rubbing shoulders with greatness and trying to avoid being verbally disembowelled for the slightest transgression. One day my writing hero David Mamet called, only I didn't know it was David Mamet – all I knew was that a man was on the line asking me to inform my boss that her Dog Psychiatrist was on the phone. I was very new, and this was New York, and my boss was a Very Important Person. It was entirely possible that this man was who he said he was. I knocked on the door and passed her the message, only to be met with a look that eviscerated and cauterised at the same time. 'I don't even have a *dog*,' she hissed, and I had retreated, only to be further ridiculed by Mamet, who to my horror identified himself, saying, 'We're making a little movie together, she'll remember me.'

Eventually I got sharp enough to graduate to all the duties of a real Hollywood assistant. I ordered in macro-Japanese and soy-protein burgers, held umbrellas over gazillion-dollar celebrities as they exited their chauffeured cars, ferried Evian in and out of offices, massaged crumbs off conference tables, and never, ever, ever confused decaf and regular. I went downtown to clean the litter trays for the Vice President's demented cat in her Chelsea loft, I picked up the President's dry-cleaning and shielded it from the snow to the Park Avenue hotel where he lived when he was up from LA. I had come so far so fast that I felt giddy with success. Paid assistants with MFA's spend years at this mezzanine level of responsibility.

After a few months of this, the weather chilled and the magic faded. Downtown, the Boy's internship was really motoring along. He was redesigning the interior of a nightclub, which was run by a group of environmental activists and owned by a man who made his fortune from a documentary about the legendary jam-band The Grateful Dead. The Boy spent his days sourcing plastic sheeting and camouflage netting in Chinatown, trying to get teenage volunteers to leave their dreadlocks and body jewellery alone long enough to paint his Earth Station.

One day I called the Boy in tears from the Vice-Presidential Chelsea loft. The cat had bailed me up in a corner and was wailing like a hellish siren, her talons slicing the air. Her owner was away at Cannes, or Sundance, or somewhere else I was fast realising I'd never get to go, and the cat had become more feral than anyone back at the office thought possible (You're tough, they had told me when they hustled me down there, you're Australian right? A Crocodile Huntress. I was the best woman for that kind of job). The cat had thrown up fishy chunks and bile the length and breadth of the house, as well leaving a trail of mucusy diarrhoea that stretched from the hall to the kitchen floor. She was not sick; she was spiteful.

Her litter box, placed in the bathtub (possibly to avoid the scenario that greeted me) had become waterlogged from a steadily-dripping shower until the tub was filled with eight inches of poo, pebbles, fur and water, on which the plastic tray floated like the boat on the river Styx. This cat was not just grumpy. This cat was a vicious beast. It had in no way been weakened by its ordeal. It would kill me if given half the chance. It wanted me to know it *would* kill me. Furthermore, I had been instructed from on high to deal with this mess as if my life depended on it. Trembling with fear, keeping the hissing, pounce-ready cat in view at all times, I knelt on the ground swabbing her violent emissions with Kleenex and tears.

So I called the Boy and explained between hiccuping sobs that there was an Attack Cat trying to slice my face off and I was using Q-tips to clean its poo out of the cracks in my boss's floor, who, incidentally, still thought my name was Sally. And I was doing this for free. In winter. In one of the most expensive cities in the world to lay your head. We decided then and there I had learned what I needed to about the American film industry. The curve had reached a distinct plateau. After the Boy prescribed a box of donuts up the road at Krispy Kreme, I felt strong enough to continue for a few more weeks, but then I stopped doing good work full-time for free, to devote myself to doing no work, sporadically, for great money.

The final reminder – if I need one – about the value of this card comes to me now as I find myself on 45th, standing in front of the gated fortress of a building where I briefly interned for mogul movie producer Scott Rudin. I was still moonlighting (if the term applies to free labour) for New Line Cinema, and one day my New Line mates asked if I'd like to earn 50 bucks by doing an hour of promo work for the new Adam Sandler film *Little Nicky*. Stupid question, really. At that point, there wasn't much I wouldn't do for 50 bucks. The event would take place outside the MTV studios, which were around the corner from Rudin's office. Starving by the time lunch rolled around, I was forced to forgo food, sneaking off instead to don a tiny T-shirt proclaiming me to be one of 'Nicky's Angels', before jumping around like a dickhead in the petrifying cold in front of hordes of Christmas tourists.

I was late coming back to an office where disapproval might literally be injurious, and remained tired, cold and humiliated for the rest of the day. That night the Boy and I discussed where the heavenly gift of 50 big ones would best be spent. I felt like such a good provider and had puffed with pride. The next day I made an early trip into the New Line office to collect my money. It was a cheque. And they needed a Social Security number to issue it. Wandering back out into the snow I clenched my small fist and raised it to the sky. 'Nothing,' I cried. 'All for nothing!'

So yes, this city feels very different with my Green Card. I'm very, very aware of it for the first time. I feel bold with my Green Card. More like a real New Yorker now. Legitimate. I'm walking around singing the 'whoa ho, I'm an alien, I'm a legal alien' line from Sting's 'Englishman in New York' song. Works much better as 'Aust-rail-yan in Noo Yawk', by the way. With a light heart, I'm thinking about how I can do what I want in this city now. No more medical testing, no hair product lies! I can make hundreds tending bar, establish some kind of real career, or just chill out working at Barnes and Noble, selling three floors of books all day. I can work in a Greenwich café or I can . . . I can. That's all. Just a shift in possibilities and the city seems so much more on my side than before. Hey sugar, she's growling, ya back. Is that a Green Card in ya pocket, or ya just happy to see me?

It's a beautiful day, and I buy some gooey gelato to take for a walk in the sun. I'm looking around with the understanding that I could be here forever now, never leave. Find a new job, somewhere to live, and just stay. This could be it, this could be me, this could be my life. Strolling through Central Park, I remember waiting there for free tickets to Shakespeare in the Park; lying on the grass with the Boy, the *Times*, and a box of Krispy Kremes. This could be my future. That's the real prize,

I think, the excitement and the thrill of it. The choice is so huge. This country is so different from mine. But can I have them both? For how long? And where? At this point my gelato falls off its cone and I'm swearing too energetically to answer my own questions.

I keep itching to call the Boy, but I've left my mother-ship-sized organiser and calling card back at the hostel. I make a detour there on my way uptown to visit with the squirrels in the park. Opening the door with a long squeal of wood and paint, I am greeted by a flood of inquiry. 'Hiya! Are you my roommate then? What are the other girls like? Have they stolen your stuff? Has anyone messed with your stuff?' A beautiful girl stands next to a monstrous suitcase, patting at her Alicia-Keys-style braids like she is calming a small dog.

'Oi!' she says. 'I hope you don't fink I'm in 'ere messing wif your stuff, because I've got my own stuff, yeah, loads of stuff, and it's good stuff too. I brought all m' best gear wif me.' Then she looks nervous. 'But don't tell anyone else about m' best gear, yeah. I'm only telling you so you don't fink I'm messing wif *your* stuff. Did you bring your best gear then?' It is impossible to marry this hideous voice to the gorgeous young woman producing it. Her name is Lucy ('Oi, please don't start singin' about effen' skies and diamonds, yeah, because me mum says that song's about drugs an' loonies an' makes er wish she'd never called me it.'), and her dad is from Ghana, but she and her accent hail firmly from Norf Laaandan.

Lucy tells me she's been in New York for 'one hour, but only if I'm allowed to count the taxi trip in – can I count the taxi trip? Did you count *your* taxi trip in?' Out of politeness I make the mistake of asking Lucy what her plans are. She sits down on the suitcase and fixes me with the wide-eyed, earnest expression you might give someone interviewing you for a job. 'I just really want to be famous, yeah, really, really famous. And I want to do it all, yeah. Actresssss, modellll, singerrrrr, songwriterrrr . . .' She ticks them off her fingers musically, like the periodic table. She squints at me. 'Are you an actress or somefink? Is there lots of actresses and models in here? People tryin' to make a lucky break, like?'

Hmmm, not so much, I tell her, reluctant to explain that most people here are en route to somewhere else, and just want to see the sights, drink some beer, clog some ashtrays, and trade travel stories. Lucy talks non-stop for 40 minutes. I keep trying to leave, but she and her suitcase are blocking the door as well as my best attempts at excuses. My addition to the conversation sounds like 'A ... bu ... lef ... bi ... a ... uh ... g ...' but Lucy doesn't seem to notice.

'If someone messes wif my stuff I swear I'll kill 'em,' she says, 'and I'm not a violent person. I worked at nice places where I worked – Selfridges and Harrods, truly – and people still nicked things and you needed a locker! And you wouldn't fink that in those posh places, but you do, people will do anything for money you know, they will, *anything*, me mum says. Oi, can I call me mum? Because it's early here, only two, but it's seven there at home, and they'll have dinner on.' At the mention of the family dinner table she bursts into tears, and then quickly stops, making a face like someone told not to scratch a particularly nasty bite. 'Do they have MTV and cable?' asks Lucy, recovering. 'Where can I watch TV? I am *especially* interested in MTV, because that's how my career will start, I fink, and I need to do research. I especially need to know what the singers are wearing, yeah, and the hosts too I s'pose. If I am ever invited on, then I can remember and compliment them. The hosts, I mean. Oi, do they call them hosts? And do you fink that would make a difference?' she asks, 'if I complimented them?' 'A ... yu ... puh ...' is all I get in as an answer.

'Where can I get dinner in New York City?' she asks finally, standing up from the suitcase settee. In New York?!

'Yeah, can I just have a McDonald's like, or is it all too fancy for a McDonald's?' I draw a hasty map to the nearest Maccas and flee. My hand is covering my mouth all the way to out onto the street and I'm shaking my head not knowing whether to giggle or squeeze out a tear.

I wander around Chelsea for a while looking for a net-café, before I remember that they hardly exist in Manhattan, and indeed, in the rest of the USA. Perhaps it's because more people have personal computers in the US, or perhaps it's how Bill

Gates gets people to buy them. After my luck in Savannah, I figure I'll try the library. A tall black man in a wizard's costume, complete with knee-length beard, enters the turnstile for the New York Public Library's Chelsea branch at the same time as me. Fifteen minutes later I see him reading quietly at the same table as a tiny old Korean woman, a turbaned Sikh and a little blonde girl dressed like Madeline. Wizard-man has a book called *Magicks and Spellcasting*, which he is reading peacefully, one foot tucked just behind the other inside glittering Merlin boots. Though sitting close enough to touch, none of the four regard each other in the slightest. Over by the photocopier a little group of people are busily making signs to protest against scam pamphleteering, while a guy at the next machine is making what look likely to be those very same scam pamphlets. Apart from occasional sniffs of mutual contempt, order is maintained.

When my turn comes up on the computer, I search 'Greyhound bus' to find out how to get to Maine. I find some unexpected information about Greyhound travel and promptly wish I hadn't. After some simple clicking and Hansel-und-Gretel-style link following, I come to understand that I am now using the method of transport most favoured by the prison systems of the United States. Apparently, when incarcerated criminals and detainees of America's mental-health lock-downs are paroled, they are issued one pair of prison-made khaki pants, one blue shirt, some lunch money and a one-way Greyhound bus ticket home. My scrolling finger is burning through material. I read testimonials from concerned citizens, concerned police officers and even concerned members of the State Boards of Pardons and Paroles. They are concerned about the hundreds of 'low-functioning, potentially aggressive' inmates and mental patients ejected from their institutional lives into the swirling chaos of crowded bus terminals, facing days of journeying home towards uncertain futures with no money. Well, no shit, Sheriff, now I'm concerned.

Los Angeles police are online complaining bitterly about their downtown Greyhound terminal, where parolees are met by drug dealers who offer false sympathy and camaraderie in the form of, 'Man, you just get out? Me too, man, I know how it is. Hey, when's your bus? Wanna go smoke some tasty crack?' By the time the parolee figures out his new friend is just a ruthless salesman, he doesn't much care, and, according to the LAPD, he wreaks havoc in the already crime-ridden area to complete his down-payments. The dealers target teenage runaways too, ensuring a steady supply of new custom, all delivered to their door.

This may sound heinous, but in a country with no public healthcare alternatives, it actually seems like a good solution to me. After all, it's still much cheaper for the nervous parolee and the depressed teen to buy their mood medication illegally than it is to see a doctor or psychiatrist – it's the ultimate generic branding with a free consultation. Americans are such an enterprising people. However, I'm a bit nervous now. My freaky fellow Greyhound passengers can no longer be given the Smiling-Buddha benefit of the doubt at 3 am, because now I know there's a good chance they might actually be as violent and crazy as they look. And I really don't want something horrible to happen to me – that would make my mum right about the bus crazies after all.

When I come back to the hostel in the late afternoon, Lucy is lying prone on the top bunk. She is fully dressed including denim jacket and high leather boots, has a head-scarf over her tiny braids to prevent frizz, and is covered from head to toe in the thin foam shroud that passes for a blanket at the Chelsea Hostel. (Why a piece of foam? And how the heck do they launder it?) It's 93 or 38 degrees, and the humidity in our airless room is set to slow boil. It may be too early to guess, but from a cursory examination of the scene, I'm tippin' total meltdown.

'Lucy?' Silence. Then an anguished sob. Yup. She sits up wild-eyed. 'It's like they're all against me, they're all looking, looking, LOOKING at me!' She flings herself back onto the bed. 'It's like they know why I'm here and they're laughing, thinking I'll never make it, thinking, she'll never be a star, she should just go home to her mum. I feel so *stupid*.' She pushes her head into the pillow and says something I interpret as, 'They're all laughing.' I ask if she made it to McDonald's but she shakes her head. I begin drawing a map to Krispy Kreme. That'll fix her.

'I went to the corner store,' she tells me, 'and found no food I could eat, nuffink! NUFFINK! Rotten meat and spinach – nuffink!' She pops up again. 'They had blue potato chips!' she wails. 'Blue! Who eats a food coloured blue?'

Lucy is also heartbroken to discover that there's no MTV in the hostel. 'That was my dream, Sarah, my dream! They make it out like everywhere in America has MTV! Especially New York, *especially* here.'

I tell her that the MTV studios are only a subway trip away, and begin another map. She sits up again. 'Oi! Could I bribe someone to get on MTV do you think? Even to get in the audience, and then I could just start singin'?' She flops back down. 'I'd be discovered then. Sometimes it happens that way you know. Only in America, though, not England, never in England. They won't give you a chance that way in England, but in America, you can be discovered doing almost anything. Even jogging, I've heard.' She's up again. 'I should see Times Square. If I have to audition, I s'pose it would be there, wouldn't it. Because of the size. So they can really test if you're nervous. I will have to go. For research.' Aaaand she's down again, face in pillow. Through the muffle I come to understand that her mum took out a loan to send her here because when Lucy becomes famous it will solve all their problems. I'm not sure which generation is more delusional. Lucy is extraordinarily pretty, though, and you never know your luck in the big city. She's up again. 'Oi, when I am famous, I spose I'll have to live here. Move all my other stuff too. Should I live on Fifth Avenue, then? I heard it was nice, but you can't trust everything you hear, my mum says, so I'd better look for myself. Can you get a place with a carport here?' She flops down again. 'Because first thing I'd like to buy would be a nice car. Like Jennifer Lopez.' She's up again. 'Oi! I'd probably know Jennifer Lopez then! J-Lo. We could do a duet. Do you think we could do a duet if we had different record labels, yeah? Or are there rules?'

Lucy tells me that her money will run out in four weeks – no, three weeks and six days – and if she hasn't got a career by then, that's it. 'Did you know,' she says, 'there's a lottery to live in America, yeah? Someone told me dad about it and he said it's true. But they don't let people from the UK enter and I don't fink that's fair, do you?' I just nod, my lotto prize burning a big guilty hole in my pocket. 'If only I could go in it, then I could have a bit longer to make it. To audition and buy a car, and a telly wif MTV on it.' She jolts up again, crying, 'An' when I was at the corner store, all these people were looking and I just thought, you don't know what you even have, just walkin' around. You can be here forever in New York, and I have to go home in three weeks and six days!'

We talk, or rather, she talks, while I change. I'm squatting underneath her in my sweltering bunk, fishing out whatever's still clean. Everything in my bag is twisted up, and damp from humidity and wet shampoo bottles. By the time I put my clothes on I'm sweaty and dirty all over again, sporting rust stains and paint flakes from under the bed. Farewelling poor Lucy before she has a chance to stop me, I'm out on the street again in a big sticky, itchy tangle.

I wander a bit aimlessly. I think I have a case of lag like Virginia. The bus really wipes you out, I hadn't really anticipated it. There are sirens rapping everywhere, like the yelp and wail cycles are tracks being scratched and spun on decks in the back. In a city full of sirens I suppose it's how you get people to pay even scant attention, but it sounds more like a hip-hop sound-off than an emergency. It makes me think again of those months of living here, where the sirens were part of a constant background track like fridge hum. I wonder if I should spare the time just to revisit the old nabe and poke around, and if I would ever live there again. I seem to be forgetting more and more how hard it all was now that I'm free to wander in the sunshine with US dollars in my pocket. I force myself to remember the elation the Boy and I felt at the end of our time here, the involuntary smiles that stretched our faces whenever we remembered we were going home to Sydney soon. But I still love this city, and its opportunities are certainly amazing.

At the hostel later that evening, I meet a group of pink-nosed Poms who have just returned from their own trip to Brooklyn. 'Yeah?' I ask suspiciously. 'What did you think?' A breathless, pony-tailed girl replies, 'You could spend all day there, you really could. It's just awful!' The whole group weigh in on how awful it is and how deliciously dangerous and crap and gory the experience was. They offer to show me their digital photos.

We sit down and go over their war trophies. There are lots of pictures of burnt-out cars, graffitied walls, and zoom-shots of guys in doo-rags smoking weed outside bodegas. There is often a big round face of the polo-shirted tourist, backpack on, smiling the same goofy smile you might use if posing near a tank full of alligators. I have to agree that the pictures of bleak, towering apartment blocks and streets devoid of greenery are unlovely, but I feel a tug when I recognise the dozens of private churches, as prolific and bland as laundromats, which pop up around the Avenue of Puerto Rico. This really is a strange and interesting town.

The Poms twist my rubber arm to lead the way to the corner shop for a crash course in American beer. We bring it back to the open-air courtyard where everyone has gathered to drink and hang out until dark. Holding court at the backpacker's cool-kids table (Birkenstocks, extra-paged-passport and hand-rolled cigs mandatory) is a handsome Brit called Daryn. He's a former London copper who has just left his stripes and police hat at Ground Zero, along with what was left of his marriage and professional life. At only 28, Daryn describes a job where 12-year-old boys demanding money and sex held knives to the throats of old women; where riots, bomb scares and dead children were the career highlights of his year; and tells how he hardened his heart against it all until there was nothing left to give his young missus.

'Wow,' I say. 'That's not really how I picture England.'

'No,' he says, miserable. 'Sounds like Detroit or something, doesn't it?'

Ironically, Daryn tells me he is now finding peace in Detroit, and in New York, Houston, LA and New Orleans. 'You can't heal in Europe, yeah,' he tells me, 'it's too old. Too fixed. Things are young in America, young and free and just . . . without limit, yeah?' He says he loves being here in the US, loves the spirit of reinvention, of energy, of space. Daryn's been travelling around by Greyhound too, and says it's actually nice to sit next to the crack-whores and crazies, jailbirds and runaways, and not have to book them.

'Uh, yeah,' I say, 'sounds great,' secretly wishing his power of arrest was transferable. 'Those people are teaching me more than anyone,' he says. 'I'm remembering how to be just human, and not a cop. No one tells the truth to a copper, Sarah, not ever. Even victims will lie to plump charges. But here, it doesn't matter if we're all lying, yeah. You can be anything you want to in America, anything and anyone at all.' Then he gets a bit weepy over his lost girl, and so I take him round the corner to the Chelsea Krispy Kreme, where Daryn marvels at the consistency of the hot dough like it's a new food group. Which, of course, it is. His eyes are dry, and once again it has been confirmed to me that there's not much in life which cannot be vastly improved with a sugary treat.

With a belly full of beer, snacks, and Daryn and Lucy's dramas, my lag catches up with me and forces a trip off to bed. In the four-bunk room that is but a few centimetres bigger than the beds themselves, I find an Australian girl getting ready to go out. By 'out' she means downstairs with the other witless 'travellers' who are spending all their New York nights getting pissed in a sweltering rec-room near the communal kitchen. I can already tell it won't be the joyful cultural reunion I shared with Kate. 'Manda from Moe says she's surprised to find that she likes New York. 'Yeah, I thought I'd hate New York ay, 'cos of all the Yanks? All the Yanks that live here? But it's a great place! Fully! Don't you reckon it's cool, like, how everything looks like a movie?' She gets conspiratorial about the location of our hostel. 'I think we're in a real faggy part of town but. I just hope no one gets the wrong idea about me 'cos there's heaps of hot blokes here ay.'

She pulls out a sheaf of photos, most taken in and around our crummy little hostel, the others in equally crummy Times Square. 'Manda finds a picture of Damian, the guy she 'almost rooted'. 'So stoked ay,' she says, shaking her head and holding the photo in front of my nose like I'm a border guard. 'He's so much better than what I pull at home. Reckon I could have rooted him too, but I'm not that kind of girl, y'know?' She considers her statement. 'Well, I might have been. Only if he'd asked, but. *Stoked* I got a photo . . .' She regards the pub lout's image again, and her brow furrows. 'Wish he'd had his shirt off but.'

Quizzing me on the status of the Boy, she informs me sympathetically that 'If 'e's not here, 'e's queer,' and offers to send a new one my way if I want. 'There's heaps of blokes down there ay, and there's some that I'm not after if you want a look.' I decline her offering with the same forced politeness reserved for when someone else's dog presents me with a rancid bit of bone, and wish her luck. I am asleep within seconds.

In the late morning, having waited for an hour to use the dank little shower, I am reborn onto the street and into another beautiful day. My body refuses to entertain the idea of donuts as its second main meal in nine hours, and so I hop the subway down to Canal Street, Chinatown. Chinese food for breakfast. Pure look-surey. Above the regular subway tiles, Canal is spelt in English and with Chinese characters using tiny mosaics, lending the grimy station a kind of antique gravity, and the passenger an immediate sensation of exotic arrival. Up, up, out of the underground and fluro lights, I find myself in a world made of smoky air and sirens and fire escapes. All around me people are not so much talking as hurling guttural Mandarin at each other, throwing it down the street and batting it back and forth at close quarters.

I walk past markets already steamy in the sun. Huge fish lie butchered on ice, wooden buckets are filled with lychees, and men shout to each other as they hack the tops off coconuts with curved blades. There are no tourists hanging around this part of the action, they have no interest in the overwhelming pong and the foreign fruit. Across the street, the Pearl River Mart sounds like a stop on the old silk trade route. The shop is near Pearl Street, the old New York thoroughfare that was named for the original oyster-shell roads. Wouldn't it be nice, I think, to do away with this gooey black bitumen and go back to crumbly, pearlised shell.

A travel agent whose sign 'Great Tours' features bold Chinese characters above a Peking-style boat, seems to suggest that if you wandered inside you would find yourself booking trunks on a slow boat to China rather than Disney World or the Bahamas. A fat green dragon sign announces the 'Original Chinatown Ice-cream Factory' with durian, lychee, coconut, tea and jack-fruit among their flavours. Jade is everywhere, along with old silks and fans, as well as the latest clothes and music from Hong Kong. Pictures of Asian pop-stars abound, and kids crowd around them, causing stout pale visitors to hang on to their wallets and 'fanny packs' with exaggerated caution, failing to deduce that the locals barely notice them. Young men and women walk two to three abreast, all holding hands or linking arms in chains, flapping their plastic flip-flops and checking their cell phones. Over everything is the tempting sour-sweet smell of frying pork dumplings and melting icees.

New Yorkers are so lucky to experience international travel via the N and R subway lines rather than the airport. The plastic crud, things wrapped hastily but expertly in Chinese newspaper, cheap gadgets and wind up dogs, Asian beauty products, food, books and pharmaceuticals recreate perfectly a quarter of Hong Kong, Shanghai, Sarawak or Singapore. I realise then that I really miss Asia; I miss my Asian Pacific corner of the globe. I miss the Asian food and people in my home town. If I lived in the US it would have to be somewhere like this, near a large Asian influence like Chinatown. This Chinatown feels authentic in the same way Sydney's does; a self-supporting bubble of culture that is magic to enter.

The corner of Canal and Mulberry peels off to become Little Italy, but I take Canal and Mott St down to Bayard St, turn the corner to find the Green Bo, a local favourite where people share tables and pile in, eating five-star delicious next to the noisy kitchen and slop bucket. At my·round table an agent is doing business over steamed dumplings and Singha beer, talking about getting De Niro for 'cawfee' in Tribeca. Two young Chinese guys are eating whole crabs and bowls of egg noodles, shovelling them in with chopsticks flying like eggbeaters. Beside me a Jersey 'soccer mom' eats roti and sips her green tea while she reads the Arts and Leisure section of the *New York Times*. She has just purchased a fake Kate Spade bag and Gucci sunnies, and looks just like Mrs Soprano. Eating my braised chicken with ginger and snow pea breakfast, my feet swing under the table, as they are wont to do when happy, and I get excited to be handed the remains in a little white cardboard box like a *Seinfeld* prop.

Back out on the street, thongs flapping in the sticky concoction of soy, rotten fruit, green tea, fish blood and fuel on the road, I briefly consider a dodgy handbag myself, but discover that they are actually quite expensive now. Seventy dead presidents for the Dolce & Gabbana that I long to sling over my arm like the world's dorkiest rock star. Perhaps it's because the rip-offs are getting so good, or perhaps it's the threat-of-prosecution tax. Belts and shoes, bags and scarves, if it can be faked and logo-ed, it's here. Do Kate Spade or Donna Karan ever wander down here and go mental? I mean, they only live up the road, after all, and I reckon if someone was splashing my name over half the block, I'd find it very hard to walk past.

The I ♥ NY T-shirts are also big sellers, and have been for years. Even after the 9/11 cash-in there's still stock to the ceiling. Both sides of Canal Street are positively groaning under the weight of all this screen-printed cotton. These are the T-shirts that cockroaches will be wearing after the apocalypse. I tumble back into the labyrinth of subways again, marvelling at the value of my little Metropass. This is definitely a great city to get around in, and its accessibility is a great leveller. The Rodenticide warning signs are still in place, but it doesn't seem to have made much of a dent. I see two rats copulating furiously under the sign. Thrill seekers.

Stepping out at Fifth Avenue, I go into H&M, a Scandinavian chain all over Europe that has graced the US with its own megastore. Three floors of clothes are arranged like post-modern fabric-candy, with plasma screens pumping music and images of beautiful, disaffected youth to the throngs of beautiful disaffected youth in the store. This is the America I used to imagine. The America from disposable teen movies and advertising think-tanks. From what I've seen so far, this is no more the real America than Chinatown or, for that matter, the trailer park in Florence. The stately homes of Savannah. Cuban food by the white sand of South Beach. Fishermens' swamp homes in

Georgia. Ai. What's next? I'm only halfway up one side of the beast, too. I'm fast losing hope of pinning this nation-prize down. What the hell have I won? How would I ever explain it at home?

On the subway I read the classifieds in the *New York Times*, where I find studios from $2000 a month and nothing at all, not even eight-people, two-room-share, for under $1300. It is expensive to keep a roof over your head here, but if you have $20 in downtown Manhattan, it's enough to make sure you aren't naked or hungry for long. Everything is for sale, in an astonishing consumer rainbow. I guess the New York City gestalt is about being broke, about finding and funding apartments against all odds, shopping at three different grocery stores every night and still finding all you need for under $200 a week. It's natural selection on a daily basis.

Swinging my little bag, flapping around town, summer here seems perfect. Outside, everyone sits in parks with newspapers and pastries, sushi and beer, flowers and art. It really is a global city. The world shrunk small with an array of its usual uglies and most of its joyful things. Again, I ask myself, could I live here? Properly? Officially? Well, maybe. She'd have me back, New York City. There's still room – studio-sized – but still room for all. You can always come back to New York City, and once you're here, you need never leave. That can be a problem in itself, I think. New York can make you into a permanent New Yorker, I'm sure, where nothing else is fast enough, new enough or clever enough, and a horizon makes you agoraphobic. Already I'm remembering how the close quarters and daily subway struggle becomes grinding, suffocating. How the city swallows you up, making it hard to leave, or even want to. It's surprisingly lonely too, isolating everyone into their own pockets, and people here do work very hard. It's a career town, or it's a three-jobs-to-pay-the-bills-while-you-try-to-make-a-career town.

Hungry again, I find a Popeye's and enjoy a delicious second breakfast of crispy fried chicken, hot flaky biscuit, red beans and rice and some jalapeño poppers (whole chillies filled with melted cheese). I am the only white face in the joint. Virginia was right. I looooves black food. Two gallons of Cherry Coke later, I suddenly remember the thing about public toilets in New York. There are none. Literally none, and the toilets inside buildings are jealously guarded. I steal two or thirty packets of 'Cajun Sparkle' seasoning for the road and slosh out onto the street uncomfortably.

Times Square lies before me in all its questionable glory. One big product placement, with school tours, chain restaurants, movie theatres and tacky crap. No one is outside. They're all crammed into stores called 'Big Apple', buying in a frenzy. 'Okay,' they say, fishing wads of greenbacks out of the I ♥ NY fanny packs they have already bought, 'so that's Susie, Tommy, Jeffrey and Casey done, now how about Judy, Billy and Cathy get the I ♥ NY Even More T-shirts, and Terry and Shari get the NYPD sweaters?' Outside, New York City moves on without them.

The reality of returning to the bus early tomorrow morning is starting to sink in. I decide to buy a full-sized pillow to combat air conditioning, bad neck and numb bum. Because it's so cheap, I buy a massive Yankees pillow at a discount variety shop before realising I'll have to carry it around all day looking like all the witless tourists I keep dishing on. Dammit. The man serving me is called Isaac Isaiah and wears a skullcap with a peace sign embroidered into it. Much is made of the fact that this is a town of Jewish jokes, surnames, food and expressions, but it all just blends from where I'm standing. Bagels and knishes, 'kvetching' and kosher dills, even Orthodox men with their ringlets and black robes don't rate a second glance here. Neither do full body tattoos, the kind of loaded piercings that make some people look uncomfortably magnetic, wigs, muu-muus or celebrity faces.

In Union Square a rainbow blanket of children under four sit on the soft grass, black as night to pale as snow, and everything in between. Their teacher gives some simple instructions, and the little corn-rowed, ringleted and pigtailed heads bob up and down like one animal. Urban living is kind of cool in this way. There are lots of parks and things for kids to do here, and, with a constant stream of stimuli, Manhattan kids seem to have it made.

I begin to picture raising my own future widgets here; I see them exploring Central Park with their kindy teacher and see myself signing permission slips for baby Broadway and museum outings. So chic! So cosmopolitan, nothing would shock my Manhattanite offspring. Mid-way through imagining Daddy and me coming home from our fabulous jobs to greet them, thoughts of flights and flights of stairs, cramped apartments and expensive groceries sold in supermarkets with aisles as wide as airline tray-tables begin to sour my vision. My New York kidlets would have the city's parks but they would never have a patch of grass to call their own. I want them to lie in their own backyard, yelling to me that they're *so bored*, Mum, as they eat melting Frosty Fruits and listen to cicadas and currawongs. There are many North American versions of this daydream, I'm sure, substituting squirrels and woodpeckers, and a lesser degree of boredom due to kiddy-cable. My babies are many years away, but unless I become fabulous beyond my wildest dreams, they won't be raised in the towering splendour of Manhattan. They can find it for themselves later on.

Sick of drinking the drip-filtered watery muck passing for coffee everywhere in the US, I experiment with different cafés around town. New Yorkers have a real preoccupation with food. Where to get it, where to eat it and how to burn it off. That I still can't get a decent latte is beyond frustrating. They are almost uniformly weak or burnt-tasting, and one was so bad that I suspected the grounds had gone through twice. Lugging my Yankees pillow and experiencing a food coma brought on by Popeye's, I succumb to the most glorious smell of roasted beans and enter a Starbucks. I am excited. Maybe, I reason, this chain is so popular because it's the only place good coffee can be found here. Sure, most people hold Starbucks accountable for the rape of the planet, but at this point I would happily trample a few acres of virgin Brazilian rainforest myself for a good cup. Globalisation? Sign me up, where's my cawfee?

'Welcome to Starbucks!' the counter girl accosts me like a drill sergeant. 'NEXT!'

'Hi!' I say, smiling at the colossal menu above her head.

'NEXT!' she shouts to me again.

'Oh, okay, I'd just like a latte, please.'

'Uh huh?!' she says, making fast little circles with her hand and nodding her head in the universal gesture of 'hurryitthe-fuckup!' What does this woman want from me? I panic, the queue pushing forward against my pillow. 'Um, a latte . . . coffee, please . . . with milk?' After an eye roll like the moon's orbit, she screams, 'MediumLatteGrand-ayLatteFrozen-LatteorSixGallonLatte?'

'Just a regular latte, whatever that is, I just –'

'Twoshotthreeshoteightshotdecaforflavoured?'

'Strong, please, just give me str –'

'Okay! Grand-DAY La-TAY! NEXT!'

I stumble along to the register where an unsmiling woman declares, 'That'll be $15.87 plus tax.' She might as well have pulled a gun. Okay, so it isn't quite that much, but it does cost the better part of a $10 note, which, after all, is 20 Australian roubles. What I get for my money is the frothy hot milk bath left over from when the littlest bean last gave himself a quick wash behind the ears. What's more, it is three cups tall, forcing me to drink two litres of warm milk before I can find the available caffeine. It takes half an hour to drink, during which time I drift in and out of consciousness, dreaming I am a baby cow and certain I can hear the 'barista' yelling 'WELCOME TO STARBUCKS! Please stand still while we screw you in the ass and steal your wallet!' Wobbling back outside, I now happily join the legions of boycotters worldwide, though mine is an entirely selfish rage.

A man sits at the subway entrance with a little sign announcing 'I'm a street musician, too hard to live, too mean to die. Give me money or I'll play something.' There are a lot of buskers in this town, but not as many panhandlers as I remember. In fact, New York actually seems to line your pockets as you walk around. It's the city of free, of marketplace and product testing. There are lots of giveaways and questionnaires. Today I am practically accosted with Body Shop body butter, test-audience movie tickets and a free drink. Test me, try me, buy me, put a dollar here next time please.

There are rumours of free pizza in the evening at the hostel. In the courtyard, four scrubbed and smiling evangelical Christian travellers are singing God-rock around a guitar, drinking Diet Coke. Young Christians are up there with Young Liberals (the Australian version of the Young Republican Party) on my conversational avoid-like-gonorrhoea list, so I skip the free pizza and head downtown.

It's a beautiful night on Manhattan Island. Just as the sun starts to set, all the lights in the skyscrapers twinkle on, and everything turns to silver and blue. A welcome breeze ruffles my feathers and I can't think of many places I'd rather be on a night by myself. Wandering Soho, I happen upon the old Angelica Cinema building and vow to take myself on a smashing date. I buy a ticket to see *Cinema Paradiso*, a jumbo popcorn (extra butter, God Bless America) and settle in. We are below street level in the theatre and can just hear the trains thundering past underground; a shaking rumble through the whole movie that is not unpleasant. There's lots of audience participation in New York. They laugh easily and readily, and many people are here by themselves.

After the movie I have seven drinks too many with an old friend uptown, deciding it will knock me out on the long trip tomorrow. I get a bit lost going home, but it doesn't matter. I feel I can move with impunity at night in New York. This city isn't scary. The bus though, the bus has now got me spooked.

Chapter 8

Mainely perfect

My drunken bedtime has made me the present of a wicked hangover. Just a few hours after I fall into my bed, I find myself out of it, propping myself up in the subway station. The only other people in here are still coming back from their Saturday nights out, making their way home for a snooze before a leisurely brunch. I decide to hate them. My new pillow is now strapped to my front and is an ugly, bulky encumbrance, but I have high hopes for how it might change my bus experience.

At 6 am, the sun is already growing warm and the humidity is still sweltering. By the time I stagger into Port Authority I'm drenched with alcoholic sweat, leaping aboard the trembling bus to Bar Harbor, Maine. It still surprises me how hot and muggy New York can be. It is invariably cold and snowy in the movies, unless it's a gorgeous springtime in the park. What bloody cheek, I think. *Dog Day Afternoon* is the only accurate cinematic portrayal of summer conditions in this town.

Our bus is an old rattletrap, but the passengers already seated politely seem ordinary enough and I don't spy any potential lunatiles. Up and out of the sooty bowels of the orange- and lime-tiled Port Authority, New York looks very fresh and inviting. I smile reflectively back at the city despite myself.

The bus actually drives through the quiet roads in Central Park, and we get a lovely and unexpected tour of New York in this soft hour of the morning. At seven o'clock on a Sunday, there are already joggers, dog walkers and people dressed smartly on trotting horses. It's quite perfect.

On the outskirts of the city I squash into my pillow and try to sleep despite my throbbing head. At precisely this moment our groggy bus comes to life, and the two people behind me discover that apart from exceptionally loud voices, they also share a number of common interests, which they decide should be discussed in some detail. It turns out they are both actors from Memphis, and this unfortunate coincidence leads to conversation like, 'Do you know Mary-Sue Cowpoke? She has kind of reddish-brownie-blonde hair and used to live in Memphis one time? No? What about Bobby-Ray Rancher? He was that guy from, y'know, the thing? That they shot in, um, that place? He has the same agent as that other girl? With the brownish-longish-reddish hair? From that time in, uh, in that other place?'

The seats on these older buses are small and terribly uncomfortable, with zero legroom. It's freezing cold too, but not as bad as the new buses. On those, the AC is elbow height on a sharp window ledge and the air jets powerfully up the glass. If you lean your head against the window it shoots up the back of your neck, under your chin and in your ear and nostril, flapping your eyelids out. Like much else riding Greyhound, it seems to be a lose–lose situation.

My seatmate is a college girl in much the same state as me. We keep looking at each other with bloodshot eyes and drool-crusted lips, shaking our heads at the horror of babysitting shrieking hangovers in our cramped situation. With no pillow, she attempts to sleep by assuming the crash position. Though dragging my pillow around is annoying, it means I can finally use my ugly yellow striped sheet for cover instead of stuffing it into the AC. I try to sleep but can't seem to remember how. Instead, I drift in and out of leaden consciousness, waking just long enough to have severe reservations about bus travel that has nothing to do with parolees.

Many hours later I come to and find the scenery to be quite different. We have passed Boston and New Hampshire, and are already at the tail-end of Connecticut – Mark Twain country. I'm angry at myself for missing it, as well as many other places I wanted to gawk at. Still, there's always the trip back down through it all again. Consulting my map I see that there will be much backtracking on the way out, as the only places west from Maine are Canadian. I sit up straight like the Euro couple, getting all excited. It is very green and pleasant outside my window and I like it immediately. Signs begin appearing which declare themselves to be 'Maine-ly' everything, as well as lots of 'Bar-none', as in 'Maine-ly Groceries, the best fresh produce in town, Bar-none!'. These jokes wear thin after the first one and a half of them.

A sign outside the little Ellsworth church announces, 'Body-piercing saved our lives!' and I snicker at the rather transparent attempt to lure the younger faithful. Faith is a big deal in the US. Religion doesn't affect daily life that much at home in Australia. Apart from turning on the news each night to see which group of pious believers has massacred the other one during the day, it just doesn't come up much. In fact, it's always been a bit of a joke at home to mimic American sports stars and movie idols thanking God for their awards. If someone did that on Australian television I doubt I'd be alone in assuming they were a bit of a nutter. There's a time and place for everything, right? And if God is everywhere, as Virginia insists, then surely the big Kahuna already knows you're grateful. No, there is very little wearing of your cross on your sleeve in Australia.

In the United States, however, even my hardest-partying friends have some kind of deeply held religious affiliation, and the ones who have sworn off any faith altogether will still talk about including someone in their prayers. They can't help it. It is almost impossible to avoid. It's such a huge part of political life here, too. I absolutely cannot conceive of a Prime Minister asking God to bless Australia. Or the Prime Minister's wife giving interviews in magazines with titles like *Faith* and *True Believer*. Religion certainly contributes to the dichotomy of how the average American lives their lives.

My sample size is far from exhaustive, but this emphasis on worship is the surprising norm amongst almost everyone I've met in this country. Apart from a few recent Yoga-Buddhists, I'm not aware of anyone's relationship with a higher being at home in Australia, but I know the religious beliefs of every one of my American friends and acquaintances. Party-boy Nick and most of his friends were raised Middle-America Christian, and he flirted with the Born-Again variety on and off during college, forswearing alcohol and sex before marriage along with vast numbers of fellow students and fraternity brothers. Kevin and his friends are all Catholic; Mike lives with a unique blend of New Orleans French Catholicism and Bible-Belt Baptist, and my Jewish friends are also numerous. Unless they were Satanists – also strangely common – I didn't meet a single person at university in Mississippi who hadn't found God in one form or another. Sunday morning would find me alone in the dorm as everyone went off to their churches, and I was left to have a quiet heathen breakfast in the echoing common room.

There are churches in America that look like shopping centres, like the White House, like sports arenas and universities; strange and massive structures where the parking lots are always filled. A particularly large church in Hattiesburg, anchored next to Wal-Mart, had a field-sized lawn in front of it with rows of tiny pink and blue crosses hammered into the earth. A sign explained that what looked like a sizable Barbie graveyard represented the 'murdered children' aborted in the state of Mississippi that year.

Still, for all the evangelical creepiness, you can find a piece of just about everyone's God in the USA, as well as a temple or synagogue, mosque or altar to worship at. Americans even started their own world religion, the Church of Jesus Christ of Latter-day Saints, known as the Mormon Church. That's a bold move for such a young nation. If the Mormon stronghold of Salt Lake City weren't such a detour, I would love to go. I'm certainly very curious.

The green countryside out the window now is where the original Puritans landed and started this whole God kick. I wonder now how different America might be if it had been founded by rough-shod criminal stock who found God in their flagons of ale, like Australia. I also wonder if religion would creep up on me if I moved to the US for a while. I've already emailed a 'God Bless' to a friend here, a kind of culturally appropriate salutation that I didn't really think about till later.

The rattling bus is much emptier now and my poor seat-mate has disappeared. Outside there are huge bushes of lavender everywhere, and, strangely, lots of motorbikes too, the Japanese plastic kind which look fairly incongruous in this gentle landscape. So does the explosion of Dunkin' Donuts franchises, where the said motorbikes are lined up by the dozen. Kids wearing pastel and outdated shades lurk and mingle in the car parks and by the counters inside. It sure looks like the place to be in Maine. Must be special donuts. There are lots of attractive Dutch barns and same-styled buildings. We pull slowly through Bangor, where a giant painted statue of Paul Bunyan leers down at us. *Anne of Green Gables* is playing at the crumbling opera house and everything is peeling and spooky in a style of architecture I decide to call 'Gothic Farm'. Stephen King lives here.

Crap olde fashionde writing adorns everything, including a big sign announcing the Acadia Zoo. I can see a paddock with a camel in it. There are lots of ads for lobster and other fresh produce, and it makes my tummy grumble. I am arriving at the beginning of the very short tourist season, which doesn't start until the first day of summer. That is today, 21 June, and here's me thinking it has been summer for whole weeks now, when it turns out I had to wait for some kind of solstice all along.

I've been on this bus since 7 am, and it's now nearly five in the afternoon as we pass a little airstrip where mountains and water are visible in the background for the first time. Lush green fields filled with tiny yellow flowers stretch out ahead of me and I tap my sneakered toes. I'm getting excited now, and hungry for a sweet treat or something. I've already eaten all my puffy dry corn cakes. The bus rumbles over a bridge and onto a majestic, fir-covered island. This is Mount Desert Island, and finally, Bar Harbor. The road to this small town runs straight through green, green grass and big dark forests before arriving at a storybook village. 'Bar Harbor,' says the driver, standing up and clicking his back and legs. 'Bar Harbor, enjoy your stay.' This is the end of the line.

I hop off the bus and hoist my life-vest of crud on, front and back. I'm like a snail now. Slow, awkward, slimy, but totally self-sufficient. With the hostel guidebook in hand to complete the picture of sophistication I've created, I walk through a leafy square to a redbrick fire station, where a fireman waves hello and smiles. Without a word he points up Cottage Street, and, turning onto Kennebec, I arrive at the Bar Harbor Hostel.

After becoming acquainted with the small, 100-year-old building and the chipper scout-master of a manager, I find myself by the kitchen tap drinking down gallons of water. The Grey-hound air conditioning dries you out like a desert mouse. A friendly Irish guy called Mark shares his choc-chip cookies and some information. He's been in Bar Harbor for a year, doing odd jobs around the hotels. 'So what's here out of season?' I ask. Mark pours a glass of juice and sits down. 'Notin',' he says, and finishes the juice in one gulp. 'Just a ghost town and a hundred 'n' one inches of snow.' He's not exaggerating.

The town is far from ghostly tonight, though. People wander everywhere, holding hands and heading to dinner, telling kids to come on and hurry up as they scamper around in the grass. Unlike New York, Bar Harbor is not an alone town. This is a town for families, for couples, for friends. I troll for a takeaway dinner, feeling like I'm at some other family's reunion picnic by myself. I buy a large pizza with mushrooms, cheese and broccoli, and take it down by the water to eat. It's delicious but expensive after New York.

It's already dusk and the sun seems to set much faster here. By the time my pizza matches the waning moon, the harbour is dark except for the swaying lights on fishing boats. In the distance are the granite-capped mountains of Acadia National Park. Swinging my feet backwards and forwards under the bench, with the warm pizza box on my lap, I look out across the water knowing that I'm right at the edge of America, and the little bus has drawn the first complete line on my map. The air is fresh and clean, and I can tell the scenery will be exciting tomorrow, but right now I'm just hoping I can make it back to the hostel before I fall asleep.

It's a chilly walk back to the hostel, but it makes a pleasant change from the cauldron of yesterday. I'm really, really tired. Once inside my room I have to add that I'm really, really sick of hitting my head on bunk beds already. I take a shower to wash off the day. The water is strong and hot, and the home-style bathroom is scrupulously clean. There is an antique mirror, good lighting and someone has thoughtfully provided a shelf for toilet bags. My heart swells. These things are suddenly very important.

When Mr Bunyan/Scoutmaster raps on the door with a cheery 'Seven am, hostellers! Rise and shine!' I have no idea where I am at all. Really, no idea. I actually have to run through a quick list of possibilities before opening my eyes to discover the truth. I am aware that I have slept blissfully, amazingly well. I slept like a baby, I think, and then wonder why we say that when babies seem to sleep like crack addicts. The windows were open through the night. In the large wooden room the temperature must have dropped steadily, but there was no breeze for a draught. Perfect sleeping weather.

At seven o'clock the sun is brilliant and jewelled on the window pane and on the lush green grass beyond it. There is a little church at the end of the lawn. My nose is quite cold but my feet are toasty. I can tell I haven't disturbed the covers since I lay down at nine, and I sigh over this piece of heaven after the sticky hostel in Chelsea. I prop myself up a bit and have a look around. There are only two bunks occupied bar mine (I'm doing the Bar thing already) and I find myself staring deep into the eyes of the girl in the next bunk before I realise we are nearly reflections of each other. Wild blonde bird's nests, pink noses and tartan covers up under our chins, looking and feeling like kids at Camp Friendly, Nantucket. We enjoy a brief fit of the giggles. Her name is Tara (second only to Molly on the list of popular American names) and she's here to meet some friends who are camping in the national park. When she goes off to shower, I dress carefully and pack for the day. Like Savannah, this hostel has a strict lockout, and so at eight o'clock I double-check camera, phone card, wallet and PEZ dispenser, and step out to explore Bar Harbor.

Outside, it's not just quaint and pretty like I had expected, but genuinely, stupefyingly beautiful. Where Savannah was heavy with humidity, a glutinous miasma hanging over the city like the steam from cooking rice, Bar Harbor is soft and fresh. The light, unfiltered by any haze or smog, has a clarity to it that is not unlike the first time I wore contact lenses. It's like instant Lasik surgery. Everything just jumps out. The edges of every leaf, the shape of tiny birds across the street – it's like an eye test where the circles turn in, getting sharper and sharper. It's a landscape of delicacy; of crystalline colours and hues where even the grass blades seem much smaller and finer than usual. They are soft and springy, and intensely green. I get the feeling that you could squeeze just about anything and produce a litre of chlorophyll in Bar Harbor.

Walking down quiet neighbourhood streets, I am surrounded by white picket fences closed by little garden gates, and planter boxes filled with the type of delicate blooms that get fried to a crisp in New York or Florida summers. You could probably store cut lettuce in the full sun here. Antique lampposts line the streets and I smile at them, goofy with pleasure at how they complete this idyllic scene. I have to allow myself a moment of early-morning cynicism, though, when I see shop windows filled with T-shirts featuring lampposts. I realise these streets will soon be clogged with tourists who exclaim over these same lampposts and buy the T-shirts, which will be worn in the garden once or twice before ending up in the car-wash bucket or on a skinny Somalian back. This old-world lighting was here before the tourists, but now I suppose it's only here because of the tourists. The lampposts have become a thing apart from themselves, a representation, a slightly Disneyfied historical 'feature' on the coloured map in the New England guidebook. They – oh shut up, you just need coffee. Leave the bloody lampposts alone.

Once just a dot on a map, at first Bar Harbor is also just a street or two, but as I walk around it slowly gains dimension, blossoming outward and revealing its true shape. The houses are all old with high, shingled roofs for snow to slide off. Most sport ornate weathervanes and massive deciduous trees. Every street is picturesque as if by city ordinance, and I'm already wishing one of them were mine. The 1500-foot Cadillac Mountain in the middle of Mount Desert Island is reportedly the first place in the US to see the sunrise each day. It must be quite a view. The harbour itself is a quiet glory, gentle and sheltered like the rest of the town. It's beautiful to walk around. Over the water, wooden boats and white cruisers roll in and out with tourists, taking them on day trips to Nova Scotia, Canada's most easterly point, as well as whale watching. There are lots of places to go and eat 'Fresh Ketch' lobster, clam chowder and other salty-sweet gifts from the sea. Fishy goodness heads straight to the top of my Bar Harbor to-do list.

Perfect sleeping weather turns into perfect breakfast weather, and when I spy a group of people sitting on white wrought-iron chairs in the sun, with newspapers and steaming cups, I make a joyful beeline. Inside the Cottage Street Bakery and Deli, I find myself hijacked by blueberries. I've never cared much for the little balls of purple-ish moisture, but somehow I end up starting the day with a giant blueberry muffin and fresh blueberry jam. I decline the offer of blueberry butter, and choose regular Joe over blueberry coffee. Craning my neck to make sure this café is not actually called 'Blueberry and Deli', I discover it is situated beside the charming timber offices of the Wild Blueberry Association of North America.

Turns out this town is all about blueberries. Blueberries and lobster. Well, and some maple syrup too. These little berries are serious business but kind of bland. I now know the blueberry is chock-full of vitamins, flavanoids and antioxidants, but quite frankly, the tart raspberry and bold blackberry could still kick its ass. These particular blueberries are mild enough that the sugary jam ends up like syrup. I drink a jug-sized serving of coffee to wash out my candied oesophagus.

From the groups of people walking past, and some spying on my fellow diners, I deduce that Bar Harbor on the brink of season is an odd mix of people. They appear to split neatly into two groups. There are the flocks of youngsters with select merchandise proclaiming them to be from Andover and their older siblings from Princeton, Harvard, or Yale, who all seem to know each other and meet on the street wearing J.Crew and LLBean. They are fastidiously understated in dress and manner, and appear to be sticking to some kind of prep-school morning regimen of jogging followed by bagels with Lite-Philly spread.

The other kids are the less moneyed kind. The half-a-pack-of-Camels-for-breakfast kind, who are here to work the season as waitstaff and maintenance personnel. Blind, you could tell the difference by giving each a vigorous shaking. The prep-school kids would produce nothing more than the delicate sound of a discreet money clip brushing against polar fleece; the hushed whisper of platinum Amex plastic separated from school colours by sensible knickers. The other kids would jangle a cacophony out of change left on tip trays, pick-up truck keys and pens for taking orders down at the pizza palace.

Some are back from seasonal jobs in Florida and there is much recognition going on in both camps, but for different reasons. An equal opportunity eavesdropper, from one group I hear conversation including 'Julia, how ARE you? Have you taken the Bar yet? Did you hear David married that Kennedy girl? How's Kitty?' and 'I didn't see you once in the Hamptons! Oh, Monaco?' I hear waitstaff kids competing with war stories from seasons past; flexing muscles (tray-carrying, cocktail-shaking muscles) in front of the new kids. 'First of July man,' the experienced group boasts. 'Watch it happen. Thirty boats a day. Buses. Planes. *Sea*planes . . . they hitya for breakfast at six-fuckin'-thirty. On vacation, man . . . Parking? Man, forget about parking. Roll your truck in the water right now and walk away.' There are lots of big old trucks parked in the street this morning, as well as a fleet of luxury cars. Dozens of mid-life-crisis motorbikes are shining in the sun, most bearing rental plates.

Sitting with a full belly, I realise I have no idea what to expect from this town or what to see, and that this is a first on this trip. After six months of Florida sun, and revisiting Savannah and New York, it feels good to be somewhere totally new. I walk over to a hilly park in front of the harbour. The visitors here have T-shirts like bumper stickers. They help me trace the

National Tourist Route. Boca Raton, Clearwater, Martha's Vineyard, Cape Cod, San Francisco, Santa Fe, New Orleans. Two of them, armed with a camcorder, are getting Pouncer the bichon frise and Buddy the German shepherd to pose and run. There are no shots of the couple, only of the dogs. 'Jamie, get Pouncer to go under the sign, Pouncer . . . gooooood girl, there you go, stay, staaaaaayyy . . . Buddy, can you show me how you say hello? There'sagoodbooooyyyyy . . .'

A young man with exceptionally attractive bed-head hair sits sketching in the sun. I wander close enough to see that he is the spitting image of the Boy – is, in fact, an American doppelganger of the Boy, who is also a scruffy-haired artist. He smiles huge and without warning. 'Hi.'

'. . . Hi . . .' I say and trundle off, all glum and heartsick. I've been away from the Boy for over half of this year already because I won this prize and not him. Sole stompin' rights to country $2000 away doesn't always seem like much of a gift, even on such a beautiful morning.

A notice at the hostel suggested riding the free LLBean-sponsored tour buses to see the rest of the island, and I make my way to the mustering point. Outdoor outfitter LLBean has a megastore in Freeport, Maine, which is open around the clock, all year long. It attracts more than three million visitors a year, second only to the natural wonders of Acadia National Park as the major tourist draw for the state. I am actually surprised that nature won out. The wilderness might be the original open-all-hours amusement, but LLBean is no doubt centrally heated and it does get icy cold out here. The tour bus sets out from the centre of town, a perfect grassy square called the Village Green. Scattered on the grass are dogs and kids and dappled sun and huge leafy trees. It is an immensely agreeable place.

Our driver is an old Maine salt, who tells me that he's troubled today because he's just had six summer drivers quit during training. 'It's tha new computah system,' he says. 'Some of them don't hold with it an' they get lawst. We've got enough drivers to get through the day, but then . . .' He peers at me shrewdly. 'You here to work in Bah Habah?' Oh, great. So my sojourn on the Greyhound is already paying dividends of shabby chic. He can tell which camp I'm in round these parts. I tell him I'm becoming a professional bus rider, but he says he has enough of those.

The bus windows are tinted heavily, which is very frustrating and totally unnecessary. This is hardly a part of the world known for glaring sun. Peeping through the scant un-tinted spaces until I get used to the sensation of half-face-sunnies, the landscape is completely different from anything I've experienced before. The trees feel luxurious just to look at. They are fairytale trees, movie-screen trees, dream trees. They are so different from the silvery eucalypt bush at home. The houses and resorts are so different too. I struggle to invent a new type of architectural phylum again and come up with Swiss/Victorian/Connecticut: sub-phylum, Seaside. I can't imagine there is a single dwelling similar to these in Australia. They would be completely out of place just about anywhere at home.

An old couple travelling in front of me sigh, 'Well, we'll say goodbye to the ocean. We leave tomorrah.' The bus driver replies, 'Oh, don't say g'bye. It'll still be here next year. Goes up and down a bit, but she never goes away.' There are my first real 'ayuhs' traded around after that. The dialectical 'ayuh' is to New England what 'y'all' is to the South. Mainers are characterised as very kind and friendly people, given to the wearing of those large foam trucker caps with netting and the frequent use of 'ayuhs'. They don't talk all that fast, either, which is a bit frustrating after New York. Local Mainers pronounce Bar Harbor just like I do. In fact, Australians and New Englanders have much in common linguistically. We both say 'Bah Hah-bah'. When I told my friend Kevin I was coming here, the west-coast boy made the same mistake as many other Americans and thought I meant Baja ('Bah-ha'), California. Which made them panic for me at the thought that I was headed to the complete opposite end of the nation.

Talking to Tara this morning, I asked her if she knew which state the Mall of America was in, which I had heard was the biggest shopping centre in the United States. She said she had no idea, but suggested I ask at the Parks and Wildlife office. Whaaa? After much to-ing and fro-ing and different inflections, I finally had to write it down, and Tara revealed she thought I wanted to see the Mole of America, presumably the best burrowing mammal in the nation. Americans are invariably embarrassed when they can't understand me. Considering that I'm the one with the accent here, I've always thought that to be quite sweet.

After only a few weeks in this country I learnt to adopt what I think of as my pirate R, turning the Aussie r ('ah') into a yo-ho-ho parrot-shouldered 'aaaarrrrrgh'. Without my r's understood in this land, my English quickly becomes a foreign language. I'm serious. I'm only a single consonant away from needing a phrasebook and an interpreter. 'Weird', is the most commonly misconstrued word, usually met with blank looks or mistaken for 'wet'. Essential services such as water, shower and beer all need pirate treatment, as does the spelling and pronunciation of my last name. After two years here, Dad has dropped the word 'car' from his vocabulary completely, opting instead to use the r-less 'vehicle' exclusively.

I don't much like my pirate r, but some things I've taken and refuse to return. Ass is one. I like ass. I like it much better than 'arse' which can sound a bit pompous and strictly *biological* in what it conveys. Arsehole is just too literally the sphincter to me. It is not usually my intention to paint that picture if I say 'ass'. Shake that ass is sexy, cute. Shake that arse means move your large and unattractive behind. I have adopted ass not as an American pretension, but as a fantastic addition. Armed with both arse and ass, I now have a linguistic multi-tool that's just plain dangerous.

The bus rounds a corner and information comes blaring electronically from above. 'APPROACHING ACADIA NATIONAL PARK!!! MAPS, PATHS, GUIDES AT THE VISITORS' CENTRE!!!'

'Phew!' the old man says, visibly shaken, gesturing to the intercom. 'Didn't see her get on.'

'Aw, that's just Elvira,' says our driver, and with that cryptic explanation they begin to discuss a recent LLBean bus accident at the Regency Holiday Inn. 'It put a crease in the top of the bus, an' it didn't help the hotel canopy much, either.'

'What happened?' the old man asks.

'Well, you got a 9-foot clearance and a 15-foot bus ... I'd put that down to pilot errah if I was made to say sump'n on tha issue.' His spanking-new radio jumps to life. 'Campground 1 to dispatch 5, go ahead, dispatch.' The old people get off and wave goodbye like we have always been friends. Now it's just me and the driver. There are seventeen buses on this single-road route, and every few minutes we get an update. The intercom system burps out, 'Well, George is leaving tha Village Green.' The driver reaches for the handset. 'Copy that.' We drive on along the empty, looping trail.

At the tidy little campgrounds on the bus route, there are small ugly pools with plastic slides, and these are jam-packed as the free bus departs for its half-hourly run past the beautiful still ocean waters. The Pirate's Cove Adventure Mini-golf is also over-full on this sparkling day when all the splendours of the natural world are in bloom. I'm not much of an outdoorsy sort myself, but the scenery here is extravagant. The weather is perfect. It would certainly be enough to make me want to buy boots from LLBean at 3 am on a Sunday and just run off into it. As we pass another full but dismal campground pool, the driver echoes my thoughts when he shakes his head and says, 'No accountin' for folk.'

We ride on in companionable silence. The massive houses give way to old Ford and Chevy trucks, ride-on mowers and red-roofed, barn-styled living. Who knows, perhaps some of them are barns. That would be novel. 'Are ya happy tah-day?' the driver asks suddenly. I'm a bit startled. It's not a question asked much outside of rudimentary psych evaluations. I have to concede that I am indeed very happy. Tooling around Mount Desert Island for the hell of it, with a pleasant – probably treat-filled – day ahead of me. 'Good,' he says. 'Ah enjoy it when people ah happy. Ah've hauled a lotta people and ah've only had one person to the best of mah knowledge be upset.' I lean closer, eager for bad-passenger gossip. 'He got offa tha otha bus, nearly had that young girl driver in tears. Well (he pronounces it 'whale'), he got in here then and stahted up, and ah thought ah hope ah don't have tah listen tah this all up Eden Street. So I say "Y'know, it's a terrible shame to go on vacation and be so upset.

So I'm gonna refund yah money for this bus."' The bus, of course, being free. I snicker, but I had been hoping for fisticuffs. 'Whale,' he continues, 'everybody else just laughed and laughed, and it buttoned him up good 'n' propah. Now, that little crack made it all ovah town, and then it was in tha newspapah and everything! But ah don't want a reputation for having a smaaht mouth.' He winks, chuckling.

All around us there are wet, quiet grasslands right to the edge of the water, with little pools and islands, and huge tall forests of firs. The geography suddenly strikes me and I can see myself as if on a map. I've come a very long way from the reclaimed swamplands on the Gulf of Mexico. Since I've been here, I've seen many instances where Maine is referred to as 'down east' but now it occurs to me that this isn't really so. 'Why,' I ask the driver, 'does everyone here say "down east" when this is about as far east as you can go at the top, like, to the north, of the USA?' He thinks. 'Whale . . . it's just is how it is. It's down east.'

I won't be thwarted. 'But only if you're Canadian is it down, surely. For the rest of the US it's *up* east.'

'Whale . . .' The driver stops talking to me, and I fear I've just crossed a line in Maine.

Just off Mount Desert Island, the bus sets down for half an hour at the Carrolls IGA supermarket in Trenton. For such a tiny place I find a glut of papers on sale – *The Maine Times*, *The Bangor Daily News*, *The Bar Harbor Times*, *Ellsworth Weekly*, *Ellsworth American*, *Mount Desert Islander*. Cheeses, no wonder the bus driver's crack was front-page material.

I am entranced by the unusual varieties of everyday foods too, which is surprising considering my last few months spent raiding US supermarkets. Deciding on a pre-luncheon snack of salty chips I come face to face with such flavour sensations as Mesquite BBQ, Honey Mustard and Onion, Sharp Cheddar and Jalapeño, Applewood BBQ and Smoked Cheddar, Sea Salt and Malt Vinegar and, my personal favourite, Buffalo Wing and Blue Cheese. I am gobsmacked, until I discover blistered pork rinds, in original or BBQ. The product mavens at Lay's potato chip company have also come to the party with a limited-edition chip series called 'Tastes of America' featuring Memphis BBQ,

Monterey Pepper Jack and California Cool Dill. I grab one of each. They look quite delectable.

On my way to the register I walk through the baked bean aisle. Correct. An entire aisle devoted to the tinned 'musical fruit'. Curiouser still, most varieties seem to contain maple syrup, an addition that seems never to have been considered in my hemisphere. Among the more popular are Bush's Maple Cured Bacon Beans, Boston Recipe with Molasses, Brown Sugar and Pork, Maple Flavour Beans 'with real maple syrup!' and Jacob's Cattle Beans with Pork, purported to be 'Maine's favorite'. There are lots with pork and beans, and with different beans too; yellow eye, regular kidney, black and kidney, bacon and onion-soaked beans – the list is wild.

At home, baked beans means beans in a can covered with tomato sauce. Here, in an aisle with every combination, I finally find three lonely cans of 'vegetarian beans' which, from reading the list of ingredients, one can only assume to be what at home is labelled 'baked beans'. They look suspiciously different though, and I'm concerned. The idea that something as simple as baked beans will now be added to the lengthening list of 'things you suppose you can get anywhere but think again' is quite distressing. The big things you expect. It's the small things that creep up to remind you that you are a stranger in a strange, strange land. Along with my chips and a maple-flavoured candy treat, I purchase some string cheese – flubbery sticks of mozzarella you peel into strings to dangle into your mouth. There is no finer food. Most bars in the USA serve them deep-fried, too. With dipping-sauce.

Back in town, bad weather starts to settle in and my elation with Bar Harbor gets a little dented. Locked out of the hostel until five, I find myself wandering up and down Main Street, lugging my string cheese and a hand-poured barley-maple-moose-pop in a straggly plastic bag. I am shivering like the entire cast of *Trainspotting* in the flimsy chiffon top I bought in NYC in a rather pathetic attempt to look like Sarah Michelle Gellar, and my toes are trying to curl up inside the hem of my jeans. Half frozen, I'm left to schlep around the newly grey town with growing understanding of why the LLBean megastore does such great business out here. Wish I had some goose-down socks and Kevlar britches myself about now. This place must be completely miserable most of the year, because the locals are still wearing tank tops and smiling despite it being 14 degrees Celsius.

When the fog rolls in across Bar Harbor, it seems there isn't much to do but take refuge inside and bitch about it. Having spent a large part of my weekly food allowance on one dressed-up lobster claw at lunch, I also discover that there isn't much to do in Bar Harbor that doesn't require opening your 'pocketbook' as the Americans call handbags. (They also call them 'purses' – your purse can be in your pocketbook, but it can also be in your purse. If you catch my drift.) I suppose I could always ride the free bus again, but I will be up at 6 am to ride the Greyhound for 24 hours to Chicago, so I'm not looking at buses as a form of recreation right now.

Cranky and sullen, I move my sorry purchases to Parke's Coffee and vow to do what the name suggests for the rest of my day. At a cosy seat, I drink about a pint of Lapsang Souchong, a smoky-flavoured tea I love that is often accused of tasting like campfire or Pinetarsol. I'm pleased to find it here and my spirits lift a bit. An old guy is sitting at the counter, drinking his drip-filter and minding his own, when two ladies who obviously don't know him tap him on the shoulder and both say 'Yes!' He is as confused as I am for a minute, but then joins in with their chuckles and waves to them as they leave. I'm totally bewildered by this exchange until I stand up to get more sugar and get a good look at him. His T-shirt has a picture of a Maine fishing boat in the background with bold letters in the fore posing the question, 'If a man speaks at sea where no woman can hear – is he still wrong?'.

When I finally get into the hostel for my jumper, it goes on like a hug. I don't think I could ever live anywhere that gets this cold in summer, even somewhere this astoundingly pretty. Nobody seems to be around and I'm bored stiff. Bar Harbor is not a great choice for solitary vacationing. Just around the corner I stop to investigate the Reel Pizza Cinerama on Kennebec Street. It appears to have been invented just for me. Tickets to their latest release movies are five bucks and you can purchase pizza and meals, beer and snacks, all served on fold-out trays attached to the cinema seats, or at comfy couches with side tables. It also appears to be a real hit with the whispering-Amex set. The conversation in the ticket line revolves around luxury yachts, senators' wives, whose kids are at Andover and who is summering with the Rockefellers.

'Bill's taking me flying now.'

'Good for *you*! It's great isn't it?'

Their accents sound like Mr Powell from Gilligan's Island.

'Absolutely! I mean, I feel like I've gone as far as I can go with sailing now.'

'Oh yeah, I hear ya there.'

They trade knowing chuckles as the wives turn their diamonds distractedly.

'And I was just in such a funk. Brokers do everything now . . . I needed *something* to use my time for, something meaningful, something I can engage with intellectually as well.' Sombre nods. This guy is all of forty.

'We flew out to the island last week and it only took us half the morning! Think of all the time we saved.'

'I know. It's so hard to fly commercial again, though, be warned!' Waggling finger, sage nods and knowing chuckles. Time saved to do what, I wonder, search for more *meaningful* hobbies? I want to mash my $2.85 popcorn down his expensively cologned neck and force him to buy me the $3.95 nachos with a side of sour cream and then fly me to my next stop.

After the movie I catch up with Tara and her friend Nicole, and we make cups of weather-appropriate hot chocolate in the hostel kitchen. There's something pure and wonderful about the school camp atmosphere of these timber rooms, our solid bunks and the feeling of being cosily tucked up at the foot of nature. After a week of Greyhound and New-York-City madness, it is intoxicatingly normal. Well, for a while. Before the thick cocoa is drained, we hear shrill, hysterical laughter coming from the women's bunk-room, followed by a little scream. Mugs in hand, we head back down the hall as fast as socks on polished floors will take us (pretty fast if you slide) and poke our faces round the door.

Instantly, I am attacked. An arm reaches around my chest and pulls me backwards, thumping my very un-funny bone against the wall and throwing the chocolate dregs over my throat and into my bra. We all scream together.

'Hiiiiiiiiiii!' yells my attacker. 'Ohmigosh, you're just the cutest thing!' She spins me to face her, thin arms pinioning my shoulders. 'But you're so dirty! Eeew! What a yukky, yukky mess! Are you a dirty girl? I think you aaaaarrrre!' Before I can beat this woman over the head with my empty mug, she scolds me, 'You shouldn't be drinking coffee at your age. No wonder you've spilled it.' She claps her hands together. 'Now let's get you cleaned up. You may borrow a nightdress from me if you wish, but not a good one, no, no, not for dirty girls!'

'Are you fucking insane?' I manage, still shocked and covered in goop, thankfully unused to being thrown around by strangers.

'You just, like, totally grabbed her!' Tara accuses.

'You could have burnt us!' Nicole says, shaking her head.

My attacker just folds her hands in front of her. 'You want me to leave,' she says. 'That's what you're saying. I offer you my nightdress but the sisterhood is unforgiving. I offer you my *nightdress* . . .' In front of us stands a woman with a huge straw hat, Anne of Green Gables plaits, fingerless black bicycle-gloves, high-top sneakers and a maiden aunt's frock from the Eisenhower years. It seems my initial diagnosis was correct. She starts to cry, and before we know it, she's been forgiven and introduced.

'Oh, I'm your new friend, Susie!' she says, and shakes each of our hands in turn. When she gets to me she giggles and then frowns. 'You said the F-word!' she says. 'But I won't tell!' Against all reason we help Susie drag her odd luggage in from the foyer, and refuse her offers of nightwear and hair-brushings. Tara and Nicole are laughing because I apparently have stripes of hot chocolate behind both ears, and I'm failing to understand how my brutal assault is now fun and games for everyone but me.

'Now girls,' says Susie, 'I have to go to the store before it closes so please don't think I'm snotty for leaving. I do so want us all to be best girlfriends! Oh, it's going to be such fun, all of us girls together! Tomorrow we'll make our friendship fast, I can't wait!' She claps the bike-gloved hands together again and shrieks with joy.

'I'm leaving at 6 am,' I say.

'We're leaving at seven,' echo Tara and Nicole.

'Oh boo,' says Susie, frowning, hands on hips. 'That's just no good at all.' Then she grabs me, lips an inch from my mouth, eyes darting. 'The guy . . .' she says.

'Yeahhhh?' I reply, arching my back like the friendly team at Sesame Street demonstrating the letter C.

'Was he . . .' she looks around, then leans in till our cheek fur is touching. Tara and Nicole slink behind a bunk. 'Was he *weird* to you?' she whispers. 'Like about not staying extra nights?'

'Um . . .'

'Because he wanted to keep MY ID!' she screams, releasing her grip and throwing me halfway across the room.

'Oh yeah,' I lie, placating this loony the way Greyhound has already taught me. 'He wanted mine too.'

'Oh good,' she says and sits down. 'I thought he just didn't like me!' she adds, shrieking with that hideous laughter again. 'Girls,' she asks us, 'do you think he's single? The boss guy? Because I *am* looking for a husband, after all.' Tara pulls up a chair. It's only 9 pm. Susie is as good as the in-house entertainment is going to get tonight.

She tells us that she's been travelling around America looking for a husband since she finished college in Maryland. 'I've been to almost all of the states!' she says. 'I won't go to Hawaii because I really don't like volcanoes and I would never marry a man who did, would you?' No, we agree, most certainly not. Poor Susie rambles on and on about her mission to find a husband and have kids. 'I don't care if he's a Maine fisherman!' she brays, glittering eyes indicating she would very much like a Maine fisherman. 'To have and to hold, girls, you know what I mean, to *have* and to *hold*,' she says as she rapidly braids and re-braids her long girlish hair. 'We all want daddies for the children now, don't we? No dirty girls here!'

When Susie finally goes to the supermarket, leaving all her stuff on the bed, we feel entitled to snoop a look. Hey, she's crazy and we're curious. It says her name is Mabel Swoosen and that, despite her girlish looks, she's 43. We whistle and hope for her sake she finds Mr Right soon.

When the lights go out, Susie sleeps next to me ('You're such a cutie-pie! You can tell me all your dreams in the night.') with the straw hat still on and the blankets pushed below her knees, showing pale legs up to bloomer-style underpants. Those knickers are hardly man-traps, I think, no wonder she's having such a hard go of it. What looks to be an extra pillow is revealed in the morning light to be a lumpy cloth doll with a little red felt mouth and woollen hair. It wears knitted mittens on each sack-cloth hand, and a hankie covers it up like a tiny sheet. Susie clutches at it in her sleep. It makes me wish I could take my F-word back.

Chapter 9

Go west

At 5.45 am the air is so fresh it makes me want to open a vein for a direct hit. I am overwhelmed by the odd sensation that my lungs are working properly for the first time. After a lifetime spent in soupy humidity or car-filled cities, I never understood how breathing O^2 this fresh could get you this high. The lilacs are scenting my morning as I'm skipping across the Village Green to the bus, leaving the quaint Yesterday Town behind for new adventure. In the midst of all this skipping and elation I have a severe buster, falling over on top of my string cheese and mushing it; my apple denting my spleen and winding me. Now gasping at the delicious air, I lie face down on the springy grass, grateful the mountainous paradise is largely empty at this time of day.

In keeping with the Perfect-Small-Town gestalt, the Greyhound which daily services Bar Harbor sleeps here overnight under a big old tree, tucked away neatly next to the small motel where you buy the tickets. Having deemed my squashed snack un-breakfastworthy, I look for somewhere to buy food at this hour of the day in the ten minutes I have before the bus departs. Running like the Michelin man with my pillow strapped to my front, I can smell promising breakfast-type odours coming from a place called Tathey's.

From the outside it looks like a modest grocery store. Inside, it is alive with early risers. Big rugged men sit lined up at a diner-style counter, all wearing baseball hats advertising 'Coastal Car Care' and the 'Down East Bait and Tackle Co.'. I order the delicious and inexpensive bacon egg roll and instantly wish I'd found this place earlier. Damn, I love a good brekkie. It strikes me as being the authentic Maine in here; where stories about moose and bad weather might be traded, where it's acknowl-edged that man is a slave to the season, the sea, and the elements, and where anyone not actually born in this state is considered simply to be from 'away'.

The sleeping Greyhound shivers to life and pulls out from under the tree, taking us up past the Village Green and out of Bar Harbor. Only two old women join me on this trip over the bridge into Trenton, watching the little boats already scudding around on the dark blue water and the huge yachts gently bobbing in the sun. An old wooden cart lies abandoned in a field of tiny yellow flowers and makes me smile. After sleeping the whole way here I'm looking forward to the scenery on the trip back down through it all. I'm going to be on the bus for a long time, I think, and get out a pen to figure my hours on the back of a Tathey's napkin.

I called my friend Nick in Denver last night (mostly to make sure Denver was still even there – months of drought have set the state of Colorado on fire), and he told me he was organising tickets for a three-day concert in the mountains. Did I want to go? Now there again is a silly question. I haven't partied since New Year's Eve and it's the end of June. Still, it would mean making a straight shot to Minneapolis – missing Chicago completely – and riding the Dawg for . . . well, for a long time, right? Definitely overnight. I decided to do it anyway. Sure! I said, and now I'm scribbling on the greasy napkin to work out my arrival time.

Mathematics has never been my strong point. In fact, my high-school maths teacher rearranged the entire school's time-table around keeping me out of his class for the last two years of my secondary education. I'm certain he quite liked me, but he said he didn't want either of us to endure my sitting a maths exam ever again. He was very wise, Mr Law, wise and benevolent, but it's times like these I wish I'd had my numeric dyslexia treated after all. At 6.30 this Monday morning on the bus, I have just redone my hasty concert-acceptance calculations to discover that with continuous bus travel I will arrive in Minneapolis at . . . 2 o'clock *Wednesday* morning? Shhheeeeit. Wait, let's do that again. I channel Mr Law. Betty and Jim have a Greyhound Ameripass. Jim wants to sleep and remain sane and clean, but Betty wants to go to a concert with her friends. How many hours will Betty have to sit on the bus to get halfway to Denver? I scribble and scribble, but for once I am perfectly correct and can only sigh as I prepare for the inevitable Greyhound flogging.

The bus is now half full and the old Bah Hahbah biddies at the front are driving everyone nuts. They natter on at top pitch, but apparently their age precludes the driver from exercising his shushing-rights. It seems I'm not alone in wanting to enjoy the peaceful scenery. There's a lot of huffing and pointed coughs coming from the other passengers, but it just seems to egg these ladies on. Three questions for old people. One – why blue eye-shadow? Especially when wrinkles mean 12 new eyelid folds instead of the original pair? Two – at what point does everything become wrong, everyone become rude and the world start generally going to hell in a bucket? Was everything really so much better before civil rights, women's rights and the right to reject polyester pantsuits and meals comprised entirely of tinned food? Three – must there be a running commentary on anything which passes your field of vision for a time span greater that a nanosecond? For an hour now it's been, 'Phyllis, what's that yellow car doing now? Where's that man going, do you think? Are those all her children in that car, I wonder? You never can tell these days. Driver, are you from around these parts? Daisy, that yellow car is back again . . .'

After a few hours of driving, the bus pulls up outside a remote airfield. We are close to the Canadian border here, so I'm not too surprised when a giant man gets on sporting a gun, flak-jacket, aviator shades and a smart green uniform. Border control. Unlike the many regular police officers I've seen in the

US, border control officers look so much alike that they may as well be the same person. Huge, cold, automated, intimidating. After a silent examination of the occupants of each pair of seats, he pulls a radio out and six-fours his twin in the car outside. Then he gives a brief speech I fail to take in, and people begin to mutter and fish for documents. I'm so excited to show him my Green Card. 'Ooh, ooh, me, sir!' I think. 'Over here! I've done my homework!'

The first time I came into contact with these immigration boogeymen I was considerably less confident of my status. Considerably less as in shitscared. On the overland trip I made to Las Vegas as a university student, I had never expected that my expired airline ticket and student visa might be called into question. Having been assured my J1 student visa was good for a month or so of travel before I left the US, even though the printed date was now clearly past, I was certain that no one was going to ask for my passport outside of an airport anyway. Australians aren't very good with the whole land border thing – we're islanders, after all. So when our Greyhound (slinking through New Mexico, hugging the wasteland of border towns and rural pit stops) was pulled over in the middle of the night by flashing sirens, my initial reaction was actually positive. If we had been breaking the speed limit then great; we weren't going as impossibly slowly as it felt. If arrests were to be made then double great. We needed the room and some of our fellow passengers were clearly deranged.

I remember the men who climbed aboard as being so hardcore that they wore *Terminator* sunglasses. At night. Their uniforms were tailored one size too small and they carried a couple of firearms apiece, as well as a heavy truncheon. Without preamble, one began poking this black bar into the overhead compartments and under seats, issuing terse orders for people to wake up, to move, to stand. He knocked on the locked toilet door and demanded the person inside come out, holding up a gloved hand for silence when someone protested that it had been broken all day. After a few more knocks, he stepped back and kicked the door in with his boot. A collective gasp rose from the bus. This was serious stuff.

Meanwhile, his partner was making his way down the back, asking each passenger where they were born. Dissatisfied with an answer for whatever reason, documents were called for and handed over to the poker-faced uniform. Anyone not born in an American city had to present their papers as a matter of course. My heart started to pound and my palms prickled up with sweat. One of my friends leaned towards me. 'Shit, Darmody. Shit. Say your passport's on the other bus.'

Our luggage had been travelling on any number of buses headed west for the past two days, and it was a pretty good idea. Four rows ahead I heard a man say, 'All my stuff's on another bus. I don't got it, ask Greyhound!' The uniform was still. 'Off the bus,' it commanded and the man had no choice but to comply. My palms were now so slick I suspected stigmata. 'Ohmygod,' my friends were saying, 'Ohmygod, oh no . . .'

I remember how sick I felt, sick with the fear that any minute now my holiday would be over before it had begun. Mum would get a phone call in the middle of the night, I would be deported and my passport shot to bits for further travel. I am white, I thought, I am white and I will lie. When the uniform whispered to a halt in front of my seat, I opened my mouth only the tiniest fraction, certain that I was about to lose my inadequate dinner onto his shiny shoes. 'Where were you born?' he asked me.

I looked up into the mirrored frames, died a little, and said, 'Sacramento.' Actually, I said 'SacREmenno,' in what I hoped was exactly the same drawl used by the tattooed man a few rows in front when he had spoken the same word. There was a long pause before he turned to the next person and asked, 'Where were you born?' Looking back, lying to the INS rates up there with licking the freezer 'just to see' as one of the more stupid risks I've taken, but those people don't exactly invite negotiation.

This time, when the officer reaches me my voice rings out to fill the bus with 'Australia'. He nods. He moves on. I deflate. My Green Card is all dressed up with nowhere to go.

Apart from the non-stop nonsense from the old women, our bus has been dead until the officers got on and now it's a free-for-all. It seems there's nothing like a brief interruption from the outside world or some kind of misadventure to get everyone shouting their malformed opinion on the Greyhound.

A sweet old hippie gets on at the airfield and keeps trying to convince us all to take an interest in the government and go to a Ralph Nader rally this weekend. He's got a tough job preaching to this lot. We have ten people representing the young and ignorant, and six for the old and whiny.

A British girl loaded with piercings tries to get on with a cigarette and is read the riot act. While the others get settled she mutters loudly to herself outside. 'Can't even have one fuckin' smoke, and I say just let me have one fuckin' smoke and then we'll go, orright? I gots rights,' she repeats 'I gots rights . . .'

'I gots rights' is a popular refrain on Greyhound – it's practically the bus anthem. It's also a popular sentiment right across this country. There are times when these rights are truly the shining beacons of hope and democracy they're supposed to be, but as far as I can see they are mostly used to sell things and sue people.

The British girl, still cursing and carrying on, throws down her bag and her sizable arse (note usage) on the seat in front of mine. A few minutes after we take off, she turns around. 'See, I'm the sort of person yah, when I make my mind up, I won't change it? Dja know?'

I look over my shoulder. An old man is asleep three rows back. It appears this girl has mistaken me for someone she knows.

'See, when I make my mind up,' she continues, 'I just will NOT change it for anyone, and that's why people say it's hard to get along with me.' Perhaps that's not the only reason. I try my usual tactic. I smile like you might at someone with an automatic weapon and a headless teddy bear, and give a bright 'Okay!' before closing my eyes to signal nap time. (In the US, by the way, this interim slumber is called 'nappy time'. At home to hear anyone over toilet-training age discuss needing some nappy time is only mildly less unsettling than the concept of 'fanny packs' – your fanny, of course, being your *front* bottom in Australia.) It appears that neither nap nor nappy time means much to my persecutor. I sigh a bit and smack my lips, but she's not buying.

'Oi. What's yer name then?' she asks, poking me in the shoulder. I tell her and she turns it over for a bit. 'Well,' she says, 'I'm Tess,' and sticks out a little black fingernailed paw for me to shake. It is abruptly clear that we are about to become bus mates.

On the Greyhound, becoming someone's involuntary bus mate is a bit like prison bitch without the benefits. Inside I moan as I calculate my miserable chances at escape. Luckily, Tess seems content to do most of the talking. In fact, as long as I remain a conscious and vaguely animate audience, my duties to the conversation are few. She begins by cataloguing her piercings, of which she is inordinately proud. Having had some experience in this area myself, I know that apart from a ready wallet, the only skill required is to sit still for approximately one second. 'I've had my tongue done three times right, because it kept getting infected? But now my piercer? Nightshade? He makes me use Listerine every day, like, practically *drink* it!' Good for him, I convey with a slight inclination of my head.

We are driving through Augusta now, a town that seems beautiful, blessed with a huge sparkling lake running parallel to the main street. Even Tess takes time out from her piercing tales of woe to exclaim that she thinks it's nice. 'Yeah, I like the States. It's good 'ere. It's a lot roomier than England. In real space, and head space too, dja know?' She proceeds to tell me how she feels she can be herself here in Maine much more than she can at home, something I find startling considering that Tess is from punk nesting-ground in London, and there are more farmers' co-ops out here than nose bolts.

Tess lives in Maine with someone 'on me dad's side' but is going to Salem, Massachusetts, with a big book about the Salem witch trials in her bag. 'I'm Wiccan,' she declares with sombre authority. 'I can even do spells . . .' She continues with her tough-kid tales, and I feel a bit sorry for her as she twirls badly-dyed hair between chubby fingers. She's about five-foot-nothing with a bloody great belly ring through her ear and a small crop of blackheads in a patch under her chin. She's shown me her passport photo to display her snarl and dog collar ('Wicked, yah?') and it tells me that she's just turned fifteen. Funny little thing, I think, wondering if her parents are contemplating boarding school.

'Oi!' she says, 'Sa-RAH, are you even listening?' I nod. 'Well, I bet you wouldn't think I had a kid, would ya?' Tess enjoys my brief look of horror, and triumphantly produces a well-thumbed photo of a small toothless chubbit. The child has its eyes firmly shut, dressed in bright green in the middle of a Kmart photo-op pumpkin patch. 'His name is Silas,' she says. 'I'm going to raise him Wiccan. Probably white, but maybe black? Y'know – black magic? Evil has more power you know, actually, bet you didn't know that! If Silas is evil he'll have power over everyone.'

She's still desperately trying to shock me, but I'm getting so bored with all her posturing that I'm only drifting in and out of her babble. 'Oi! Sa-RAH. I'm talking to you, orright? Now, see, I can do anything I want with Silas's religion, because he's my kid. And no one can stop me. Because he's my kid. And if his fuckedupevilbaptist grandma – his dad's mum – if she says anything, we'll run away. And I can do that. Dja know why? Because he's my kid.' I nod. 'Oi! This is important.' She leans over into my territory and traces a pattern on my knee. 'I'll do a spell on you!' she giggles. 'Oi, c'mon, I need to talk, to get it straight in me 'ead.'

I exhale loudly and shake my own head, hoping to express my outrage at this bit of cheek. The little brat forced herself upon me 36 minutes ago and now I owe her a shoulder? Tess continues on regardless. 'Me kid's dad's orright though. Says I can do whatever, he'll leave it up to me. Like, I want to get Silas a tattoo for his first birthday? Maybe a bat, I'm not sure, and first his dad said no, but I said fuck you, whatever, and so he said yes. But then I found out that it's, like, totally illegal and no one would do it, but *then*, his dad found a guy who would. Cool, eh?' Tess gazes proudly at the Kmart pumpkin kid. 'Soon as we get some money he'll be a real Wiccan baby.'

I've really had enough now. I close my eyes and rest my head on the window. 'Oi! Sah-RAH, you liss-en-ing?'

'Yep. Just thinking.'

'Oh!' she squeals. 'I could tell! I know what you're thinking too. You're thinking I'm radical.' She stares at the stained bus ceiling, lost in self-contemplation. 'Dja know, I've always been radical. It's why it's hard for people to get along with me. And anoth–'

'Actually, Tess, I was thinking I'd rather we didn't talk about your spawn anymore, it makes me think about my own two.'

She's bouncing on the seat as if to break it now. 'Oiiiiii! You got kids!'

'Had kids,' I correct.

'Aw, not like stillborn or whatever? Or that cot death? Dja know you should never –'

'No, they're in Utah. Twins. I gave them to the Dark Lord on their first birthday.'

'You *wot?*'

I sigh, struggling to look forlorn and asleep simultaneously.

Tess is quiet for a bit. 'I didn't know you could just, like . . . do that.'

'Oh yeah,' I say. 'They're my kids, I'll do what I want. Batlugs and Bastard, little darlings. Oh well, easy come, easy go.' This time the silence lasts a full five minutes. There is a rustling as Tess shifts a few rows ahead and introduces herself to some unwitting stranger.

By the time we reach the next town, she and Courtney, who the whole bus now knows has three young boys of her own, multiple sclerosis, a false hip and husband in a South-American prison, are whispering about me and pointing, incensed at my bad parenting.

At this same stop we pick up a new weirdo, dressed in a fishing jacket and Girl Scouts hat. Smiling and extremely smelly, she plonks her bag on my lap and then sits next to me, grinning every few minutes. At one point she pinches into my shoulder. 'Excuse me, excuse me.' I am ready to kill. 'We're in New Hampshire now.' I look out the window as we come into a small town.

New Hampshire is pretty in the same way as Maine, with huge trees and bridges and stately old houses, and an excellent state licence plate: 'New Hampshire – Live Free Or Die'. The area seems quiet and conservative for such a proclamation. Texans have 'Don't Mess With Texas' but I get the feeling from every Texan I've ever met that they mean it and are ready to prove it to you at a minute's notice.

My seatmate, pleased with my positive response to New Hampshire, tries again. 'Excuse me. Excuse me.' I lift my brows in acknowledgement. 'Do you ever wish you could take a part off yourself? To clean it? It can be hard to clean some parts because they're attached, don't you think?' From the smell I would say that she's tried and found it nearly impossible. Tired of playing games with creeps, I go textbook.

'Look,' I say, 'I don't feel comfortable talking about this. I'm sorry.' She nods and I feel much better. Easy. The minutes tick by, pregnant between us. Then a whisper. 'What about your girl's part . . . do you ever wish you could take that off and just clean it?'

'Oh, for crying out loud!' I yell, and stomp my possessions to the back of the bus, where the remaining seat next to the toilet has been left empty for obvious reasons. I can't do this for two days straight, I'll go mad.

Sitting on a Greyhound smells like being locked inside a bag of Doritos with three old apple cores, two unwashed marines, one brown banana, half an anchovy, a splash of urine, a gob of bubblegum and a hint of vomit. There are other noxious smells, which may or may not be present, depending on your luck, but those ones are consistent. Also, without fail, about three hours into any trip, empty water and soft-drink bottles will begin their death rattle along the aisle toward the driver. From that moment, they will continue to travel backwards and forwards, the noise just loud and random enough to keep you from sleeping, until, five minutes short of your final destination, the driver takes a corner and they make a final, clattering rush for the front steps.

We roll into Boston at 1.30 pm, among much discussion from the original old biddies on who's driving what, where and why. Boston has an inviting harbour running in and out of the city and looks quite lovely. I warm to the city even more when I hop off the bus and find their Greyhound terminal to be a real treat. My first stop is to the huge bathroom designed with waiting seats and ample counter space, where I would very much like to take off my mind and give it a good wash. It's hard to keep clean while it's attached to me on a Greyhound bus.

There is a good but expensive sandwich shop too, and even a McDonald's. I clap my hands together at all this splendour. Strolling around in the new space, it feels very much like a terminal belonging to real travellers, not us lowly Greyhound losers. I approach the airline-style counter to double-check my travel time figures.

'Hi! I'm travelling to Minnesota and –'

'Where in Minnesota?'

Hmm, good question. I pause, mouth open, squinting at the map behind the attendant. She clicks her nails on the desk. 'You're not going to make it there today ma'am, that's why I'm axing you.'

'Yeeeah,' I say, peering at all the states in between me and Minnesota and remembering this choice having been made for no other reason than an enforced stop across the great, vast middle of this country. 'Let's try for the capital,' I decide.

'Minneapolis, ma'am?'

'Sounds good to me.'

On the outskirts of Boston a Spanish-accented girl squashed into Christina Aguilera's questionable wardrobe gets on and, out of the endless possibilities of empty seats, takes the one next to mine. I curse my bad luck for being young, white, female and thin. While this has occasionally been a problem in a rowdy pub, it's a demographic that has largely served me well. Until now. I am everyone's ideal seatmate on a Greyhound bus. Hell, I would want to sit with me too. I can already tell that Greyhound travel will push me to wish I was a fat, ugly-ass man of dubious ethnicity. Those lucky bastards get all the room they need.

My seatmate's name is Jessica. She tells me she's going to meet her three kids in New York City for a few days. A few years ago, in Puerto Rico, they were taken away from her because she was letting them run riot ('They kids, choo know, only small! I say, let them do what they like, it's a life of do dis do dat after they older!'). When social services discovered Jessica had tried to commit suicide at 19 over some lousy guy, they decided she was unfit and gave her kids to her childless aunt. She was so angry that she left Puerto Rico, and is now onto husband number three at the ripe old age of 27. I settle back. This is good and juicy. I even offer her a barley sugar to keep her whistle wet.

Jessica's latest husband is Guatemalan. He loves her very much, she says, but he doesn't know any English still, and if he doesn't learn some soon, she's going to leave him. She hates that he sounds like a peasant. He works illegally for thirteen hours a day at a laundry where the chemicals are so strong that he has nosebleeds all the time and has lost his sense of smell.

Jessica works at a cookie shop and a maternity store. She sees a lot of babies and kids at those places, she says, which makes her sad. Her aunt is bringing the kids to the US for a week, and it's been a year since she saw them last. The aunt says she could have them back, but Jessica tells me she wants to live in a rich world, even if she has to be poor in it, and she has no money for kids here. When pressed, she says she likes Boston better than Puerto Rico because the dancing is better and she loves to see people wearing clothes from magazines and driving beautiful cars. Eventually her stories peter out and we fall into a contemplative silence.

When we wheeze into New York at 6.30 pm, it feels strange to be back after having said my heartfelt farewell to the place at dawn only a few days ago. It feels much the same as when you say goodbye to someone and then walk off in the same direction as they do, eventually forced to have that second, awkward, salutation. I get a very different view of the city this time. The bus travels through what must be miles of shitty apartments on the upper, upper, upper East Side, which I could never live even close to. Sometimes it doesn't even look like a first world nation.

Surely not in America, not in New York City, would you find these huge towers with tiny windows fifty storeys up; with rusted barbed wire, and postage-stamp-sized patches of grass the colour of tinned lima beans. The sameness and the lack of pride or signs of ownership is depressing. This is also New York City, I think, and she is hot and beat and dirty.

Off the bus once again at Port Authority, I watch Jessica collect her one small bag. Out of the top sticks a Barbie doll in its pink Mattel box and a bag of cookies from the chain store she works at. She walks away slowly, tugging at her ill-fitting clothes. I think of her bloody-nosed husband and my under-appreciated Green Card feels ashamed to belong to me instead.

Up and out onto the street with all my junk strapped to my body, I find out the hard way that New York is no place to be a fat, slow pedestrian. I push through the crowd, getting hot and sweaty and trodden on. Walking the few blocks to 45th and 18th, I stop and inhale a delicious Caesar pizza from a hole in the wall near all the stores selling adult videos, Taiwanese watches and cheap luggage. Fresh salad on hot pizza is still a fabulous idea. This one is very good, and reminds me of the big square slices eaten on a dusty doorstep during my travels with the Boy. I miss him badly. This is something we should be doing together, I think. It's harder alone. Not the eating of course – now I just get more – but certainly the carrying of my kilos of stuff.

I go into a Duane Reade, a 'drugstore' chain that sells some groceries and cards and things too. I had long wondered about the American pharmaceutical baron Duane Reade until I was told the original store was on the corner of Duane and Reade streets. Oh. I buy some water and some corn cakes. Corn cakes pack-up small, last on the bus, need no preparation and eat more like a cereal meal than a salty party snack. I'm all about salty party snacks, don't get me wrong, but not for breakfast on the road. I'm not in a hurry to get back to the station, but my luggage-related girth is making me a liability in the cramped retail spaces of New York City.

The Port Authority terminal is disgusting and depressing. I prepare for the next two nights to be spent on the bus by having a quick cat-wash in a toilet block under a big sign that says 'No shaving, no bathing etc'. Bathing is a little hopeful in here anyway. The tiny sinks are beyond scummy and it stinks like a Bombay giardia clinic. I brush my teeth and wash my face, put on a woven head cover on which I fancy makes me look like Lauryn Hill (if she was pale and scrawny with much smaller lips) and change my socks. Doing my best to remain clothed in polite company, I attempt to make use of my newly purchased baby wipes from head to toe.

For half an hour I remain the only white face in the room even though a hundred women and children must have come and gone. Most are Latin-American, and there are identifiable groups of Pakistani, Chinese, Vietnamese and even Eritrean women as well. All of them make the same face upon entry; a multi-ethnic grimace of 'phwaaw!' Pity there are no cheery 'Tell us what you think!' forms here so I can write 'Ponkering House of Stink, Port Authority'.

In the waiting room/holding pen, I sit next to an older guy who is waiting for the same bus. 'Pretty grim down here,' he says. Ayuh, I think. 'Shame the Twin Towers didn't take the whole damn island with 'em.' Whoa cowboy! Steady on. 'C'mon,' he says, 'it's dirty, it's nasty and it's where 80 per cent of the country's prison population originates from. For violent crime that is. Damn ambulance officers gotta wear bulletproof vests. This town disgusts me.' He shakes his head. His attitude towards New York, while heinous, is actually not surprising. The rest of the world seems to exclude New York when they give the US a verbal pounding, but Americans themselves are still often critical and suspicious of the place, though much less so after 9/11.

This New-York-hater's name is Jeff and he's from Alberta. He's going all the way to Nevada on Greyhound for his job because he is too afraid of heights to fly. 'I get so sick from fear I just crawl across the tarmac on my belly and cry for my momma.' Jeff works for a company in Nevada that has a government contract transporting weapons for the FBI and the DEA. He can't wait to be out of the 'Greyhound thing', as he calls the cycle of buses and bus stops on his marathon journey, but he says it's still quicker than driving himself and having to stop overnight. It's Monday night tonight, and he won't reach his destination until Thursday morning.

I have quite a way to go myself. Tonight will be spent crossing Pennsylvania to Ohio, where I'll change buses for one that will continue to take me west through Indiana and Illinois, before veering up north a bit through Wisconsin and, finally, to Minnesota. When I reach Minneapolis, I'll still be a big state or two away from halfway across the country. I can certainly see where they might stash 300 million people in the USA.

There is an absolute sea of humanity down here in the bowels of New York. In an atmosphere still thick with tension and suspicion over recent terrorist attacks, it's strange that I don't see a single security guard or police officer amongst these itinerant masses underneath Times Square. I do see lots of young guys in military uniform. It's not so cute when there's really a war on. This current conflict is shaping up to be the Vietnam War of my generation in terms of useless and unpopular conflict. Many of these young marines are sitting cheek by jowl with women in chadors and bearded Muslim men, and both parties seem very uncomfortable at the obvious irony. I wonder if everyone will behave themselves on the bus; it's like fans from opposing football teams forced to share the last cab home after the game.

We show our tickets and some ID to get on the bus, and our belongings are wanded with metal-detectors. Many go off, including mine, but we are waved on with limp gestures. This half-hearted attempt at security is backed up by photocopied notices instructing us to leave the seats behind and beside the driver completely clear 'due to the events of 9/11'. A few weeks after those 'events', Greyhound suffered an event of its own. On 3 October 2001, an unstable passenger slashed the throat of a bus driver outside of Manchester, Tennessee, causing a crash in which six Greyhound passengers were killed, including the attacker. The event halted Greyhound services around the jumpy nation, due to its similarity to the airline attacks, but the perp turned out to be a mad Croatian sailor living illegally in the USA, who had a criminal history in his homeland. According to witnesses, he became 'agitated' during the journey, and asked repeatedly how much longer, further etc, prompting many off-colour jokes about what Greyhound travel will drive people to do. One year later this incident was repeated when a driver had his throat cut outside Fresno, California. Two people died, including the poor driver this time. I don't blame the drivers for fighting to keep the seats behind their necks clear.

As the bus leaps away, Jeff and I trade gagging faces as we are forced to eat gallons of 'Just like Armani's Aqua!' deo-cologne, sprayed by some German tourist jerk ahead of us. The chemicals make me dizzy. I feel giddy too from the improbability of finding myself riding through the night to the destination Cleveland, Ohio. I'm strangely thrilled. Yep. Off to Cleveland, that's right. Don't mind me, I'm off to Cleveland. He he! The place has never really existed for me before now, except as the butt of a few American jokes regarding its apparent dullness, and as the start of the Drew Carey show.

I lean in heavily against the unforgiving chair, squirming around to avoid the pointy base of the seat dividers. We won't be arriving until the sun does. One week into my grand excursion and I've had to become less streamlined and more bag lady; gaining headdress, contact-less squint, pillow, bottles and bags of snacks, so that I'm looking ugly, moving slowly, but feeling comfy. Maybe that's why people on the Greyhound look like they do. On the sliding scale from snappy to comfy, we end up socially unpleasant.

Our bus driver has a heavy, indeterminate accent, and seems to be a pretty cool guy. As we hoon around the corner from the station he shouts out to us, 'Okay, now I don' have I mike workin', so I gots to express myself this way, but for you, please jes' come down here, don' be shoutin' from the back, it's being annoying! Now, this is a bitch of trip. Lots of stoppin', not so much sleepin'. So jes' all be quiet like mice, don' be rude, use your head, and I will not be using any lights at the rest stops unless some blind lady ask of me, okay? Try to sleep. Leave me to driving, I try for smooth. Good dreams for you.' It works, too. Use a bit of common sense and get it back. Treat your passengers like cattle with mad cow disease and you get Port Authority.

I had always imagined Cleveland, Ohio, as a place of winter coats and grey skies. Evicted from the bus at 6 am, it is already unbearably hot. Inside the attractive station, designed with acres of blonde wood, high ceilings and lots of light, a human freak show has collected in spiteful contrast to such moderate architecture. I am bumped out of the toilet line by a large pale woman covered in an unearthly constellation of spots and scars and freckles; her eyes almost lost in two pink piggy rolls of flesh. I am about to protest her rudeness when I realise she just didn't see me. The poor woman is fat enough to need those 'If you can't see my mirror I can't see you' truck signs stuck to her generous flank. I fall back in line beside two small black kids. They watch her moving with open-mouthed fascination, and so do I. We can't help it.

Waiting for an east-bound bus is a sizable group of Rabbinical scholars ranging from five to 55, all decked out in identical black, with hats, holy books, ringlets and strange lengths of cord hanging off their shirts. Next to their blackness stands a Hindu woman in a bright-pink sari who is sporting a delicately curled and filigreed gold nose-ring the size of my front tooth. A bald man walks past with a huge roll of neck fat like an in-built travel pillow. Mmm. Handy. He is wearing a T-shirt with a picture of a big dog collapsed in the heat, which reads 'Fort Lauderdale'. Most of these people are speaking shyly around mouthfuls of missing teeth. It turns out bad dental care isn't just a hokey joke if you're poor.

Over by the ticket counter, a fight breaks out between two drivers and a station manager that appears to be over routes and pay. With stubble, sweat stains and untucked shirts, none of them look like they've slept all week. There seems to be some huge hassle over our bus to Chicago, and I find myself at the back of a very long line after waiting, exhausted, in the wrong one. I figure it out just in time to see the express bus roll away without me. 'I *hates* de local buses,' says a guy to his friend behind me. 'What you wan' is one of dem hex-press buses. Now we going to stop at every damn mailbox in Sandusky.' Fantastic. It's the fucking Carolinas all over again.

I sit down on the floor in front of the west-bound gate and dig for some corn cakes. I'm so sore after a night on the bus that the hard floor is really punishing, but at least the dry, scratchy cornies are doing a good job on my furry teeth. The poor piggy woman is now marooned in a puddle of gristle propped up by the wall, crocheting a pair of the tiniest mittens. Their stripes and elongated shape are reminiscent of the weird Tim Burton world of *The Nightmare Before Christmas*.

We are all finally shoe-horned onto a packed bus, where we sit for an hour without a driver. I'm starting to get worried about my connections. I'm also dying to get somewhere and go exploring again. Just to be vertical for a while would be nice. Or at least properly horizontal. Making the miserable discovery that I've left my good Australian skin cleanser and the attractive maple-moose-pop in Bar Harbor, I'm struck by how long ago and far away it already seems.

Two overgrown third-graders are telling dumb stories and arguing over, of all things, which one is the hardest sleeper. A little Hispanic girl sings her own composition entitled 'Ees No Bus Dryer' over and over and over again. Two hours after our bus was scheduled to leave the Cleveland depot, a very cranky man gets on and hurls the vehicle into reverse in under two seconds. Startled, we react as though kidnapped. 'Look,' he says, 'I slept for three hours. They called me, they begged. Now you all sit still,' (and he makes the word sound alarming, like *steel*) 'and we get there, capiche?'

Capiche. The only time I've ever seen a Greyhound station manger is here in Cleveland, and up and down the aisle we all trade knowing looks of the 'shit must have hit the fan today' variety. Burning bus rubber on the way out, Cleveland goes by pretty fast. It's misty or smoggy, hard to tell, with a lot of construction. There are some old buildings and old signs and some kind of waterway – a river, a lake, a pond, I don't care enough to ask. The entire bus is unconscious almost as soon as we leave the city. We've all been lining up since six, and the vibrating rhythm is hypnotic. I try to fight it for awhile, but I can't.

I wake at the first stop, where a skinny girl-woman gets on and charges up and down the aisle muttering to herself before she goes to the front two seats, rips down the 9/11 sign and lies there, curled into a quivering question mark. Everyone smirks delightedly at each other. A fight will surely ensue and provide an entertainment break. It doesn't happen though. The driver is too preoccupied to notice, half-asleep himself and fielding random abuse.

The next stop is a place called something like Scrotum, Ohio, consisting of a Wendy's burger outlet and the 'World's Biggest Fireworks Warehouse! Fireworks inside, no smoking.' The 9/11 seat-stealer leaps to her feet. She isn't dwarfed, but is still strangely small, like a grown woman in the body of a ten-year-old girl, and she walks pushing out her tummy and chest like a toddler. Her outfit – pink satin cropped pants and a matching top – look custom-made to fit her, but she shows no other signs of care. She has also had the mean jitters the whole way. I wonder if it's recreational or prescription meds. I wouldn't mind some of either.

She pushes to the front of the line at Wendy's and, producing two battered dollar bills from her pink plastic shoe, she orders off their '99-cent' menu. The bill comes to $2.08 – there's sales tax just about everywhere in America. Pink girl-woman clearly doesn't have it and the Wendy's girl is being overly smug. Although I'm in no mood to be charitable, this whole morning has been so pathetic that I feel our bedraggled busload should avoid at least this one disgrace. 'Miss,' I tell her, 'you dropped this,' and I hand her another note. She grabs it like a little animal and sends the bill sailing over the Wendy's counter like a dirty moth.

Back on the bus I discover those jerks at Wendy's have sold me a bowl of sloppy chilli and an equally sloppy salad with no fork or spoon or even so much as a straw with which to stab at it. A kindly schizophrenic man stops conversing with himself long enough to lend me his chewed red plastic spoon, and I'm so hungry that I actually use it. Truly. Though I soon find eating salad with a spoon to be highly unsatisfactory, there is much to keep me occupied on this particular Greyhound route. It's like a zoo where the keeper has squashed animals of very different needs and sizes together to experiment on their behaviour. Cruel, but interesting.

For my lunchtime viewing entertainment I stay tuned to the seat just in front and to the left, where sits a Korean man so small I begin to suspect that he and the pink-clad crazy are from the same nuclear testing facility. He is sitting next to a black woman so large that her thighs have forced apart her knees to nearly the entire width of the seat space. In order for our hero to read his Korean newspaper, he must keep it tightly rolled, jamming it upright in his crotch and turning it slowly around like a barber's pole. Reading all the way to the bottom requires a yoga position Madonna would be incapable of performing, before turning the page and starting over.

The fields outside are large, flat and quite lovely. Ohio is very green, and the miles of crops look lush and fresh. Huge sprinklers on wheels move imperceptibly forward over stalks carrying grain and big trucks thunder past us hauling produce. This country looks incredibly rich and fertile. The houses – when there are any – are neat with Dutch barns or sloping roofs. After a while it gets a bit dull. I try to stretch and psych myself up for the push at the next big station.

Just before Gary, Indiana, it starts pelting down with rain, absolute sheets of it. We are now driving so slowly it feels like we are barely moving. Angry passengers get angrier as the bus crawls into the storm. I peer out the window at Gary, a town I have long been curious about. Every other year it seems that Gary has led the nation in murders per capita, a factoid that always seems to crop up somewhere in articles about violence and the US (which is another common combination). The Gary I can see through the rain confirms my prejudice that it would be a bleak and ugly place. With burnt-out cars, smashed walls and derelict streets, I start to wonder if suicides ever get confused for homicide and push those stats up. We stop just long enough to release two passengers. A perfect blond boy-child gets off with his gargoyle of a mother who has one eye closed, her left breast twice as long as the other, dragging to her knee. She hits the kid three times down as many bus stairs.

We rumble along through Indiana and into Illinois. Outside Chicago the driver attempts to calm the now very late and furious passengers. 'Okay,' he starts, 'traffic on the Dan Ryan Expressway is going to be what it is. Traffic on the Dan Ryan. So y'all remember when you get off, you're mad with Greyhound now, not with me. So try to smile, 'cos I'm gonna smile reeeal hard.' Protests and accusations are hurled. The rain and traffic worsen. We witness two car accidents as they happen out the window. In the second one, the men involved just get out and commence fisticuffs in the middle of the rain on the expressway. Who are these mad people? Chicago looks sprawling and gloomy too, and even accounting for rain the traffic is appalling. It takes two hours to get in and another two to get out.

Rivalling Port Authority for worst/ugliest/most inefficient/ most effluent bus terminal in a city so far, Chicago is another shit fight. I'm slowly deteriorating too. Stinky, with grey flaky skin, oily hair and dirty clothes. It occurs to me that perhaps most Greyhound passengers are probably very normal, but without the benefit of some real food and some sanitation, humans just get like this. Tired, ugly, hungry, and mean. I'm in the line to leave Chicago. I had wanted to see the Windy City. Well, sort of. It's probably unfair, but all of its tourist drawcards sound like 'New York has one, so do we!' – theatre, galleries, restaurants, a baseball park. Yawn. Everyone says it's a great place to live, but the weather sounds appalling. It's much worse than New York City in winter.

I've seen the winter weather reports in America, and Chicago is always gruesome, grey and biting, with schools closed due to snow. Foul weather causes so many airport disruptions that everyone tries to avoid connecting flights via O'Hare. No, I could never live in a town with weather like that. I know I should go and have a look, but what I've seen so far makes me set on my course of action. Off to Minneapolis and then to party in Denver by the weekend.

My field of vision is suddenly obscured by pink satin. I look up into an old face; black skin dry and freckled. 'Me,' she says, 'I'm done with Jersey. Gonna start a new life, a new life in Chicago. Get my shit together.' This is another common refrain on the bus, second to 'I got rights' in the Greatest Greyhound Hits and Memories. Up there with 'it was like that when I got here' and 'move your fuckin' stuff'. I'm wondering how to respond to this unsolicited epiphany when she points a tiny finger at the Coke machine. I get out another dollar bill and she's off like a flash, bashing at the plastic buttons and scrabbling her arm around inside the dark plastic mouth.

Loaded onto a new bus, I go through the now familiar motions of stashing my grubby gear, arranging my pillow, and establishing my-half-of-the-seat rights. The girl beside me is a sweet blonde from Wisconsin, crying into her mobile phone and wishing six ways to Zanzibar that she'd never signed her military contract straight out of school. I am reminded again of my

Mississippi schoolmates strolling all over campus in their sharp uniforms, arms slung around each others' shoulders, impromptu press-up sessions greeted with shouts and hoots and smiles in the sun. Most of those kids were more interested in paying for college than gettin'. their war on. I offer a barley sugar to the choked up blonde, but she just shakes her head and closes her eyes.

I wake up after a few hours of tormented sleep to find new people on and old ones off. Blink, blink. A woman sits opposite me in a black micro-dress and clear stilettos. She has perfect high breasts – largely visible through the fabric-free sides of her lycra costume – which are patterned with delicate stretchmarks like the cracks in an old painting. She must be six feet tall, with legs that run forever. We shamelessly gawp at her for the rest of the trip, and she's certainly dressed for our attention. She has an impenetrable Mona-Lisa smile and moves very little. Who wears that kind of get-up? Okay, so she's a workin' girl, but she's certainly not working on the bus, so what about a bag? Sneakers? A jumper for the chill? Staring at her beautiful face, I doze off, these lapses of consciousness contributing to the twilight-zone effect of Greyhound travel.

I open my eyes as a woman gets on with what must be a rare and very unfortunate pigmentation problem. She is black except for two white circles around her eyes, one on the tip of her nose, and another long circle around her mouth. Her poor arms are two-toned as well; from elbows to wrists they are completely white. From a distance she looks like she has purposely applied clown make-up. I drift off again, promising to cease all the bitching I do about my own small patches of eczema.

The next time I wake, a little boy is running up and down the aisle crying out, 'I died! Me! Five years ago! I died! Me! Five years ago, yes, five years ago! ME! I died. DIED!' His mother beckons and he sits down. We all look at her, alarmed. She just smiles and they both close their eyes. It's getting very David Lynch in here. I understand now that cabin fever is a real disease and highly contagious. I've run out of water and I'm very thirsty. Thirst is a real curse on the bus. The air con dries you out like a cornflake, but using the toilets is to be avoided at all costs.

Finding a balance between dehydration and a trip to sensory hell is a game we all play. The walls get closer every minute.

So.

Bored.

Kids play games with bus detritus, adding to it with their singsong nonsense.

'I found a dir-ty so-ock!'

'I found a apple! A piece of apple!'

'A hair, a little haii-iir! A curly haii-iir!'

'A chee-ese, I found a cheese!'

'I found a . . . eew, Mommy, wha's this?'

'*Baby doan touch dat*!'

At 6 o'clock we hit Milwaukee. We sit up and start looking at everything – all the regular crap around a Greyhound station – with great excitement and absorption. I begin to understand what those old biddies in Maine were up to. There's nothing much to look at on the big interstates in the USA. Way out in the middle of Nowhere, Milwaukee, we pass an enormous, white, barn-styled building topped by a giant waving cut-out of Santa Claus advertising the Olde Christmas Megastore.

What is it with Americans and Christmas? They have year-round Christmas shops in this country, huge Christmas parades, and even a Christmas theme park. Holidays in general are big news. Halloween and St Valentine's Day are among the occasions when schoolchildren must buy cards and lollies for all the kids in their class. You can buy these cards (actually cardlets, they are very small) in long perforated strips, and they even include a master-card for the teacher. This type of thing is only a fraction of the evidence indicating there is a distinct and organised commitment to fun in America. A feeling that calendar holidays are rights to be exercised and that the weekend is a platform for recreational success. I'm such a sucker for the hype and the excitement of it all. Maybe I'll grow out of it, but life's short. If you want to party properly, be advised to find some Yanks to help you out. They see their good times as a high point of cultural pride.

At seven o'clock, the fuzzy, coral-coloured sun creeps very low over green grass, red barns and black and white cows. It's strange to thunder across such a peaceful landscape in this smelly silver bullet, which has become like a mobile time capsule from the rest of the trip. My comrades don't match the outside world. None of us do. We look out the windows like tropical fish in a tank; secure in this false world created for our exotic needs. Just like fish, if we tumbled outside now we would stand little chance of survival. Most of us have no provisions, no shelter and no idea. We're like a biosphere project in here. We have our own temperature and our own smells, our own time and reality. The outside world can never be touched, felt, smelled or interacted with. We view it like the world's slowest reality TV program, things occasionally piquing our interest and then slipping away.

Opposite me, a guy who looks like the real Slim Shady is talking a mile a minute to our favourite whoo-or, and behind them, fast asleep, is the giant black woman sans Korean. Maybe she ate him. She is taking up the full two seats now. She wears a red tartan top and pants, with a blue hospital scrub thing on her head. Her hands are folded peacefully on her girth about a mile from her lap and she has long red talons, which are delicately painted and inlaid. I see that even these fingers are hugely, immensely fat. She has long ago lost anything which can be referred to as a wrist, and her watch looks cruel as it squashes flesh out either side, like string drawn tight on fresh salami. With my feet tucked underneath me, head pushed into my seat, I watch her like a movie, entranced by the bulging fingers in particular. I picture some kind of internal storage process going on, populated by invisible characters not unlike beleaguered Greyhound employees.

'Ah, Jose, we got no more room back here, we overloaded, man.'

'Sheet. Gimme minute. [Thinking] Okay, okay. Start loading the fingers.'

'The *feengers?*'

'You heard me! It's that or nothin', man, all we got left is eye-lids. Ai, *mis huevos*, if they don't stop sending us this stuff soon . . .'

Coming into Madison, Wisconsin, we drive up to a bridge and over a huge flat lake with lots of bright canoes and small fishing boats. It's beautiful, but after hours and hours of driving it seems like we are still next to nothing and nowhere. My prize stretches on forever.

Chapter 10

Cereal Adventure Land™

At 2 am in Minneapolis I find myself on a gracious, tree-lined suburban street, breaking the silence with hesitant knocking on a huge front door. Nothing. I look behind me. The taxi driver, a sweet-faced Nigerian, is still waiting to make sure I'm all right. I'm standing outside a large white house which looks like it belongs to the cast of *It's A Wonderful Life*, peeking into a coat room lit up with delicate fairy lights like a private Christmas. Just beyond it I can see a lovely living room with a wide wooden staircase covered with Eastern rugs. This is *so* wrong. I've checked the address several times before approaching, and it seems to fit, but there's no way this is a hostel.

I knock and knock. Then I remember the Japanese exchange student shot to death by a jumpy American homeowner, and I pause mid-knock to check the address again. Oh for pity's sake, what's going on? Where am I? Suddenly, a cheerful young Liverpudlian happens along the deserted street. In his thick brogue, he confirms this is indeed a hostel, and lets me in with him. Overtired, sweaty and totally strung out, I tell him I left a message from the road, trying to book a bed. He just shrugs and tells me that the owner is very relaxed and probably hasn't checked the answering machine in days. Sorry, he tells me, there's no bed, but I'm welcome to hang out. Do I want a snack?

DO I WANT A FUCKING SNACK? Freaked out and defensive after no sleep and two and a half days of Greyhound, I can't believe I've come all this way to find no shelter. A few days living with ne'er-do-wells on the Greyhound seems to have destroyed my trust and goodwill; I feel suddenly poisonous toward people and have begun gnawing on my own elbow.

The Liverpudlian, sensing a breakdown, is quick to come to my rescue. It's now 2.30 in the morning, but he enlists the aid of three other wakeful guests and they ramble around the big house working out what to do with me. After nixing several of the cat-furred couches I attempt to lay claim to, they tell me to have a shower and they'll find something. 'Go on,' he says, 'goooh and have a long, hot wash an' you'll feel brilliant.'

After showering like a goddess in the antique bathroom, it's nearly 3 o'clock when I tiptoe back downstairs. The house is still gently lit and filled with quiet, attractive and super-friendly people making snacks, using the net, reading books and doing other solitary things. They all wave and smile at me, silently offering herbal tea and a cozy collection of blankets. Tears form and my lip quivers. I really am in shock from days of Greyhound. I feel like I need to detox my soul. The bed-scouts tell me a cot has been discovered in the basement, but there are six boys in there, they say, wringing their hands, and that's never been done before . . . I just growl and drag the tomato-pack in with my teeth, before falling asleep on the narrow little camp bed like it's a puffy cloud.

In the morning, I discover it's a good day to be alive in Minneapolis. Making use of the clean and efficient public transport, my city bus window looks out onto wide streets, green trees and nature strips kept neat and filled with flowers. I find it odd that so orderly a people elected the six-foot-four WWF wrestler Jesse Ventura as their political representative, which was the only thing I really knew about the state of Minnesota before now. Through a perusal of the bus timetable, I add to this short list of known facts that Minneapolis is extraordinarily close to the city of St Paul, explaining why they are called the Twin Cities.

The buildings are a nice mix between carefully restored and spanking-modern, without too much fugly in between. In my limited experience of a few streets and a few hours, I've already come to deduce that people here are extremely friendly, patient and courteous. We are about halfway through this bus trip when a young woman runs up the front to the driver and says, 'Well, I forgot to pay yew!' They share a deep and hearty laugh, as if she's just confessed to putting all her clothes on backwards, and she pays. There are at least seven thank yous from both parties. I count them.

Nothing can touch my good mood this morning. To begin with, I have breakfasted at McDonald's, where the American version includes one of my favourite snacks, the egg and bacon biscuit. This, followed by hotcakes with whipped butter and maple syrup, makes it very hard to be at odds with the world. But the real reason for the spring in my step, the wiggle in my wobble, is that I'm on my way to the Mall of America. This shopping centre is so big it actually appears on my map of the USA, as if it's a town, or a canyon or a marvellous geyser of hot sulfuric water. In fact, the Mall of America attracts more tourists each year than Disney World, the Grand Canyon and Graceland *combined*. This is staggering information. It is the largest enclosed shopping and entertainment complex in America, and while I've heard that there's something like it in Canada with an artificial beach, I doubt there's too much global competition.

According to the hostel handout, the Mall of America has over 500 stores, a full-sized theme park and even a wedding chapel inside its 4.2 million square feet of retail therapy. It has a million-gallon aquarium whose promotional material promises 'two touch pools which allow you to pet sharks, stingrays, crabs and other critters'. I'm so excited I can barely sit still, flapping my happy foot on the ground like a kangaroo rat.

Inside the Mall of America, I head straight for the huge adventure park called Snoopy World. I never was too excited over the *Peanuts* comic strip anyway, but after a few minutes I'm sad to add theme parks to the growing list of 'things that aren't much fun by yourself'. I'm struck by how white everyone is after the Greyhound mission. Not just white, but blonde, with big blue eyes and rosy cheeks. All the Scandinavian last names (you can't say 'surnames' in America, it's up there with 'fortnight' as terms least likely to be understood) give hints as to the rootstock of these people, as if I needed any after a quick look at them. The phonebook here reads like the Helsinki *White Pages*, and everywhere around me walk people called Sven Larson or Lars Svenson. It's really quite startling. The crowds of milling teens look like a Norwegian high-school assembly, and I get the feeling that if I shouted 'Olaf!' at least 20 people would turn around.

I spend a comfortable hour in Legoland, sitting at tiny tables constructing new worlds from plastic bricks, and then I happen upon a store which gleefully attempts to sell my eighties childhood back to me. Rainbow Brite, Jem, Care Bears, Transformers, and He-Man – the gang's all here with T-shirts and accessories. With this many shops, specialty stores can really afford to specialise.

Up in the sky on the fourth or fourteenth floor – who could tell – I stumble upon another amusement park. Now, Snoopy World wasn't that flash, but scraping rock bottom in wacky theme-park concepts has got to be the General Mills 'Cereal Adventure Land™', tag line – no kidding – 'Where your favorite cereals come to life!'. What freaky kid is going to buy that as a good-time scenario? The thought of crunching down on friendly Cornflakes or being confronted by a life-sized Rice Bubble is really quite disturbing. Connected to the park is the Cereal Adventure Café™ where you can mix your own cereal. Gee Willikers! Will the fun never stop?

A little wooden sign posted in oversized stage-prop grass declares that 'All 300 million pounds of oat flour used by General Mills™ is milled right here in the Twin Cities!' Wahoo! Mum, let's go! Quick! Into Cereal Adventure Land™! '46 per cent of land in America is used for farming!' announces another fun-park sign. I feel like I've stumbled into an episode of the Simpsons. I'm mildly disgusted to discover that most of the cereals displayed here are really just confectionery dressed up as breakfast to placate parents. There are Reeses Puffs™, after the chocolate-peanut-butter candy; French Toast Crunch™; Boo Berry™, featuring tiny ghost-shaped marshmallows; Cookie Crisp™, mini cookies in milk for breakfast; Trix™, coloured balls of junk; and Lucky Charms™, with leprechaun-themed candy chunks and marshmallows.

There's cinnamon too. Oh, lots and *lots* of cinnamon, enough to empty the Spice Isles and your nan's famous teacake. There's Cinnamon Toast Crunch, Cinnamon Grahams, Apple Cinnamon Cheerios, Apple Cinnamon Oatmeal Crisp. This obsession is not contained to your average cereal adventures either. The American people have a real love affair with cinnamon. There is a giant chain here called Cinnabon, which sells hot cinnamon buns in airports, shopping centres and public places all around the country. The smell of warm cinnamon turns ordinary Americans into mindless lemmings like a trigger, and I actually suspect the CIA might be involved somewhere.

Within my first few days in this country, I unwittingly sampled cinnamon gum, cinnamon lollies, cinnamon Tic Tacs, cinnamon toothpaste and burning cinnamon drops called Red Hots, favoured as Valentine's offerings. Even homes and hotels have cinnamon-fragranced everything, including soap, shampoo, household cleaner and garbage bin liners impregnated with 'Cinna-scent'. I don't even really like cinnamon, so imagine if one actively sought out cinnamon products in this nation. It's overwhelming. However, over the last few days of Greyhound travel I've noticed a distinct trend towards fragrancing public toilets with an artificial cinnamon smell, and I think this stomach-churning association might just spell the end of the cinna-craze.

All the dubious cereals on offer Cereal Adventure Land™ claim to be 'part of this nutritious breakfast™', a nutritious breakfast being, as featured, two bits of toast, a piece of fruit, milk and juice. So, I wonder, the Trix™ features as precisely what part of this nutritious breakfast? The useless crap part? Anyway, for most American kids, it is the only part, and that much is evident from the heaviness of most American families. With all my packs on I'm still very much lighter than most of these giant people, but it still feels terrible. For me the extra weight is unwieldy, embarrassing and annoying, and I'm so relieved to get rid of it at each stop. But even with this constant lesson, I've been taking full advantage of my metabolism and find myself biggie-double triple-cheese-chocolate-fudge-saucing everything I come across. It just tastes so damn good.

All over the Mall of America there are giant roly-poly kids, and otherwise healthy-looking people struggling with walking canes and motorised scooters to heft their weight around. Over the past six months I've become used to these scooters in super-markets and shopping malls, where they are provided as a matter of course. I know that Australians are getting heavier every year, but I would hope we are still a long way off from needing to drive our bulk down the chocolate-bikkie aisle. Much has been made of American chub-chub, and, from what I've seen, not without reason. I still can't figure out whether it's just that there are so many more people of all shapes and sizes in America that the volume of the terminally obese is greater, or if the problem is as epic as it appears to be on the street. After all, I have seen far more beautiful people in this country too; whole cities overrun with starlet material like no other place in the world. Perhaps it is just the concentration of human beings. A family of four wobbles past me into Cereal Adventure Land™, sweating with the exertion of placing one foot in front of the other. They are all eating large waffle-cone sundaes, dripping with syrup. Hmm, nah.

When the crowd begins to swell outside Cereal Adventure Land™, I feel I must be missing something. I go over to take some pamphlets. One includes an article boasting, 'Visitors can also pose for their own souvenir Wheeties™ box and create their own cereal brand – talk about bonding with your breakfast!' Is there really a market for breakfast bonding? Two Asian tourists walk in looking confused, asking halting questions of the sporty, monogrammed attendant. 'What is this place?' they ask with much gesturing and shrugging of shoulders, palms outstretched feeding invisible birds.

'Ma'am,' the attendant says, 'it's a cereal-themed amusement arcade with educational videos!'

'Ah,' the tourists say, and then politely ask each other in Japanese, 'What the fuck?' They look to me. I make a face to tell them, yeah, I don't get it either.

'What to do here?' they ask, still bewildered. 'Well . . .' the attendant says, 'have fun! And learn about cereal!' Silence, then more polite chatter.

'Ci-we-ah?' one asks, just to be really sure now. 'Yeah!' the attendant motions eating from a bowl. 'Cereal! Sure!'

There is much raising of eyebrows as this strangeness is confirmed, before they say, 'Oooh, no sank you,' and leave. At least I'm not alone.

Confirming my earlier observations on the local bus, everyone in the Mall of America is very friendly, or, as they say in America, 'real friendly'. I'm collecting compliments left and right, and everyone I speak to exclaims at my accent and asks where I'm from. This has hardly happened at all on my trip so far. These people make a real point of welcoming me to Minnesota, which they pronounce 'Minesooooota' in accents that sound like a casting call for *Fargo*, and tell me that yah, it's real nice to live here, you betcha. When I tell a girl how noticeable the friendliness is, she actually blushes and calls over two more staff to tell them how this Australian girl thinks Minnesota is the just the gosh-darn friendliest place in America that she's been so far. They are all so happy and giggly at this. These are girls of my own cynical and self-absorbed age group, too. There must be something in the cereal.

I pass a free-standing stall selling eucalyptus oil as the 'Down Under Wonder', with koalas and kangaroos adorning every available surface. Eucalyptus oil is really great stuff and I wander over. An American woman is doing the hard sell on the oil for arthritis and allergies. 'Just go on and spray it on his pillow-case,' she tells some curious customers, but the family look unconvinced. 'It's really great for getting sticky labels off stuff,' I pipe up from behind. 'Gets rid of adhesive in seconds. No mess. Nice smell.' The woman turns to her hubby. 'Well, we do have those marks from Billy's stickers on the fridge.' They take two bottles and I beam with ambassadorial pride.

The mall is filled with a hordes of young people in denim pants big enough that you could fashion a tent pole from a broomstick, run it from crotch to cuff, crawl inside with three of your closest friends and unzip the fly to stage a sleepout. These aren't your regular, low-riding, baggy, rap-star jeans. These are mammoth triangles of cloth as big as boat sails. Their owners shush past in little groups of fabric and punky hair, struggling under the weight of their sizable piercings. There is an adorable sameness to their getups, rigidly adhered to but still bizarre, like geisha in their kimonos. They all wear the same kind of death-to-rich-fat-white-capitalist T-shirts, which can be purchased at a chain store here called Hot Topic.

The fact that they are all, in fact, rich fat white capitalists is something they are desperately trying to ignore, and good for them too, I think. Their counter-culture hearts are in the right place even if their accessories are costing them a fortune, and their cigarettes are only making the bastard capitalists at Philip Morris richer every minute.

I don't make it back to the hostel until 6 pm, but it's still light, and on the veranda of the house people gather to hang out, watching the sun set over the large park across the street. Some of them are setting off for a late afternoon swim in the lake, and I learn that Minnesota is called the Land of the Lakes. There are apparently over ten thousand of them in the state, with many of these waterways winding in and out of the city. It's a nice atmosphere and a great place to stay. Everyone is exceptionally generous, including the young owner, who can be found all over the house with his cute Russian girlfriend hanging off him like a noodle. Like a pair of housecats, they turn up everywhere, just cuddling and smiling, curled around each other tightly and lying around.

I'm still in the guys' room, but no one seems fussed. In the bed next to mine lies a young Japanese man massaging blistered hands. His name is 'Tommo', Tomoaki Ishii, and he tells me that he too is off to see America. In fact, he set off from New York City on his bicycle in the middle of May. *Bicycle?* Are you crazy? 'I know!' he says, laughing, 'maybe I sink I Samurai, somesing like dat!' With his cool topknot and beard Tommo actually looks very much like a Samurai. 'What happens if it rains?' I ask him, thinking back to yesterday's downpour. 'Ah, is good. Rains is better than suns for riding in summer.'

I'm struggling to understand what would possess someone to ride a pushbike across America, but Tommo can only shrug in response to my questioning. 'It's my dream,' he says simply. At night he just hops off his bike, walks it off the road, climbs into his sleeping bag and goes to sleep. 'Many people sink of me as beggar! One time one man saw me outside gas station eating beef jerky. I have no shave. He talk to me for a while, ask few question. Then, he give me five dollar!' Tommo roars with laughter. 'He say, next time eat McDonald! But I like jerky!'

In Pennsylvania, Tommo was stopped by police in the Appalachian Mountains. 'They say, "Where are you from?" I said, "Why, I am from Japan," and he say "Nahhh" and then I said "Yes! Of course! Look at me! I am Japanese person!" But they sink I lying!' He rolls back on his bed with the giggles. 'They sink I terrorist! ON BICYCLE! So long to get out of that one,' he says, shaking his head, 'so when I try one time to ride on interstate for short cut and police stop me, very angry, I just pretend I speak no English. Then it's too difficult for them. They don't even ask for passport!'

After days of riding these roads on the bus, I am boggled anyone would attempt to cycle them. It seems terribly dangerous, for one thing, and Tommo doesn't even have a helmet. B, a Thai student whose real name is very long and much less user-friendly, pretends to be unimpressed. 'Ah, he just a cheapskate,' he says, grinning. 'Pedal power is free. Buy a ticket, man, pay for some gas!' This banter has obviously been going on for some days now, because Tommo has finally bought a tent at the Mall of America after pedalling there and back today. He says he bought his new 'hotel room' just to stop B calling him cheap. Tommo produces some riding gloves, too, which I can tell he is very excited about.

'Did it hurt your hands?' I ask, 'before the gloves?' Tommo nods. 'Oh yes,' he says, smiling. 'Very, very much.'

Attached to Tommo's bike is a homemade white flag, which reads 'PEACE from the W.T.C.'. He set off from the block of rubble where the World Trade Center once stood to bring this timeless message from one side of the country to the other. 'I don't know if people will notice,' he says, 'but I have many hopes.' The three of us sit on his creaking bed going through the photos of his journey so far. They are filled with Tommo, his bike and his flag, beside different landmarks across the US, his beard just that little bit longer in each spot. He is often surrounded by smiling people, invariably giving the thumbs up and pointing to his flag. 'So many new friends!' he says, shaking his head and smiling. 'I always am ask people to come too, but so far,' he sighs, 'no taker.'

The next morning, finding myself at a bit of a loose end, I fish out the *Lonely Planet* and flip it open like a Magic 8-ball. Soon afterwards I am seated on a local bus to St Paul, a woman with purpose.

After fifteen minutes of motoring along in the sun, it occurs to me I don't know how long the trip should take or where to jump off. 'Excuse me,' I ask the driver, 'is this bus going to Kellogg?'

'O, Kellogg,' he booms. 'Why do you need to go there?'

I'm slightly embarrassed. 'Uh, the uh, Science Museum.' The bus just erupts – businessmen, bag-ladies and young trendies alike. 'O, the Science Museum!' they exclaim. 'O, you'll love the Science Museum.' There are lots of encouraging nods and noises of approval regarding my choice of destination. The driver nods too. 'Just stay on the bus, hon, and I'll drop you as close as I can,' he says, joining in the general commotion regarding the jolly time that surely awaits me at the Minn-es-O-tah Science Museum.

'They have those interactive things, you know, where you can touch stuff!' cries an old man. 'In the cafeteria,' offers a teenage girl with a black trenchcoat and pink hair, 'you can see right over the river! And the food, mmm, it sure is pretty good too.' The young guy sitting next to me actually takes off his hat and sunnies to formally introduce himself and shake my hand. As we cross over into St Paul, I admit to the questioning crowd that it's my first time in this particular Twin City, and the young man says, 'Really? Your first time? Welcome! You know, I think I speak for everyone when I say that Australia is very highly regarded in St Paul.' There are nods and smiles all round.

I'm looking for hidden cameras and catching flies in my mouth. I feel terrible, a smirking cynic, heading off all sly-chuckles to see the Museum of Questionable Medical Devices, once free and located downtown in Minneapolis but now recently ensconced in the new Science Museum. I have no desire to see interactive kiddie toys, wave machines, lava lamps or whatever, and no interest at all in St Paul. I'm actually annoyed to have to shell out for the museum, because I rarely visit a city's museums until I have exhausted all other options. I never willingly consort with hordes of other tourists, and museums are consistently filled with high-school tour groups flirting and squashing and sweating together like weasels in heat, creating kilometre-long lines to pay $15 for a watery fizzy drink with old fries. I am always forced to buy inadequate snacks when hunger overcomes me after getting very lost (which I inevitably do) and turning up on some mezzanine level that serves as the janitorial station. After some hours I'm usually discovered, pale and panicked, pulling at doors that won't open, by some bewildered official asking, 'Wow! Did you, like, rig the service elevator or something?'

So I don't often find my way to museums in foreign cities out of choice. I'm only heading to this one for the promise of a few cheap laughs and a hint of gore from the medical devices. After all, what could a museum teach me about the city that couldn't be better learnt on its streets? Right? So as the sweet Min-nesoootans give me painstaking instructions on how to see their favourite exhibit (the pickled albino vole being top of the list for many), there is no grateful excitement swelling in my breast. I am smiling a plastic smile, thinking, 'Fuck, if they're this excited about it I'm going to have to open my "pocket book" reel wide for the entrance fee.'

The driver drops me off last, and points out the huge new museum, rising clean, shining and immensely proud of itself by the banks of the river. Enormous Snoopy figurines are everywhere. There's giant Marcy, and Snoopy and Woodstock, oh my, as well as a huge Lucy statue at the entrance to the museum with a sign above her that says, 'The doctor is in the house.' I hope so. I might need one. A little girl posing with Lucy, whom she declares to be her 'total hero', informs me that, like, *duh*, Charles M. Schulz was from St Paul. Y'know, the Snoopy guy. And boy does St Paul love its favourite son. They've taken the Snoopy thing and run with it, right down to that Peanuts amusement park inside the Mall of America yesterday, which now seems a little less lame.

Inside the museum I realise the wallet will have to be reached for. With many days and nights left riding the Dawg from sea to shining sea, I'm already beginning to stress the greenback – this country ain't cheap to hoof around in. In the ticket line I see the hordes of kids are everywhere as expected, but they are uniformly polite and attractive little bobbins, most of them wearing T-shirts proclaiming them to be part of some summer 'Camp Geewillikers' daycare program or other. As for the museum, were the kind folk on my bus right? As they say in Minnesota, o yah, you betcha! Two hours later I find myself pushing kids out of the way for my third turn in the Cell Lab and trading Barbie gossip with my new friend Cindy as we learn to weave using organic yarn, when I suddenly remember what I came here for. O *yah*, the medical devices. It seems that my inner cynic has briefly deserted me for the wonders of this first-rate fun park. The Minnesota Museum of Science is everything Cereal Adventure Land™ failed to be. It also impresses me with its remarkable cultural sensitivity, and I feel guilty at my own surprise; I had expected much less from America's white-bread heartland, having always imagined that things out here would be backward somehow – conservative and insular. Sometimes it feels really great to be wrong.

Around the corner, a group of little blonde kids from America's wheat belt line up patiently to learn how to say Çatalhöyük ('Chat-ahl-who-yook'), and identify with a life-sized cut out of Sadettin Dural, one of the Turkish guards who works at Çatalhöyük, an archeological site in Turkey. Inside the exhibit, pictures of young Muslim women in headscarves invite them to 'İşimi dene!' (try my job!) from a poster beside their very own sorting tray, where, like the young villagers, they can sort through excavation dirt with tweezers and a lot of patience. Here, on the edge of the Mississippi River, in pasteurised, homogenised Snoopy-town, these kids are lapping it up, asking insightful questions of understanding adults, and identifying with Turkish people, language and even archeology.

At the 'Tree Cookie' exhibit, a massive slice of Douglas fir tree is on display, with a plaque explaining how its 552 concentric circles had once been used to tell the story of America's history over the course of the years the circles represent. A picture of the slice from when it was first exhibited in 1932 shows the original tags attached to certain lines used to identify events occurring during the tree's long life. Under the heading 'Whose History Gets Told in America?' the museum discusses how these labels were removed in 1992 when an exhibit was produced that took a critical view of the 'discovery' of America by Columbus. Walking by on their way to meetings for the exhibit, a community advisory board including several Native Americans pointed out the exclusively eurocentric view the labels on the tree took, including Columbus' discovery in 1492, the landing of the Pilgrim Fathers in 1620 and the Battle of Waterloo in 1815. The museum staff agreed and removed the labels from the now bare chunk of polished wood, which has instead become a permanent exhibit to the question 'Whose History?'.

The museum poses questions about its own viability all over the place, with big signs constantly asking, 'Whose is it?', 'Should it be here?' and 'What do you think?'.

It goes even further, with revolutionary concepts printed in huge type intended for very young readers. In describing the old stuffed lion diorama, it asks, 'What's wrong with this picture?' and a small girl reads the rest out loud in a breathy little voice. 'Completed in 1929, the diorama depicts an adult male and female together with a cub. In the wild, however, females and cubs tend to stay together, while males associate with other males. The display of this "happy family" says as much about contemporary American social values as about lion behavior.' Wow! Put that in your lunchbox!

A little Asian boy runs into my leg. 'Hey!' he tells me, too excited to be embarrassed, 'you should go in there, it's a mummy!' In Minnesooota? O yah, you betcha. Served up by the banks of the mighty Huck Finn raft-way lies a veteran of civilisation, an ancient Egyptian some 3500 years old, beautifully preserved down to his still pearly teeth and the waxy nails on his slender fingers. The story that accompanies his relocation to Minnesota is fairly amusing.

In 1925, a Mr and Mrs Simon Crosby of St Paul bought the mummy while they were vacationing in Cairo (a plaque notes Cairo, *Egypt*, just so we don't mistake it for Cairo, Illinois, or Cairo, Georgia where Aunt Petunia might be from, and call her pestering for mummified remains). The Crosbys thought it'd be neat to have a mummy in Minnesota, and donated it to the old St Paul institute for display. The mummy didn't come with a case, though, just a few dark shreds of its burial shroud. It must have lacked drama, because the exhibit tells us that in 1925, Marion Rasnussen, the institute's director, travelled to several other American museums to see if a case could be purchased for the mummy to rest in. No luck. Well, that didn't stop these irrepressible Minnesotans, who decided to have local artists build and paint a mummy case right here.

'We don't know how they came up with the design,' the plaque reads, somewhat apologetically. I have a good long look at the case, with its startled eyes, Marilyn-Monroe full pink lips, and flapping folk-art birds. The lumpy scarab beetle looks like a fat house spider. I look closer. I swear I can see Snoopy in there too.

There is a suggestion box here asking, 'What do you think?' next to several scathing letters reprinted for the exhibit, which have been sent to the museum citing racism and disrespect for the dead. Good call, member 658, Minnesota Museum Science Board, whose tactful answer to these letters invites suggestions on this yet-to-be-resolved issue. The sign reads, 'Many of us would object to displaying the remains of a relative or member of our community. Is it different if the remains are those of an unknown person long dead from another culture?'

Here's what the youngsters – primarily youngsters, judging from the tenuous grip on the HB pencil obvious in most replies – of St Paul had to say.

Kristin says, 'Well, it would be different (bad) if you did not have him privately covered. We are still respecting him, but this way we can learn from him. We know Egyptians were smart and knowledge consuming, so I think he'd want it.'

From Freddie: 'I think it's wonderful. Maybe some day I can be put in a museum by aliens so they can learn from me too.' Someone else has answered, 'I'm stunned and appreciative that you would ask, but find I can't answer this dilemma.' I, too, am stunned and appreciative. I get the feeling that I am learning something about the folk of the Twin Cities in here after all.

When I finally reach the exhibit that was once the mighty Museum of Questionable Medical Devices, I'm disappointed to discover it only contains a fraction of the tons of original curios once housed in the downtown Minneapolis space. An attendant commiserates, telling me, 'Yah, they're like, in the basement or something. O yah, it's really sad.'

Among the curiosities still displayed is the electric Battle Creek Vibratory Chair created by Dr John Harvey Kellogg, breakfast cereal legend and total crackpot. Kellogg claimed his chair cured all manner of ills including headaches (which it would seem to induce) and constipation, presumably by literally shaking the crap out of you.

Detroit king of quackery Albert Adams championed a radio wave treatment offered by his Electro-Metabograph Machine, which he claimed could cure about 300 illnesses, including nymphomania, thirst, sunburn, sweat, sweat without relief, jaundice and even jealousy, all by using radio frequencies. The real catch was that the spanking new machine didn't even have a radio inside. The only things that worked were the lights, and apparently some impressive ping-like noisemaker.

Taking a break, I enjoy a delicious lunch of grilled chicken Caesar salad overlooking the Mississippi River, with a fresh M&M cookie and strong coffee to polish it off. I am inordinately pleased with myself for coming here. A quick trip to the loo presents even more excitement. A door-sized cartoon diagram called 'Portable Toilet Adventures', tells me all about what happens to the waste from Twin City porta-loos. Gracious! I just can't leave! Will the fun never end? Minnesooota, what a great place to be a kid. Poo, cereal – everything's an adventure!

Six hours later I'm all learned out. As I leave the museum I can't resist going up to tell the staff how much I liked the place. 'O yah, you betcha!' they beam. 'It's a great place!' We all stand around and smile for a bit. So this is how it happens, I think, this 'Minnesota Nice' I've been experiencing. Everything here is lovely and unobjectionable, and pretty soon it just creeps up on you despite yourself.

On my way out I run into B in the foyer. 'Hey!' I say, 'I didn't know you were coming here!' He just shrugs like it's hardly surprising, and tells me he's been here heaps of times. '*Hello,*' he says, 'everyone has.' We walk to the bus stop together, trading highlights of our visit, and back in Minneapolis we're still talking about it as we walk towards the downtown piazza, Nicollet Mall. We pass a huge army surplus store, which is closed, but in the window, amongst many odds and ends, is a hideous electrocution chair, complete with a straining mannequin, shirtless and seizing next to a sign that boasts 'includes sound, smoke, tape player and strobe!'. It can be ours for just $3000. There's lots of war memorabilia and general evil gadgetry on display. B makes a face and says, 'I hope to never meet the Americans who like these junks.' I'm with him. In the window, an advertisement for an upcoming gun show promises 'Concealed weapons permit classes all weekend long!' as well as the latest military and 'specialty' items. Shudder. I hate being reminded of the things I find despicable about this beautiful country I've won. The death penalty and firearms head a short but very ugly list.

B and I trek to the giant Target building on Nicollet Mall. The store itself is immaculate and exceptionally well staffed, which is probably due to the corporate head offices being located in Minneapolis. This is Target town. We each go in with clear missions – cheap food items and laundry products. We emerge over an hour later, overwhelmed by the sheer volume of attractive and attractively-priced goods. B has done well: fast-drying towel, Clorox, milk, chips, Vanilla Coke (by Jove that's some good thinking from the Coca-Cola people) and new shoelaces. We inspect my purchases gravely. Streak-free sunless tanning foam by Neutrogena, hair serum that promises to distribute gold shimmer through my hair along with a pleasing coconut fragrance, Mossimo volumising and conditioning gel, and four shades of eyeshadow (particularly useful seeing as

I never apply any). 'Oooh,' B says. 'Mmm,' I answer. We walk on in silence, understanding that I've just fallen off the hostel-travel wagon in a big way, clearly choosing beauty over dinner and possibly breakfast as well. Sometimes I'm such a damn girly-girl I just hate myself. Oh well. At least it will be a tanned, volumised, conditioned, pleasantly fragranced, gold-flecked kind of self-hatred.

We ride the number 18 bus back through Nicollet Mall, where, underneath the bright blue sky and shimmering office windows, Minnesotans are out in droves at the very many outdoor pub-restaurants, leaning back in their seats with faces upturned to the afternoon sun. It's always a wonderful thing to behold. Citizens out in their downtowns, using their public spaces for food and chat and just *being*, instead of trapped in offices or commuting. The dining here is far more European and al fresco than I had expected of the Midwest. In the Mall itself, down near a large fountain, a jazz band plays and Italian sausages sizzle at a concession stand while people gather on stairs to enjoy these hot, juicy treats that I could also be enjoying if not for my sudden commitment to volumised hair. Everywhere I look it seems that people are young, beautiful and revelling in it.

B tells me that the University of Minnesota is huge, with about 50,000 students, and there are over 100,000 students among the roughly half a million people living in the Twin Cities. No wonder everyone looks so youthful. No wonder there's so much beer. A large banner announces that Gay Pride week will kick off tomorrow with a huge block party at 4 pm. 'All the city is invited!' the banner reads. Man, what a town. O yah, you betcha.

There's only one problem. The thing is, Minneapolis may look sunny and beautiful, but I know she's lying harder than my streak-free sunless tan. I know this because her nickname is Minne*snow*ta. I know this because beside flower beds and shady trees, quiet lakes and sun filled piazzas, are big signs that read 'Snow Evacuation Route' (pronounced 'rot'), showing a comically tiny truck attempting to plow through what looks like twelve feet of ice. And I know this too because the temporarily discarded window fillers at our fabulously breezy hostel read 'Remove this and DIE! Don't ya know it's WINTER?' The coatroom I found so quaint when I arrived is a life-or-death necessity, as two-stage entries are essential here to keep the cold out.

It doesn't just get cold in Minnesota, it gets arctic. In winter, it's apparently de rigueur for many residents to turn their lush green yards into home skating rinks, hosing down the frost-burnt grass each day to maintain a thick, solid layer of ice. The Minneapolis Park and Recreation Board freeze over about thirty impromptu rinks for public use as well. Such distinct and totally oppositional seasons are mystifying for a Sydneysider. Yesterday morning a slim girl at the bus stop told me she hoped to bulk up a bit before winter this year, because she's had hypothermia a couple of times now, and 'O, it just really sucks.' You *betcha*.

After two pleasant days, I wake up sickly on my last morning in Minneapolis. During the night I have had an attack of vertigo for the first time in two years – a revolting condition associated to my body's propensity to motion sickness and all forms of nausea in general. Motion sickness even in the absence of motion seems especially cruel to me. All through the night the floor was stable, but in my head the little bed went up and down like popcorn in a blue movie theatre. Feeling very sorry for myself, I decide I'm to be allowed two servings of hotcakes at Macca's when I get my balance back.

Out on the street I notice again how many Muslim women wearing traditional head-coverings there are in Minneapolis – many more than I remember seeing in New York – and I realise that it's more of a multi-ethnic community than all the Andersons, Brodersons and Scandinavian-ness might imply. Instead, I have been intrigued to find a very cosmopolitan city filled with exotic food and interesting people. There's a quiet young man who speaks nothing but Arabic in the hostel. Perhaps I should take him up the street here and point him in the direction of all the small Arab markets where his compatriots can be found. Every time I come back to our room he's still there, sitting on the end of his cot, reshuffling the things in his backpack rather listlessly, or picking at his fingernails. Today he's taken to staring at the 1950s map of the USA on the wall, occasionally standing up to trace a path across a group of states with his fingers. I wonder at how much more confusing and amazing his America must be compared to mine.

After a syrupy and satisfying brekkie, I go downtown to the post office to get rid of some stuff before setting out on the bus again tonight. In line, I am again struck by how polite everyone is. No one here abbreviates their social transactions to save time. It's not 'Next!' or even 'Next please!' in the city's central post office, but, 'Whoever's next in line, I'm ready over here for ya.' This is typically answered with, 'O great, that's me. Hi!' There are about fifteen of us, too, in a queue reaching back to the door. Everyone is smiling and there's no watch-checking. These are city folk mind you, the suit-wearing kind, in the heart of the bustling CBD.

When I finally reach the front counter, I do everything wrong and out of order, until the plastic bag from Legoland that I'm trying to stuff into an envelope bursts open, revealing a bright yellow Chinatown T-shirt, a General Mills keyring, a few beat-up bags of maple candy and some pamphlets that look like junk mail. In short, it looks like I've just cleaned out the passenger side of someone else's car and am now paying big dollars to priority mail it to the other side of the country. The postman surveys my junk. 'Well, bless your heart,' he says, and he means it. I hold up the line again, as it takes nearly five minutes to cram all my crap into a bigger box. I turn around occasionally with that wild animal look of the bad pedestrian, but everyone just smiles encouragingly. It's Friday, and at the close of sale the postman leans over, laces his fingers together and says, 'Well, you just go on and have the best weekend you can make for yourself.' The only reason I know he's sincere is that this is Minnesota.

I still have time to kill before my Greyhound trip to Denver, so I set off to find a supermarket for some road provisions. I walk straight ahead from the hostel into the downtown neighbourhoods. There are huge houses here, houses that look like all the family homes from the American sitcoms of my childhood – *Family Ties*, *Who's the Boss?*, *Leave it to Beaver* (the short-lived eighties remake), *Eight is Enough* and countless telemovies. I'm starting to get that movie-set feeling again. All around me are huge lawns so soft and fine they feel like cool green fur. People wave to me and say hello, walking dogs and watering grass as I struggle on, sweating under my awkward pack with my striped sheet dragging behind me. Despite my rumpled and slightly crazed appearance, a little girl actually stops to say, 'I like the colour of your hair,' before skipping on. I look up to a street sign to confirm something I already know – this is Pleasant Avenue.

I soon come to a little collection of cafés where heavily tattooed and ornamented punks share latte-sipping space and smiles with the urban gentry. Pointed in the direction of a supermarket, I almost walk past it due to the lack of fluoro-lighting, abandoned trolleys and sterile white aesthetic. For some reason, in Western society, our food always looks like it lives at the dentist's.

The Wedge, a fresh food co-op and supermarket, is another small treat from Minneapolis. I step inside and it smells like . . . earth. Where food should come from. I stand there sniffing like a customs beagle. Rich, heavy soil, wet from new rain, hit by full sun. The cynic in me is sure they pump it in like the cookie-smell in Coles, but this is something else. Something very, very good. Like beeswax and peach. I've never really been a whole-foods-macrobiotic-fava-bean kind of a girl, and I've long ago come to terms with the fact that I'm a salivating sharp-toothed carnivore at the top of the food chain, but this supermarket is food heaven. Everything is so fresh and new that it squeals when you touch it.

I gorge on California rolls made with real crab meat rather than seafood extender (a difference I note to be not unlike that between Dutch chocolate and brown shipping wax). I sink my teeth into fresh, golden felafel, crisp as tempura on the outside, green and fragrant in the middle. Lining up to buy my non-perishable bus provisions, I realise that none of the sales assistants are wearing uniforms. They all look like completely normal human beings. It's astounding. My line is a special line too, with a sign that says, 'For the comfort of others, please do not use this line if you are wearing or buying scented products. Thank you!' My heart grows heavy when I realise that coming into Denver tomorrow, lunch on the bus will surely consist of 12 varieties of cheap deodorising sprays all deployed at once until the air is chewable.

Walking back with my tummy full of ethnic treats and my ears full of birdsong, I realise something quite startling. I could live in Minneapolis, Minnesota. I mean, really. It's a beautiful, friendly, clean, livable city populated by kind and attractive citizens. I can't shake the vaguely European feel of the place; from the Parisian capitol buildings in St Paul, to the Italian corso streetscapes downtown, the Scandinavian influences, the German and Irish brewhouses, and the many waterways and parks. And unlike much of Europe, it's spacious, welcoming and pretty cheap. It would be a great place to raise kids one day. You could ride a bicycle around in this city. You could picnic near your office. Okay, so I'm not a winter person, but who knows? Maybe bobsledding could become my thing. It is a strange feeling. *Quelle surprise*! This is the Midwest? This liberal, forward-thinking city of culture, al fresco dining and that special long baby-hair grass? Am I really ready to move to the *Midwest*? Man, I need to leave. I hurry back to the hostel and pack the last of my stuff just in case.

Chapter 11

The Boonies

The Minneapolis bus station is clean and light. A giant, three-dimensional greyhound is suspended leaping gracefully over the hemisphere of silver chairs, all as clean as the large shiny windows, which are a feature I hadn't realised has been missing from most Greyhound terminals so far. The ticket counter is surrounded by a large curved bench, presumably on which to place small children or bags while queuing, and there is a whole wall devoted to framed black and white photos of Greyhound through the ages. I check out the first Greyhound bus, built in 1914, and the 1927 Ohio to Pennsylvania Coach – the Great War- and the Great Depression-era buses. I wonder idly what era of American history my bus will feature in, and how much worse this current War on Trr might get.

In 1936, Greyhound got swanky with the super-moderne double-decker 'Nite Coach', complete with a black porter in his bell-boy cap and jacket to hold the door. In 1937 the 'General Motors Super Coach' appeared, followed by the smashing World's Fair edition bus from 1939 in New York City. These old photos are like a snapshot of the nineteen hundreds. Motor cars, rock 'n' roll, space rockets and skyscrapers – I forget how much of last century's defining wonders were born, or at least heavily fostered, in America. The United States has held sway over the global imagination for a long time now. I'd been thinking of cultural imperialism in terms of the movies, politics and soft drinks of the past 30 years, but there's much, much more to it than that. All roads seem to lead to this modern Rome at some point. I am suddenly aware, and grateful, for my brief inclusion in a unique chapter of this motorised history.

I look at the buses for a long time. There's the long, bendy 'Capacity Flexible' from 1942, an advancement in engineering no doubt benefiting from wartime ingenuity. You can get all train-spotting technical with the model numbers too, which are listed through the eras for the serious enthusiast. The GM 4506, the 4104, the MC1MC-7. My favourite is the 'Sceni-cruiser' pictured in '54 right here in downtown Minneapolis. It has a special raised roof with extra windows for sceni-cruisin'. Finally I get a load of the MC1G-41, the boring-ass 2000 model that I'm usually tortured with. All bland efficiency, pointy edges and zero romance. Give me the bump and rattle of the Sceni-cruiser any day (especially if it still comes with a porter and a shoe-shine kid).

Many people note my avid interest in the photographs, including some of the heavy-set security personnel, absurdly guarding the 50 people in here at a ratio of five to one. A black-suited Rambo approaches me. 'Ma'am, do you have a ticket?' I fish out my folded Ameripass, which he inspects like it's fake ID. 'This doesn't explain your destination, ma'am.'

'I'm going to Denver,' I tell him, 'but it's an open ticket.'

'Uh huh,' he says, looking me up and down. 'An' that's all the luggage you have? To travel around the US for –' he checks the ticket, '45 days?'

I nod, bemused. My gear seems like rather a lot of crap to me.

'Travelling alone, ma'am?'

'Yep,' I say, smiling with what I imagine to be my most winsome expression, 'no one would come with me!'

'Uh huh.' He's still staring at me, holding my ticket. 'When are you expected back, ma'am? Forty days?'

'Yeah,' I say, ''bout then.' I'm getting annoyed now. I hardly look dangerous and no one has bothered to grill me in big stations like Chicago, Boston or New York City.

'You able to support yourself on this trip, ma'am? Cash? Credit? Traveller's cheques? You got all those?' he asks. 'You're not a bum now, are you?' he says, with the hint of a smile at last.

'Yeah, no, I mean, of course. Look, I have credit, and I don't –' but he cuts me off with a hand held up in the Stop position. He passes my ticket back slowly, and leans in when I finally take possession. 'What you just told me?' he growls. 'You don't ever, ever tell anyone else that stuff for the rest of your trip, do you hear me? Do you understand? Not a security guard, not Greyhound desk people, not a driver and definitely not other passengers. Do you understand me?'

I nod, feeling suddenly cold. He's right. I just told a perfect stranger that I'm alone, with money, travelling to indeterminate destinations and that I won't be missed for about a month. Any psycho can become a security guard, I think. I've looked at the uniform and failed to see a big, muscled civilian with a gun and shifty eyes. I nod again, deeply, to show him I really do understand.

'I don't wanna scare ya,' he says, 'but you're a nice lookin' girl, and Greyhound people,' he sweeps his hand around the worn-out, scratching mass of waiting passengers, 'most of the time, they aren't your regular, decent Americans, okay? They're people lookin' for trouble or runnin' away from it, do you understand? Don't forget that. Have fun on your trip, but don't forget that, understand?'

'Okay,' I squeak, and head over to the south-west departure door, tail between my legs.

I sit down at my gate next to a girl called Katy from Texas. Apart from my own name, I endeavour to tell her nothing else. Like most people on Greyhound, she's more than happy to do all the storytelling herself anyway. Sweeter than spring honey, uglier than winter toes, Katy has a huge black hole out of her front tooth and a figure with ice-cream scoop proportions. She talks at great length about the coyotes in Missouri, before revealing that she has an Internet boyfriend who says he's from France, and she's meeting him this Saturday. With the security guard's warning still ringing in my ears, I deliver a big lecture on the need for Katy to let someone know where she's off to, but she just laughs. 'Pee-airr is French! Everyone knows they're just lil' sissies at heart, right?'

'Well, what if he's not even French?' I ask.

'Duh!' she says. 'He writes all *bon-jor* and stuff, and he has trouble spellin' in English sometimes.' I'm considering how to argue with such watertight logic when we are joined by a nice young guy called Clem, who offers us each a stick of gum. Clem is originally from California, but he says he's from nowhere now. 'I'm from the night places, I think,' he says, and it doesn't even sound pretentious, just strangely childlike. 'Yeah. From the night and nowhere.' Clem has home tattoos on all his fingers, and a few professional jobs scattered around. A group of beautiful shattered stars fall from his forearm and a full head of garlic – yes, garlic – is delicately drawn behind one ear. 'Vampires?' I inquire. 'Nope,' he says. 'Just really like garlic.'

Clem tells us that he has travelled all over the US since he ran away at fourteen. He says there's a huge network of people just like him who travel all over America, usually by hitching rides on freight trains, finding each other quickly in big cities along this well-worn route. 'There's a lot of drugs usually,' he says, 'but I'm not about the drugs, I'm about community. It's like a family when you find them. You know how they say there's safety in numbers? Yeah, and plus it's better than freezin' your lonely ass off in winter. There's more of us in every city now,' he says. 'It's like a growing force. Seriously, like a force. The economy is totally shitty and the world has all gone to hell since 9/11. People like us don't give a fuck about living by the rules now.' Clem's a nice guy. Under his black punky hair, clothes and industrial accessories, is a sensitive 17-year-old boy. He says he's terrified of being a grown-up. 'I'd rather be homeless my whole life and stay positive, stay who I am, than sell out for the so-called American Dream.' He doesn't look bitter when he says this, only earnest. Katy takes another sip of her Dr Pepper and tells Clem she thinks he's 'brave as heck.' I'm beginning to think that the guard-guy is wrong. There are lots of decent Americans on Greyhound; they just don't look the way a Fourth of July department-store catalogue would like them to.

Katy takes pictures of Clem and me and each waiting bus in turn, to show her friends that she was actually in Minneapolis. Then she disappears for a few minutes, returning to announce that she has bought one of everything from the concession machines and she is throwing us a little party. We sit in a nursery-school circle on the sparkling clean floor, surrounded by a technicolour picnic of Wildberry Skittles, Homestyle Grandma's Vanilla Mini-Cookies, Austin Lemon-Ohs!, Ritz-bits, Cheese Sandwich Snax, Oreos and Andy Capp's Oven-baked Hot Fries, which are in fact cold, small and meanly spicy.

When our bus turns up the security check is long and silly. I am incensed at the invasion of privacy as these big hired-guns go through my dirty knickers and ask little old ladies to produce prescriptions for their medication. I very much doubt they have this kind of power, but they keep pleading 9/11, which is presently enough to shut everyone up in this country. Of all the places to go to such lengths with bus security, I can't help thinking that Minneapolis is the most ridiculous.

Clem is in trouble. His back pocket reveals a pearl-handled folding spoon, fork and can-opener combo, a beautiful set that is seized because it could be used as a weapon. My Leatherman multi-tool, underneath a box of tampons in my toiletbag, has been fortunately overlooked. There is something very Huck Finn about this gentle boy, despite his black clothes and garlic ear, and even his eating utensils look like they belong on a raft going down the Mississippi. I decide to intervene and eventually the boofheads agree to let the tool on if it goes in my bag and Clem is not allowed near it during the ride.

During the midst of the debate, I find myself subconsciously posh-ing my accent up a notch, something I have begun reflexively whenever I need to deal with problems here. For some reason, Americans find that British and Australian accents (which they rarely distinguish between) make their speakers sound intelligent and authoritative regardless of what they're saying. I use my accent again on the driver, coupled with what I hope to be puppy eyes and a convincing buckling on wobbly legs under the weight of my bag, pleading illness to get at the restricted seat behind him. I'm ruthless now. Totally without ruth. Ruth can sit somewhere else, baby, because I need the room. Ruth can walk to next-stop Des Moines for all I care. I need to sleep.

The driver accepts my protestations of motion sickness and lets me ride in what we refer to as the 9/11 seat. Yeah-heh, this is more like it. Now I've got the best seat in a far superior bus to any I've had so far. It's what we would call a coach at home, with higher, more comfortable seats, more room, huge windows and even a little TV. I tell the driver that this is the best Greyhound I've been on so far, and he chuckles. 'That's because it's not Greyhound,' he says. 'This here's a Jefferson Line bus. We run a few regional routes for Greyhound, but that's all.' He tells me that Greyhound is currently under Chapter 11, which is American-tax-speak for bankruptcy. The dawg is bankrupt? Yipes! It must be due to dodgy management, because the customers sure are there. 'I wonder what went wrong,' I say to the driver, but he just snorts. 'I wonder what they can get to go right!' he says, and I'm inclined to agree.

Up high with a 180-degree view from floor to ceiling, I'm in a great spot to see everything, which, on the outskirts of Minneapolis, is largely a lot of cool green grass, a band of purple freeway and the swollen orange sun going down. I'm on my way to Colorado now, travelling due south through Iowa, then west across the big middle state of Nebraska and on into Denver, the Colorado state capital. For some reason Aussie television was once peppered with gleeful re-runs of the American wild-man show *Grizzly Adams* and I've always wondered about the Rocky Mountains. I'm excited to be headed there and pleased to be making such a big stretch of westerly progress, too.

In front of me, the bus driver begins to share his many philosophies; educating me on the vagaries of right and left thumb thinking, nuclear arms in Syria, shortcrust pastry and the unqualified benefits of ingesting Gingko biloba. 'Now I'm gonna let you alone to sleep,' he says, 'but first I'm going to put to you a single question. It's the same one I've been asking for many years, an' so far no one's got it right.' We share a few seconds of silence for dramatic effect and then, 'What was the name of the whale in Pinocchio?' That's the secret question? 'Uh, Jeppeto!'

I shout. 'No, wait, um, the blue fairy was the . . .' After a while I give up, but he won't tell me. 'Does the whale even have a name?' I ask, exasperated. 'Oh yes,' he answers, 'the whale has a name. So important in the story is the whale. Couldn't have the same story without it, but does anyone remember his name? Never. Never.' He shakes his head, and drives on into the glow.

With the whale question signalling the end of our conversation, I figure my chances of the toilet being usable are greater on this kind of bus and balance my way down the back. This toilet is much more like an airline loo, with little metal flaps that open and close instead of the yawning cesspool of dysentery and despair on Greyhound, but one thing here is very wrong. The seat and lid have broken and somehow become fully detached. They have crossed over each other and are covered in misfires, leaving a hole about the size of a teacup to pee into. That's a fair-sized area to aim for, but take into account please, even after 20-something years of practice and subsequent expertise, this is a bus pelting along the Minnesota interstate at serious speed. I'm busting though (peril of the Big Gulp and the never-ending refill), so I decide to give it a big Aussie try.

Things are progressing nicely until I hear a, shall we say, *dropletting* sound. Thud thud, patter patter, rather than a continuous tinkle. Looking down I see that the river has forked on impact and split across state lines, one on Leaking Lid Highway, the other in Broken Seat County. They meet up again to form the Jefferson Bus Falls, now heading towards the door at a rapid rate. I yelp and leap involuntarily, wetting the back of my hipster jeans, and, with all my secret-agent quick thinking, hurl the entire toilet roll at the offending waterway, heading it off at the pass. Suddenly I'm alone in a broken toilet; wet jeans, bladder half-empty, a soggy roll of grey toilet paper blocking the door and nowhere to place it now that the lids have closed off the hole forever. I try manoeuvring the lid with my shoe, to no avail, and now I don't even have paper with which to concoct an emergency barrier on my hands. I squelch back to my seat, my nice-bus travel bubble having burst already.

Watching the sun retire its last winking glimmer for the day, the bus leaves the freeway to roll through an ugly-looking town called Owatonna. It appears to be populated entirely by staggering drunks reeling between flat concrete architecture, with pokey shops invariably called Christian Book and Gift, and a grocery store called 'Hy-Vee'. We pull in beside a cheap motel and pick up some hard-looking men and another Jefferson bus driver, who is obviously a friend of our own whale-man. The drivers spend a good half-hour talking about routes and payroll codes, and I'm getting kind of twitchy. I start pulling things out of my backpack to read the instructional labels, and by the time I'm done with my new suncream bottle, I'm very bored.

'Excuse me,' I say. 'The TV? Do we get a movie later or something?' I can spy the video case for *The Poseidon Adventure* next to his foot.

'Oh,' he says, 'I'd like to, but the VHS in this bus had its cord removed on account of the plain folk, and someone musta forgot to put it back.'

'The whaa?' I ask.

'Well, this bus came via Pennsylvania and Ohio and such, and down by Harmony in Minnesota. That's where a lot of plain folk are,' he says. 'You know, plain people? Amish and such?'

'Oh,' I say, 'like *Witness*, right?' Both drivers laugh to each other. 'Yeah, that's right.'

They tell me the Amish can't watch television, and that out of respect for these people, the TVs are deactivated along routes where there might be Amish passengers. 'Okay,' I say, 'but if they can't watch TV because it's a twentieth-century gizmo, how come they can ride on the bus?'

'Well,' says the driver, 'they don't have cars of their own, and I guess sometimes they need to . . . Hon, I'm not real sure of the rules, only that they're nice people and we don't like to offend them.' The bus drivers begin chatting to each other about the plain people they've met over the years, and the things they've learnt about them. These are fascinating stories, and certainly better than second-rate TV. Maybe the Amish are on to something after all. The driver corrects my idea that the Pennsylvania Dutch were Dutch migrants and tells me that they were in fact Swiss-German. The Dutch part was a corruption of the word *Deutsch*, or German, which is what these religious settlers spoke. This would explain the obvious lack of windmills and clogs.

The driver says he has an Amish friend who he's been pestering for years to collaborate with him on making a tasteful calendar of photographs explaining the Amish way of life, but the Amish abhor photography. 'I've been tryin' for a while now,' he tells me, 'but I don't think he'll cave. He always says "O, maybe next year. We'll see."' I ask him how long it's been. 'O, 36, no, 37 years,' he replies, 'but I'm hopeful.'

At exactly 10 pm we make our meal stop in a town called Albert Lea. Ah. Burger King. Great. Better than the truck-stop scenario, but only by a soldier's whisker. My stomach has a real aversion to burger chains, mostly because I can never seem to get myself fed at one. If it's before ten in the morning, sure, I have no problem. Breakfast at these places is largely just real food with added grease – there's not too much you can do to hotcakes, bacon, eggs and an English muffin to make them objectionable. Dinner is another story. Apart from hard, oily potato slivers, there's never much on the menu for someone who dislikes the idea of taking a thin cardboard coaster of maybe-meat and hiding it inside that sweet fake bread with the texture of tissues, covered with a slobber of sauces like artificial condiment soup.

A real hamburger is a gastronomic force to be reckoned with, but this rude approximation of food always makes me gag. That gherkin and plastic cheese smell that wafts from the flapping 'Thank you' of the man-high garbage receptacles is a constant argument against eating. The 'Thank you' flap bangs open again and I decide I'd rather go hungry for a few more hours than eat next to our own waste.

Outside, I spy a buzzing neon sign across the parking lot. It announces The Panda Bowl. It looks open, but there's no one around. I heft my tomato-pack up and go to investigate. The front door, glass with a pink curtain closed behind it, displays a cheerful 'OPEN' sign, and I push on it tentatively. Inside, a lone Chinese family sits around a table stacked with folded napkins and soy-sauce bottles, shovelling mouthfuls of fragrant rice and chicken. 'Oh,' I say, 'sorry. Your sign says open . . .' The parents and a teenage boy all speak rapid Chinese to a tiny little girl, who slides down off her chair and comes over. 'We open! You want tasty snack?' Did I want a – 'Yes!' I cry, 'That's me! I want a tasty snack!' and I order some special fried rice with chicken soup for my bus throat.

The mother disappears out the back and I smell a pleasantly blackened wok spring to life on a gas stove. The little girl runs around collecting takeaway paraphernalia for my meal, before standing on a stool behind the cash register to take my money. She carefully counts out the change and I thank her. 'How old are you?' I ask her, and she holds up six fingers proudly, telling me that she will have her first American birthday next month. Her mother comes back with my food, nodding and smiling at my heartfelt compliments for this hot and delicious snack, which is still cheaper than Burger King.

Walking across the lot again I can see that the Burger King line is still snaking along without relief, so I sit down at a bench outside it to wait for the others. I eat my meal alone at the closed plastic playground, under prison-yard-strength lights, next to the roar of the Interstate. In the time it takes for the last Greyhound passenger to get their floppy burger, I am investigating the final crumbs of jasmine rice on my fork and opening my fortune cookie. My fortune is the most obscure I've ever had, and reads – no kidding – 'Next time, you should sit down.' Huh? When I think of my still damp jeans I shiver as if the Fates themselves are watching me.

Riding on the bus after a burger-chain stop is a bit like crawling into one of those gherkin bins, and the constant gaseous belchings force me to apply eucalyptus oil under both nostrils to block the stench, finding yet another use for the miraculous unguent. With 16 hours to go, I crunch down two Kwells and drift into what has become my usual Greyhound daydream, which consists of getting off somewhere and checking into a hotel, where I draw the blinds and remain quiet and restful for about a week before flying home. Just before unconsciousness, I note that our bus is in the Boondocks. Official Nowheresville. I never knew that 'out in the Boonies' was an actual place, but here it is. Boondocks, Iowa, just off Interstate 35. The middle of nowhere.

Coming out of a chemical coma against my will, one eye pissing out fluid, armpits prickling with sudden heat, I find myself out on the bitumen wearing my backpack on my chest, trying to remember who I am and what I'm doing here. And where, for that matter, here is. Ah. I see. Through the one eye left that's working, I figure out that the Greyhound bus pulling out beside our newly parked Jefferson is headed to Denver. Why is it leaving? I check my watch. It's half an hour early, what's going on? 'Schmy buhsh!' I cry through a fog of dramamine. 'Buhsh 'eaving!' and I begin a crazy-footed scramble towards it. A shout goes up and a little Denver-bound posse is on my heels. We stop the bus and leap aboard. The bus is packed tighter than King Oscar Brisling Norwegian Sardines, and the squeaky-voiced driver begs us to find a seat or get off. 'I'm late!' she screams. 'Really late, okay! Sit down or leave! I can't answer your questions, I don't know! Okay? I don't know!' We fill the remaining seats and she takes off backwards at about 50 miles an hour, before hopping forward for a mile or more.

I turn to the guy next to me and say, 'What on earth –' but he just shakes his head, saying, 'Oh, don't even . . . don't even . . .' A big sweaty guy who had been the first to follow behind me leans over to the driver. 'Hey, so will our luggage be on the next bus then?' 'WHAT?' she screams, pulling at the steering wheel like a pilot trying to heave his plane out of a tailspin. It becomes apparent that this is not, in fact, our bus to Denver. This is the previous bus, which is about four hours late, and I'd put that down to pilot errah if I was made to say sumpin' on tha issue. The big boneheaded guy and his friends leapt off our Jefferson bus with their luggage safe underneath and followed me blindly onto this one. He's pointing a meaty finger at me now, waggling it around, saying, 'She did it first! She got on and she said this was our bus! She said it! Hey,' he yells at me, 'what's gonna happen to our luggage?'

'How would I know?' I shout back. 'I took mine with me!'

'That's not fair!' he yells, like I have somehow cheated. 'That's not fair!' he repeats to the driver. 'Hey! Call them on your microphone and say where's Pete's luggage, okay? I need my stuff!' The bus driver looks like she's going to spontaneously combust. The more upset she gets, the higher and squeakier her voice becomes, until we can no longer hear her. She turns the mike on and starts screaming into it. 'NEW PASSENGERS, I DON'T KNOW ABOUT YOUR BAGS! I'M JUST TRYIN' TO DO MY JOB! YOU ARE RESPONSIBLE FOR YOUR STUFF!' She leaves the mike on, or perhaps she can't figure out how to turn it off, and yells into it for the next few hours. We groan and flinch and shout, 'Turn off your mike!' and 'We can hear you! Don't yell!' but it just seems to make it worse.

Her shrill and shaky voice reminds me of High Top from the *Police Academy* movies, and this whole situation would be pretty funny if our senses weren't being so assaulted. This new driver has screwed up her routes and timing so severely that we are nearly out of petrol and need to make an unscheduled refueling stop. We make a crazy, lurching trip across five lanes of traffic, finishing up at a truck stop where a few other buses are already waiting. I look around me to see people unwinding bits of tissue and even shoelaces from their ear cavities, and my seatmate tells me that the mike has been on and off for at least two states. The little driver flings herself from the opening door and runs inside the gas station. 'Don't worry,' Boneheaded Pete addresses the crowd, 'I think she's just going to see about my luggage.' He flashes me a triumphant grin, and I raise one eyebrow in the universal gesture for 'Yeah. Right.'

Half an hour passes and there is no sign of our driver, or any gas for the bus. Little camps are set up on the grass outside, cigarettes and gum are passed around along with baby photos and even a wedding album. An hour later a woman in a smartly-pressed Greyhound uniform approaches the bus. It's nearly 3 am. The woman gets to the door and smiles. She has honey-coloured hair in a loose bun, and stands like a policewoman. 'I understand you folks have had a rough trip, is that right?' Something about her voice is soothing and we just nod a bit, with a few 'damn straight's thrown in for good measure. 'Okay,' she says, addressing our sorry gathering. 'In this neck of the woods, I'm the one they call when things go bad. Now,' she pauses, inspecting us, 'things have gone very bad. I can see that. But I need your help to turn them around. I'm going to ask you to stand up, to re-board this bus as quickly and as quietly as you can, and then I'll see about some gas. We should be on the road again in ten minutes, and then I promise to drive so fast you'll feel like you *flew* to Denver, is that understood?' A hopeful giggle erupts. 'Now, driving fast is dangerous. We all know that. But I'm a good driver and well rested. So what I ask is for you to get on this bus, get in your seats, and do not move, do not speak, do not distract me in any way. Okay, everyone,' she says, 'now get on my bus.'

Seven minutes later we are hurtling west at a speed I hadn't known these rattletraps were capable of. I am asleep in minutes. When I wake, the sun is up over the flat plains of Nebraska. The bus still feels like it's rocketing along, but there isn't a single hump on the landscape for me to judge our speed against. Our driver's lovely voice penetrates my thoughts. She is reassuring Boneheaded Pete about his luggage, and I itch to kick him. She said don't distract her, moron! I begin to fashion our driver as a modern Annie Oakley; an immensely capable frontier woman. It's quite easy to substitute a covered wagon for our bus across these harsh yellow plains. Poor Nebraska has little to recommend itself. Dead flat, it just drags on and on, the entire state seems to be little more than a giant prairie, inhabited by no one as far as I can see, and I can see a long, long way.

We are in a new time zone again. I think America has about twelve of them. The mechanism on the side of my watch now moves like it's been greased. About an hour after I wake, we stop for food in a town called Ogallala, originally a hard-bitten cowboy outpost named for a tribe of Sioux. We pull off the freeway into the massive car park of the Country Kitchen restaurant, attached to a rural Ramada Hotel. The Greyhound fleet has converged here, five filthy buses lined up side by side, expelling their wretched cargo in stumbling, multi-coloured waves. Once inside, we all make for the toilets. The unspoken rules that govern groups of humans thrown together do not apply to Greyhound buses any more than United Nations food trucks. I hold the toilet door for a woman with a cane, and 12 others take advantage of my position to throw themselves through, squashing me behind the door. When I struggle past, people are still trying to jostle in front of me and being first in line means diddly. These people must be from kill-or-be-killed communities. Their kids grab and push and swear and, far from stopping them, their parents are doing the same. Some are even pushing kids out of the way.

A row of little kids has assembled near the sinks. They want to wash their hands but they can't reach anywhere near the taps. No one helps them. People tread on them. They cry. One little girl is particularly frantic. 'You gotta wash you hans!' she insists, howling. 'You get sick! You gotta WASH YOU HANS!' Cursing loudly, I lose my place in front of the so-far stench-less cubicle I had pole position for in order to lift her up. I look around, swearing a lot, asking the kids where their mums are in the hope of shaming people into assisting, but no one even looks. These kids are unlovely, covered with sticky foodstuffs like war paint, with dried snot, sullen mouths and dirty words, but someone, somewhere has at least managed to instill that, Greyhound bus toilets? Hey, might be a good place to wash those hands!

I spend 15 minutes in the toilets, washing the hands of squirming children who climb up my weary body, kicking with their filthy shoes, until I'm wet and dirty and busting to use the now disgusting toilets. I'm tired of these people, I think. Tired of travelling with people who are cruel and careless, slovenly and pathetic, tired of smelling their smells and listening to insane babble. Out of the toilets, us Greyhound passengers sit in a separate section of the dining hall, but still manage to terrorise hotel guests with our proximity. As we leave, 'Closed' signs are hung on both restroom doors.

We are delayed outside by the number of people getting on the wrong buses, and a constant reshuffle is taking place. Our Annie Oakley driver is sharp and accounts for all of us at a glance, subtracting a woman with leopard-print shoes and thick white socks, who wears a swimsuit with running shorts and studiously reapplies coats of glittering mauve eyeshadow. 'Ma'am,' says the driver, 'I think you might be on the wrong bus. Where exactly are you headed today?' But the woman can't remember and so the five buses are grounded while we try to match a luggage tag with the name on her Social Security card.

Nebraska drags on. I didn't have time to eat at the Ramada, and I'm hungrier than a cover girl. I've been on and off these buses for 20 hours now and I'm tired, sore and sticky. I have a single corn cake left in my supplies and dig it out. *Phtha.* My mouth is too dry to eat it. My nose has been blocked from the air conditioning and I must've started breathing through my mouth without realising it. My tongue feels like the under-belly of a leprous armadillo – a very tired, filthy, cranky little armadillo. I scold myself for having such a low threshold for discomfort, but I'm sick of the bus filth and the dry, barren landscape, I'm sick of the passengers and I'm tired of smelling my unwashed self. The bus makes a stop outside a run-down motel and a gangly teenage boy lopes off. He's all of 19, with a shocking case of dandruff and jeans held up by a pink elastic belt. A woman of at least 45, with bleached hair and tattoos, is waiting to meet him. The bus looks on, bored. He walks up to the woman we all assume is his mother, until they pash, wetly, as the bus rolls away. A collective 'eeeewww' goes up and I'm gladdened. All hope is not lost for this crowd.

I consult my map and am further excited to discover that I'm almost at the halfway point around America. What's more, our driver is the speed demon she promised to be, and this bus should still make it in to Denver by 2 pm, which is precisely when I told Nick to expect me. I lean back in my seat and replay our phone conversation, pondering such delicious phrases as 'guest bedroom', 'shower' and 'friends'. It's been a long time since I hung out with friends. After half a year on the island, I don't think I will ever again take for granted a steady stream of people my own age with similar interests to pal around with.

Missing my friends has put the biggest dampener on this prize of mine. I do love them, but I didn't really expect to feel this mopey for them all the time. I'm actually a fairly grumpy and independent kind of person; the kind who pretends she's not home so she can finish making macramé handbags in the bath. After all, your friends are always there, but adventures come and go. Right? Well, maybe. Maybe they're always there. Maybe not if you leave them alone for a few years. Friends and lovers come and go, but rarely do people give all of them up completely for the sake of something else. That something, in my case, is not a distant war on terror like it is for all those young marines, nor some lama-esque religious calling, but simply an unforeseen future in this very distant land. My prize. Unless I just let it lapse, of course. Unless I don't bother playing Guilia's tag-you're-it game with the INS, and give Chance back her favour. I close my eyes; Nebraska is not the sort of place to be having this conversation with myself.

Chapter 12

The hills are alive

The bus hoons into the Denver Terminal at five minutes to two, amidst much clapping and the bestowing of high praise on our driver, who still looks remarkably fresh. I buy a cold drink and catch sight of myself in the mirrored refrigerator. I am a ponkering mess. Oh well, I console myself, nothing that some hot water won't fix, and I'll do some quick laundry at Nick's place too. While Nick's a bit of a hottie, I'm not too concerned that he should lay eyes on me in such a state. Nick is mildly narcoleptic, and falling asleep unbidden provides ample opportunity for you to render yourself disgustingly uncool in front of large groups of people, no matter how attractive your wakeful self might be. The last time I saw him he was a backpacker asleep at the top of a cliff, shirt twisted under his chin, dribbling into his stubble with his tongue nearly frozen to the rock face. Friendship, as they say, is an exchange of vulnerabilities.

Nick doesn't answer his home phone, so I try his mobile. He's driving. 'Hi!' I say, 'I'm here! So, the concert starts at seven, plenty of time for a long shower and an American-sized meal, eh?'

'No time, my friend,' says Nick. 'I'm en route as we speak. Come as you are and we will try to meet the Party Bus out there.'

Whaaa? But no! I am the definition of skank. Let us not forget the subtle odour of urine wafting from my grimy seat. Forced to do the quickest clean-up ever, I make something of a spectacle even for the Greyhound toilets. I'm throwing everything on and off in public because my bag won't give me a turning circle in the tiny cubicles. I don't care anymore, and I can't see that some skinny pale flesh is going to be more offensive than anything Greyhound passengers have witnessed before. I peel my sticky bra from my chest and grab a bikini top, the only clean undergarment I have left. Throwing a graying singlet on over the top, I wash my face in the sink under the sign that says I can't, trying not to think about the dried suds and curly hairs in the plughole just millimetres away from my mouth. An eighth layer of deodorant is the height of Greyhound chic and I apply it now. My undies are like a small wet sock curled inside my filthy baggy jeans. Yeech. I whip them off and ping them into the bin. There will be no knickers today.

Outside the station the air is so dry it crackles like newspaper, and it's blasting hot. I had expected Denver to be very green somehow, perhaps even snowy, but the grass and trees are crispy and brown. There's a smoky haze lingering from the forest fires that have been raging around the state, and I remember that there's a drought to explain this lack of fresh vegetation. I check my watch and sigh. I'm starving.

A big black man saunters over. 'Hey sister,' he says.

'Hey,' I reply.

'You a redneck?' he asks.

'I beg your pardon!' My thrift-store belt buckle has two tiny silver cowgirl guns crossed over it, but how he could see this detail of my ironic fashion statement at ten paces I'm not sure. It has to be something else. 'I'm Australian,' I announce, hoping to exonerate myself from any of the rules pertaining to his culture.

'Hey,' he puts both hands up, 'jus' wanted to know if you got any rolling papers, needed to check you weren't a redneck first.'

'Oh. Okay. No to the redneck and to the papers. Sorry, mate.' I make a show of looking up and down the street for Nick.

'You intimidate all these guys, you know,' the man says, hand sweeping around the menfolk of the Greyhound exit, a group comprising two very small Mexicans fighting over a plastic raincoat, three skinny black teenagers so stoned they can barely keep their heads up and an elderly man attempting private conversation with the only leg he has left. 'Yeah,' he continues his awkward line of flattery, 'uh huh, I bet you intimidate a lotta guys too.' I deliver a half-nod and go back to looking.

'So,' he says, 'you smoke dope or what?' I don't reply.

'So,' he says, 'what are you doing in Denver?'

'Visiting a friend,' I tell him. 'He's coming to pick me up.'

'You and your friend smoke dope or what?'

'Or what,' I reply, getting annoyed. Come on, Nick.

'You smoke anything else?'

I just shrug, and he looks angry, frustrated.

'Aw, c'mon,' he says. 'Whatcho doin' down here then, sister?'

'What do you mean?' I say, exasperated. 'It's a bloody bus station, what are *you* doing down here?'

'Business,' he replies, flashing me a handful of rolling papers that he had all the time. I suppose the caches of illegal narcotics are close by in his drug den. Wow! My first pusher! This is so hard-core! So authentic!

'Jeez,' I splutter, 'you're, like, trying to sell me drugs!' I'm so excited. I've never been this cool.

'Man, fuck you,' he says, as he wanders off. 'I knew you were a redneck.'

Greyhound is awash with drugs, but until now I've suppose I've looked clean enough to be left out of the loop. Since Miami the toilets have been filled with hundreds of small transactions; clattering syringes, desperate swearing when rocks of chemicals or baggies of powder, goop, or plant life fall from trembling fingers and hit the floor. I couldn't care less (or, as they say here, I could care less, which doesn't make sense to me but apparently means the same thing). Getting off a long-haul Greyhound makes me feel like I need a habit too. I don't understand why people on drugs get such a bum rap. I'd rather all my seatmates were stoned. It keeps them quiet and usually well provisioned with snacks.

Nick comes cruising up just in time to represent a totally different America. After all my bitching and moaning of the past

24 hours, he might as well be wearing a T-shirt that says 'I am the Greyhound Counter-argument'. He squeals to a halt when he sees me and throws open the passenger door of his huge black SUV. The sunroof is open, windows are down, music is blaring. He pushes his aviator sunnies back across his blond hair and blinds me with a megawatt smile. I climb in gratefully, aware with every inch that I'm polluting Pepsi-commercial perfection with my grossness. Luckily, Americans are unfailingly polite and Nick pretends not to notice. We burn along as he gets directions on the cell phone and radios ahead to the others, 'You gonna make it? No, I'm gonna make it, are you? Well is he gonna make it? Okay, but we're gonna make it. Hold the bus!'

Nick's car is massive and I'm delighting in the comfort of my squishy seat, pushing at toggles and buttons and switches, wiggling my toes with pleasure at the leg-room and the speed and fresh air. Suddenly we're there, leaping out and dashing across the street. 'Another bus,' says Nick. 'Just what you want, huh?' Huh, I think, trying to keep my jeans from sliding off as we climb aboard. The big bus is packed with lip-glossed and summer-tanned college grads gathered around a keg of beer and some coolers filled with icy beverages.

I'm in culture shock. In total contrast to the last bus ride of wakeful discomfort with the terminally disenfranchised, I find myself surrounded by beautiful and healthy people, urging me to sit and relax with kind words falling from amazing teeth. The bus driver yells, 'Okay, welcome to the Party Bus! Express service to Widespread Panic, Red Rocks Amphitheatre!' Huge cheers go up, and there is much shouting, chugging, hugging and picture-taking as we set off. I'm in such a daze. I feel disgustingly dirty and my lack of knickers is making me itchy everywhere I can't scratch. The bus makes a quick supermarket stop where everyone buys massive tanks of water, which makes me nervous about impending conditions. Along with water I buy a truly enormous sandwich and wolf it down in three bites, establishing myself early as Nick's feral friend from Oss-traylia.

'Hey, don't worry,' he says, 'you look fine! And uh, I like your perfume too, that's ... nice ...' He sniffs closer. 'It's just deodorant,' I tell him. 'Really?' he says, 'It's interesting, kind of . . .' his brow furrows and I step away, pointing my jeans downwind.

The Party Bus reaches Red Rocks and I'm reunited with Tom and Sarah, more friends met on a post-uni backpacking adventure (the ubiquitous Aussie rite of passage) in Egypt. Nick, Tom and Sarah are all originally from Kansas. It has always tickled me to have made friends from Kansas. It just seems like such an improbable place to be from. This trio were always quintessentially American to me in many ways. They fit my old preconceptions of what it meant to be American – they are blonde and tanned, equipped with perfect smiles, expensive college educations, lovely manners and lots of lifestyle accessories. They enjoy outdoorsy stuff like hiking and skiing, they are very familiar with one church or another and they try not to swear in public. They are ambitious, effervescent, drive nice cars, wear nice clothes, understand the stock market and party like their world is in immediate danger of ending. They represent to me the wide, privileged, upper-middle class of this country.

When we get exchange students in Oz, these are the kids who usually come and I think this must be the America the world typically gets to meet. Despite my high-handed demands to friends and family that they cannot, and must not, generalise about the people and culture of my newly-won country, I find myself unable to stop myself from degenerating into the same lazy thinking. It's always dangerous to stereotype, but after you meet a hundred 'typical' Americans, it can be difficult not to.

Still, after being in the US for a while now, I can't help feeling that these very 'American' Americans get a lousy go of it. I've met so many of them in Australia and abroad, and the criticisms levelled at them are repetitious. They're airheads. They're self-centred. They're ignorant. They're insincere. They're phony. They're shallow. They're all the same. Hmmm. I made a great deal of Tommo, my 'sweet little Japanese friend', in one of my increasingly long and rambling emails home. It is understood that Tommo, being Japanese, will be unfailingly polite and concerned with saving face in public. It's a cultural thing, right? Most of my friends have at least a vague understanding that there are rigid social codes at work in Japanese society. I don't think Americans are given the same benefit of the doubt. In fact, I'm sure they're not.

What I have come to realise is that these middle-American friends of mine were raised in a culture where an immeasurable degree of importance is placed on being friendly, complimentary, accommodating, polite and transparent. Until you get to know someone, there is absolutely no room socially for anyone to be moody, aloof, dry, witty, incisive or confrontational; traits which Australians and many Europeans equate with 'personality'.

Americans have personalities. There are 300 million different personalities living in this country, in a culture that considers it extremely impolite to impose that personality on someone you've just met. You can spend all night at a party with Americans and learn nothing much about them as individuals. You will have your drink refilled constantly, your comfort inquired about frequently, and your ego stroked pleasantly, but the true personalities of your excellent hosts will remain elusive. Don't get me wrong. You may well learn the most intimate details of their lives. Much is made of the American share-how-you-feel, Oprah-style confessionals, and it's nothing for someone here to tell a perfect stranger how they were sexually abused as a child, just got a messy divorce and have a brother who is dying from testicular cancer. These are details, though, just an extension of the idea that you should endeavour to be honest, open and transparent.

It has taken me a while to get to know my American friends. They have very little cultural room for 'taking the piss' and, being Australian, I find it perfectly natural to compose entire conversations around the concept. I'm surprised they still like me (perhaps they don't, they're all too nice to let me know), but these three make it easy for me. They are long-term travellers who have been far afield for long enough to see glimpses of the America that I do. They have seen a large part of the world and have even set up residence in countries as diverse as Argentina and Iceland between them. I liked them well enough in Egypt, but I feel like I understand why now. My Green Card has loaded me with cultural questions and baggage that I never anticipated and I can feel myself dissecting our conversations and the smallest interactions, clinging to them like the new kid at school, while rejecting some of their ideas miserably in turn.

Despite the smoke haze in the distance, the air is so thin here that I feel like everything looks much sharper than it should, and I keep blinking, shaking my head. 'This is nothing,' Tom says. 'On a good day you feel like you could see forever, see the whole *state*.' He's right, it's really quite amazing. My hair feels crackling and crisp, even under layers of bus grease, and my eyes are sore and dry. I sit down heavily on a boulder in what I think is shock at the air clarity. I have a slow stinging headache and queasiness that is immediately explained away as altitude sickness. 'Hydrate!' they tell me, and I start a continuous chug.

Denver is known as the Mile High City for its 5,800-foot elevation. Here at the canyon we are even higher and I feel almost drunk just from breathing. The dusty car park at the foot of the giant red rocks is filled with an odd mixture of high performance cars, giant SUVs, a grand collection of hippie vans and impromptu tent cities. On my way to a port-a-loo (port-a-potty here) a bearded guy in a caftan actually says, 'Hey, baby! What's your sign?' Man, are you kidding me? I'm intrigued, though, and, realising that the dryness is such that I no longer need to pee, I sit down while he does my sign and my numbers. 'Whoa . . . you've come a long way in short amount of time,' he tells me, and on account of my accent, I'm underwhelmed. 'You are making difficult decisions with no one to guide you.' Spooky. Welcome to the twenty-first century, I think. 'You miss your love . . .' he tells me, looking directly into my eyes, 'a water sign, whoa . . . that's funny for you, Capricorn Sister, choosin' a water man, a fish friend. Dude, you can't leave a fish alone, they swim away.' It must be the altitude, but I start to cry. The Boy is a fish, a Pisces.

A long-haired guy auditioning for the role of Neil from *The Young Ones* comes up and says, 'Dave, you aren't reading people again are you?' He peers in, as I dry my eyes with a grubby hand. 'Dude . . . Virgo? No, wait . . .' He has a Grateful

Dead tattoo the size of a grapefruit on his arm. Widespread Panic, the group we are going to see tonight, is an extension of that jam-band sensation begun with Jerry Garcia and the Grateful Dead in the late sixties and continuing with current acts like Phish. Legions of fans travel all over the country, following these bands on Pied Piper missions of drugs and song and all manner of intergalactic affirmation. It makes for an interesting crowd.

Money and tickets and drugs fly freely, and the crowd, composed predominately of college kids, soon has bloodshot eyes, saucer-like pupils or twitching noses. People keep nodding and smiling at me, saying 'Chronic nugget!' The linguistics of this statement confuses me. I decide it's a compliment. 'Hey! Sure! Thanks!' I tell them, 'You're ah, pretty chronic and nuggety there yourself! Yeah! Have a good night!' I'm winking and waving, yeah, back atcha, man. Chronic, yeah, all right, good times. 'Dude,' the Party Bus crew are telling me, 'we already got some, you want some more?' Ah, whaaa? Turns out it's just lumps of pot and I'm not being complimented on my chronic nuggets after all. Americans love, love, love flashy lingo for their drugs. The things they call cocaine over the course of the evening make me cover my smile and look away. Australians saddle drugs with the kind of slang that make them sound like your ugly mate who lives round the corner and farts on command. Americans name drugs like they are hot chicks or superheroes, and employ all manner of ritualistic ingestion involving expensive and attractive props.

Once inside, the canyon is immense and beautiful. Huge slabs of burnt red rock form a natural amphitheatre, with a raised red-rock 'stage' at the bottom. It's really spectacular. What a venue. I am sure if this place was in Europe I would have heard about it before – it would surely be one nation's big tourist drawcard. There's too much to choose from here. The US is spoilt for natural beauty and I never really knew about it before this trip.

Tiered bench seating covers the undulating rock and people sprawl or stand on these wooden platforms, drinking alcoholic lemonade from the concession stalls and sharing gallon jugs of water. It's hot, but so dry that I'm never sweaty, just kind of wide-eyed and leathery, unstable on my feet. When the sun goes down the sky turns instantly black beyond the canyon, depthless in this thin air.

Later in the evening it becomes Red Rocks Island, floating above the world on a night cloud. There is perfect blackness past the canyon until the twinkling lights of Denver way down below, a false horizon like the edge of a continent as you come in on an aeroplane. It is an unearthly view anyway, but such clear and still air makes it even more ethereal. The crowd cheers and sings, dancing, stumbling, floating, falling, hugging, and it's a crazy, wonderful night of music and madness. By the time my body remembers that the last time it rested was three states ago in the opposite direction, I'm done. I manage to stagger through the thin air to the bus, where I fall asleep on any lap that will support me until I crawl into the back of Nick's massive car. The mad Americans continue until 5 am while I sleep blissfully next to the toolbox, waking every hour or so to pee on someone's well-manicured lawn.

The next morning I wake up and announce to myself that I'm in Colorado. I have officially left the Great Plains of the Midwest behind with Nebraska and am now in the Rockies, in the middle-left-hand side of the country. I look at my map and decide to call it halfway. No one else is up, so I go snooping around the house Nick shares with his friends. All over this modest suburban home are the signs of the casual affluence of the middle class in the US of A. There are skis and snowboards, motorbikes and mountaineering equipment, pool table and weights, TVs by the dozen, computer games and piles of expensive clothes, all just thrown in together by the people who live here. They work hard, but they party a lot, eat out a lot and spare no expense. Casey, a friend of Nick's and a former exchange student in Sydney, wakes and agrees with my findings, telling me, 'Hey, unlike you Ossies, Americans only get two weeks vacation a year. We work hard because we love our easy life, and it takes cash. But if you work that hard, you're gonna play hard too.'

The boys have roused themselves from unconsciousness with the agenda of doing it all over again and before I know it we're back on the road to Red Rocks. I've had the benefit of a shower and the smug protection of clean undies, and now the guys are looking at me as if for the first time. 'Oh,' says Casey, 'you're a blonde?' Illustrating his play-hard philosophy, Casey is ingesting the breakfast of champions and administering various narcotics with the skill of a medical practitioner. With the War on Drugs in America up there with the War on Trr as expensive and unwinnable shadow boxing that is nevertheless likely to get you nuked for flirting with the opposition, I'm consistently frantic about being deported for using so much as hemp-seed-oil lip balm. All hemp products are illegal in the US now. Seriously. It's a wonder you can still buy orange poppy-seed muffins. In many states they can lock you up and throw away the key for possession of a single, straggly marijuana plant. Life imprisonment, I shit you not. Even teenagers, unable to buy so much as a light beer until they turn 21, can go to jail for almost a decade for succumbing to curiosity and buying a solitary tab of LSD.

The US government has been in a manic froth over its citizens' illegal drug use for decades now. Despite seeing more drugs here at a suburban McDonald's or a downtown laundromat than at 3 am on New Year's Eve in a Sydney nightclub, no one seems willing to concede that enormous numbers of otherwise law-abiding Americans enjoy a truly astonishing variety of drugs. Luckily for me and my nervous discretionary Green Card, alcohol is ridiculously cheap here, with hundreds more taste sensations on offer than could ever be supported by Australia's meagre population.

It takes ages to organise a group of assorted hangovers and by the time we pick everyone up it's time for lunch. Three cars squeal off the freeway into Wendy's, a national chain famous for the Pippi-Longstocking-like girl in red pigtails on the sign, and the square burger patties. My wallet feels reassuringly full, but I open it to find that I've been duped by the thick and grubby paper money again. The mighty greenback is really the grimy greyback and every cash transaction seems to leave me with a growing collection of ones, which look the same as notes of considerably more value. A wallet feels dramatically fat with seven dollars in it and this can break your heart time and again.

Beside me in line, one of Nick's friends opens his wallet to reveal 11 one-dollar bills. He shakes his head in disgust. 'Dude, did I go dancing last night?' he asks, alluding to the practice of stuffing cheap strippers' garters with the least valuable of the dead presidents. I complain about these wads of worthless cash to Casey, but he's having none of it. 'Oh, like your Ossie gold is so much better!' he says. 'In Australia, you lose some change down the couch and there goes the fuckin' rent!'

I wrestle with an ATM outside and when I come back in the posse is right where I left them. There are five people serving and ten customers in line, and it still takes us over half an hour to get our food. I wonder aloud why fast food is so popular here when it's never, in fact, fast. 'She's right,' says Casey, 'fast food in Australia is actually fast. And it's cheaper than regular food too.' I grin as if I invented this myself. 'But,' says Casey, using a dangerous tone, 'what do you have to say about this?' He waves a sachet of tomato ketchup slowly and triumphantly in my face. Americans are constantly aghast at having to pay for condiments in Australia and react as though some vital code of hospitality has been broken. Now, lips turn thin with bitterness as the lack of free drink refills is recounted and I hang my head when Nick remembers his stinging shock at having to pay for mustard and three glasses of cola during his own trip to Oz.

A coffee war breaks out next, which illustrates much of the dining expectations of Americans compared with the rest of the Western world. From London to Sydney, Paris to Rome, if I buy a cup of coffee, be it espresso or – if I find myself at a police station or hospital waiting room – drip filter, this is the one and only cup of coffee that I receive. If I want milk in it, it will come with milk. In America, when you buy coffee, you will almost invariably get a cup of black, filtered coffee (even in shops selling nothing *but* coffee) and you must then repair to a nearby 'beverage station'. For your whitening needs there will be a buttery mixture called half and half, which is basically pouring cream, as well as 2 per cent fat milk, 1 per cent fat milk, and 0 per cent fat milk, but never, ever regular milk from a cow, which is rather awkwardly referred to as 'Vitamin D' milk.

After concocting a mixture of half and half and skim milk into a dodgy aeroplane-tea-tasting liquid, there are still a few choices left to make. There are various sugars and artificial sweeteners, along with flavoured syrups, vanilla sugar, chocolate powder, and, of course, the national favourite, cinnamon. If you're not exhausted by the time you stir your bubbling witch's brew and down it, you can always go again, for free. After months of enduring such caffeinated struggle, I dream sometimes of a single, hot, whole-milk latte, a few straws of sugar on the side, three bucks, no returns. We spend a long time discussing whether less is more, and I can't help feeling that this may be at the crux of what is so different about a life in America. This tyranny of endless choices.

Today's concert at Red Rocks starts and ends much earlier. After nursing hangovers in the blistering full sun, an executive decision is made that two days is enough Widespread Panic for our bodies to handle and we allow ourselves to be carried out of the canyon on the tidal crowd. Nick is a champion of Denver and is keen to show me everything at once. Americans are often extremely proud of their cities, however different they are from each other, or whatever they might have to offer. I've never met anyone from Gary, Indiana, but I'm sure I would encounter swollen chests and teary eyes there, too. So, despite our fragile conditions, we retire to the open-air rooftop lounge at the Little Buddha Bar downtown and I have to agree that Denver is an attractive city. The streets are wide and clean, the inky sky is star-filled, the weather is dry and perfect and mountains line the horizon. We have just enough energy left to lift vodka gingerly to our mouths and fill in all the blanks from the last two and a half years.

I discover some things I never knew about this down-home Kansas sweetheart. Nick is one of the heirs to a family gunpowder business and has an uncle on the board of the National Rifle Association. He owns a couple of guns himself and has even fired them competitively on his college shooting team. He believes that guns don't kill people, people kill people, that the rights to bear arms is sacrosanct and we'd all be better off with a Smith & Wesson in the kitchen near the kettle.

(Actually, I made that bit up. Most Americans don't own kettles. Truly. In a society where hot tea is a delicacy, boiling water means in the saucepan for pasta or eggs.) I smile, nodding and sipping for as long as Nick's host-rights dictate, before instinct decries that I attack the enemy and I tell him he's a big jerk. What follows is the inevitable argument you have with someone who believes that guns are a great idea, or that whale meat sure is tasty, or peanut butter should be smooth. Some people can't be reasoned with and you bust ribs just trying.

What upsets me the most is that this is precisely what I've spent the last year of this Green Card process defending America against at home. I get furious with people who ask me why the hell I'd want to go to America when it's filled with, well, crazy Americans. Nothing made me crankier than the worldwide generalising that the millions of souls inhabiting this country are all ignorant, gun-toting assholes who think George Bush is a great world leader. Nick is a really nice guy. He's kind and friendly, well read and widely travelled, interesting and articulate and good to his mum. And now he's terribly upset that I'm reacting like I just found out he has a white sheet and pointy hat in the cupboard or that he clubs baby seals in his spare time.

'It's a cultural thing,' he protests. 'You eat Vegemite and surf or whatever; I ride horses and Harleys and shoot guns.'

'No!' I insist, 'not all Americans support guns, and you don't all vote Republican and think public healthcare is a bad idea!'

'That's right,' says Nick, 'but a lot of us do. I do. It doesn't mean we're bad people if we disagree about some things. Nothing is ever that simple.' No, but . . . but I don't want any of that to be true. I don't want my prize to be *Bowling for Columbine*, I want it to be the liberal world mix of New York, the friendly beauty of Minneapolis, the charming grandeur of Savannah, the vibrant ethnic salsa of Miami. There is no room in my vision of life here for those other things. Not school shootings, not marines raping school girls in Japan, not Kyoto-kiss-my-ass, Dubya's crusades or the cross-eyed war on drugs, not woeful inequality in health and education, not psycho-paths and unabombers, anti-abortion murderers and white supremacists. Not any of that continuous stream of bad-news-

America that hits the press at home every day. I finally realise that I'm scared that my Green Card means I have to somehow collude with this or apologise for it. That's what I've been scared about since the letter with the eagle and stars emblazoned on it arrived in the post. I fake a tummy ache and we go home, where I fall asleep with a vodka-numb tongue and a heavy heart.

The next morning Nick must have forgiven my brutal assault on his country and character, because he lets me sleep until lunchtime before delivering me to the mountain city of Boulder on his way to work. Just outside Denver, Boulder is a city of 100,000 people, 20,000 of whom are students at the lively university there. I like it instantly and flap around in my thongs with the air of someone off to her own birthday party. Denver and Boulder experience more than 300 sunny days a year, even in their snowy winters, a fact that locals proudly present to me every five minutes. People are really proud of the beauty of this state and exalt at living here, especially to each other. I can see why. I wander the pedestrian area for hours, revelling in the novelty of walking around underfoot of mountains. Denver is nice but it's just any old city compared to Boulder, I think. Boulder is a special place.

The drought has intensified, though, and at one o'clock, the temperature in the central Pearl Street corso has reached 40 degrees C. I spend ages coaxing droplets of water from public drinking fountains before spending fortunes on bottled water instead. I do not sweat. I do not pee. My lips recede and my eyes refuse to blink, citing lack of lubrication. For lunch I discover a great supermarket called Wild Oats, a precious-gem store of food like the Wedge. It's packed, and I get the feeling that the citizens of Boulder are of the platinum-Birkenstock variety. There is a lot of money in this town, that much quickly becomes apparent, and a lot of Earth-mother-crystal-Zen-Buddhist-stickered Beemers and Lexus SUVs being driven around. Being summer, the college students should be thin on the ground, but everyone still looks remarkably young. Boulder is exceptionally mellow. It's a pricey college town and a town for people whose sports involve a lot of gear – skiing, trail riding, mountain climbing, kayaking.

The attitude here is distinctly 'West Coast', and the University of Colorado at Boulder (UC) is often referred to as the University of *California* at Boulder. It looks like a great place to go to school, I think, shaking my head in wonder. University costs a fortune in the US, but if you've got the dough or the brains, you're really spoilt for choice. There are lots of kids here from 'Cally'; beautiful girls walking around with the long-legged, honey-haired look typifying that state.

It's not hard to tell that this is a community championing alternative lifestyles, politics and religions, but it seems to have some negative consequences. This laid-back, each-unto-their-own vibe means that the Pearl Street Mall is littered with groups of very aggressive panhandlers; mostly chubby teenagers wandering around in expensive punker gear, with multiple piercings, harassing everyone for money. They go into a pizza place ahead of me, demanding, 'Gimme a piece for a buck,' and sneering at the other customers, including *moi*, who has herself had to forgo an extra topping on account of miserly funds. Motley groups of all ages blast crappy music from spendy sound systems, sitting in circles next to shops, glaring at people and snarling out random insults. A girl crosses the street to push at my shoulder, giggling with red eyes, saying, 'Hey, bitch! Don't you remember me? I was at your house last night,' before walking away whistling. Hmm. Maybe it's just the altitude.

Still, the shops and restaurants are lovely, and most of the shopkeepers and pedestrians wear colourful clothes and ready smiles. It's treed and gorgeous, with lots of people riding bikes and walking everywhere. They have an Urban Outfitters here too. Oh goody. I flap inside, unable to resist such blatant niche marketing. This is a giant shop that is trés cool and trés expensive, full of gadgets and books, accessories, shoes, clothes, and even furniture, which all look like they've been handpicked by your super-coolest friend and priced at a 300 per cent markup. Boulder is kind of the same.

On my way to meet Nick's friend Casey, who has kindly offered me a tour of his town and alma mater, I fall in behind a group of tourists that I'm sure I remember from Bar Harbor. The kid has one finger up his nose drilling intently and another pointing at various things he wants his parents to buy. 'Mom, kite store! Kite store!' Mom is wearing a Boulder T-shirt to match her son's, and Dad, taking up the rear laden with shopping bags, has a preemptive Fourth of July commemorative T. I feel a surge of irrational rage toward these tourists on the same trail as I am. The ones who get off at Canal Street in New York to buy a T-shirt and then leave; the reason that stores selling plaster statuettes, window crystals and general tat will be interchangeable in Boulder, San Francisco, Miami and NYC.

Casey's Best Tour of Boulder begins with a crisp Sierra Nevada pale ale upstairs on the deck at the West End Tavern. The view of the mountains is stunning. I can see how easily people become intoxicated by their presence. We hop in Casey's car and head around the corner to Boulder Creek, which has a nine-mile bicycle trail running beside it. Huge trees line the banks, and people sleep and picnic there, escaping the beating sun. The creek is far from raging, but I'm surprised to find the water to be freezing cold despite the heatwave. This snow-melt seems like a great relief to the scores of people lolling about in inner tubes, splashing in the dappled light, big dogs bounding everywhere.

We spin past Casey's house and I can't help thinking how nice it would be to live there. The street itself is gorgeous, like all of the streets I've seen so far, and the lovely house has an outside hot tub at the foot of the mountains, which the guys are keeping as a 'cool tub' now, due to the searing temperatures. Casey seems almost embarrassed by my enthusiasm and says, 'Okay, this is *nothing*. You should see some of our friends' places, especially the mountain homes. Dude, it's amazing up here.'

I think he's right. Driving straight up the mountainside, the trees are uniform and beautiful, straight and green like Lego trees. Like Acadia National Park, the Rockies have awakened some regrettable instinct in me for outdoorsy behaviour. I suddenly crave hiking boots and trail mix.

Less than five minutes out of town I enjoy an uninterrupted view of stillness, pines, spruce and wilderness. There is no one within sight apart from a family of hummingbirds, with wings beating so fast I think they're insects. I don't understand how they don't dash their little brains out. The air up here is so thin that you suck and suck and nothing seems to happen. I'm trying hard for great lung-fulls of pine scented, Nordic-fresh type air and am coming up with little more than dry nostrils.

Back in town we meet up with Nick and the others at an open-air bar called L'Iguana, where we make our way through icy buckets of Mexican beer. Snowing down from huge trees, sheets of cottonwood seeds are blowing in the breeze. They look like soft little cotton balls, but shine like silk threads when they catch the afternoon sun. It's such dramatic scenery here in Boulder, and so different from home. I really like it, I think, feeling considerably more grateful for my Green Card than I did last night.

At six o'clock it is still terribly hot. The heatwave here is really intense and with the Fourth of July coming, talk turns to the sad fact that all the fireworks are banned as a fire hazard in such dry conditions. Nick's friends are heading to resorts in Vail, Aspen and Tahoe for the holiday and I tell them I'm not sure where I'll be. This is instantly deemed unacceptable and before I know it, I've agreed to attend an Independence Day festival in the ski town of Steamboat Springs. 'It'll be great,' Nick assures me. 'James Brown is playing! It'll be totally American,' he adds with a wink. At this point, all four boys' 'cells' go off and I'm left to inspect the salsa while they all try to sell stuff.

Everyone seems to be buying and selling in the US. Everyone seems to be on the take, and cheerfully so. All my American friends are so entrepreneurial. Even the gentle hippie ones with no money behind them are still incredibly driven and have more than one job. Casey was in IT but is now doing something I don't quite understand involving reconditioning machinery from the former Soviet Union and selling it on to South-East Asia, as well as setting up a time-share scheme in Thailand. Nick has had so many jobs I can't keep track. His latest business venture – a grisly crime-scene-cleaning outfit – has turned him into a local media darling. Casey is right. They work hard, they play hard. I wonder if that's me. I have a sneaking suspicion that it's not.

There are huge houses all over, mansions really, set into the Rocky Mountains. The wealth of this land is quite staggering.

Even on the bus, though, even amongst the poorest quarters, there seems to float the idea that this station in life is achievable for anyone who works for it. The American work ethic is very strong and the desire for material success is intense. Even the tofu-eating Dead Heads at the Red Rocks concert arrived in Saabs and Range Rovers, in Jeeps and Audis. The kids here have cars that most adults can't afford to buy in Oz. There is an entrepreneurial spirit that is encouraged and heavily rewarded in America; a shameless pursuit of fiscal gain. It scares me a bit.

At 25, Nick has just settled on his three-bedroom home in a trendy neighbourhood in downtown Denver and Casey has just bought the brand new Audi that we've been tooling around in. Even the waiters I worked with in Sanibel were homeowners in their twenties and drove new cars. America can make me feel poor and strangely shabby. I never feel that at home in Australia and I'm struggling to come up with reasons why I should now. My thrift-store finds and relaxed attitude towards a career trajectory never felt out of step in Sydney or Melbourne, but they do in the US. I feel my student-lifestyle poverty here. I also feel the need for a nice car and an expensive handbag.

I'm not sure I could settle for the simple life in America. I'm scared I'd work too hard. I'm scared I'd relax too hard as well. The Boy and I and our Aussie friends are happy to drift along a lot more. Until now, I had considered us all to be pretty ambitious, but that seems laughable here. We're practically bums. When people here ask me what I do, I have developed a tactic I like to call lying, and tell them that I'm on a fact-finding mission for the Australian Department of Foreign Affairs and Trade. 'We're thinking of farming kangaroos in Idaho,' I tell them, or else I just announce that I sell ugg boots, which are somehow the hottest cultural export since Mick Dundee fashioned a boomerang from the tail of a limo.

For a special treat, Nick has offered to take me through the Rocky Mountains National Park. I smile and thank him, secretly keen to spend another day sourcing cunning accessories at Urban Outfitters, breaking for artichoke and sundried tomato cous cous and soy-honey-chai. He must sense reluctance because he assures me that, like many things in American life, a trip to the great outdoors need not require us to leave the comfort of his vehicle for any longer than it takes a camera shutter to click open and closed.

It's high summer, the week of a public holiday, and I expect the park, just on the outskirts of town, to be jam-packed with tourists. However, for a long while we are the only car on the wide road to the foot of the mountain and, once past the toll booth, it becomes apparent that there's room for hundreds more of us while still leaving the impression that the park is totally empty. We drive for a while in silence, awed by the space and beauty. Higher and higher up the mountain we climb, through thickets of trees until the trees give way to rolling grass, rocks and groups of silent, mysterious animals. My *Grizzly Adams* tutelage allows me to recognise them as elk. Clouds gather briefly, feeling close enough to touch. Up high on the mountain the air is clear and cool, and we stop the car to wander near the grazing elk.

I feel like I'm starring in the opening shots of *The Sound Of Music*. It's absolutely jaw-dropping. 'This,' I tell Nick, gesturing wildly, 'this is what I want.'

'You want an elk?'

'No!' I shout, although, having never seen an elk before, I have to say I'm now rather taken with them, 'This is the America I want. This, *this*, is really special.'

'Yeah,' he agrees, 'I get the feeling people don't realise how amazing the wilderness is in the US, or how much of it there is. People, like, come to see Vegas or New York or LA,' he shakes his head. 'That's kind of crazy.' I snap off a roll of film while I debate a new career as a US Park Ranger, mentally designing a cute cargo-pocketed uniform and a solar-heated hut, before we hop back in and drive to the top of the mountain. At about 13,000 feet above sea level, Nick snaps out of his Mountain Man moment to discover that we are almost completely out of petrol. Not just gee, there's not much gas left, but the needle is dipping out of the red and trying to detach itself from the dial so as not to go down with a sinking ship.

Pulling in to the visitors' centre at the summit, Nick inquires politely if they sell emergency fuel, or just the really useful things they have on display, like commemorative pens and wildflower hair-bobbles. 'Gosh,' says the salesgirl, as if we've asked for a Klingon interpreter, 'maybe the ranger could help you but he's off shooting something right now. I don't know when he'll be around . . .' A woman behind us says that she has a hose in her car and a full tank. 'You could just suck out some of mine,' she says, tapping her smiling son on the head. 'The Good Lord asks us to help those in need, Ezekiel, remember the Good Samaritan?' Ezekiel nods vigorously and they beam at us. Praise the Lord for useful Christians, I think, wondering for the millionth time why they can't all be more like Ned Flanders and less like Fred Nile.

We all troop back out to the car park, where it is now getting cold. At this altitude the air is so thin that it's very hard to breathe, and I start to feel uncomfortable and claustrophobic despite the incredible space. Nick puts one end of the hose deep into the tank and the other end in his mouth. 'Be careful now,' I say, checking my nails and wondering how big a baby elk is. Nick inhales tentatively, expecting a rush of nasty liquid. Nothing. He tries again a little harder. Twenty minutes later I'm standing above him as he lies on the ground, pounding my fist into my hand, exhorting like a rowing coach, 'Pull, Nicky, *pull*!'

The Christian woman and her son stand together in prayer. 'God bless him,' she says loudly, waving her hands above Nick's head. 'God cover him now, cover him in this task.' Nick, green and wretched, wheezes, 'Uh, I gotta say, I'm, like, really, really high right now and I don't think this is going to work.' It turns out that every vehicle in the large car park is too new to have pre-siphon-proof tanks and we are, as they say here, shit out of luck. Ezekiel gives Nick a bottle of Sprite to wash his dry mouth and Nick gives a rambling thank-you speech, still high as a bug in a pint glass. 'Well,' I tell him, 'looks like you'll have to walk for help and leave me overnight with the elk herd,' hoping he's vulnerable to suggestion in his current state. 'No,' says Nick, wild-eyed and giggling, 'It'll be totally cool. It's downhill now.'

He leaps in the car, still laughing like a madman, sucking deeply on the purloined Sprite. It's taken us two hours to get up here and now Nick throws the car in neutral and we roll faster and faster down 13,000 feet. Elk and chipmunks, trees, birds and icy glacier streams, everything whips past me as we spin around and around down the mountain-side. We pass a tent city named Never Summer Campground, which strikes me as an unusual marketing angle, and in the distance I can see Grand Lake. It is beautiful, that water, and the whole scene is like a dream. Down at the bottom we are back in the good chubby air again and my anxiety disappears as a gas station appears on the horizon. 'Hey!' I say, pointing, 'there's a –'

'Can't talk,' Nick rasps, ashen-faced, 'coming down.'

The night of the third of July, I join my Kansas trio and we set off for Steamboat Springs. I've burnt quite a bit of time in Colorado already – unwilling to spend Independence Day on a bus – and I'm becoming shamefully addicted to being driven around, entertained and generally treated like visiting royalty. Each morning I've woken to the reproachful gaze of my much-abused pillow, still strapped to the tomato-pack where I abandoned it almost a week ago. I know, I think, I know. There are still at least 40 states out there that I haven't seen. But it's also been a very long time since I've had a girlfriend to talk to, and I can't discount that either. Now, on our way up the mountains to the little ski resort village, I practically devour Sarah's every word, pathetically grateful to natter about boys and summer skirts and the consistency of my new lip gloss. My Greyhound skank has dried and peeled off me like a scab.

The holiday is already in full swing, with an 'All-American Weekend' announced on most radio stations, providing us with a constant soundtrack of Creedence and Cougar, until I'm convinced we all live down on a bayou with Jack and Diane. We burn along through the night, singing and laughing through Springsteen anthems, loving the holiday before it's even begun.

At 2 am, the four of us crash out in a big room at the Nordic Lodge motel, but I can't sleep. I've had an email from the Boy, just a brief hello, but it feels like a missive from another world and another time. I've been in a bubble for all those months on Sanibel and now I feel very disconnected from my former life across the sea. It's only been less than a week in Colorado, but there have already been enough shared adventures, drunken escapades, bar-room bullshitting and private wanderings that I've begun to feel at home. I even have a little routine of sorts. There's also the thrill of making new friends and the comfort of seeing old friends, the easy job offers and the share-house rooms waiting for me if I want them.

This is a nice place, I think, this is good fun with good people. It's all very new and exciting, and I feel like I could easily take this place and make it mine for a while. Why go home? Australia isn't going anywhere. Why go home? This is a new chance, a new adventure. This is my prize. Why go home? I'm turning it over and over until I feel sick with it, auditing my life, my loves, and my dreams for the future.

I don't remember sleeping but I wake up early to sounds of sirens mustering for the small town parade. I head out with my little camera. It seems that every emergency vehicle in Steamboat Springs has been assembled, with their lights flashing round and round in the morning sun. As if on command, the handful of large horses lined up behind them begin to spray the bitumen with spectacular lashings of pee, causing the curious addition of a group dressed as cardboard Lego men to stumble awkwardly into each other as they try to keep clear. The kids go wild with laughter, hurling lollies and grubby tissues at the hapless Lego men. There are a few people in uniform and some baton twirling, but after sucking diesel for half an hour with no forward motion from the parade, I allow myself a big yawn of fresh mountain air and retreat.

Since the events of 9/11, Independence Day is considered a likely time for terrorist activity. When I return to the room, we click on the TV, expecting to see some kind of bad news. A newscaster is rehashing last year's Fourth of July airport shooting at the El Al counter at Los Angeles Airport. The Arab gunman responsible, announces the solemn-faced reporter, was a resident of the US through the little-known immigration practice of entirely random selection via the Green Card lottery program. Three faces turn to me with wide-open eyes, and I flick the channel.

After a fortifying snack on the picturesque main street, we join the jubilant townsfolk and tourists heading towards the holiday concert. I'm surprised to find that the big drawcard of the day isn't the venerable James Brown, but a band called The String Cheese Incident, which seems to have attracted the same wild crowd as Widespread Panic. In a small arena surrounded by the towering peaks of summer-empty ski runs, I manage to get close enough to Mr Brown to photograph his breakfast. Dancing and wailing like a man much, much younger than his 70-plus years, he belts out 'I Feel Good' and 'Papa's Got a Brand New Bag', and I'm overwhelmed to be a metre away, listening to him sing the songs I've heard throughout my lifetime. It suddenly strikes me that this is American music and a particularly American celebration, but just when I start grinning at how much I love it and how comfortable I feel, a chant starts up.

It's the Fourth of July, the country is at war, and a great deal of beer has been chugged in summer heat. U . . . S . . . Aaaaa, U . . . S . . . Aaaaaaa. The sound is distinctly masculine and threatening. It's a war cry, national pride like a banner waving. I feel my Green Card melt away inside my pocket where I'm required to carry it at all times that I'm wearing clothes. It hits me like a plank – the certainty that I will never be a part of this nation enough to join that chanting. I'm already starting to realise that I can't ever be – don't ever want to be – an American. I might want to be a New Yorker, or a Savannian, perhaps a New Orleanian, or even a very occasional Sanibel-Islander, but I never want to stop being Australian, or a Sydney girl. Is that possible or is that like polygamy?

A dust cloud rises like smoke from the parched brown earth under our feet and swirls around us with the music and laughter. As the last chords echo to the base of the mountains, the drought breaks, pelting the scattering crowd with fat droplets of water and turning the dust to mud. We run back to everyone's huge rented ski-chalets and condos to party, ruining at least six kilometres of white shag-pile carpet over the course of the night.

All the people I meet here are moneyed, privileged and universally beautiful. This is the wealth of Middle America – the

Infidels, the Western devils. Playboys with performance cars, party-girls with silicone breasts. It's a blast, too, I can't lie. Parties and booze and fun and games. There is nothing casual about these good times. There is an unwritten rule here that if it's going to be done at all it should be done *big*. Huge. Bring your video camera. Rent a Hummer. Hire an attorney for the morning after.

This whole week amongst it all has made me feel very young and lucky and free. It's intoxicating. People talk deals and dreams and life plans, and there is the overwhelming sense that anything, *anything* is possible. No one is afraid to stand out; in fact, it's the goal here. It's not Australian at all in that way – the flash cars, flash clothes, the instant smiles and the boundless energy. I want to hate it but I can't. I'd snicker and sneer but I'm having too much fun. Watching this lifestyle on screen is one thing, being caught up in it is quite another. It's not obnoxious so much as infectious. These young Americans are living as large as they can, as fast as they can, with no apology. In a way, I'm beginning to respect that. Life is short. Maybe being so coolly Aussie and casual about it is a bit of a waste.

The next morning we drive back through the stunning Colorado scenery, as more drought-breaking clouds gather at last. We stop at a gas station in a tiny place called Granby, where a Greyhound bus has also pulled in. The usual suspects are hanging around the toilet, smoking like it's their last for life. Tattered cowboy hats, shirtless, smelly, dejected. I keep close to Nick's shiny black SUV, fearing I'll get sucked in through the door. I can't escape, though. These are my people now. Very soon that will be me by the truck-stop toilets. Their smell will be my own.

Having woken up with the last of my Colorado hangovers, I force Nick to drive to Denny's so I can shout us the cure. Just the thought of Denny's makes me smile. It's not great food. In fact, it's often pretty crap, but in my book, a restaurant can get away with almost anything if they are willing to serve breakfast 24 hours a day. 'What?' the waitress says. 'You don't all got 24-hour breakfast in Australia?'

'No,' Nick confirms, shaking his head, 'barbarians . . .'

There are a couple of similar chains to Denny's in America: the fancier IHOP (the International House of Pancakes – some kind of governing body which no doubt includes the renowned Maple Syrup Institute and breakfast aid agency Toast Sans Frontières) and the simply inedible Waffle House, both of which have outlets scattered far and wide, serving breakfast till Armageddon. There can be no fault found with this idea whatsoever, and it thrills me now to be a legal resident of a nation with 24-hour breakfast chains. I believe that cultural exchange at its most fulsome would be the opening of such establishments on Australian soil, and the immediate cessation by Americans of pouring maple syrup over their bacon and toast (barbarians).

After breakfast, we stop at the grocery store to do Nick's household shopping and buy my Greyhound supplies. The reality starts to dawn as my water and corn cakes hit the trolley and I begin psyching myself up to leave luxury and get back on the road again. Even being in a car for a week has been an unexpected pleasure and I'm starting to understand that this cushy detour was a bit stupid. I've gone soft now. I'll have to start all over like a new recruit. Snap out of it, man! *Find the edge*! But instead I'm just chewing on my bottom lip and hyperventilating through my nose. I hate that bus, I think, passionate fucking hatred. I remember that I still have a good 150 hours of bus travel left (in go two packets of aspirin and Tylenol Night Caps) and I'm only halfway there (four Snickers, six packets of Reese's peanut butter cups). Oh, God – I forgot about Texas (*National Enquirer*, box of Oreos and some Mitchum oilrig-grade deodorant).

Nick's weekly groceries consist of pints of Gatorade, boxes of microwaveable lumps of gross called Lean Pockets and a *Maxim* magazine. Nick is a grown man. This is shameful behaviour, but before I berate him, I have to concede that there is a different cultural emphasis here on cooking, i.e. none. The household oven is remembered faintly as that archaic piece of equipment capable of making Pillsbury instant cookie dough rise and last night's pizza crisp again. Go into most houses in America and ask the inhabitants to light a moderate oven in under ten minutes for a hundred bucks. Go on. Your money is perfectly safe.

Back at the Denver Greyhound Terminal, I feel like it's been a month or more since I woke up from Nebraska. I wonder vaguely if my undies are still here somewhere. Nick looks around at the relatively normal collection of passengers and drivers, his lip curling up over shiny white teeth. 'Okay . . .' he says, 'you really going to do this?' I surprise myself by feeling defensive. 'Hey, it's not that bad,' I tell him. 'It's pretty fun if you . . . well, some of the newer buses even have toilets that close off! And this one time? I slept for, like, four hours!' He smiles politely at my boasting and says goodbye, leaving me in line next to a man with a live chicken asleep on his hat.

As soon as Nick drives off, I'm not in Denver anymore. I'm in Greyhoundland, and back in the swing. Far from feeling bratty and miserable, I'm pleased to discover that I'm actually excited to be off on my own again, master of my own destiny and destinations. It's strangely comforting to saddle up with the big tomato-pack, and my ugly pillow even gets a special smile and a little squeeze. I've burnt eight days in Colorado and I'm boggled by how much of my prize is left out there undiscovered. 'All right, Pillow,' I say, 'off we go! Next stop, Big Sky Country.' From the hat in front, the chicken agrees.

Chapter 13

Big Sky Country

Our bus thunders away confidently, starting another little line on my map of America, this time headed north. After Minnesota, way up on the Canadian border, I moved steadily down and across to the middle of the continent and now I'm making the other arm of the letter V on the way back up to the border again, this time in Montana. Although I can't remember why I'm going to Montana, I do know we have to pass through Wyoming to get there. Unfortunately, that doesn't help much either. These are two states I have absolutely no preconceptions of. Big Sky Country is what I've been told, but what that means, I'm not too sure. Big Sky as in Dead Flat? Lots of sky because . . . not much ground? Or is Big Sky some kind of Native American thing, I wonder, Big Sky and his ancestral lands perhaps? How can the sky be any bigger there anyway? Is it possible that just over state lines you get an increase in horizon? Do Coloradoans ever complain, 'Oh sure, *Wyoming*, those guys get all that extra sky,' or is it just some snappy state tourism motto kind of thing, like the way Missouri is officially the Show Me State and Ohio the even more incomprehensible Sooner State.

This bus is big, and the driver is friendly, apologising when he tells me that my Greyhound ticket is a problem because the Big Sky route is taken by the Powder River Line. At each stop, I will need to line up with the rest of the herd, present my Ameripass, get a re-printed Powder River ticket and come back to line up at the bus. When I venture that this is quite an annoyance, the driver agrees. 'I've been dealing with this same problem for nine years now,' he says. 'They thought we would fold back in June of '94 and tickets have been a problem ever since.' The ticket hassle seems a small price to pay for the fact that I have two whole states – big states too – with the pleasure of non-Greyhound buses. I recline my seat a full inch and a half and sigh contentedly. As the miniature TV hanging above the aisle zaps to life, I throw my hands up in ecstasy at my further good fortune. But my hopes of viewing pleasure are quickly dashed.

Tonight's feature presentation turns out, rather incongruously, to be a dragging episode of *The Man From Snowy River*, an ancient Australian TV show that would now have a hard time screening in a tele-shopping timeslot at home. This episode, 'The Race', features a young Guy Pearce, as well as a lot of actors with stubble saying 'streuth!' while they kick around in Blundstones and ride horses in and out of herds of sheep. The yawn factor is high. It seems to be a real hit with the enraptured bus though, particularly when the brash American cowboy arrives to make some kind of impudent challenge involving the usual – horses, money, women and national pride. I spend the next two hours rumbling through the Rocky Mountains looking at the Victorian bush.

At the first stop, a big man gets on with two children aged about nine and 12. It becomes immediately apparent that he's a few Smarties short of a lollybag and I wonder how he came to be left in charge of the kids. He smiles and waves at the driver, telling the bus in a booming great voice that he's picking up a car in Fargo. 'My brother got me a car! But we gotta go and get it first! Then we can drive it back! So I won't be seeing any of you on the way back! Cause we'll be driving! In our car! That my brother got us!' I expect the kids to be mortified, but they're just grinning as they lead him to their seats. 'C'mon, Dad!' the elder says, 'gotta be quiet now because it's night-time.' 'Oh sure,' says the dad, nodding. 'Sorry!' he says, waving at all of us on the bus. The little family chat quietly amongst themselves for an hour or so and it becomes obvious that the kids love their simple-minded father to bits. The rest of us keep smiling at each other, jerking our heads towards the contented trio.

At Cheyenne, the bus stop is giant and odd, sparingly constructed like a huge demountable trailer plonked out of the sky into the surrounding nothing. Outside, the landscape is black and still, the air fresh and silent. Under the harsh fluorescence inside, there seems to be at least a hundred people, all so strangely formed and attired that together we look like some kind of extra-terrestrial migration plan. Back on the bus, it becomes apparent that we've picked up a few rowdy passengers, and the driver is snippy as he announces, 'No alcohol once we leave Cheyenne.' There are a few throaty chuckles. 'Hey now, I mean it!' the driver says. 'There ain't nothing out there but cay-oats, prairie dogs and their critter friends, and they've all got little lunch pails. I got no qualms about puttin' you off to join 'em if there's booze on mah bus.' Things quieten down then and I use my new pen to scratch the usual pathetic ramblings on a postcard home. I found this pen inside the station by the phones. It's purple and says 'West Rock, Cheyenne'. My last pen was from the bakery selling blueberry treats in the cool Bar Harbor morning. I wonder where I'll be when this one runs dry.

A few hours later we tumble from the bus, entering the Gillette bus depot at the same time as the first few rays of sunlight. I'm so tired I can barely see straight and I'm sure I would cry if I could find the energy required. With some dry blinking and squinting, I can see that this terminal is by far the weirdest I have seen so far, but given my current needs, the best. Resembling some kind of aircraft hanger, the Gillette terminal is huge and largely empty, with what look exactly like ripped-out car seats lined up in rows. Like the backseat of a car stretching for the length of an Olympic pool, these comfy oddities are arranged in long lines so that you can lie out fully and sleep. Pressing my face right against the musty fabric where hundreds of indigents have parked their filthy arses before, I'm so grateful I think I really will cry. All the other stations have had the requisite plastic bucket seats or metal benches with thigh-high railings to prevent any kind of sleep except upright and twisted. My fellow passengers are all muttering appreciatively and stretching out for naps. The big simple guy is still with us, his thick hair resting just under my shoes as we snooze. His kids wake him when it's time for their next leg and they have to gently remind Dad of their purpose. I wish someone would remind me of mine, I think, calculating how many more bus-sleeps there will be until home.

Lying down head-to-toe in long lines like an army barracks, I am treated to an hour and a half of dreamless, dribbling peace before piling onto another Powder River bus; an older one this time, a dented, rattling hulk. Engine running, the bus driver takes some time to check his calibrations. He stalls out six times in good humour, muttering 'Jezzum Betsy!' before figuring it out at last. Two women and a man watch him from the terminal door, smiling and waving encouragingly. One woman motions for us to stop. She goes back inside and then comes running out to the bus. 'That's Jenny-Sue,' he tells us. 'She must need ta tell me something.'

'Yew forget your phone!' she says, as she reaches the door, handing him the brick-sized gadget and a bottle of water. 'Good luck now! God Bless!' As the bus pulls away, we all wave back at Jenny-Sue and she blows the bus a kiss. Once we're on the freeway, our driver figures out the mike. He taps a few times and says, 'Well, we left Gillette only about . . . eight minutes late, which I've been finding out in this business is pretty darn good! Buffalo and Sheridan, Wyoming, will be your next stops. Apart from that, not a whole lot I can tell you.' He turns it off and we descend into silence.

The countryside spreads out warm and flat around me, before turning into gently rolling hills. As time goes by, these hills begin to grow, turning into a wide sea of canyons with small green oases wherever water collects between them. I put my contact lenses in again and my mouth hangs open. 'Ohh . . . I see,' I say to no one in particular, 'Big Sky.' The sky is suddenly huge. Just like that. Two thirds of my world is now a mammoth stretch of atmosphere.

To amuse myself on the long straight roads, I begin a version of I Spy that is only possible in American traffic. This is where one or multiple players watch the roads waiting for any car that appears to be over five years old. It's a slow game, but it never fails to leave me gobsmacked. There are only two types of car on American roads: new and big. It is so rare to spot a small car like the humble Australian city hatchback that they are worth triple points. This excludes the very occasional new Beetle or Mini Cooper, even though they look so comical on the roads here, small enough to be side-cars on one of the many Harleys that roar past (piloted by owners whose hair whips out freely behind them in a country without helmet laws). Two-person sports cars don't count either, there are plenty of those.

America has a cultural love affair with SUVs (Sports Utility Vehicles) that runs deep enough to be accused of influencing domestic and foreign policy. Despite recent world events, petrol is still cheaper here than anywhere else in the world. At home in Australia, Dad's Jeep Cherokee would be a big car, a large 'four-wheel drive', as we call them. Here, thundering down the freeway in his more-than-substantial vehicle, I actually worry the 'big' cars won't see him sometimes. Big cars like the Navigators, the Humvees and the trucks (utes, actually, utes on bull steroids) hauling one or two humans encased in tonnes of steel the length and height of a road train. There are Winnebagos galore, too. There are lots of war-time stickers and flags on all these vehicles, evidence the nation is feeling the collective pain of September 11, Afganistan and the new war in Iraq. Most read 'Proud to be an American' or 'USA all the way', with a few of the more hardline 'Get US out of the United Nations!' variety. Some stickers are shaped like yellow ribbons, engraved with the patriotic directive 'Support Our Troops!', others with the small, hopeful 'Keep Daddy Safe'. There are newspaper cutouts of flags taped to rear windows, as well as cloth and plastic flags, now faded and ripped from their months of sun and speed. There are flags or coloured ribbons on at least every second car, and some have two or more full-sized Old Glories waving madly.

My Petrochemical Excess version of I Spy comes to a halt as we pull off the freeway, into a service station in Buffalo, which seems to be a cowboy town. 'Mountain Man Meats' a sign proclaims across the street, 'custom slaughter and game processing'. It must get cold here too. There's a clothing store with little but what looks like wearable bedding in the windows, and a sign saying, 'Snowmobilers! We fix your rides here!' We drive out of this tiny town past the 'Bare Bottom Laundry – Ma's a washin' and we're a waitin!' and a grog shop called 'Wa-HOO Likkers!' I stare out at the road for a long time, blinking in and out of consciousness.

I wake up on the outskirts of Billings, Montana, to find the entire bus asleep. There are kids stretched out on floors and under seats, and even people lying bowed across aisles. This is the ultimate Greyhound offence, but there's more than one seat for everyone on this old bus and the driver doesn't seem to care. How civilised. We must have been enjoying this giant, contorted slumber party in the sun for quite some time now, because trees suddenly populate the hills as if they have sprouted while I slept, as if they were always there just under the crust, hiding. Billings is small. All these places are small. I consult my guidebook for a benchmark and learn that Wyoming, the Cowboy State, has the smallest population of all fifty states. Only 500,000 people live in the 100,000 square miles of rugged and beautiful land we just passed through.

Montana is enormous. It's the fourth-largest state and yet this low-key township of Billings is the largest city it has to offer. I look out the window at Scary Larry's Pawn and Used Goods, and the Muzzle Loader Gaming and Saloon. Ninety thousand people are supposed to be here somewhere, but I can't see any-one just yet.

The Billings station is an attractive old Art Deco building, with Greyhound spelled out in bold letters. Inside it is small and clean, with very little going on. I try for a second lunch of instant noodles, and Billings provides. Ooh, chicken and vegetable. I decide I like Montana already. The Pearl River bus gives way to a Rimrock Stages coach, and I notice there are only a few of us left from Cheyenne and we don't gain any extras in Billings. It is such a change from the crowded insanity of the other bus trips so far. The people on the bus through these states have been different too. Nicer. Cleaner. Regular folk. I say as much to the driver as we leave the terminal. According to him, bus travel is pretty much the only way to get around Montana if you are temporarily without a car. Despite its massive size, the small population means there are no flights into this state other than through tiny regional airlines or via charter to the university town of Missoula, which accounts for buses being regarded as a thoroughly acceptable mode of transport.

Just as I'm beginning to revel in the comfort afforded by the absence of Greyhound bus seats and passengers, it becomes apparent that it is stupendously hot in here. After another half an hour of zooming along the open road, the driver announces an unscheduled stop. 'Folks, as you may have noticed, we've got no AC,' he says, 'and I don't know about you, but I'm dyin' in here. I'm gonna try an' fix it. Won't be long.' Spilling off the bus, covered in sweat, we kick around a tiny service station, buying the usual gum and cold drinks, too overcome with heat to concentrate on newspapers or magazines. As the time drags on, we take our purchases on little walks around the bus, pausing to kick a tyre or pull at a loose bit of trimming.

The gas station – like all the others we've passed so far in Montana – is also a casino. In fact, there are about six more casinos across the expressway, and most are attached to a second business. There's one next to the Road Kill Café ('Friendly family dining!') and another joined to a tannery. There must be lax gaming laws here. There must be a lot of the other kind of gaming too, because tanneries and fly-fishing stores with seductive names like The Sweet Cast are also plentiful. Strangely, though, the miles of nothing have been dotted with tiny espresso stands everywhere – wooden huts as big as tollbooths advertising a sophisticated array of beverages. On the horizon is yet another small hut with a carefully hand-painted sign, offering fine espresso, gelato-smoothies and Italian sodas. I wonder how the hell rural Montana got so hip when the only people I see for miles are the kind of rugged men who look like they'd hit you for even suggesting they'd drink that fancy European shit. Do cowboys really pull off the road for a Chinnoto instead of a Big Mac and a brewski?

Eventually the driver rounds us up and delivers the bad news. 'Well, I don't think it can be fixed, folks,' he says, wiping his big hands free of grease. 'It's gonna get hotter than Horatio, hell 'n' horsenuts in there, and I'm sorry 'bout that. I don't know what else we can do.' We hang around together for a few minutes like pallbearers, squinting at the defective machine with heavy hearts, before filing back on board.

The interior of the bus is largely made up of red and orange velour and plush carpeting, with metal trim around the windows that has heated up like a skillet in the sun. Without any air-flow, it soon becomes sickeningly claustrophobic. Everyone moves to one side of the bus, away from the sun, which solves one problem and magnifies the other. 'Driver,' croaks an older woman, 'it's not just tha heat, I don't seem to have enough air. I can't breathe in here.' The driver opens the front doors and we drive along with the rushing noise of our own progress but hardly any circulation. It is intolerable. We begin to strip off as much as we can and fan ourselves with anything on hand. The smell of our unwashed bodies is heavy in the stagnant air. One by one, we begin to drift, entering a kind of hibernation caused by the slow combustion of our brains in the heat. When the driver pulls off the road again, most of us are still cooked and don't respond.

'Whass happen'?' I ask, pushing a little warm air past my larynx. 'I have an idea,' the driver says, making the word sound like 'eye-day'. Standing on one of the front seats, he pushes open the emergency flap on top of the bus. I can feel the air already, and join the others in making a kind of keening noise in response. We start off again and there's a measure of relief offered by the two-inch gap, even though the air is hot and dry. Climbing back to 85 miles an hour, the wind suddenly picks up. Within moments, it lifts up the emergency door and rips it clean from the bus, with what seems as much effort as flicking a bottle top out the window. The noise and magnitude of this event are not dissimilar to what you might expect if you tore the back off a family sedan and sent it hurtling down the freeway behind you.

The almighty bang is a great shock, stirring us from our sweltering torpor like a slap. Instantly we are all sitting up and looking around at each other, reliving our moment of terror excitedly and speculating on our fate and that of the missing flap. We are completely awake and united for the first time in

21 hours. The driver yells, 'Hold on!' and we squeal off the road, jumping out with hands shading our eyes, standing on tiptoe and scanning the empty road behind us. There is nothing to be seen. 'Dang,' offers the driver.

We stop for about 15 minutes to un-bend the twisted hinges and wake ourselves up. The drama of the moment has given way to great big belly laughs, and we lean against our hellish stink tank, trading strangers' conversation.

'Where ya goin'?' we ask each other. 'Sure was hot in there, huh?'

'We almost at Missoula?'

'Missoula! Ha! Go back ta sleep, yer dreamin'!'

Back on the road again the air streams in through our new convertible coach and I start to appreciate the scenery. Through the roof, the smell of baking green grass is sweet and warm, strangely similar to fresh Anzac (oatmeal) biscuits (cookies). Some of the large silvery trees remind me of the eucalypts at home, but the rest are pure mountain town. Ranches dot the green hills and plains. The Mission Ranch W, the Lazy J, Circle K Ranch, Special K Ranch, the Circle R Dude Ranch. I remember the movie *City Slickers*, a recycled prime-time favourite, and realise it must have been shot out on the cattle ranches here. This is definitely how I imagined cowboy country. Out the window, Montana stretches huge and majestic. This state combines the massive green fields of Minnesota, the mountains of Colorado and the wide pure skies of my own beloved Australian countryside. Stunning. We pass massive fast-moving lakes and silver, ribbon-like streams. Occasionally the air fills with cottonwood buds like paper snow, floating like laughter against the blue sky. Colorado struck me with its beauty too, but now it seems a grim and stifling landscape compared with Montana; hemmed in jealously by its mountain ranges. In Montana, space just rolls, luxuriantly.

I can picture myself here immediately. Under the stars, cooking up chilli in an old black pan over a crackling fire. Fishing in quiet streams, going to bed with the sun, waking to silence. It strikes me as certainty that I could get a tiny shack out here and just *be* for a while. The countryside fills me with an unusual feeling, a sensation of fullness. This is enough, I think, the rich land under the enormous sky. Of course, I could always run off and fulfil this same agrarian fantasy in Australia, but the Aussie bush is somehow less exotic to me. Familiarity does breed contempt. I'm sure a native Montanan would find it hilarious that I could look out onto these gentle hillsides and bright forests with more wonder than I might give to the eerie fantasia of towering eucalypts and precious marsupials at home, but the novelty is seductive. Just like my bright-eyed forays into rural Australia, I find myself wondering whether these feelings of completion would wear off and I'd eventually want a public library and a good Thai restaurant.

This is awesome country, though. Blowable dandelions are as big as fists here. Red barns and houses are nestled Heidi-style amongst peaks and valleys, which are covered in purple and gold, green and white. I understand the line about 'amber waves of grain' in 'America the Beautiful' (one of their many anthem-like songs) – it does crash and roll like waves. 'O beautiful for spacious skies,' I mouth to myself, 'for amber waves of grain, for purple mountain majesties . . .' Yep, I think, got it. This scenery is intoxicating like no other state yet. It feels like nothing bad could come from being out here; it's a pure poetry of space.

Who would have thought it? That America could be this impossibly beautiful? How did we miss it? The poet Walt Whitman's America is here too, I think, I must have found the real America at last. There aren't many American *people* here, but maybe this is what they think of when they talk about their country. Part of the popular imagination, like the Australian outback is for a city girl like me. So far, the Rocky Mountain regions are what I most wish I could share with the Boy and my family, but it's such a long way to come, and such a useless destination for Australians with the dollar the way it is now. It isn't a holiday spot as much as a romantic lifestyle dream.

The road passes a little ranch-style house with majestic views and a tiny stream running through it. There are no neighbours visible for miles. A small hand-painted sign on the log fence reads 'God Bless America'. Usually, this kind of appeal to divine favouritism really pisses me off. Looking at the view though, I kind of get the sentiment. They love their land, these wacky, God-fearing Americans. They love this country; they love their home. And how can they not? It is exceptionally gorgeous. It's just that it comes across as a challenge, as jingoism, instead of the small prayer of thanks that I can now see it might really be. Many media and political personalities, including the President and even former New York City mayor Rudy Giuliani, have recently called America 'the best nation on Earth' and 'the best country in the world' in televised speeches explaining why it is important to go to war on Trr. Two words, I think: shut up. You're not helping my cause, guys. Because so far, I have discovered this about my prize: America is without a doubt one of the most physically beautiful nations on earth. It has a large, diverse and interesting population, environmental and material wealth galore, a rich and multi-faceted culture despite its McHollywood image problem, a strong democracy, endless opportunities in countless areas and what are possibly the best *donuts* in the world, I'll give them that. But calling this the best nation, the best country? Sorry, boys, that's too suspiciously Taliban and Saddam-y for me. Y'know, all that we're-the-best, blow-up-the-rest business? Best, best, best? Best country, best religion? Sound familiar?

Besides which, it's really a bit like standing up and saying, 'I'm the best kid in the whole school.' Not only are you denying all the other kiddies their own special worth, you are just *so* cruising for a bloody nose. Who wants to be friends with someone so busy declaring that they're better? Clearly not a large chunk of an embittered world. But it's a strange situation when the countries burning the American flag with the same regularity as taking out the rubbish are the very same countries on Guilia's decade-long waiting list to come and make lives here. It really is like school, I think. Everyone hates that glowing, popular kid, the kid whose one-eyed parents say, 'Don't worry, honey, everyone's just jealous,' that kid who is so caught up in themselves they can't consider that anyone else might have an opinion worth a damn. But people also want the easy life of that golden child, to stand in the sun and have it all land at their feet.

Hate it, want it. I read a newspaper article about this dichotomy once, entitled 'Yankee Go Home! Take Me With You.' I think I can see what they were getting at.

The wide-open beauty of Montana seems a long way from all that nonsense. All the global strife and posturing, bombs and blood and rhetoric. I think genuine peace could be found out here, something simple and whole. Driving through all this natural splendour makes me exultant. It's not about the fact that it's America or American; it has nothing much to do with the Green Card either. It's the unravelling, the exploring outward of places on earth I hardly dared conceive of, never quite imagining the size and majesty of the planet we live on. I do feel finally as if I have won something wonderful. My prize has brought me this far at least, to see this place with my own eyes. That would be something special in anyone's life, but the right to step off this bus right now, to get lost in this place for a few months or years, is spectacular.

After nothing for miles, the town of Livingston gets me very excited. Under the mountains in the aptly named Paradise Valley, the tiny KPRK radio station building sets the tone for the town, which looks like it's remained safe and cozy in 1938. The whole place is in a delightful time warp. Near an old railroad, odd machines of industry are collected together like a twentieth-century trading post. By a dusty general ranch-supplies building, painted signs advertise upcoming rodeos and a dance at the main hotel. Everything has a name. Olsen's dry-cleaning, Pete's Place, Ricci's Thriftway Food Store, Chathams-Thomas and Son, Dan Bailey's Fly Shop, Bob's Outdoor. We pull into the small bus stop, which has a faded poster in its window depicting a Greyhound bus, curled in at the corners. The bus stands proudly under a sign proclaiming it to be 'America's Dream Machine'. No one gets on or off, but we sit for a while as the driver makes another attempt at the air conditioning.

Outside, I spy the Whiskey Creek Saloon near an antique cinema, and it could be 60 years ago; downing a few shots of likker and heading over to watch John Wayne kick up some black and white dust. There's an eerie old hotel too. I briefly consider hoping off right here and now. I could spend the night and explore, play Frontier Land and drink at the convivial tavern promising to have been Calamity Jane's favourite watering hole. Something about its antiquity is almost intimidating, though, and I'm suddenly certain I would stand out in a most uncomfortable way.

And so, I am stupid. Rather than go with my gut and hop off in Livingston, I hang on for Bozeman, where there is the guidebook-promise of a hostel in this college town. A few hours later I arrive in the middle of bland suburbia, with the charmless university looming stark and incongruous in the background. It takes me ten minutes to pull my crap together and set off down the main street in the heat. Trucks blare past, gas stations appear, distant and unpretty on the wide horizon, and I feel very low. Twenty-four hours on a bus to spend a night here. Great, I think, you dickhead, Darmody. Nothing will do having glimpsed the quirky glory that was Livingston.

All this sudden concrete feels way out of step with the rambling ranches and nature I have been so enamoured of in the rest of Montana. I turn to see my stinky hot bus rolling out of the lonely station behind me. When it finally catches up, I impulsively stick out my thumb. Well, I try to, but it gets stuck in my tomato-pack straps and so I end up flagging the bus down with a vigorously bobbing head and some fancy footwork. There is a low moan of brakes and a short hiss as the door opens. 'Changed m'mind,' I say to the driver. He nods. 'Where ya headed now?' he says. I lean around to check the destination card at the front of the bus. 'Missoula?' I read. 'Okay,' he says, 'jump back in.' Inside the six remaining passengers smile, pleased to see me back. We've come a long way together, after all.

Within 20 minutes I have ascertained, with the help of my two guidebooks, that there are no more hostels until the western seaboard. I consult the map. This is not good news. Running into horrific traffic because of an overturned cattle truck, the driver takes us on an inspired shortcut that works fine until we end up on a single-lane road, stuck behind a grader for over an hour. We crawl along. I'm starving and my water has run out too. I think about this time yesterday – fresh and clean in a good restaurant with Nick, as we discussed our youth and general fabulousness over a Negro Modello beer. I suck. Reading over and over again the short paragraphs my guidebooks have apportioned Montana, Butte begins to sound promising. It is described as an old Wild West mining town in the midst of an economic downturn. Translation: cheap, close, possible photo ops with gnarled locals and quaint signage.

When we stop in Logan, I call the Capri, which looks to be the cheapest of the scant motels in Butte, Montana. The man who answers is both ancient and insane.

'Yes,' I say, 'hello! I was wondering what your rates are for a single, please.'

'Our WHAT?'

'Your prices, sir, for a single room.'

'At the CAPRI?'

'Yes, please.'

'Y'mean at the *Capri*?'

'No, sir, on the stoop outside it. Yes. Of course. Rooms at the Capri. How much?'

'How many?'

'One.'

'Well . . .' he thinks about it. 'Okay.'

'So, how much will that be? For the room?'

'WHAT?'

'The price, sir, the cost of the room. What money will I have to give to you in exchange for the room, sir?'

'No.'

'No?'

'Yes.'

'Yes?'

'CAPRI?'

Hmmm.

I'm running out of time now. I'm back on the bus and somehow heading up even closer to Canada when I need to be going down towards Eugene, Oregon, where my old friend Erin will soon receive a smelly visitor. I look at the map again for ages with no real idea of what I'm seeing. I guess I could go to Seattle. I'm certainly high enough up on the continent. I hadn't considered it before, though, and I wonder what's there.

'What do we know about Seattle?' I ask myself, because everyone else is asleep again. I come up with cold, some kind of water/ocean, Starbucks, anti-globalisation protesters, the Space Needle, grunge bands, *Reality Bites* and *Sleepless in* the city of that same name. It's happening again. The bus exhaustion that leaves me without the energy or inclination to do anything at all. A Motion Stoner, that's what I've become. We drive on and on. The driver shows no sign of slowing, but I have no plans to get off anymore. We spend hours on a straight road past mountains and through fields of grass so large and undulating our bus could be a ship on the high seas. This is just one state. One out of 50.

A place called Townsend is just that. Bleak and remote, it looks like an eerie film set. The bar on the corner is called the Corner Bar. The Seventh Day Adventist Church is called the Seventh Church. The video store is called Video. The streets are wide and bare. There is no graffiti, no wandering dogs, no life. A tiny kid doing lazy circles on his bike rides up to the bus to check out the action, regarding us with a slack-jawed fascination. We hop off for a quick stretch, perusing the limited noticeboard at the Conoco gas station. There will be a quilt show here in a month and then nothing until Christmas. I get back on the bus and as we ride away, I see another perfect little espresso stand, beautifully painted with sunbeams and steaming hot coffee cups. The line is six deep.

Big Sky gets even bigger outside Helena. Now it looks like our bus is driving through one of those novelty shake 'n' snow liquid domes. All of us are staring out the windows into the sky, our upturned faces gazing heavenwards like novice Jesuits. There is something very peaceful and reassuring about our place in this world. Our passage is no longer fretful. We are reduced to bugs and our restless, skittering lives seem comical out here.

In Helena, we stop at the local Town Pump gas station, which is also doubling as a casino. 'We're still pretty late from that grader,' says the driver, 'so back on board in a few minutes, okay?' I rush in to buy a bag of Chex Mix, which is a salty version of a popular breakfast cereal, with mini-pretzels thrown in, and the stupendously bored crowd in the bus station perk up at my interruption.

'Look, honey, quick!' says a woman to her bored toddler. 'Come and watch the lady put the money in the machine! She might let you press the buttons.' She smiles hopefully at me and I freeze, quarters in hand. The child in question is approximately 2.7 kilometres away from the chip machine and is slowly making his way out of a dribble coma to move toward me on legs as short as my forearms. I estimate I have about 12 seconds to get my snack before the only bus in Montana tears off down the highway without me. I pause, trapped. The child moves four tenths of an inch. The crowd coos encouragement. The bus rumbles to life. 'I'm sorry!' I yell, as I throw in my silver, hit E12, grab my Chex and go. 'I'm sorry!' Behind me the kid starts to wail. Safe on the bus, I rip open the pack, and the driver begins to reverse. 'Sir?' comes a voice from the back. 'Can I use the facilities real quick?' 'Well, sure!' says the driver, and stops, getting out the paper while the woman wanders off for the loo. I eat my Chex under the weight of a bus stop full of accusing eyes.

Further down the freeway, the town of Drummond offers little apart from a used-cow lot and I start to pin my hopes on Missoula as the sun goes down. By the time Missoula arrives on the horizon, I'm ready for a night in a motel and an extremely long shower, but a brief exploration reveals that there's nothing much to get to on foot in the so-called town centre. The folks at the Greyhound stop are slower than justice and helpful as tetanus. I finally threaten to hold one man upside down and shake some shreds of information out via his aural cavities, and he reveals that the next and only bus headed west is less than an hour away. At eight o'clock, all the odd-looking restaurants are already closed, and so I struggle across the six-lane freeway to a McDonald's for dinner.

After 40 minutes in a three-person-long queue, I receive a small bag of food and dash back across the road with it. The fries are stiff and inedible due to cold, but I'm so hungry that I try dangling them in my thimbleful of reconstituted orange juice to soften. Still hungry, I struggle back across the six lanes, and beg them to give me whatever is immediately ready to eat, as the bus is due to leave in ten minutes. Running back across the freeway with another small bag, I open it to discover a chicken burger that is identically stiff and cold, but I force myself to swallow the congealed grease anyway, dressing it heavily with bright yellow mustard.

On the verge of tears, I call Erin. It's getting cold now, I tell her, and I'm tired and still hungry. 'Okay,' she says, 'who is this?' Then I remember to introduce myself. It's been about a year since we've spoken on the phone. Having lived with me on two continents through numerous crises (first as my uni roommate in Mississippi, then as a reciprocal exchange student in Sydney), Erin uses what I recognise as her Soothing Voice and tells me to get my ass to Eugene where everything will be all right. 'What are you craving?' she asks.

'Food and shelter?' I snivel in reply.

'You must be pretty gross by now, huh?' she says, but it's not really a question. Erin announces that she's setting up an irradiator to scan me for bus-bugs before I enter her home. 'I have a cat to consider now,' she tells me, 'oh, and a man, too.'

The bus to Spokane, Washington, is a regular Greyhound crap-mobile again, and we fill every last seat before leaving Missoula. The regular nut jobs start arriving too, and I begin to accept that sleep will be a scarce commodity this evening. Why is everyone always injured on Greyhound, I wonder, as the motley crowd piles on. Wrists and ankles, arms and legs and eyes, someone always has at least one huge and improbable bandage on these buses. At times we look like outpatient transportation. I manage to look pissed-off enough to avoid a seatmate until the last possible moment, when a fishy-smelling man plonks down next to me.

'Do you know Jesus?' he asks, as we pull away from the station. 'Yeah! Sure I do,' I answer. 'Puerto Rican guy, little moustache . . . hangs out in Miami.' Everyone is called Hay-sus in Miami. He opens his mouth and then shuts it. One more word, I think, just one more word and you will wear my mustard. Fishy-man goes quiet, rubs his pate once and bothers me no more.

From the back of the bus a man begins a loud, blow-by-blow account of repairing his truck in Anchorage, Alaska. 'It was the axle, man, I knew it was the axle, but he just kept on and on, just kept on and on, but the whole time, I knew it was the axle, man.' At first us vaguely normal passengers trade grins and shrugs, and then thin-lipped grimaces and arched eyebrows. When he moves on to the carburettor, we stare off into the distance, dreaming of acid dripping slowly into his ear. A heavy woman in a faded housedress has been with me all the way since Cheyenne, Wyoming, and I overhear her say she started off in Shreveport, Louisiana. Where the heck is she going? There are a few others I can tell have been on buses awhile; we make up a ragtag, smelly bunch, fiercely protective of our seats.

Housedress finally strikes up a conversation with the Anchorage-truck guy. 'Yew look like my friend in Texas,' she declares, and he is ecstatic. 'Wow!' he shouts. 'It's true, I know. When I was in Texas I noticed there were so many guys who really looked like me!' The pair of them carry on like it's an actual reunion for the next half-hour. Just when I manage to tune out the freak-frequency and drift into the usual dreams involving king-sized beds and room service, there's a tap on my shoulder. I glare at Fishy Jesus-man, but he's convincingly asleep. The tap comes again from behind me and a woman leans over, her plastic bracelets jangling in my ear. 'Mah trailer's in Gillette right now,' she tells me, 'but I'm lookin' whars to move it. My name's Jay-NEECE,' she says, but before I'm forced to respond in kind, the driver's amplified voice booms over us.

'Okay,' he says, 'we're comin' in to St Regis. Now, when I drop you all off in St Regis, you'll see me drive away and leave you behind. Don't nobody be panickin'. I'm just going over with the bus to a motel to change drivers, then we'll be back. If you should see this same bus drive away twice ... well, they're always looking for dishwashers in St Regis.'

'St *Regis*!' says Jay-NEECE, 'don't that sound pretty?' She stands up and begins gathering her bags together. 'I'm sorry,' she tells me, putting her hand on my head for balance, 'we'll have ta talk some other time. See, mah trailer's in Gillette right now, and I'm lookin' whars to move it.' The bus stops and she gets off, looking around the interstate like a newlywed in a display home.

The bus is freezing and I rug up tightly, dozing fitfully with my head against the window's chill. A few hours later I rouse myself to find that the heat has been on for some time. Parched and sweating, I flop to the front to beg mercy. At 3 am I finally loose my fishy seatmate, contorting myself and my trusty striped pillow into a position that invites sleep to take me like a two-bit whore. Mercifully, she does.

When I next wake up, the sun is creeping into a much smaller sky, and it seems that we are in Big Tree country now, where tall pines and conifers dwarf the bus on either side. We are winding along next to an impressive lake, which is the kind of deep, dark blue that suggests it might be cold enough to stop your heart. Mountains jump up behind it, jostling each other for space, covered thickly in dramatic alpine vegetation. This matches my guidebook description of Washington State, and I realise I must have crossed another border.

I struggle to put my contact lenses in for a better view. Still without glasses, I have been using my contact lenses in precisely the ways my optometrist suggested might lead to profound orbital dysfunction. I test-drive them for hours on tired eyes in blasting AC, before repeatedly falling asleep in them, so that I wake with eyeballs that couldn't be more dry and aching if someone had stretched cling-wrap tightly over them and left them on the front steps in summer. Moaning in pain and irrigating with fingers and morning-breath saliva, I inevitably pry them lose and accept temporary blindness. This has started a pattern of frantic behaviour at Greyhound terminals, where I run up to things really close and press my nose against them like a madwoman. I can't see the signs that will mean the difference between a bus to Dungareeville or Drunkendogville, and so I wander with my arms outstretched and circling, perfecting my open-mouthed squint.

I place my lenses in now to bring the outside world into sharper view. Once again, there is almost no sign of civilisation around us. I feel like I've driven through most of Europe and seen barely a dwelling in the last few days. By the time I get off these buses and get to Eugene, it will be 48 hours of continuous travel. My clothes already smell from the heat of yesterday's bus, and the cuffs of my jeans, sweeping the floors of public toilets, have long since been exiled by the rest of my outfit. My hair hangs in greasy threads at the front and the back is an impenetrable nest of knots. I can't wait to meet Erin's fiancé.

A clumsy map of the Greyhound route tells me that we are driving alongside the Columbia River. Little tree-covered islands jut up here and there in the water, some with strange buildings on them. We pass a bridge called the Bridge of the Gods, and given the scenic majesty it extends across, it might not be an empty boast. I find my heart swelling yet again. I picture a small house, probably wooden, definitely heated, with a mountain garden and a couple of chickens to keep my nanny-goat company. Could I really live out here? And just like Montana, Minnesota and Colorado, the incredible natural beauty might make it seem like an easy yes, except that I have always watched the global weather reports. In my favourite American places, I am certain I would shiver for three months and freeze to death for seven. I'm also worried about that good Thai restaurant.

Washington State turns into Oregon at last and the ponky little bus passes under the exit sign to Portland. This is the state capital and the global headquarters of the Nike Corporation, which was founded in Eugene. It is a very attractive city with lots of trees, colourful flowers in large tubs, clean, crisp air and a river running through what I take to be the downtown. At least six large bridges are immediately visible, so that this small city looks more covered in them than Manhattan. The Greyhound terminal we arrive at is big, clean and quite efficient, though it favours the wide sea of chocolate brown tiles shared by my least-favourite waiting places.

There is a long, drab, food-service counter, which is populated by two women who look and sound like they used to run a prison canteen in Estonia. The lukewarm trays of congealing sauces are unidentifiable under dim lighting, but I line up hopefully anyway. One of the women is cooking fresh hotcakes on a greasy grill plate and it seems as though everyone in front of me has wisely chosen to order them. There's not much you can do to hurt a pancake, I tell myself, pleased at the thought of a newly cooked snack. When my turn finally rolls around, the woman wipes her forearm across her wrinkled, perspiring brow and turns the batter jug upside down to show me that it's empty.

I howl with rage, kicking at the counter as she points to the vats of floating protein. Three sandwiches are stacked up together as well; greying tongues of ham lolling from gash-like mouths of stiff bread. I have never trusted bus station sandwiches or reheated lumps of anything. It's asking for trouble when no one has been seen actually eating it and the one toilet you all have access to is in constant violation of World Heath Organization protocol. Once again, I choose the Maruchan instant noodle cup in chicken flavour. Instant noodles, salty juice, four dehydrated peas and some dried carrot shavings.

After a few days of soup and fast-food that is neither fast nor food, I always find myself dreaming of impossible foods on the bus. Tomatoes. A whole plateful, with fresh basil and baby mozzarella. Corn on the cob and even tinned corn were yesterday's favourites. Tinned corn, creamed corn, corn niblets in water – I craved it with helpless ferocity, but can't even remember the last time I ate it, and doubt it was this century. As long as the food in question is fresh, natural and wet, it fulfils all bus-food craving criteria. We get as dried out as the Maruchan peas.

On the way to Eugene I see my first Jack in the Box burger joint. I've discovered that you can split America up along its fast-food borders. Some chains are jealously protected as regional cuisine – Krispy Kreme donuts, Popeye's Chicken, In-n-Out Burger and Checkers – while some, like White Castle, are nationally derided. Apart from a noticeable change in the fast-food culture, I notice that the people wandering into these plastic menu-board establishments look different, too. The mix of faces include those with Asian features for the first time in a long while. There are also lots of hippies here – real ones this time, not the $30-shampoo variety of Colorado. Everywhere there are shops selling multicoloured glass bongs and miscellaneous psychedelia, employing cunning names like 'The Grateful Thread – Fabrics that Rock!' At last we come to the dark little station in Eugene and I lump my battered gear off the bus. I stand outside in the sun, waving at every second person who comes toward me. Everyone seems to look like Erin in this town. At least seven girls walk past with her distinctive long dark hair, milky skin and blue eyes. When she turns up ten minutes later, the real Erin is treated to a half-smile and a suspicious wave. 'Yeah, nice to see you too, Australia!' she says, as she hugs me despite the filth. 'Let's get you a shower!'

Freshly washed, courtesy of the attractive bathroom at Casa de Erin, I put the undies I've been wearing since I woke up in Denver into a ziplock bag and bury them deep in the tomato-pack. Erin lives with her husband-to-be in a sunny walk-up apartment on a wide tree-lined street, with a bouncy little cat, colourful décor and enough photographs of our old house in Sydney to make me weepy. Driving and walking around town, I realise that most of Eugene is much the same as Erin's shaded street, with pleasant, low-level buildings.

Eugene is a tie-dye heavy college town. The people who live here are politically active, socially aware and keenly interested in recycling. The cars beside us in what traffic there is in Eugene are often small and usually old. Many sport stickers that say 'SUV – Stupid Ugly Vehicle', denouncing them as environmentally ruinous and even internationally dangerous, charging that gas-guzzling cars affect foreign policy. 'Wow,' I say, and Erin proudly points out a variation on the popular pro-war bumper sticker that spells out, in red, white and blue, 'These Colors Don't Run!' The Eugene-modified version adds '. . . The World!' The politics, the general relaxed attitude and the thrift-store inspired outfits on twenty-somethings lounging outside cafés remind me much more of home than anywhere I've been in the US so far. 'Yeah, really,' says Erin, who lived in Sydney for a year, 'welcome to the West Coast!'

I met Erin at the University of Southern Mississippi. An Oregon native, she was in Mississippi on a full scholarship too good to turn down, but she was often frustrated with the South and always maintained she was just as much of a cultural and geographical exchange student as the rest of us foreign-nationals. 'I told you there were a lot of different countries that make up the United States,' she reminds me, 'but I'm sure you've figured that out by now.'

When Erin came to Sydney, she brought with her a huge book about Oregon, filled with pictures of dark-pebbled beaches, rugged coastline and dark, quiet forests. There were photos of the state's many vineyards, rich brown soil covered with rows of green, roping vines, of soft winter gardens, of snowy trails and of the grand explosion of autumn leaves. I always imagined her home town as vaguely freezing, so it's a surprise to be so hot and muggy on summer-green grass, listening to a distant buzz of insects as we pull our hair up high off our sweaty necks. For relief, we sample some of the many microbrewed ales so popular in the West and then tour the shaded campus of the University of Oregon.

Erin's school is one of hundreds of universities in America, and though it is only a small state school in a moderate-income area, it's still immediately more beautiful and impressive than the best – publicly funded – universities at home could ever hope to be. It's a beautiful campus filled with old stone buildings, ivy-covered walls and majestic trees. Still, Erin has had to put herself through school, which has involved years of juggling multiple jobs, grant applications and constant financial stress, and she is certain to graduate with massive financial debt as well as her degree. I decide I was better off at a school that looked like a military hospital, but left me with a HECS debt akin to the price of a dented second-hand jet ski.

We spend a lovely day together in the sun, flapping around town and parking ourselves at numerous coffee-houses. The coffee here is fantastic at last and Erin explains that the Pacific Northwest, Seattle in particular, is an area known for their commitment to excellent Joe. She thinks that might be why Montana, bumping against the Coffee States, seemed to have an inexplicable fondness for espresso.

After a good, fully horizontal sleep, the next day is filled with many of the same joyful activities – eating, drinking, wandering and the unparalleled pleasure of being with a good friend. Erin has made a lovely life for herself in this laid-back town, and it boggles me once more to think of how many similar places in this country there are that I have yet to discover.

Chapter 14

The path well trodden

The next evening I enjoy a delicious Pacific-Northwest meal of Atlantic salmon and a local microbrew called something like Spanky Squirrel, before having a slightly drunken shower back at Erin's place. Squeaky clean but covered in bruises from my inebriated connections with soap dishes and shampoo organisers, I finally declare myself ready to go.

Erin drops me at the line for the San Francisco-bound Greyhound and wishes me luck. 'Be careful, Greyhound Girl,' she says, hugging me tightly. 'Try to keep away from the lunatiles and, uh, wash when you can.' As she leaves, there is some excitement at the Eugene bus terminal. Two senior drivers run up, yelling and waving their hands. 'Move 'em back! Move 'em back! We got a newbie coming in!' We squash flat against the wall as a tiny Mexican man jumps the big bus into the narrow, covered parking bay. This miniature driver looks pale and shivery. Someone at the back of the line whistles, saying, 'I'd say buckle up all the way to San Fran, but Greyhound don't got no seatbelts!' There are a few nervous giggles.

'You should have taken the train,' someone suggests to their friend behind me. 'Nah, took Amtrak once. Train was late three fuckin' hours. They hit a cow. Think it was a big 'un, or preg-en-ant. Took em all morning ta clean it off.' A little girl waits with her young mum and her grandma and a boy in military uniform. His boots have a price tag only half removed near the sole. His mum keeps touching his thick mop of hair – which will soon be a crew cut I guess – and tearing up. They have been joking along with us about the jumping bus, but now it's time to say goodbye, and the rest of us pile onto the bus quietly, aware of the gravity of the moment.

All is going well until the little girl stops sucking on her root beer and begins to wail, clinging to the boy. 'Uncle Aaron, stay with me! Stay with me!' Both women start crying then and so does the boy. Big honking tears. It is up to the poor driver to hasten the farewell, and soon half the bus is in tears too as the sobbing young woman hugs her brother and begs him to be careful. The boy cries all the way to his seat and then stares out the window with shaking shoulders as his little family recedes, wiping his eyes with the back of his big hand. He looks so young, sitting there, a big boy in a too-small seat his uniformed knees up around his ears.

The international news (when I get it) is worse every day. Although I'm still struck with the same desperate pity for the people of Iraq and Afghanistan, I'm also increasingly miserable for all these uncertain American kids in uniform. My Greyhound touring has allowed me a window into the small towns and family lives of young marines that makes it hard for me to dismiss the soldiers on telly as the unfeeling and ignorant killers I once supposed they must be. I hope poor Aaron makes it back to Eugene in one piece. I hope he brings back the news that Iraqi boys have sisters and mothers too. I hope this whole ugly mess comes to an end very soon.

When the sun has gone down, I can see that it's going to be a boring trip. Black all the way to San Francisco by early morning. I'm not too excited about getting there, either, I must admit. Although I'm nostalgic for the place because of a drunken trip there with the uni friends I miss so much, I'm also starting to remember that it was cold, expensive, touristy, and filled with aggressive panhandlers. Will it be easier to discover the city on my own, I wonder, or just less fun?

As I settle in with my trusty pillow, a little girl comes up unbidden and plops down her Hello Kitty backpack on the seat beside me. By now, I'm used to wandering Greyhound children. Left unattended to roam bus aisles and terminals, they stumble and cry, put filthy things in their mouths and hit out at each other with a kind of grim lassitude. It stupefies me that people would get on a bus with a kid for three days, or even one day, and not bring so much as a scrap of paper and a crayon. What do they expect them to do? I'm very pleased to see that this kid's mum has the right idea and has allowed her to equip herself for the journey. I'm not very pleased that she's allowed to pester grownups who have just swallowed enough dramamine to knock themselves out till next week.

Unzipping the backpack with a solemn little face, she takes out a colourful Hawaiian lei, two butchered Barbies, some headless texta pens, a lump of grey Play-Doh, a single pink sock and an action man figurine. She arranges these possessions carefully and pushes my pillow out of the way, before seating herself and straightening her ponytail. Sure kid, I think, make yourself at home.

'Did you know Hello Kitty has no mom?' she offers, ''cos she's a cat.'

'True story?'

'Yeah-huh. And the Powerpuff Girls? They aren't lez-di-ens. They're just friends from school. They never would kiss or anything, just play and fight. A lot.'

'Man, you've got the inside scoop.'

'An' Barbie? See? My Hawaiian Barbie? She tried to make it with Spiderman, but they can't have no kids.' She sighs dramatically, shaking her head and crossing her arms in frustration.

'Yeah?' I say. 'They ever think of adopting?'

'Um, I don't know. I could ask.'

So she does. With one eyelid open each, we sleepily discuss the fertility crisis and interracial adoption issues stemming from the fruitless romance of topless Hawaiian Barbie and her unfortunate Spidey-lover. Barbie grins disconcertingly throughout the entire conversation, making my drugged self mildly anxious.

Hawaiian Barbie has no pubic hair, which this perceptive child understands to be a prerequisite when it comes to filling the Mattel dreamhouse with heirs, and Spiderman is clearly incapable of maintaining a 'he-REKSHUN' (she says like a sneeze) – also vital. She's only seven, but she's cleared up some stuff for me, that's for sure.

'Do you have kids?' she asks.

'No.'

'A husband?'

'No.'

'A fee-yon-say?'

'No.'

'A boyfriend?'

'Yes.'

'Does he have a he-REKSHUN?'

The bus looks on.

'Where's your mum then, hey?'

At the front of the bus sits another little girl, with her tiny hand flat against her pregnant mum's belly. She won't take it away for even a second and long after her mum is asleep she sits there, staring intently and alert, occasionally changing hands. I fall asleep dreaming that the Boy has run off with that strumpet, Hawaiian Barbie, and I am heavily pregnant to some unknown suitor, unable to take my hands from my swollen belly and give chase.

I'm almost relieved to be woken from this nonsense, as we struggle off for the changeover at 1 am. After 40 minutes of leaning against a cinderblock wall and sipping carbon monoxide, our new bus driver arrives. He wears a big bomber jacket with a Greyhound bus as big as a Christmas ham embroidered on the back, under the legend 'Leave the Driving to Us'. His hair is slicked back and his trousers are firmly pressed. He inspects us with the glare and gait of a drill sergeant, and we unconsciously straighten.

'Okay!' he booms. 'Good morning! Now, listen up, folks, 'cos this is how it's gonna roll! Until we hit Sac, we're gonna be a team. Now, I'm gonna be in charge of that team, and what I say goes, so listen up. At some point I'm gonna give the signal, like this –' he motions sharply, with stewardess-like precision, to the door of the bus. 'That's the signal. Now, commit it to memory. When you see that signal,' he demonstrates again, 'you're gonna move SINGLE FILE and you're gonna give me your tickets in a calm and professional manner, and I'm gonna take them, in a calm and professional manner, and then,' he says, jerking his jacket forward at the collar, pulling it down tight and zipping it up fast, 'we *ride*.'

The crowd looks around and we smile nervously, waiting for evidence of irony. None comes. This man is serious. Our backs straighten. Children are hushed. 'Okay, so lissen up! Remember the signal.' We wait, lissenin' and rememberin'. He stares at us. We stare back. Then, finally, the signal. We line up and hand him our tickets. I believe my manner to be especially calm and professional, and puff my chest out when I receive a slow nod of the well-done-soldier variety. Safe in our seats, we watch the driver as he checks his controls like a pilot. He uses his cell phone like a CB radio, holding it upside down a few centimetres from his mouth, shouting. 'Yeah, Tom, this is Greyhound 287 local to San Fran and LA; luggage is loaded, passengers are loaded, I repeat, passengers ARE loaded, rolling out on schedule . . . nnnnnow.' He shuts the phone in one hand with a snap and the bus lurches forward. 'Okay, people! Lissen up!' It's too late for me though. I am dramamine unconscious in seconds.

I sleep uncomfortably all the way to Redding, transforming my seat into a small island of sweaty yellow-and-white-striped sheeting like some demented hospital ward. As the bus enters Sacramento, so does the sun. The driver turns on some local radio and an excited newscaster announces that the ambient temperature in Sacramento is climbing to 114 degrees F, breaking a hundred-year-old record. People groan and wave listless hands across their faces in anticipation, but I grin. The last time I visited San Francisco it was the beginning of summer, but the city had, rather surprisingly, required two layers and a light jumper just to keep your teeth from chattering. My sneakers had become saturated in a sudden downpour and I was then reduced to wearing socks and sandals in order to maintain the basic functioning of all ten piggies. San Francisco had been bloody cold. Less than an hour's drive away from this Sacramento heatwave, San Francisco will surely be toasty warm today. My memories of howling winds and chilly damp begin to evaporate. I tuck my dirty fleece back into the tomato-pack and stretch out the kinks in my back like a lemur.

Sitting up and staring out the windows, we know we've reached San Francisco at last when we can no longer see it. The rolling fog the city is famous for is immensely heavy and the buildings and harbour are now completely obscured. Still, when the driver says, 'San Francisco', I believe him and hop out at the massive terminal with a smile. It feels good to be back somewhere familiar at last. My euphoria lasts about three minutes, which is as long as it takes for the city's icy, grasping fingers to reach up my back, into my ears and right down my pants. It is 68 degrees F. San Francisco is still bloody cold.

I take a number 42 bus to Pacific Street and walk to Broadway, where the Green Tortoise Guesthouse shares its neighbourhood with nudie clubs, Korean restaurants, bad fast food and a smattering of nice cafés. It's a hop, step and a jump – or in San Francisco a shiver, a shudder and a huddle – from the ornamental archways of Chinatown, where I plan on consuming breakfast.

Every street in downtown San Francisco looks like a car chase. Improbable vehicles have bumped down these hilly roads a thousand times on film and whenever a taxi heads toward me at beeping speed, I unconsciously look around for the Humvee full of baddies behind it. I can't help feeling that San Francisco is a bit like a movie set in other ways, too. As with my first visit here, I am fast feeling the same vague sense of disappointment that comes from walking amongst the painted props and fabricated streets of a production lot.

The hordes of tourists surrounding me now are the same ones who might wander back lots at Universal Studios, clicking cameras and exclaiming, 'Morty, look! It's just like it is on TV!'.

Some people think that's fun, but I don't. I'm a grouch. The San Francisco I always see on screen is revealed to be kind of small and flimsy, lacking dimension somehow and, just like a film set, it becomes obvious that any real action takes place behind the few showy props.

For such a famous city, I'm struck again by how small it actually is. It doesn't lack big-city pretensions, but it lacks the population. Only 250,000 people live here, but they've somehow pushed the real estate prices into the stratosphere, battling it out with New York each year for the most expensive sales and rentals of any American city. With New York, silver-screen showpieces like Times Square are pretty disappointing too, but the thrill comes with discovering the blocks and blocks of authentic New York that unravel with every step beyond the landmarks; the New York that is even more outrageously New York than fiction arranges it to be. There is no sense of that going on at all in San Fran. Just a dutiful, aimless, watch-checking wandering after you pay your admission fee.

I check into the Green Tortoise and begin poking around. This hostel is on the fringe of the Italian North Beach area and began as a crash-pad for travellers on the infamous Green Tortoise bus tours. The antithesis of Greyhound, these buses are basically big mattresses on wheels, designed for comfort and drunken party fun. Since 1974, they have been filled with patchouli-scented, dreadlocked travellers who are ferried on sightseeing trips up and down the coast, out to the Grand Canyon and even as far as Central America. Each bus has its own name and they boast, 'You won't fall asleep leaning against a window, but lying down, listening to beautiful music . . .' Waking, no doubt, at a location that will not include group-crapping in a Greyhound station full of parolees and outpatients twitching for chemical breakfasts. Just looking at the pictures of these smug little buses makes me jealous.

It's a nice enough hostel, a sociable dive that's a good place to be with a group. It's probably why my uni friends and I spent five full days in San Francisco after we had seen all there was to see before lunch on the first day. We dragged it out, unwilling to accept that this was it and unable to remain sober long enough to drive off. We hung out in the old ballroom downstairs, nursing cases of beer with a United Nations grab-bag of Green Tortoise passengers, before drinking ourselves stupid on tequila in the Mission district and coming home to befoul the inadequate toilets. By the time we got up each day, dressed for the arctic winds and moved the car seven times to avoid the obsessive-compulsive street cleaning hours in this city, it was beer o'clock again and we were just pleased to get back inside out of the cold. One morning the fog had lifted high enough for us to read the freeway signs and we left without a backward glance.

I set off now for Chinatown with my hands tucked under my armpits, consoling myself with promises of fried dumplings and steaming hot, fluffy rice. San Francisco is at the heart of the Chinese-American population and the ethnic mix on the city streets here is much like downtown Sydney. Add to this the large harbour with its famous bridge, lots of city buses zipping around and Asian grocers tucked into every side street, and it feels comfortingly familiar. Passing under the dragon-covered arch-way called the Pagoda Gate, I find myself on Grant Avenue again, the paved, pedestrian-friendly beginning of Chinatown.

San Francisco's Chinatown is not the Chinatown of New York, nor of Sydney, which it more superficially resembles. It is not the Chinatown of fish being butchered on hunks of ice, of raised voices haggling in Mandarin, of crowds of Chinese kids drinking bright green liquid in tied plastic bags with little straws. If you were the director of the John P. Thistlewhistle Performing Arts Academy and had to stage six simultaneous productions of Madame Butterfly, this would be the Chinatown for you. Fans, dresses, chopsticks and those little boxes with wooden birds making singing noises in them: that is the essence of San Francisco's Chinatown. With such a delicious history of oriental intrigue, opium dens, gold rush gambling and those wonderful Amy Tan books, fifty identical stores and restaurants spruiking for your custom is a bit of a letdown. Hungry for warmth and sustenance, I spend two hours and $20 on soup and dumplings in two different but equally flavourless restaurants before swearing loudly in Thai (the only vaguely Asian profanity I could muster) at the Pagoda Gate, vowing never to return.

On my way back to the hostel to see if my travel towel can be fashioned into a lower-back warmer, I pass Jack Kerouac Alley. Kerouac loved San Francisco. He travelled all over America too, and this is where he kept coming back to. It must have been a special town then, and again in the sixties, when it truly became a centre for social change in the Western world. Everyone loves San Francisco. Just *everyone*. It consistently polls as one of America's own favourite cities, and I can only assume this is because all the people polled are gay, or perhaps covered in vital, warmth-bringing blubber.

People are nauseatingly nice about San Francisco. San Francisco can do no wrong. 'Oh, the Bay area,' they gush, 'the bridge, the harbour, the food!' and they'll invariably smile as if they invented it. 'It's fucking freezing!' I'll say, but these people just chuckle like San Francisco has perhaps been a little naughty in the weather department, but is otherwise exceptional. 'Well, yes,' they say, 'it's kind of cold, but it's nice not to be hot all the time, don't you think? So European!' It's nice not to be so cold all the time, is what I think, and I struggle to come up with a single city in Europe that suffers such constantly foul foggy damp. Even the Brits get a real summer, and they don't have to deal with the San Franciscan panhandling cartel. 'Ah,' say the San Francisco supporters (which is everyone except me and, well, me), 'yeeeesss, that's a bit of a problem. Y'know, I'm not sure why it's so bad, but it's not as bad as it used to be I don't think, and anyway, some of them are pretty funny!'

It's true. Some of the panhandlers are pretty funny. Some hold amusing signs that read 'Need money for beer/drugs. Can you help?' or 'Too lazy to work, pls. support my life choice'. My friends and I had once pointed and chuckled at the apparent wit of these signs, giving money for the giggles provided. But it soon got old. After all, we too wished for money for beer, drugs and laziness and, being impoverished students in a foreign country, we had close to none. Our little group was so broke at that time that we had just chipped in three ways to buy a card for someone's twenty-first birthday, and it wasn't even key-shaped. We were badgered from sun-up to sundown, with an average of one request for money every eleven minutes. Now, I'm a pathetically soft touch. It's no secret that America has a lousy welfare system and so a decent cough, a bit of a limp, dodgy lip-liner – any small effort to appeal to my sense of social justice – would have relieved me of my lunch money. But no. Although there were hundreds of drunk, toothless, babbling citizens collecting on corners and bus stops all over San Francisco, these people were to busy conversing with God or their radiator fluid bottles to think of asking for money. The people insisting that I open my wallet for them looked just fine. They looked better than we did (although this wasn't hard considering that we had packed for summer and were now climactic refugees).

The same kids are still here, listening to their MP3 players while they jump in front of you demanding beer or pizza or five bucks to visit their grandma. These over-accessorised halfwits inspire in me a thundering desire to drag them by their expensive laces down the streets of the rest of this planet and show them what poverty actually looks like, and how out of balance their McWorld-view must be. The original hippies who tuned in and dropped out in San Francisco – who started the Summer of Love with a concert in Golden Gate park in '67 – would surely be appalled at this apathetic, visionless crowd of slackers, at the Silicon Valley yuppies and the clumps of fat-bottomed tourists snapping away at the Haight and Ashbury street signs like the gates of Graceland.

Now wearing my stiff travel towel as an extra undergarment, I sit on the edge of my newly checked-in bunk and consider my options. My roommate, an odd-looking man called Petr from somewhere in the former Soviet Union, is on his way to Alcatraz. He speaks little English but still manages to convey both his enthusiasm for the adventure and his insistence that I accompany him and so we set off together. 'Oh is graat!' he tells me, clapping his hands over his head. 'We go to prison as frrrend!' Petr laughs and does a bouncy jig. Despite the cold and my crankiness, I can't help smiling. He reminds me of Cousin Balki from the eighties sitcom *Perfect Strangers*.

Alcatraz sounds like my kind of fun, and it is. First of all, the boat trip out to the prison-island is heated, and on the edge of the fog I manage to snap off a couple of photos that actually look like San Francisco. Once inside the draughty old building, we rent Walkmans with guide-tapes that allow self-touring of the old prison cells and the . . . well, the old prison cells. It's a penitentiary, whaddya want? Petr somehow starts his tape off at the wrong point and I enjoy a ticklish few hours watching him rewinding and fast-forwarding, counting his paces and then reversing, walking around and around with his face screwed up, nose pointed skyward like a spastic with vertigo. Every so often he looks over to me in panic and, cruelly, I point to my own Walkman while shaking my head as if to say, 'Wow! Bloody amazing stuff, isn't it?'. With his belt up around his chin he so closely resembles Mr Bean that small children have begun to giggle.

He falls asleep during the short return voyage, before we spend a tiresome hour together dragging around the famous Fisherman's Wharf, perusing T-shirts that say 'Beer – Helping Ugly People to have sex since 1738', as well as used licence plates fashioned into ashtrays and other cunning souvenirs. Petr has collected an extraordinary array of promotional literature and I have a good go through it, trying to get enthused, but it seems I've covered most of the landmarks already. Lombard St, the 'crookedest street in the world'. Check. Chinatown. Okay, trying not to be cross now, trying not to be cross. Well, we could always tour the Civic Center. Sounds neat, as they say here, but . . . pass. Golden Gate Bridge? Actually Rusty Red, aaaand crossed it. Yawn. Petr announces a second trip to Alcatraz and I'm forced to leave him to his merry antics.

Back at the hostel, I go down to the corner store to buy a packet of Pepperidge Farm Bordeaux cookies and I take shelter from the wind in a phone booth, where I consume the lot. I decide to ride the tram to Haight-Ashbury, which, unlike the cookies, is a bad decision. It sadly confirms what I feared the first time, that the Haight area is a cynical, touristy shadow of its original beatnik, counter-culture self. I wander San Francisco for hours, on and off trams and buses in the cold, trying to see past the scores of broken-down people littering the streets, trying to find a place to sit for a while which doesn't involve purchasing something. The people who love San Francisco – all those other billions riding the planet alongside this small cranky Australian – rave on about the Mexican food over thataway, the nightclubs over thisaway, the gay culture and the art scene, the trams and the pretty houses on Nob Hill, and maybe they're right. But the bottom line is that there are better cities in the US and I don't want to waste any more time in this one.

My old friend Kevin has returned home to Los Angeles before starting law school in a few months and I go back to the cookie-phone-booth, calling him to see when he'll be around. 'Hey!' he says, 'good thing you called. We're going up to our cabin in Big Bear tomorrow, so I won't be in LA, but you're welcome to come with us if you want to.' Using his own vernacular, I tell him that would be supercool and check out of Green Tortoise immediately. 'You can leave the sheets,' I tell them, angling for a partial refund considering I won't be costing them laundry or a continental breakfast bagel with a scoop of strawberry jam, 'I didn't use the bed.' The counter girl is uninterested though. 'Cool,' she says, without looking up.

At the door, a group of Scandinavian adventurers ask me if I found a better hostel. 'No,' I tell them, 'I just . . .' Oh, why not? 'I just don't really like San Francisco. So there you go.' To my surprise, the guys nod vigorously. 'We are so cold,' they tell me. 'We want to go back to Canada,' says one. 'Ya, it was much warmer there, and there was some good stuff to do.' But when I tell them I'm off to LA, there is much recoiling and hissing. 'That is a crazy town!' they say. 'You must have car, and if you are so having, it is so, so bad to drive. Do you have car?'

'Nope,' I say, hefting the tomato-pack high, 'I have friend.' I head off to the Greyhound station with a heart made light by escape.

I go overnight to LA, the bus winding through famous Highway 1 in the dark, arriving in the early hours of the morning. The Los Angeles Greyhound terminal is like a staging post for the end of the world. There are boxes and suitcases as big as small cars, stuffed hefty-bags and rolled mattresses, there is wailing and waving, sobbing and clapping, and people standing on crates and chairs to scan the crowd. It looks like a multi-ethnic refugee camp. It smells like I imagine death might, if you came across it one hot week later.

Over it all blasts music and I realise this is the first Greyhound station I've visited that has music. I can see why they don't now: it really doesn't help. The soundtrack to this scene is particularly incongruous. 'I'm Not in Love' blares until it distorts, followed by the seductive 'Nobody Does it Better' from *The Spy Who Loved Me*. This rather glam James Bond anthem kicks in just as an elderly black woman in flared lacy pants throws up wretchedly over someone else's boxed luggage. A wild scream of Spanish erupts as vomit begins to soak through the cardboard. The music continues at full volume over the top of the drama, a fine soundtrack for transit hell. Not for the first time in the US, I really wish I could speak Spanish. It feels like all the good stuff gets said in Spanish, all the things requiring heads to be wiggled and hands to be thrown around. I want to know what's going on too.

I enter the toilets to perform my morning ablutions and discover them to be equally huge and insane. Women crowd the long strip of mirrors over the sinks, which are clogged with hair and wet toilet paper covered in make-up and mucus, in beauty wax and blood. Gagging, I take my place among them as we all primp and change our clothes in the heat, stripping off and clamouring for space in a half-naked comedy of errors. A redheaded kid from the San Fran bus is here, pushed into a corner, staring open-mouthed at the array of swaying breasts as big as satellite dishes, flat as plates, with nipples dark as wine. People emerging from the toilets – a continuous cacophony of flushing cisterns and banging doors – are forced to duck the line of hairbrushes and the arms that direct them, which are flying backwards in short vicious stokes. There is big hair, coloured hair, nappy hair that won't sit still, knotted curls and plastic wigs. Once again, I belong in the greasy strings category, subphylum: cradle cap.

The redheaded kid's mother has changed her bra and is turning her infected earrings around painfully, making funny faces to her child in the mirror, before yelling, 'Shut the fuck up!' as he twists and turns in his pinching stroller. She must be about 17, I think, and her toddler is clearly somewhere between pet and hated burden. She seems to figure that this fetid toilet block is as good a place for a meal as any. Crouched down together, they snack on three packs of Doritos for breakfast. The kid finds a melted cookie he has stashed in his stroller, but his mother steals it, taunting him with it while she eats the whole thing. He screams and cries and is unlovely. I feel sick. In contrast is a woman who can't be much older than me, with five, repeat, five girls of her own, ranging from zero to seven. It takes her half an hour to wash all their faces and brush five sets of baby teeth, but she remains smiling and so do they. That, I think, is courage. I don't even speak to *myself* for the first hour of the morning, especially not after a night on the road.

Feeling even grubbier after my sojourn in the somewhat hopefully titled Ladies Room, I place a quick mercy call to Kevin. Outside, the Los Angeles sun is magnificent. The sky it sits in would be a perfect and intense blue if it weren't for the fact that the lower half has been dipped in what looks like grey chalk dust. With more cars than people and more people than sense, LA chokes each morning like a six-pack-a-day smoker in a phone booth. The palm trees shoot straight up in the air – presumably to breathe – and are stunning. They are so cool, these LA palms; they look like they should have sunnies on. Everything in LA looks that way. I spy two girls from Washington State who were on my bus in tracky-dacks and cargo-pants (according to my rapidly filling Legal Alien dictionary of terms, they would call them sweats and khakis). They have emerged giggling from the toilets, their blonded hair long and glistening, mouths dripping with heavy gloss, heels stratospheric and new outfits straight off the hanger. After a nasal argument about whether to head to Rodeo Drive first and see the fountain where a pivotal scene in *Clueless* was shot, they head off in a cab to the Melrose boutiques. It's clearly an adventure in beauty. I sigh heavily up at the too-cool palms, wishing one of my girls were here to do some shopping and sightseeing.

Kevin arrives, smiling, appointing himself my knight in shining khakis by battling the LA freeway system at peak hour to come and get me. 'There's this diner that's a totally LA thing,' he tells me as we drive away from the terminal. 'The Mayor eats there and stuff, it's supercool.' Los Angelenos really pride themselves on local knowledge, especially when it comes to traffic and dining, so I resist telling Kevin that it doesn't matter – I'm a breakfast whore and will take it anywhere I can. The morning heat feels so good after that one day of chill in San Francisco. LA smells of sun and heavy perfume, of burritos and gasoline. After a triple-fried grease breakfast with a side of lard and eight cups of drip filter, we set off for the 'burbs.

I am only half a stranger to this city. We moved to Los Angeles for two years when I was about six. During this time I remember little other than being slightly bewildered on a daily basis, despite developing what has become a lifelong affinity for cartoons, snacky foods, driving fast, sunshine and Disneyland. Los Angeles stamped its cultural footprint on me at an early age, but it also worked the other way. I was always defined as The Australian Girl, called upon to answer second-grade questions like, 'Is your Mom or Dad a convict? And is that like regular jail or do they have bigger chains?' and 'Was there an earthquake which separated Australia from England? If so, were you scared and did you cry?'. I didn't know the answer to any of these questions but I lied with creative abandon, thus assuring my position as professional Australian.

We lived in a nice, typically Californian suburb then, at the base of a canyon, surrounded by palm trees and thirsty green lawns. No one seems to live downtown in LA, and you could almost argue that there isn't one. A collection of suburbs in search of a city is a criticism often levelled at this town. It is incredibly spread out, that much is true. Like New York, I'm so used to seeing LA in all her manifestations on TV and in films that even a fleeting visit gives a sense of homecoming and met expectation that is kind of thrilling on its own. What I remember of LA from my childhood is very limited compared to what has snuck its way in via television. I find I know the street signs – Hollywood and Vine, Melrose, Sunset Strip – as well as the names of suburbs, the cat-calls appropriate to them, the bad places to live, the good places to shop. Somehow I know the names of bars and clubs without trying, of restaurants and beaches too. Think about it. The Viper Room, Pacific Palisades,

Malibu, Encino, Orange County, Beverly Hills and Brentwood – in most parts of the world it must be hard to watch telly or read a newspaper without coming across a reference to some LA landmark or another.

The studios based here have unwittingly created the world's longest running and most effective infomercial for a city. Everywhere you look there's evidence that this is an industry town; the industry being, of course, film and television. Here, it's simply referred to here as 'the business', as if there is any other. Advertisements for editing space and equipment, for entertainment lawyers and new television shows are everywhere, stuck to endless billboards like wallpaper. These same billboards reveal that Los Angeles is a place of constant self-congratulation, with millions of advertising dollars spent by studios announcing their own awards and nominations, pilot programs and block-buster successes. On every corner it seems that someone is filming a commercial or a movie scene, with small crowds and clapper-boards, bodyguards and buxom blondes.

Oh yes, this town is blonde. Girls in some areas are so uniformly blonde and plastic that entire city blocks look related. I think they shoot old women here. That or save them up somewhere out of sight to play 'Starlet's Gram-grams' or 'Starlet – returns to Titanic, add 70 yrs'. It's a transparent town, with miles of shining glass and sparkling fountains, especially in the many pricey malls and pricey neighbourhoods. Down on Melrose, on Rodeo Drive and the beaches, everyone is blonded and nature is tweaked. Venice Beach, with the pumped muscle men and their Barbie admirers, is much like South Beach in Miami, but there is a taut earnestness here that stems more from the desire to make it than make out. There are terribly young girls with obvious breast implants, and either the button-nose fairy has sprinkled far and wide, or there is rhinoplasty aplenty. Like most Los Angelenos, Kevin finds it possible to describe his city as superficial and slightly insane, while loving it proudly at the same time. A bit like having Hugh Hefner as your favourite uncle.

Kevin's dad is a dentist, a good one, which means that Kevin has perfect teeth and two beautiful family homes, one in San Merino, South Pasadena, and one in Big Bear Lake, a resort town outside the city. Kevin's lawn is the size of my high-school oval. You could land a crop-duster on it and this is nothing out of the ordinary in Los Angeles, despite the fact that it is essentially a desert. The Casa de Kevin is a Spanish-style mansion with a large aqua-coloured pool, and it is so completely like television that I squeal upon entry. After a luxurious post-bus shower, it's back in the car and around the corner to where his girlfriend, Kelly, lives in a matching family manor. All this casual glamour has gone straight to my head and as we set a course for Big Bear I collapse quietly in the back of the car, sweating profusely. We head off through shocking traffic and blistering heat.

It strikes me now that everyone I know who has visited the US has visited Los Angeles and San Francisco almost exclusively. Perhaps it's because the West Coast is the drop-off point after 14 hours across the Pacific; perhaps it's all the great free advertising I mentioned earlier. Either way, it's a bit of a shame. This is the path most travelled in America and it's hardly representative, compared with all I've seen so far.

Leaving the city, Kevin's car takes us on a winding drive up some mountains, through Smoky Valley. 'Look at all that smog!' I shout, gesturing back at LA, but everyone insists it's just the natural . . . smokiness. In beautiful Big Bear Lake, Kevin's 'cabin' is revealed to be a five-bedroom house with the grandest of views. Whereas Spanish-style architecture and palm trees typify LA, Big Bear looks more like Colorado in style, a small town of mountains and a deep lake that is exceptionally beautiful. After an indulgent trip to the supermarket, we spend the next two days making sure there is as little blood as possible in our alcohol system, shooting the breeze with Kevin's various friends and family who have joined the weekend exodus from the city.

On Sunday morning, we breakfast at a cutesy place called Teddy Bears. It seems there's nothing in Big Bear that can't be vastly improved by adding bear to its title somewhere, and I remember the Bar and Mainely-s of that other resort town, which now feels very far away. We are in Big Bear in time for an annual rally of dune buggies, and the brave, brightly-coloured little cars zip around everywhere looking very Californian. It's lovely here and I'm very grateful to have had the invitation. Big Bear doesn't exactly feature on the Greyhound route map.

Three of Kev's old school buddies offer to drive me back to Pasadena, fascinated that not only do I intend to ride a Greyhound bus, but that I have in fact been doing so for weeks now and am yet to bear too many visible signs of this social transgression. 'I don't know what you were thinking,' my driver says, 'but, dude, that's not, like, the real America.' If I had a dollar . . .

The four of us are the collective definition of a hangover and, by the time we wind all the way down the mountains in the hot sun, a remedy is called for. In Los Angeles, it's Mexican food. They take me to a cactus-green restaurant called Margaritas for plate-sized burritos with hot tortilla chips and fresh, tangy salsa. It's delicious. The boys know their Mexican food intimately and even those who confess ignorance of the Spanish language have perfect accents and can hold a decent conversation.

Buying food in Big Bear, Kev had remarked that it was good to be back in 'Cally', where there are 12 types of tortilla in any given supermarket. Much is different here, and very 'Californian' – from the avocado-spliced sushi rolls of the same name to the ever-present health-food obsession and the faddish incarnations of everything that's edible.

LA is a town of crazes, with an elusive cool-factor that dips and soars and can be attached to everything from pets to tattoos, vegetables to medication. Los Angelenos love a good gimmick. 'What's the hook?' is all they want to know, straight up. Kelly told me about the new 'Nail Bar', where you get your nails done while getting drunk, and the current rise of spray-tan booths. Even people are not immune. This is the city of the overnight celebrity sensation. Personal stock is rising and plummeting daily, with global reverberations.

Everyone is on a diet in LA. Everyone. The guy who parks your car and the woman who does your laundry are just as ready to spend three hours discussing the merits of the Zone over Atkins as your agent or personal trainer. Despite all the drugs and surgery, there is an inverse emphasis on clean living, with juice bars, yoga centres and fitness freaks galore, and the new state law prohibiting all smoking in clubs and bars seems to have been widely welcomed. Stars, clothes, money, cars. It's a fun but exceedingly shallow town. After we have discussed said stars, clothes, money and cars, talk turns back to food as we plough through litres of melted cheese and guacamole.

'Anybody read *Fast Food Nation*?' someone asks.

'Nah. I really want to though.'

'Yeah.'

'Yeah.'

'Me too.'

There is much quiet nodding. 'But I also kind of don't want to *know* . . .'

Laughter erupts all round and the boys look at me. 'I bet the whole world thinks we're fat and disgusting, huh.' It's not a question, they already know the answer, but like most Americans I've met so far, they are intensely curious about what I think of the US. I tell them first how I'm surprised to find that none of my American friends seem overly defensive of their nation despite the high level of chest-thumping pride and flags wopping you in the face all the time. 'You'd have to be stupid not to see all the shit that's wrong with America,' they say, 'but what, Australia's, like, perfect? And it's still your home, right?' Right. And unfortunately it's very far from perfect at the moment: caught up in controversy over the indecent haste to join the War on Trr, under fire from the UN over refugees in detention centres, Medicare and public education emaciated with rattling change cups, and child obesity rising to levels where all school uniforms will soon need to be elasticised and girdled. I can see the problems, but I can't help feeling that if someone informed me my country was evil and Aussies were all dickheads, I would fire up and wallop them immediately. My American friends, however, are used to it. They love their country and their American lives, but criticise most aspects of it with a candour and casualness that I rarely see at home. There is still a measure of superiority attached to this, though. A wide-eyed 'Don't hate me because I'm beautiful.'

With lunch distending my belly and my much-abused brain threatening to push my eyes out of their sockets, I'm not in the mood for another Greyhound run. The suburban Pasadena bus stop is small and it's not until I wave goodbye to the retreating car that I read the sign telling me its doors will remain closed until the bus actually arrives. Cupping my hands to the cool glass, I can see empty seats in rows and an inviting soft-drink machine. I check my watch. I have two hours and fifteen minutes to wait outside. There is no kerb to speak of, so I rest the tomato-pack against a wall and squash myself back into it on the ground. My hairbrush pokes into my ribcage and my tail-bone is already sore from dancing into a pool table at Big Bear. (My drunken interpretative dances often leave me injured. I get the feeling they might not be very good.)

I want to call the Boy from the payphone, but it's occupied. There's a man talking loudly into the receiver, reliving his abusive childhood at the hands of his demented father. He is talking to his mum – blaming her for being a silent witness to his years of torment. It's harrowing stuff and I eavesdrop contentedly for almost an hour. He finishes abruptly and rides off on a bright orange push-bike, his long ponytail swishing behind him. When I dig out my phone card and pick up the phone, I discover that it's completely dead. There's even an out-of-service sign posted under the handset. This is La-La Land all right. Maybe he was just an actor like everyone else in this town.

The bus arrives and delivers us first to the main Greyhound station, which is forty minutes back into town, in the opposite direction of Las Vegas. Blaring music inside and clouds of cigarette smoke outside beat at my hangover, while I shift on the dirty ground, waiting for a bus that will take me back past where I've just come from. 'An ow-ah!' the woman behind me cries, reading the timetable like it's a ransom note. 'An ow-ah 'n' foddy-five minutes! It doan take no *ow-ah* 'n' foddy-five minutes to get to San Berdoo! What kind of messed-up shit do dis bus do?' My question exactly.

In front of me stands a Mexican woman with a huge tattoo on her ankle depicting Speedy Gonzales having sexual relations with Snow White. She also has what appears to be a Soviet-made toaster-oven balanced on one shoulder, which turns out to be an early-model video camera, and she is filming every second as her family prepares to take the bus. Three men and a boy stand and talk, then stand in silence, then shuffle their bags. Using the massive video camera to zoom in, then out, in, then out, she captures every second of the riveting drama. If she only turned a little to her right, I think, she could become a home-entertainment-package winner on *America's Funniest Home Video Show*. There, a woman has bunched a bright yellow towel into a pillow shape and is holding it in her arms. Her husband stands, bends at the waist and drops his face right in, and sleeps standing up for the next half an hour. It's incredible. That, I think, is the magic of Greyhound.

Chapter 15

Pennies from heaven

When the bus pulls up it flicks the destination sign over to 'Las Vegas' and I begin to get very excited indeed. I stand up and begin a little toe dance of joy, tapping one foot and shugging my shoulders along to an internal rendition of rhinestone Elvis. Bbbrright light city, gonna set my soul, GONNA SET MY SOUL on fi-yaaah ... VIVA LAS VEGAS (*by-ow, by-ow, by-ow*) ...

On the bus, I discover for the first time that Greyhound seats are actually on tracks so that they can be moved backwards and forwards. This is ostensibly for wheelchairs, but this time it seems allowance has been made for a quartet of exiting fatties. I pick a seat with zero legroom before the seats are hefted up and locked back into place. I do this intentionally with high hopes that I will be left alone on what looks likely to be a very crowded bus. The Greyhound attendant moving the resistant upholstery is sweating like a Romanian weight lifter and he looks at me skeptically as I motion that he can leave my pinched seat where it is.

'That gonna be enough room?' he asks, frowning. I smile sweetly as I explain, 'If anyone wants to sit next to me, they'll have to be very, very, very tiny.' He smiles too and we chuckle together as only people who understand the world of the Dawg can. Sure enough, people pass me by time and again on account of the pitiful lack of room. A big cranky couple gets on and start hollering about how there's no seats left. There are lots of seats in the back half of the bus. I am hungover and suffering food-coma interruptus from the burrito. Eventually, I stand up and point the seats out. 'Nuh uh!' the woman says. 'We want to sit together. We hain't no sittin' with no stranger.'

'Ever ridden a Greyhound before?' I splutter. Everyone moans heartily in agreement. I sit down very pleased with myself, for I have thus established myself early as the bitch not to mess with on this trip. A final snarl and some furious scratching seals the deal. I will be left alone. I settle in comfortably and doze with my feet tucked up on my microscopic seat.

Half an hour later we're in Hollywood. Four plump, sun-burned Brits with voices like foghorns get on. The bus is now filled with vowels and squeals, and every five minutes, 'Ooooooh, Kaaaaay-teee, whot's that then? Isn't it beeeuuuuutiful! Ooh, oooooh, look at thaaaat. Ooh, I love thhhaat, that's so pretty. Me mum'd 'ave one of thooose if she could!' To use their own vernacular, they were doin' me 'ead in. Shrieking with giggles, they turn our world into some alternative-reality *Spice World* movie, where Spice Girls mate with Teletubbies and their obnoxious offspring are left to travel the country via Greyhound. Unbelievably, the largest of the group bounces up and sits right down next to me on the smallest bus seat on this continent. She promptly squashes us both. 'Haafffarrrh!' I say, as the last of the oxygen is expelled from my constricted lungs. She turns her bulk to face me so that my head has no choice but to crack against the window. 'Oi!' she says, 'oi! Do you think they moved our seats? I'm right squashed in 'ere! I'm soooo uncomfy liiike!' I try to nod. She keeps asking me if I think the seat is too small and do I think they moved it, and am I a bit sick, by the way, because I look a bit sick. After the third time she asks, I utter my low Greyhound growl of warning before she completes the question. 'Oh,' she says, gawping, 'I s'pose you're squashed too then.' A few seconds silence. 'Are you wondering why, though? Wondering why they moved the seat like?'

'Not really,' I wheeze out. 'I'm trying to sleep. So mostly I'm just wondering how to stay asleep.' She stares at me, mouth open, eyes narrowing as if I'm some kind of possum-like creature talking Swahili, and then laughs in my face. 'You'll never get to sleep pushed all over the window like thaaat, don't be daft!' Mercifully, someone gets off at the next stop and she scoots over to sit with her fellow Teletubbies. Much shrieking and primary-school hilarity ensues. One of the girls burps involuntarily, and this becomes the source of endless repeats of the incident and how funny the noise was, and how it smelled of chicken salad. My fingers are itchy with the urge to slap each one of their pink and yawping cheeks.

It takes two hours just to get out to San Bernardino, on the outskirts of LA, a place I passed coming back from Big Bear some seven hours ago. I'd shake my head if it wasn't filled with electrically-charged cement. Fighting reflux and swearing off alcohol until my future children's graduation drinks, I have five minutes to myself before my skinny seat is hijacked. A large Mexican woman and her husband get on. She is yelling at him in a steady stream of Spanish while raising her arms high in the air to reveal tropical armpits. I close my eyes and pray hopelessly. I've played Greyhound chess so many times before that I can see this woman's move before she does. I know without a shadow of a doubt that she's headed to the seat next to me. Although no bigger than a cat-box, it is now the only spot with an empty seat adjacent to it where she can park hubby under her watchful glare.

I play asleep. Actually, I play dead, which isn't hard to do considering the extent of my hangover. I have learnt that if you open your mouth and loll your tongue slightly, you look more unconscious than peaceful, indicating you've been asleep for hours and are therefore probably smelly and beat, or under the influence of some intoxicant – liable to become dangerous or lose your stomach's contents at a moment's notice. These are all equally undesirable qualities in a seatmate. The fat woman's screeching continues up the bus until my amputated seat, where it stops. Shit. I manufacture some drool. I really, really need to sleep off Big Bear. Suddenly there's a noise that I slowly connect with a sharp, stinging pain on my exposed leg. *Penne del Perro!* The whore has slapped me! 'Hey!' she yells, spittle flying. 'You! Lazy! Wake up!' I open my eyes and fix her with the stare

I reserve for people who use almost all the peanut butter and put the jar back with a lone, pathetic scraping. 'Hey!' she says again, 'you! Why this seat so small, ah? Why so close to the other, ah? Ah?'

'Your guess,' I hiss, 'is as good as mine, madam.'

'You need to move, ah! Move over. I sit *here*!'

'Sure!' I say with a smile that I hope conveys every inch of my fervent wish that she contract an incurable disease involving flesh-eating bacterium. She squashes me against the window and complains energetically in Spanish for the next 12 miles. Abruptly, she ceases and begins to doze, head back, mouth wide open. Her breath pours out, a hellish effluent that fills the air for a square metre, making me wretch and gag. 'Shut your mouth!' I scream inside, squashed against the greasy window, hungover and too hot, fighting for air. I deliver a quick jab to the ribs and she wakes, snorting, closing her trap. Oh, thank God. But God doesn't really care, apparently, because now she's started to yawn instead. Each putrescent yawn requires me to struggle against my instinct to join in and then to hold my breath for one full minute. Fury burns and boils and roils inside me, along with all that sour cream and the refried beans.

At 2 am the driver flicks the interior lights on and we are schussing into Vegas across the barren Nevada desert. The Teletubbies start up a chorus of chatter so loud and inane I would happily bash all their heads together for an American penny and half a postage stamp. The driver turns the mike on. 'First stop is the Stratosphere,' he says. 'Stratosphere Tower Hotel and Casino, highest point in Nevada . . .' He could be announcing the county sewerage works for all I care: I want out.

The driver pulls the bus in slowly and I stand up. Beside me, the fat woman, who has foolishly jammed herself into the tiny legroom of my seat in order to bitch at the poor idiot who married her, is now trapped. She moves pointlessly against the solid armrest for a second or two and then stops. She looks at me and makes a faintly disgusted noise, as if it is I who have somehow conspired to make her so immovably corpulent. The driver, watching in his rear-view mirror, asks if she needs help getting out. 'No!' she says, 'Not me, I no need to get out! Is her! Is she!' she keeps pointing an accusing finger at my face. 'She need! Not me! I not get out until Plaza Hotel!' She wedges one big thigh firmly under the armrest and stays put. Now we're both trapped.

'If you would just spin around and stand up ...' I suggest lamely, stating the blindingly obvious. The driver concurs. 'Now, ma'am,' he tells her, 'neither of you can go *through* the armrest. That would be impossible, *comprende*? So just back-up and we'll get you out.'

'NO!' she screams, 'I no need to get out! Is she!' This time she points her finger until it hits my nose. That's it, I have had it with the busload of lunatiles. 'That's right!' I scream back. 'It's me! I need to get off! Me! NOW! So stand up or I'll squash you like a BUG on my way out of this seat!' I stand up on my half of the seat, face pressed against the light and the little air vent; one working not at all and one too well. I lift my grimy sneakered foot up and place it on the armrest, threatening an imminent squashing. She squeals and swivels around, hefting herself out of the seat in the space of a nanosecond. 'THANK YOU!' I scream at them all. 'THANK YOUUU!' throwing my luggage off onto the street, kicking past the Teletubbies in a blind fury.

Inside the heavy, brass revolving door of the Stratosphere's side entrance is a quiet telephone lounge and coatroom. Oozing into a comfortable chair, I flick through the Las Vegas *Yellow Pages* and make a call to the inexpensive looking Sahara Casino Hotel. I ask my questions and there is a clacking of computer keys on the other end of the line. 'With tax, your double room will be $28. Will you be staying with us tonight?' Hell yeah.

I stumble from the Stratosphere, still buckled into my fleece and bag, sweating and gnashing my teeth in the dry desert night. I cross the bottom end of Las Vegas Boulevard, the fat, glitzy avenue better known as 'the Strip', and head on into the Sahara. One of the older hotel-casinos, the Sahara is outfitted with an Arabian Nights theme and would still be lovely if the amazing new casinos weren't around to make it look like a truck-stop. I have come looking for price, not grandeur, but I still think it's a fun place, swinging my room key round my finger in delight and singing an improv medley of tunes from Disney's *Aladdin*.

Everyone is still up, playing the slot machines and tables, so that downstairs at 2.30 in the morning on a Monday, it looks like ten o'clock on a Friday night. The Las Vegas hospitality staff in these low-rent casinos have a distinct look. Careworn and weary, with hair and make-up reminiscent of high glam in the former Soviet Union and teeth thrown in haphazardly by a poor man's God at the end of His shift.

I glide past it all to the elevators, dying to see what kind of hotel room can be had for such small bucks. My room is massive. I drop my bag and cover my mouth with my hand, tears prickling, like a girl who's just found nine carats in her champers. There are two queen-sized beds, a large marble bathroom with a big tub, hairdryer and small packets of nonsense, as well as a giant TV and what appear to be enough towels for each body part to be dried separately, including digits. I strip off, set the AC for Bar Harbor, pull the blackout curtains tight and hop in under the heavy covers for one of the all-time best sleeps of my life so far.

The next morning I shower like a coal miner and sit on one of my beds, in an island of fluffy towels, planning my day. It feels good to wake up in Las Vegas.

I came here four years ago as an accident, an unavoidable detour to pick up a Rent-a-Wreck Dodge. Driving in on a Greyhound across the glaring desert, we had passed tiny towns with tumbleweeds, where main streets offered little but porno shops and chiropractors, before miles of rocky nothingness. 'I thought Las Vegas was near a big city,' I had said to my friend and seatmate, 'or something.' She had been looking out the window for hours with a wrinkled nose and echoed, glumly, 'Mmm. Or something.' The plan had been to pick up the car, hop straight in and drive away, but after three days and nights on Greyhound, we knew we had to revise that idea. The only one of us who could legally drive in America had been telling himself jokes and laughing with surprise at the punchlines for half a state now, and continuing the journey to the West Coast seemed like folly.

Las Vegas had risen out of the yellow gravel like a giant lunar colony. Gleaming silver and green, with pyramids and palm trees, spires and satellite dishes, it was plunked arbitrarily amidst a wasteland of harsh geography. I had expected to hate Las Vegas immediately. A tacky tourist town of poker machines and tawdry entertainment, of pensioner tours and quickie Elvis weddings. Girls with fake boobs and feathered hats. Those two creepy guys called something like Sven and Sinbad with their white lions. Ewww.

What we had found instead was a magical wonderland of cheap and colourful fun. We wandered for hours down the strip, through temples at Luxor, the pyramids at Giza, Arthurian castles, Manhattan and Monaco, a big-top circus and pirate's lair, before resting at the base of an erupting volcano. We drank dollar daiquiris and ate dollar shrimp cocktails, before discovering all-you-can-eat buffets that started at three bucks. Frank Sinatra sang to us from every direction, telling luck to be a lady and imploring us to watch for pennies from heaven. Drunk, full and comfortably bedded, we had barely touched our wallets. Las Vegas, I had decided, was my kind of town.

Today it's much hotter than I remember it here and so bright that it's hard to open my eyes past the point where my lashes meet. My first stop is the tacky souvenir shop over the road for some plastic sunnies. A chubby guy perusing the aisles in front of me cries out 'Honey!' to his wife and holds up a pair of 'I Crapped Out at Las Vegas' briefs. Next he finds a T-shirt proclaiming 'Loose Slots', as well as some other tasteful craps merchandise. I soon leave off my own investigation and follow him around. He has a nose for the good stuff. I leave without sunglasses but a significant number of pens with ugly men on them, whose clothes slide off cunningly when tipped upside down.

Down in the heart of the action, Las Vegas is even bigger and better than I remember. Three sprawling new casinos dwarf the others, gleaming with a sophistication that seems unlikely for a town never accused of being sophisticated. The stunning Bellagio, the new 'it' casino for the big-moneyed set, has a theme I can't really identify apart from Luxe. It's surrounded by miles of still, clear water behind a long balustrade suggestive of ancient Roman glory, and has a shining frontage evoking Mediterranean palaces. Up close, the marble seems to whisper *cha-ching*! Music is discreetly piped in all along the waterfront like it's your own private cinematic theme. I play Audrey in *Roman Holiday*, pretending that my grubby Sketchers are ballet flats, and then have to work a stubbed toe and grazed knuckles into the script.

Across the strip is another new casino and hotel, the Venetian. Jaunty gondoliers ply their antique boats around the waterways, which lap past old trattorias and other convincing Venetian buildings. I lean on the rail and gaze down into the exquisite water. Beside me, a couple in matching Bermuda shorts are catching their breath. 'Hey, Deeel-ya,' says the puffing man, holding his guidebook at arm's length, 'says here that tha Veneeshun is now the world's largest hotel, with 6000 suites.' Deeel-ya just nods smugly and says, 'Dinnin I tell you we should come? Dinnin I?' He ignores her and reads again. 'Says here that tha owner of the Veneeshun flew to Venice, Italy, after it was built, came back to Nevada and ordered tha whole damn canal drained and repainted. Said it wasn't tha exact same shade of aqua as Venice, Italy.' He wipes his brow and whistles. 'Ain't that somethin'?' And it really is. The water is magic, like cloudy green glass, and the attention to detail in all of these new places is quite breathtaking.

Las Vegas seems to have gone beyond being Disneyland for grown-ups and become more like *Lifestyles of the Rich and Famous*, without the pesky, velvet-roped no-go zones. For very minimal sums, you can play-pretend that you live in a mansion all day, kissing your sweetheart on a Venetian canal after lunch in Arabia, before dinner in New York City and dessert on the French Riviera. In dire need of air conditioning, I enter Paris, another brand-spanker, and flop down onto a red velvet chair in the registration area. It looks like Versailles. In fact, with its impossibly high ceilings, crystal chandeliers and cold marble desks, it looks more like Versailles than Versailles. Classical music tinkles in from somewhere and it's so romantic, so European, so . . . *clean*, that I want to cry.

Content to sit dribbling in my velvet cradle, I watch the scores of tourists checking in and out. There is only a smattering of shining, plastic trophy women amidst a sea of matching velour pant-suits and wide shorts attached to 'fanny packs'. White sneakers cover every pair of feet as if it might be Nevada state law, and I can see why visitors get disappointed at the lack of glamour on the floor. All the grown-ups are dressed like children and there are hardly any children in Vegas. That's a good thing really, as there's nothing much for them to do. They can't go anywhere near the pokies, and the casinos make sure that you can gamble in some way every 2.4 metres.

In search of nourishment I head off to find the Excalibur, an older casino with a Knights of the Round Table theme, which looks like a Disney-princess castle. I remember their buffet as being particularly cheap, and it still is, but the food looks pretty bland. Peering past a pissed-off Lady Gwenivere at the register, I spy oily lasagna, stodgy chow mein and some kind of bulk pasta, as well as trays of iceberg lettuce salad and some gloopy pink desserts. At about four bucks for all you can eat it's hardly falling on your sword, but without the dollars or sense needed for gambling, I have little to do but explore my dining options anyway.

After a two-hour tour of Las Vegas comprised entirely of its buffets, I learn much about ice sculpture, napkin art, and how best to plump up your fruit platter (whole pineapples). My previously growling tum has now shrunk, confused at all the sumptuous imagery. I think it thinks we've eaten. Tired and hot, I stop back in at Paris, because their toilet signage is the most obvious, and then end up quite lost. It's very easy to get into a casino, but nearly impossible to get out – I get the feeling that the insides of entrance doors are all painted like wall panels. After wandering confused for a bit, I resign myself to an afternoon in the French capital.

There is no dog poo on the streets of Paris, Nevada, a tiny fraction of the second-hand smoke and none of the pissing in corners of Paris, France. The old joke about Paris being a great place except for all the French might just be true. This Paris has climate control. Everywhere I turn there are people who smile at me and say pleasant things. There are no triple-espresso drivers trying to mow me down, and there's no stumbling over these painted cobblestones. But, just like the authentic Paree, it's still filled with American tourists who, as Erin would say, look like they've dressed themselves at the Teachers' Shop.

I happen upon La Village buffet and jump in line despite the shocking price. At $12 for the 'regional French cuisine' it's the most expensive buffet I've seen so far, but I figure I might not find my way out of Paris for a while yet, and I'm an instant sucker for the kind of fakery they've employed here. La Village is created as an outside-inside village square, with a false courtyard filled with little tables under a high painted sky. Dotted around the pretend open-air pretend village square are fully enclosed pretend cafés with their own tables, and open windows with views of the pretend outside. If this level of cubby house ingenuity doesn't make you tap your toes with gleeful anticipation, then you've missed the point of Las Vegas entirely.

Once inside the village walls, I take a seat in the middle of the action and look around. A charming patisserie is open for business and I head over with my plate, suspending disbelief in order to fulfil a recurring fantasy of mine. A little cake shop just for me, where I can have anything I want, over and over and over again. I sample two or nine things right away, before eating three mini raspberry cheesecakes, a slice of sachertorte, a warm chocolate croissant and a freshly fired crème brûlée. Waitresses float around dressed as mademoiselles from some kind of story-book French countryside, which is very cute except that they all appear to be far from Gallic in ethnic origin. My waitress is Hong Kong Chinese, but she manages to look oddly darling in her *Les Misérables* ensemble. She brings me a little individual pot of coffee with cream, milk and sugar, and replenishes my choc-cream splattered china.

Wandering the village, I find what must be the local fish-monger's and make the switch from pastries to prawns. There must be whole rivers of seafood flown into this town, absolute buckets of the stuff. Laid end to end, there are surely enough crustaceans in Las Vegas to cover the entire desert state. Sadly, I'm almost full by the time I discover the cooked-to-order crepes, so I only eat three, all with lemon and sugar. My waitress sees me struggling on the last one, and comes over. 'More coffee?' she asks, and I signal no, but she pours anyway. 'The food here is so good,' she says, leaning over me with her milk-maid bodice, curled plaits and Asian eyes. 'Just have a rest, okay? You've hardly tried anything!' After giving me a breather, this marvellously kind woman even lets me go out, buy a magazine and return to continue eating, which clearly violates every written and unwritten rule pertaining to all-you-can-eat establishments. I think she's bored with the French countryside, though, because she keeps coming over to chat. She tells me that someone leapt to their death from the Stratosphere last night and the whole town is abuzz. 'Wow!' I say, 'I should have bought the newspaper instead.' She just laughs. 'Oh it won't be in the *paper*!' she says, as if this was the last place to find a breaking story, and shoos me off to the food again.

I switch to savoury now. Farfalle pasta with tomatoes, basil and fetta, duck with brandy, three kinds of smoked fish, four kinds of soft cheese, soups, salads, saffron-infused wild mussels. More prawns. I have some warm crusty bread with pâté, and finish my magazine along with two bowls of fresh strawberries dipped into side dishes of double cream, another round of pastries, a few petits fours and a final pot of steaming coffee. I stay for three hours. The food is so good that I disgust myself by wondering if a trip to the bathroom, spinning around and around thinking thoughts of road-kill, might make some more room to go again. I remember studying Roman orgies, shaking my head at the ornate vomit receptacles on hand to allow neverending gluttony, but now I think those toga-tycoons were really onto something. By the time I roll out of La Village and back onto la street, I'm so full that I can feel the food tickling my back teeth, but it's no good. My body demands we keep it all. I pat my swollen stomach. It's okay, Tum, I console, we'll be back.

I hang out at Treasure Island for a bit and watch the huge fake pirate ship sink into the fake Caribbean sea it floats on, before securing a good spot for the spectacular fountain display at the Bellagio. At Caesar's Palace I have a cold drink in the Forum where the painted sky changes gradually from dawn to dusk every few hours. Passing Harrah's Casino, a car talks to me. Rather suggestively, too. 'Ooooh,' it says, 'I can tell you're lucky [low giggle]. Why don't you go on inside and *win* me . . .' The

Harrah's tagline – 'Luxury and excitement are closer than you think!' – combine with this AI automobile to give the place a creepy, *Blade Runner*-ish feel. Bits of that dystopic movie come flashing back to me. 'A new life awaits you in the off-world colonies,' and Las Vegas does feel like an off-world colony. A patch of scrabbly, uninhabitable moon-rock covered with a false paradise, containing snippets of earth's favourite things all conveniently close together and climate controlled. The splendour of the ancient world, the marvel of modern cities, all specially re-created with the nasty bits left out. A sinister shadow falls over the strip for me then and I run off to the Fashion Show mall, annoyed at the intrusion of reality in my fantasy vacation.

It's early when I decide to leave the mall and head back to my room for more rest. I love my room. I am inordinately pleased with it and I'm surprised at how shattered I am from the past few weeks of Greyhound seats and itchy hostel bunks. The Sahara is away from the main drag, so I stop in at a Walgreen's (one of many American super-pharmacies that sell everything except light aircraft) to pack myself a picnic for later.

I buy some Salsa Verde Doritos, 39 flavours of Jelly Belly Jellybeans, a packet of Cool Dill chips, a six-pack of Coors beer and a Vanilla Coke chaser. I keep forgetting you can buy beer at the supermarket here. And at the gas station, the corner shop and the pharmacy – which is where it really belongs anyway. You can buy wine, too, but not the hard stuff. No, sir, you can't buy real likker anywhere but a likker store. That kind of 'Well, we wouldn't want anyone getting drunk now' logic is a bit dubious, but Australia is worse. I don't know why we can't buy beer in the supermarket at home.

For a nation that loves its booze as much as Australia, I never understand why our access to it is so restricted. Going to all the trouble of attaching separate liquor shops to Aussie super-markets seems particularly anal, transparent and, well, American. Like America's laughable over-21 drinking age. Heads-up to the generals fighting the War on Drugs: American youth now find it much easier to snort a line than chug a beer. If you have to check ID anyway, I wonder why it matters so much where our grog is sold in Oz. Cigarettes are age-restricted but you can by them at the newsagency with your school pencil case and – this just in – they fucking kill you. I have to admit, though, putting frosty brewskis in the same aisle as chips and dip is a little too effective at cross-marketing. In America, I'm drunk every time I feel like a few Pringles.

The TV in my room has three channels devoted to teaching me how to gamble my money away downstairs, as well as a polite smattering of free-to-air channels and CNN. I guess they don't want anyone hanging out in the room for too long. It doesn't matter. I'm asleep in my clothes after only one beer, my body struggling to maintain basic functioning and process 14,000 calories at the same time.

The next morning I wake to a curious conversation taking place outside my door. A man operating what sounds like a cleaning cart is trying to explain to another that he is in fact from Pakistan, which is definitely not India, land of the treacherous, leprous dog. He goes on at some length, his insults becoming ever more creative, until he is forced to pause and ask his companion, 'I am sorry, which language do you speak?' The other man replies haltingly, in a heavy Eastern-bloc accent, that he is learning English. Las Vegas is America's fastest growing city and the people who live here and work to sustain the dreamscape come from an incredible lolly-bag of cultures. There are lots of recent immigrants in this town, no doubt attracted by the low cost of housing and the semi-skilled labour needed by all these hotels. The Las Vegas phone directory is filled with immigration services. I know this because I called about half of them the last time I was in this city. The time of my student-visa scare, just after my knock-kneed fibbing to the INS on the Greyhound in New Mexico. Thinking about it now makes me realise again what a golden ticket my Green Card is.

After another gastronomic orgy at La Village, it's time for me to leave. On the local bus, the CAT 180 to the Greyhound stop downtown, I meet some real Las Vegans. 'Hey!' I say, 'I heard that someone jumped from the Stratosphere yesterday. Is that just a joke or what?' Each of the other four passengers has heard this too, and one of them says he knows for sure because his flatmate works the rides there. 'But it's not in the paper,' I say, and everyone just laughs the way my waitress did. 'Hon,' says the oldest of the bunch, a part-pensioner who works at the Plaza, 'this is a *casino* town. The casinos hide everything and always have. Ya couldn't have Las Vegas if they didn't!' Everyone nods but I'm still unconvinced. Like I've said before, Americans love a good conspiracy theory.

'Lotta jumpers in Vegas,' says a hairdresser from the Mirage. 'People were always going off the car park at the Mint, but it's not there anymore.'

'Yeah,' the old guy from the Plaza agrees, 'we used to always say, "If I lose another twenny, you'll find me at the Mint!"' There are knowing chuckles all round. 'Car parks are still favourites with the jumpers,' he says. 'They're mostly high enough to kill ya for sure, but without the security of the hot spots, the visible places.' The hairdresser is emphatic. 'It happens here all the time! As well as all the rapes and murders. There's too many strippers and call girls out here, and they ask for trouble in that line of business.' She points at me. 'A tourist? Like you? You will never, ever see it in the papers or hear about it on the Strip. Las Vegas protects itself. It's marketed very carefully now. It's protected.' Everybody nods, and the old guy takes the baton. 'All you gotta do to make money in a casino is open your door. But you gotta keep your nose clean to keep your doors open.'

'Okay,' I say, 'but how do *you* know about the Stratosphere story then? And the other stuff?' A burnt-out woman with bleached hair and cracked make-up is the one to answer. 'The grapevine is thick with fruit,' she says. 'If you work at McDonald's you know about makin' burgers. If you work in Vegas you know about keeping secrets.' Everyone nods and falls quiet. She clutches tighter to her M&M factory bag. 'Good luck on your trip,' she whispers to me hoarsely, 'I'm leaving Las Vegas too.'

'Yeah?' I say.

'Yeah. I'm leaving for good,' she says in the same thin whisper.

'Hey!' I say, 'just like the song . . .' I hum a few bars of Sheryl Crow's Vegas anti-anthem, but she doesn't know it, projecting a blank look on the wall of the bus as she steps off and we drive away.

I'm two hours early at the bus stop and resign myself to the recurring Greyhound protocol. Gate navigation, followed by line-squatting. When you figure out which door your bus is heading from, you must plonk your bags down on the tiles or cement in front of that door and start waiting. No matter how early you are. No matter how filthy the floor. The last person in this line gets a seat next to the toilets or no seat at all. No seat at all is also referred to as the Next Bus Nightmare, which could mean a 24-hour wait at the same gate. The rules of engagement are always the same. There will be no actual seats anywhere near your gate and if Hades ices up and there are, they will already be occupied by some permanent, babbling greasies. Sitting on the floor is thus always a requirement, and while trying to sit on hard, grubby surfaces for hours is excruciating, it is also mandatory. There are limited positions possible. There's Indian cross until your legs go to sleep; then both legs under; then one leg side, one leg under; other leg side, other leg under; then both out in front; then standing. Repeat. You may not leave once committed. I sit down Indian style.

Behind me are some trench-coated, metal-studded, dyed-hair Marilyn Manson wannabes from 'middle school' who entertain me with conversation in squeaky voices like, 'Dude, he was the guy who started the rumour that I crashed his site. I didn't crash his lame-ass site!' They continually adjust the laces on their shoes, so they're undone just so, and tease one of their party for a scorch mark on his shiny pants. 'Dude, it was my mom! Do you think I would, like, iron stuff?' These guys are great. When their bus comes I curse out loud for the entertainment vacuum they will leave behind them.

A young guy gets off an incoming bus with a giant backpack and a VB beer T-shirt. Australia's finest. Homesickness washes over me in a clammy wave. I get out my map and fold both legs underneath me while I look over it. My eyes find Las Vegas and trace a line going down in a low arc swinging to the right, on and on, then down again into the finger-shaped state of Florida. And if I keep going right, right, right across the world, through Africa, Asia, then right across the lonelier half of Australia, I'll be home. I tap at Sydney a bit with the end of my pen, and I feel better. It's still there. I can still find it if I need to.

But first I have to get to Tucson, Arizona, a place I know only from a Paul Simon song and a brief moment's embarrassment when I pronounced it 'Tuck-son' instead of 'Two-sonn' while reading aloud a newspaper article about that Biosphere dome they built there in the nineties. When my bus pulls up I discover that I'll get to travel by coach all the way to Phoenix, the Arizona state capital, before I have to sit in the old Greyhound tinnies again. This is very good news. The coach has big, roomy seats that recline and we'll be travelling overnight.

Once we're all aboard and headed south, the driver clears his throat a few times and clicks on the mike. 'Good afternoon,' he says, and the ten of us mumble an awkward series of replies. 'Now,' he says, 'let's see if anyone can tell me about the liquid in the toilet bowls there at the back.' What? 'Anyone? Don't be shy now.' An uncomfortable silence follows. 'Is iiiiit ... blue?' a woman from the back asks in an I-Spy voice. 'Mmm, could be,' the driver says, 'but something else too. Anyone?' 'Ah, is it disinfected?' someone wonders, 'for germs?' The driver nods and takes one hand off the wheel, which he waves in a circle indicating that more information is necessary. After about twenty minutes of concentrating our thoughts on the bowl of the bus toilet, I'm starting to regret my farewell date with La Village.

'Okay,' says the driver, 'I'll tell you. The liquid in the bus toilets is highly *flammable*, and what does flammable mean?' He answers this for us. 'Flames. It will burst into flames. Now I'm gonna go ahead and connect the dots for ya. Don't smoke in the toilet, not even a drag, because if you do, we'll all know about it very quickly and it ain't pretty I can tell you. In fact it's dis-GUST-ing.' There is silence for a while punctuated by a few giggles as the driver turns off his mike and we are left to contemplate explosive ka-ka. Ugh.

I won't need to visit the flammable hole of stenches on this bus though. I ration my sips of water carefully and break out the Cheezits whenever osmosis needs a hand. My seat is exceptionally comfortable. It should be easy to fall asleep but I find myself trapped in a sluggish, stary-eyed wakefulness, unable to dribble or doze. I put it down to being spoilt at the Sahara. My body is sulking now, demanding horizontal. It will soon learn, I think, grimly remembering the map. Out the window I get the sense of a grand voyage, a true continental crossing, as we drive for miles of dark nothing edged by a deep horizon. There are so many towns and names unvisited, never even heard of or considered. This is a country as vast as my own and it often feels as empty. I squash my faithful pillow in towards me as we whisper on into the night.

Chapter 16

Road Runner

I awake on the outskirts of Phoenix to discover that the driver has played the usual trick of turning the heating up to equatorial after we're all tightly rugged up against sub-arctic and fast asleep. I'm boiling hot and terribly slimy, forced to apply an itching fifth layer of deodorant. Shining silver in the dawn, the Phoenix Greyhound terminal is pretty classy. Inside, above the ticket desks, big panels blink with electronic readouts for arrival and departure times. They aren't even remotely acquainted with accuracy, but they look very techie and I am impressed. International flags hang from the ceiling and across the road is the airport, where huge planes are taking off into a postcard-perfect sunrise.

I wait in line to find out when the Tucson connection leaves, yawning and stretching and shuffling along with a few hundred others. I have plenty of time to peruse the two large and evocative Greyhound posters that are affixed to the front counter. 'Go Greyhound', the text implores in dreamy, freehand script, 'and leave the driving to us.' There are a series of rich, hand-drawn images in which two bus seats are repeatedly visible, with loads of legroom and no other passengers around. Outside huge clean windows, the people sitting in these twin seats point out various scenic wonders to each other. A woman and child smile out at lush green fields and cows, a Hispanic man explains the nation's Capitol building to his son. A black guy in army fatigues and a blonde college student with a courteously-volumed Walkman are happy together as they look out onto a bright cityscape. An elderly woman sleeps peacefully by herself and two girlfriends watch the turning of autumn leaves to a festival of red and gold outside. Laid out like a children's book, this poster ought to be titled 'Fat Fucking Chance', I think to myself, and I notice that other people are also sniggering.

The next bus is very full by the time I climb on board, but this trip is only a short one. Scudding across a desert towards the new sun, I can see already that it's quite different from California or Nevada. The houses in this arid region are painted warm yellow, with red roofs, and tall fluffy palms like poodle tails, like cocktail straws, are thrown around without pattern amongst low-lying scrub. We pass signs for towns called Lone Butte and Wild Horse Pass, and this looks suspiciously like Hollywood cowboy territory to me.

The air is dry and pleasant when I hop out in Tucson. The sky is particularly blue and cloudless and, like Boulder, I know this city enjoys 300-odd days of sunshine a year. That, I think happily, is extravagantly good weather. The hotel suggested by my now filthy but indispensable guidebook, is only a block from the bus station. Or it would be, had I not just walked six blocks in the wrong direction before looking it up. This is nothing new for me. I always travel with a few extra snacks and some appropriate swear words up my sleeve, factoring my lack of internal compass into my calculations.

It's late morning when I arrive at the Hotel Congress. It's a beautiful place, a real antique from the time of railroad travel and steamer trunks. The desk clerk tells me that the Gangster John Dillinger checked in here with his gang in the early thirties. Looking around at the brick and marble, the stained glass and the private, mahogany phone booths, I can't think why management have allowed some rooms to become share accommodation at eighteen bucks a night. Seems foolish to me, but I'm certainly not complaining.

Once inside my room, I kick the door closed with my foot, dropping bags and sweaty clothes on my way into the shower. I'm the only one in here so it's quite the bargain. The narrow bed has crispy white sheets under a slow moving ceiling fan, with an antique radio on a small dressing table. I dress from the least dirty of my clothes and realise that laundry is once again in order. Gathering my rags into the striped pillowcase, I hoist it over my shoulder and step out into the corridor. It's cool and dark in here. There are old carpets and hall runners across the creaking boards and the whole place feels wonderfully mysterious in the way particular to creepy old hotels.

I don't get much further than the café downstairs where the smell of warm piecrust grabs me by the nose and demands that dessert be called breakfast. After gobbling a giant slice of fragrant pecan pie with lashings of cream, I order some coffee to face the day with. Once the coffee cup is drained, the clock has ticked over into the luncheon hour, and I have no choice but to order and consume a big BLT on rye, extra bacon, Spanish onion, hold the mayo. I'm still hungry. I think La Village must have ruined me, but I order half a chicken sandwich and the gazpacho anyway. I can afford the extravagance. The end of this trip seems inevitable now that I've reached the far side of the country and am looping back down across the bottom. By the time I finish all my food the end of the trip is even closer, and I have to scurry off to make the most of my day.

I head over to the laundry a few streets away before exploring the town. Inside, under the many signs imploring us not to wash clothes with tar on them, there is a little collection of silent and beautiful women. These people look very different to me from the Spanish-speaking grab bag labelled 'Hispanic' in other big cities. I'm very curious and do a lot of staring. There are mothers and daughters whose faces seem as old as time, Inca faces, faces that belong on *National Geographic* covers, faces that I never see in my country. These aren't the city-slick girls from Brooklyn with their hoop earrings and bandannas, nor the Puerto Rican moms with their American magazines. These are South American people, I tell myself, awed by their long, heavy hair, their suede skin and inky eyes.

Mexican art and motifs appear everywhere in Tucson, scattered amongst the small, white-rendered houses and the old Spanish architecture of the churches and public buildings. Splashes of bright colour leap from walls and desert gardens in the dry, sun-bleached town. The sky remains huge and sun-filled, the temperature constant and hot throughout the day. I'm struck by how much it looks like *Road Runner* country. Cacti appear all over the place in an astonishing array of shapes and sizes, including the large saguaro cactus that is peculiar to Arizona and parts of Mexico. They're the giant ones with an extra prong on the side that makes them look like a child's drawing of a Gumby-man waving. They can live to be 200 years old – the stately old trees of the desert. Tucson is another college town and it's filled with lots of beautiful young things and trendy places for them to go. It's cheap, too. A full load of washing has just cost me 75 cents, local buses cost a dollar and soft-drink vending machines can be found for 50 cents a can.

I walk past the Greyhound stop again on my way back from the laundry. A big, full bus is heading out, safety lights on, the driver moving his mouth, no doubt giving the usual spiel. Unlike my civilian-life Greyhound encounter in Colorado, I suddenly have the urge to just hop on and go too. I might hate bus-life, but I realise that I'm also getting used to it. I've got some kind of battered wife thing going on, or Stockholm syndrome, where I'm over-identifying with my kidnappers. I'm going to end up the Patty Hearst of Greyhound. I've become pretty good at bus-hopping too, checking to see which buses are running early or late and changing my connection or re-routing accordingly. I also go to great lengths to make sure that I only have carry-on – no luggage under bus – as that seems to be the best way to slow you down. Carry-on prevents you and your luggage going somewhere on separate buses. Swinging on and off of that bus, going wherever I want, is getting quite addictive. I'm already spending less and less time in each city. Like Tucson, I can often tell they're worthy of much more exploration, but the more I see the more I realise how much is still out there. There's so much more I want to see now. This country is huge and waiting for me. My feet twitch for the shudder of the bus.

I set off downtown to catch a local bus to the University of Arizona campus, which is Nick and Tom's alma mater. The boys picked the U of A for its party record and were apparently well rewarded. It seems popular in the US to avoid going off to college anywhere near the town where you grew up. No wonder there are so many American students in Australia. On my way to the SunTran bus stop, I get quite stupidly lost. That's twice in one day for Tucson, but nothing out of the ordinary for me. After eleven city blocks in the wrong direction, I realise the error of my ways, and end up waiting half an hour for a bus back to my starting point to begin again. I waste entire days this way. I probably wouldn't mind so much except that my lonely, misinformed walks inevitably take me to the wrong part of town. I don't just mean the wrong direction, but the wrong side of the tracks, the ugly parts of a city that no one ever wants to be from, let alone visit.

After my ill-fated trek backwards up Sixth Avenue, I collapse gratefully onto the northbound number six bus, panting in the air conditioning and cursing myself for the lost time. The best thing about travelling on my own, I think, is that there are no witnesses. Of course, when I do something spectacularly cool, this quickly becomes the worst part, but for me, it still works out much better. I'm just not that cool. The SunTran bus has a sign announcing that continued passage requires, amongst other things, no smoking, no eating, no gambling and no four-letter words. I entertain myself with scenarios involving passengers whose journeys are terminated after constructing sentences beginning, 'I bet you a fucking sandwich and this cigarette . . .'

When I finally get there, I find that the U of A is another humungous American university, featuring a lovely, if somewhat parched, campus as well as a variety of great bars, restaurants and shopping opportunities. I wander around enjoying the atmosphere of youth and energy before hiding out in the temperate oasis of another Urban Outfitters franchise. Tucson appears to be very laid-back. It's a relaxed town, low-rise, and beautiful in an unusual, elemental way. The cacti, blue sky and beating sun dwarf the man-made characteristics of Tucson, rendering them all but insignificant. It's very exotic for me, a town that feels oddly foreign even for the US.

On my way back to East Congress Street, I pass a St Vincent de Paul store and stop in for some necessary purchases. Back in my room, I spend an hour fashioning an old cravat and a double-ringed belt buckle into a device to teach my falling-down pants a lesson. This invention requires a substantial amount of my essential travel store – Tarzan's Grip glue from home. I can't go anywhere without the Tarzan's. So far it's fixed bags, earrings, shoes, wallet, parcels home, my watch, a hang-nail, a cracked driver's licence and I've even been using it to 'sew' seams back together on T-shirts otherwise destroyed by hostel washing-manglers. I'm glad I only have a few weeks left. I have the sensation that my small, dusty universe of ponk is being held together by dabs of this adhesive and, now that the tube is down to the final metal curl, I'm nervous.

The belt dries quickly and I try it on. Looking in the mirror at my private *prêt-à-porter* experiment, I realise why the belt is needed. My pants have been falling down for a week or two now and I thought it was due to the fact that they are the only bottoms I brought with me. Jeans give – especially if you sit and sleep in them for three and four days in a row. But that's not all. Despite the constant gorging, the girl looking out of the cigarette-burnt silver of the antique mirror in Tucson is waving with chicken-bone arms and laughing inside accordion ribs. My eyes have pulled a Big Sky country, taking up much more of my moon-face than I remember. Jeez, I look like shit! I do some quick disco moves and it looks like jerky puppetry. I'm thinking of promoting the Greyhound diet. Somehow eating crap food and sitting on my bum on the bus is making me shed body weight like the supermodel cigarette diet. I move another string-bean arm. Hm, I've been a skinny kid since my *Play School* days, but this is still unusual.

I put my shoes back on and go down the street to the chemist. I pretend to test some digital scales and discover that I weigh less than I did in my last year of high school. I'm worried now. I briefly consider the possibility of a terminal illness before I remember that I can't afford to ask a doctor, so I push those thoughts from my head and write myself a prescription for fried chicken. Tired and sunburned, I throw myself a nerd-fest and get an early night with a big bag of Snickers mini-bites and the tattered guidebook for company.

The next day I strap the tomato-pack up tight and walk the few quiet streets to the Greyhound station. In contrast to the dry, attractive stillness of the desert city outside, the station is muggy and chaotic, filled with rambling and wailing, yawning and stretching, and the high-pitched moan of a broken water tap. Sorry, *faucet*. Having recently breakfasted on an American-sized ham and cheese croissant (requiring a wheel of fromage and a whole suckling pig), I settle into one of the plastic bucket seats, concentrating on little more than digestion.

A small snotty child is crying on the floor in front of me. He's actually very cute but incredibly filthy, lying face down on the cement, clad only in a damp cloth nappy, crying like his lungs will burst. His mother, who after five others should probably know better, looks on dispassionately as an elder brother steps experimentally on the baby's fingers. The screams get louder. The older boy grins and steps again. Sighing the way strangers do when they wish to convey strong indignation, I pick up the little grubster and balance him on my now bony hip. His mother looks away. He stops crying and makes the universal da-da-ba-ba noises while he pats down my face and hair with his wee hands. I can feel the germs crossing this small flesh bridge in droves. I can also feel the moisture of his nappy transferring to my jeans. Abruptly, he sneezes in my face just to seal the deal. Eww. I put the baby back out of harm's way and feel a tugging on my jeans. A little girl with a nose full of fluorescent green has her sticky hands in the air, saying 'Up! Up!' She sneezes too. With self-preservation a priority on the road, I pat her little head and fish out my morning-tea Snickers bar to create a diversion while I slip away. It works, but now I have to buy a new snack.

Greyhound have their own restaurant concessions in each big city terminal. More often than not, these are called 'the Travellers' Grill'. Nothing is ever grilled in the Travellers' Grill. Gloop is often mildly reheated to temperatures favourable to Hep A, but there is no grilling that I'm aware of. The snack machines change from station to station, but the staples are always there, with Doritos and Coke making up the Greyhound explorer's regular diet. In Tucson, however, there are no Doritos. I'm aghast. I push my nose against the clouded plastic window of the Conveni-Snack dispenser and search for replacement carbs.

There are three different kinds of tortilla chips in the Conveni-Snack dispenser, including a bright green variety claiming to be made with avocados. I put my money in cautiously and out falls a pack of the El Sabroso 'Guacachip' tortilla chips, made with corn and '100% Calavo' avocados. I crunch. They are bloody amazing. Tangy, salty, crispy, crunchy, with a hint of lime and creamy, zesty avocado, they are also excitingly greener than an Irishman carrying a houseplant in Dublin on St Patrick's Day. I am in snack-food heaven, but also miserable with the irony of discovering the world's greatest corn chip in a place so far from anywhere I'm ever likely to be. How will I ever consume the humble, wooden Dorito again? I buy four more packets – all that's left in the machine – and munch away by myself.

A stary-eyed guy wearing a filthy white tracksuit keeps walking the length of the station, raking his hands through his long curly hair. He periodically strides to the front of the snaking ticket line and adopts the manner of a gentleman who has never heard of the Greyhound bus company and is checking in at the marble lobby of a fine hotel. 'Hi,' he says, smiling. 'How you doin'? So, did my wife leave any messages or anything? Crystal, that's my wife, and I'm expecting a message.' At this point the passengers he has queue-jumped begin outraged hand-waving and the attendant recoils. 'Back of the line!' she will splutter, to which our resident loony always nods and says, 'Oh, I see,' as if she has said something else entirely. He looks around a bit, ignoring the furious patrons behind him and leans over. 'Well,' he says, 'just be sure and let me know the minute she gets in.' Then he winks and pretends to give the attendant a tip. In air dollars.

Us seated folk are all fascinated. We watch these repeat performances with interest, shaking our heads together on occasion, as if we are enjoying the same daytime soap. Mr Crystal-wife's routine slowly expands. He will walk to the pay-phone now and then, pick it up and 'close business deals', then go back to the ticket line to inquire about his wife's luggage. She has her dress for 'the opening' in there, he'll say, and it's very important. 'BACK OF THE LINE!' the attendant is now shrieking, and we get alarmed that Mr Crystal-wife is beginning to look chastened. None of us want him to stop. He quietens down a little, so I go and buy him a Coke from the vending machine, just to see what adding a bit of sugar and caffeine will do to our only entertainment. Sure enough, he starts right up again and I bask in the warm approval of my peers.

In true Greyhound tradition, my bus out of Tucson to Santa Fe is running two hours late. Also, according to the staff, the quickest way for me to get to New Mexico involves travelling another two hours in the opposite direction when it does show up. I consult my own charts and line up at the counter. 'Hi!' I say, bright and perky, but the attendant only growls a little in response. She knows who gave the loony that cola beverage. 'I'm just looking at a map of your fine country and it seems to me that a bus to Los Angeles via Phoenix would in fact be the exact wrong bus to get to Santa Fe.'

'Nope,' she answers, 's'goin to Santa Fe.'

'Uh, do we have the same map? That's the opposite direction.'

'Yah huh.'

'Right,' I say. 'So I should travel away from where I'm going in order to get there?'

She nods, and then peers down at my map, thinking.

'Weeell,' she says, unconvinced, 'I s'pose you could go towards El Paso, but that might take longer.'

We consult the map together.

'But how?' I say. 'El Paso is in the right direction.'

She considers it thoughtfully.

'Yeah. You could be right. It's just that, well, we never sent anybody that way before.'

I sigh and retreat. I don't have the energy to be a Greyhound guinea pig today. It looks like I'm going back to Phoenix.

Once on the bus, I settle back with my usual companions. The smell of apple cores, bubble gum, cheap cologne and choking toilet fumes. Someone pulls out a browning Dalmatian banana. Oh look, I think, the gang's all here. I am the only *gringa* in the bus and this greatly excites me. I feel like we are over the border. Mexican music blares from somewhere up the back, but no one seems to mind. The music consists of English songs belted out loudly in Spanish and I find myself in a sudden language tutorial, guessing the Spanish words for things while listening to 'Eleanor Rigby' and 'Those Were The Days, My Friend'. Speeding across the blistering black freeway, the ancient, clumsy saguaro cacti saluting me all the way, I allow myself a moment of satisfaction. I should be at work today like millions of other people, but here I am. Burning across the Arizona desert headed for a fresh adventure.

At one stage we drive close to the Mexican border, where the road signs turn abruptly from miles into kilometres. There is no dual signage, no announcement of the conversion, but everything is just suddenly metric on the outskirts of Arizona. The realisation that I am about to get a brief respite from imperial measurement is oddly thrilling. I've been in the US for over half a year, and I still have no idea what the weather will be like tomorrow, how far away the next city is or how much milk should go into the Betty Crocker brownie mixture. I am never really sure if I want a quart of juice or not, how much I should be paying for a gallon of fuel or whether the subject of some hilarious anecdote is fat or thin based on the poundage explained up front. I just smile and wait nervously to see if the bank robber was sumo-sized or skin and bone. I resort to asking questions like how many cows, end to end, away would that be, and if you had to let small children walk to school in that weather, what you dress them in? If I want a pound of butter, would that be say, for my own toast? Breakfast for six and a baguette? Or a tri-county bake-off? 'But what's that in Celsius?' I find myself asking, phone squashed between ear and shoulder, oven-mitts on. 'Just subtract 32 and multiply by .55!' people tell me, the same people who should have to eat my sawdust cake and salmonella chicken.

Americans even *know* their measurements are archaic and faintly ridiculous. If you study chemistry or physics in high school here, then (apart from being miserable) you would have to work in metric measurements. What happens next of course is that you graduate, get a job with NASA and program the Hubble telescope in an interesting mixture of both systems of measurement, thus flushing millions of dollars down the dunny when the poor little robot gets as confused as its creators. I miss a lot of unexpected things in this country, but I never imagined units of measurement would be one of them.

Outside the Phoenix terminal is the leaping Dawg himself in silver relief, the symbol of my secret club, more potent to me now than the bat in the sky for Bruce Wayne. I swing on to the next bus headed east and fall asleep before the engine even starts. I've done so much snoozing on these buses that I'm beginning to worry the only America I'm seeing is in my fractured dreams.

Countless hours later we pull into Flagstaff, where outside it's black with night and see-your-breath cold. I break the icy crust on my eyes and peer out. We have slowed to a stop near KFC and Chinabowl Express, and I sit up straight with snack excitement. Chinese food and crispy fried chicken! Now we're talkin'. To my horror, the bus lurches forward, and I can see that it was just a red light. At the next stop, I look out the window to see my first Thai eatery since entering the United States, with a salad bar restaurant opposite. Real food! I clap my hands together but we move away again. As we drive on the food prospects get dimmer with each red light until we reach our final stop, next to a grimy-looking Dairy Queen, with soft serve ice-cream, and a dubious-looking fast-food chain called Jack in the Box. After a Mc-Flatbread McFuckingdisaster for second breakfast and the usual vending machine Doritos for road snacks, I feel something like grief for the real meal that could have been. Unable to see frozen vanilla-flavoured pig-fat as a dinner solution, I walk into the fluorescent plastic bunker that is Jack in the Box.

I have prepared myself for the usual onslaught of burger patties and snotty coleslaw and so my lip actually wobbles with relief when I read the kindly menu. So much is edible here that

I over-order quite severely, gobbling down a Teriyaki chicken bowl, a BLT on a sourdough bun, curly fries and two lots of French toast strips to dip in maple-flavoured syrup. I keep grinning as I eat, looking around and nodding at everyone, waving sticky toast soldiers and raising my eyebrows. 'Pretty good, eh?' I say, mumbling little comments to myself like, 'Ooh! Look! An extra saucy bit of chicken . . . You can run, but you can't hide, bacon-boy . . . What should I do with all this extra syrup? Do I need *more* special toasts? Oh no, surely not . . . well, all right. If you *insist* . . .'

The Flagstaff bus stop contains the usual squash of dirty kids and ratty luggage. I see my very first cowboy here. He buys a ticket to Amarillo, Texas. He can't be more than 21, but he wears a black Stetson hat like he was born into it and a tan shirt with a little stock-whip emblem on the pocket, fastened with pearl snap-buttons. His dark-blue jeans ride up to his armpits, belted by black leather and a massive silver buckle. This cowboy has huge boots and even bigger blue eyes. He looks like he's auditioning to host MTV's country music awards. He says howdy. Truly.

Two small Mexican kids are pressing the buttons on an ancient Mrs PacMan arcade game, where a single computerised blob blinks uselessly, waiting for the money they don't have. After fifteen minutes of this, the cowboy gets up and approaches them. He swipes a few quarters from his change pocket and spins them in the air before handing one to each of the kids. They are terrified. 'Go on,' says the cowboy, but the kids are frozen. 'Go on,' he says again, 'play!' Like a command issued from the Almighty, the petrified kids slot their money in and play shyly. The cowboy nods his approval. He spins on his stacked leather heel, measures the length of the room with his stride and sits down. My god, I think, he is *Shane*!

By 2 am we are on our way, jammed in tight on the old rattletrap headed east. I have my map out again, spread between the window and my knees, and I'm looking to see what's next. Goodbye Arizona, hello New Mexico, home of the . . . well, I'm not too sure. There's a Post-it note stuck to the city of Santa Fe, but on whose (and what) advice, I can't remember. I'll be grateful to get there, though, I know that much. This bus is full and overloaded with luggage. Bags threaten to spew from where they dangle overhead onto our narrow seats. I am pushed up against the window, with five unwashed heads in knocking distance from my own. There is no air conditioning and the atmosphere becomes stuffy and stale. Humans are really disgusting animals, I think. In a zoo we would be the 'eeewww' exhibit: graceless, hairless, lumpy beings with spidery limbs and unfortunate odour. Unwashed humans are so incredibly stinky. I have watched enough David Attenborough specials to know that there is something very wrong with the fact that our own rank smell should be so gut-churning to our fellows. The pong of this many humans in their natural state is too much to bear and I wonder if the human population explosion of the last century was parallel with the rise of personal hygiene products.

My seat is at the back of the bus, over the heat of the engine block, near the slosh of the toilet tureen. My legs are very hot and swollen and I feel like I can't breathe properly, like I can't find enough oxygen. This panic and sweltering build and build until I feel like I will explode. I strip off layers of clothing in frustration, panting and thrashing, and try to get rid of my pillow. There's nowhere for it to go. I shove it behind my back, but it pushes me forward until I am breathing the wasted hot breath from the men in front of me. All I can think about is how packed the bus is and how many people are taking my air.

I put both feet on the seat and boost myself higher, trying to get above it all. The bus is crawling along. The guy next to me is getting closer and closer, and suddenly I hate him, him and his wide aisle seat. Him and his big shoulders, who does he think he is? Doesn't he know I can't breathe? MOVE OVER! GET OUT, EVERYONE! I'm screaming inside. I try all kinds of things with my pillow, working myself into a snit, but each new position seems to make me hotter, more claustrophobic. My seatmate wakes up.

'Can't get comfy?'

'THERE'S NO AIR ON THIS BUS!' I say, shaking a fist in his face. 'They took it! Took the air! How can you breathe, man, HOW CAN YOU BREATHE MY AIR?'

I thought I had experienced cabin fever on the never-ending bus to Minnesota, but that was nothing. That was palatial night-sweat. This is it. Up on my feet again in a frog crouch, I somehow manage to fall into what passes for sleep. After what feels like an eternity of crazy, uncomfortable dreams I wake to discover that a mere twelve minutes have elapsed. I feel like crying but I don't want to waste the water. We are four hours from the next stop and I am desperately thirsty. So thirsty that I'd sell an ear for just a sip, a tongue bath. So claustrophobic that I debate forcing the driver to stop so that I can get out and run away. I'll sleep on the side of the freeway, I really don't care. It looks delicious and cool out there in the desert blackness.

The aisles are packed with kids and crazies wrapped in blankets, fighting for space with empty soft drink bottles and luggage packed in plastic stripy bags. To each hysterical complaint from those who can reach him, the driver keeps saying, 'I know this, I'm just trying to get you all there. I'm just trying to bring us all in and this will be *over*.' I spend a frantic ten minutes searching amongst the filth and grime on the floor under my seat for my water bottle, finding it with shaking hands. It holds one warm mouthful of desert tap water, which tastes of ash, lime and paint. I need to rip off my shoes, I think, maybe my jeans too. Yes, definitely my jeans. I'm beyond caring. So thirsty, so impossibly thirsty. Damn those curly fries and their attractive seasonings. Damn the bacon on my spicy sandwich meal.

At this moment my travel miracle occurs. I believe there to be a ration of one per trip. There are always lucky breaks and chance encounters, but only one gen-u-ine miracle. The travel gods giveth and taketh away on a much grander scale than domestic deities. When they smite it is with a particularly vicious abandon, but the balancing miracles can be just as dramatic. At precisely the moment I lose the last of the birds in my belltower, when I am about to scratch my own face off and start licking the sweaty man next to me for moisture, the bus abruptly slows down, pulls onto the shoulder and makes a sharp exit off the freeway.

We lurch to a stop at the West End Donuts and Deli on Route 66. I leap my neighbour and use children as stepping-stones on my run off the bus and into the store. Harsh fluorescent lighting illuminates the lone employee, an Indian man whose large, floating eyes have heavy panda circles around them. The donuts for sale are massive wobbly wheels of batter and all around us the ancient groaning machinery that produces them is on and humming. It's like Willy Wonka's factory in here, with huge cogs and wheels and bright lumps of icing stuck to sticky trays and baking sheets. Neon signage is buzzing on and off and Elvis sings lonely from a room out the back. Hell, this is Route 66, all right. I have stumbled into Road Trip USA after all. I slam my money down in front of the Indian man.

'Water,' I croak.

'I am sorry?' he says, wobbling his head like a Bollywood heart-throb.

'Wah-*terr*,' I say again, using my American pirate R.

'No,' he shakes his head.

'You don't have WAH-TERR?' I say.

'No.'

'*Agua*?' I say, trying out my Tex-Mex.

'Mm, no.'

I run to the fridge to grab anything liquid, to lick the catchment tray if necessary. There are three shelves filled with water. I grab the biggest bottle there and heft it to the counter. 'Oh,' he says, 'water,' exactly like I had. I drink the whole thing in under a minute even though it's so cold I get freezer-burn down my oesophagus. Behind me our bus driver is talking to another driver over their styrofoam tumblers of coffee. I realise that I'm the only passenger in here, which is very odd. Still, it's past 3 am, and we're all jammed in so tight that perhaps no one else could extricate themselves from the pack. The drivers don't seem to notice me as they chat.

'Yeah,' says our driver, stretching out and scratching at his breast pocket, 'I got a big fat one too. Fuckin' e-norm-ous. Says all, "Oh, I gotta have the front seat, I got ADA." and I'm all, "Oh yeah? You show me the card and we'll see about it." So of course he left it at home. I'm all, "Buddy, buy two seats if you need 'em and put the pork crackle snacks away, I got a full bus here."'

'He move?' asks the second driver, blowing on his coffee.

'Nah. He can't. No one wants to sit next to the flesh wall, and could ya blame 'em? Damn bus is packed to the ceiling already! I got cripples and kids and a nun, crazies and the Hulk himself. I tell you, it's all kinds of hell back there.'

They chuckle and shake their heads.

''S'nice up front though,' our driver says, smiling a little.

'Yeah?'

He nods. 'Got that little battery fan Denice gave me.'

'Mm hmm, she's a good woman.'

'Yes she is.'

I take a deep breath and I'm about to return to the 'all kinds of hell', when the second driver says, 'Well, my ride's all right tonight. No sir, I can't complain."

'Yeah?'

'Lost a few in Flagstaff and my rig's so new it hurts your eyes to look at it. I like drivin' the new ones. Roomy. Keeps everyone calm and out of my face.'

I venture out into the car park then, squinting through contact lenses made from sand and diamond files. Dwarfing our tin of unhappiness is a huge, shiny Greyhound coach, a brand-spanker, transportation that NASA could be proud of. I quickly count the number of heads greasing up the windows – they are few and far between. My heart thumps. I run back inside and train wild eyes on the drivers.

'Mr Bus Driver, sir?' They stop talking and look at me. 'Are both these buses going to Albuquerque?'

'Well . . . uh huh.' They're hesitant. I look at the second driver and smile my best Bambi smile. 'Can I please get on your bus sir?'

There's a big sigh from both men, and the second driver pokes his tongue into one cheek, pushing it around before he answers. 'Well, hon, if you do it, everyone will want to do it, you see? And I can't be swappin' a busload of people and their stuff in the dark at 3.30, in a place we ain't even s'posed to be stopped at. What with the luggage and the "that's my seat" and all . . .'

I try tears; small, semi-genuine. 'But the man sitting next to me is creepy and I can't sleep . . . He just keeps getting closer and closer and there's nowhere to move . . .' I trail off, eyes cast down. *Give me that seat, you bastards.*

The driver sighs. 'You on your own, sugar?'

I nod balefully.

'Okay. You go and get your things, but be real quiet and quick about it.'

In five minutes I'm safe on board the luxury coach, which is clean and only half full. I select a double seat about two rows back and set up my little bed. Pillow on aisle armrest, jumper balled against the sharp point at the base of the retracted middle armrest, sheet unfolded halfway to crawl into like a papoose. Out of all possible combinations, this one has been refined so often and is the only one that works really well. I set up camp in a minute and twenty. Like a good boy scout I know the drill and have all my equipment handy. The overhead compartment on the new Greyhound has an extra three inches, which allows my bag to slide in with the ease of the greased donut trays at the West End Deli. Fifteen minutes ago I was a distraught, dehydrated and desperate woman, and here I am, heading off to sleep in the best bus I've had all trip, with a belly sloshing full of H_2O. It wasn't even a scheduled stop. It must be my miracle.

Chapter 17

Adobe wonderland

After three hours of good sleep, the bus slows into a nameless town in New Mexico. A bedraggled dawn is rising like a headache over the smutty buildings at the side of the Greyhound station, which is large and unremarkable apart from the poo-brown tiles and glaring orange seats that someone inflicted on this country's public spaces in the 1970's. I can only imagine the brown-suited, bell-bottomed designers deciding to go with this way-out, happenin', groovy colour scheme with no thought to the subsequent decades of usage.

We pick up seven passengers with wheelchairs at this stop. The word has obviously gone round disabled communities that there has been a user-friendly bus added to Greyhound's questionable fleet, and it seems that partially paralysed people have been driven here from all over to ride the new Dawg. Manoeuvring the aisle on crutches, a passenger collapses beside me, telling me she hopes the energy of Santa Fe will help her, because the doctors sure can't do nothing no more.

I am suspicious of words like 'energy' attached to a place. I bought one too many crystals in the New-Age nineties, as well as posters of diaphanous creatures experiencing enlightenment, which left Blu-Tack stains on my walls and a creeping scepticism in my heart. Now, ragged, pissed-off, underslept and overdressed, I decide to shoot through Santa Fe. I'll skip straight to Truth or Consequences, or maybe I'll just ride this fresh new bus to the end of its line and go home. This idea makes me smile for the first time in days, and I realise how much my energy to continue on this trip has dwindled. The fifth week of sleeping on buses has been the killer, robbing me of the little things like tolerance, compassion, the spirit of adventure and the will to live. I close my eyes.

On the outskirts of Santa Fe, with the disabled passenger asleep on my shoulder, her poor smelly hair a few days filthier than mine, I throw in the towel. Fuck it. I've seen the USA haven't I? Arizona had enough cacti to embroider my New Mexico imaginings – can't I just give this other dried-out state a miss? What's the difference? The last town looked bland and dusty from the bus and all I've gleaned from my flick through the *Lonely Planet* is that Santa Fe will be 'exorbitantly expensive'.

The woman shifts. Drool starts. Seeing as she was in a head-on collision at 80 mph and died three times on the way to the hospital last year, having broken seven bones across both legs and splintered her spine, I figure it isn't really my place in the world to deny her a few moments peace for the sake of some drool on my shoulder. I've let far less deserving college boys drool on that same shoulder before, but yeech, y'know? Just as I'm think up creative ways to skip three or four US states and go home to bed, the bus stops and so does my heart. I find myself stumbling off into the *Star Wars* planet Tatooine, mouth agape, knees trembling. 'You've gotta be shitting me,' is my first articulate utterance in Santa Fe.

Now, I've heard all about adobe, the mud-brick buildings that prosper in these dry places. I've seen pictures and even the odd mud-brick dwelling in Tucson, but before me lies an entire adobe city. The houses up and down the oldest streets look like Hobbiton, like something from a fairytale. In the morning air I sit down on the tomato-pack and revel in Santa Fe's very existence, in its possibility. As far as the eye can see there are houses, gas stations, hotels, grocery stores and cafés, all fashioned from dried, mushroom-coloured mud. Some of the buildings are huge, with castle-like turrets and long, high walls surrounding hidden gardens. There are Moorish windows cut into elaborate hotels, and tiny old houses with rounded edges and dwarf-sized doors, their gardens filled with soft grasses and flowers like a Beatrix Potter illustration. I half expect Squirrel Nutkin to emerge from one of these and ask me in for tea, or a troop of Spanish conquistadors to march out of the cool mud palaces in curved and shining armour. I can't believe this place exists.

It takes me about half an hour to walk to the hostel, which is just on the outskirts of the city centre on a main road. My heart cracks to discover that it's not adobe, but what it lacks in mud walls it makes up for by being filled with free snacks in the large central kitchen, including fresh strawberries as big as my fist. It's much more like the well-established hostels of Europe than the slightly confused or embarrassed American versions.

I'm desperate to go and explore, but I vacillate over a quick change. I decide on new socks as the bare minimum and get a nasty surprise when the old ones are peeled off. I have bright orange feet. My streak-free sunless tanning foam leaked into my sock bag some days ago, but it dried colourless and I assumed that my socks were now merely pleasantly fragranced. They must have been sweat-activated. My tootsies are a deep burnt orange from ankle to the tips of my chocolate-brown toenails. I'm a good week away from flip-flops again, I think, and judging from the intake of breath around me in the foyer, I'll have to pass them off as birthmarks or get used to changing in the dark.

I set off up Cerillos Road into the town centre, an enchanted adobe wonderland. There are ancient churches fashioned from earth, with intricate detailing and solemn gravity. It's very dry here, which is why the mud stands up as a viable construction material, and I can tromp around shower-less without my own sorry smell overpowering me. The Santa Fe air dries out my nose in two quick breaths, but it's actually kind of pleasant. Heady. Invigorating. My hair has gone stick straight and crispy. I've grabbed a sheaf of handouts from the hostel, which cause me to twice walk into wooden electricity poles as I learn the reason behind this vapour-free air. I am currently at 7000 feet above sea level, in America's highest capital city. I'd whistle but my lips are too dry.

The desert has been continuously wide and flat and there was no sense of climbing a gradient during the torturous bus trip. I had no idea that I was up so high. I would have been confident in announcing that I was only about ten feet above sea level, but when I see the mountains in front of me it starts to make sense. I literally have to stop and crane my neck back to view their ice-covered tips. The Rocky Mountains are impossibly tall and green around this desert city and I wonder just how much luck one town can have. How is it that I have never even heard of this place before? How can I know twenty people who've been to ponky San Francisco and none who've been within a state of Santa Fe?

I soon find that Santa Fe has no shortage of impossibly hip and accommodating cafés to while away the days with great coffee, company and suitably eclectic soundtracks. I choose the Cowgirl on Guadalupe (pronounced Gwada-loo-pay), and experience my first breakfast burrito, deliciously smothered in 'Christmas' chilli made from the red and green varieties. I sit out in the morning sun, listening to bluegrass, drinking bottomless American coffee, wishing not for the first time that I could share my happy discoveries.

My waitress studies at the small university here, St John's. The school is a few hundred years old, but it only takes about 450 students. The coursework sounds as exotic and precious as the city itself. Each student, who pays up to $140,000 in tuition and board for the four-year undergraduate degree, studies the Great Books. This consists of an A to W (apparently literary greatness doesn't favour the surname challenged X, Y and Z) of the biggest texts of the Western world. Imagine that. An entire university tucked away in this adobe city, devoted to the study of Great Books.

It's not just works of Western genius that are celebrated in this town. Evidence of a deep reverence for all kinds of Eastern mysticism keep popping up alongside the Hopi Indian flutes and native turquoise adornment. Santa Fe gets curiouser and curiouser still. Out here in this largely barren, little heard-of region of North America, Santa Fe is an official Tibetan resettlement area, with many Tibetan refugee families finding homes in this tiny community during the nineties. 'Free Tibet' bumper stickers look like the state licence plate here. There's a great deal of Japanese influence too, with sushi, origami and kimonos turning up in unlikely places. Odd, but perhaps it's a hangover from the Japanese internment camp that I've heard was set up here during World War II, although I don't see any Japanese people anywhere, just their tasty snacks and glorious fabrics.

My waitress tells me that there's lots of 'Hollywood types' out here too, lots of media moguls and high-techsters have adobe houses and use this area as a tranquil hideout. Taos (which rhymes with mouse when pronounced correctly and is 'Tay-os' only to the Hollywood-wannabe vacationers people snicker at) is where Julia Roberts lives and staged her private, ranch-style wedding. Santa Fe is also one of the world's largest art markets, despite its small size, and there are impressively stocked galleries everywhere. The waitress urges me to go and have a look.

I ask her and the other super-friendly staff at the Cowgirl what it's like to live here. Their eyes light up when they tell me how much they love it, but they say the rent is high and the only industry is very tourist-oriented. It's a resort town. As much as it would like to be about art and fly-fishing, it's really about selling rich people more stuff and a week away from reality. Sanibel, Bar Harbor, Santa Fe; all amazing places that exist for the sake of themselves. You'd need to be a professional waitress to make your home here, or have a freelance career or a million bucks to retire young. We all sigh a little together as we look around at a beautiful place that can only be borrowed for a while by the likes of us.

I'm very full when I set out to do some more exploring, and so I have to curse when I find a Wild Oats whole-food supermarket like the one in Boulder, Colorado. This one's even adobe. Like Boulder, whole-foods and interesting ethnic nibbles seem to be a fresh air, Rocky Mountains thing, and wherever there are mountains there are also lots of Harleys, big dogs, rich hippies and outdoor sports. And a great deal of New Age spirituality.

Unfortunately for these places, they attract too many wealthy people who, just by flocking to the natural beauty and cosmic spirituality, are making those things much harder for the average person to experience. There are too many tourists carrying too many bags in Santa Fe; Texan oil-dollar wives exclaiming, 'Way-all, I'm not going in another store, I sway-uh!' on every corner of this town.

There are lots of day-spas and retreats advertised everywhere and the town centre is beautiful, but very boutiquey. There are three outlets of the up-market, forty-something, women's clothing store Chicos in the small downtown area alone. That's just crazy. The tourist shops are high-end too, stocking lovely but expensive ethnic home-wares, Hopi Indian jewellery and craft, as well as a diverse range of New Age products. There are lots of workshops going on in Santa Fe, on everything from chakra cleansing to Morris dancing and learning to speak to your inner Smurf.

I can see all this but, as they say here, I can't help diggin' on Santa Fe. I want to be a part of this place instantly. Buy an old truck and a big flobbin' dog to love, build an adobe hobbit-house of my own outside town. Fish. Walk. Eat whole foods. The Boy has a long held interest in constructing a house from mud and hay bales (he also has a strong interest in metal eskies from the fifties, so I never take it too seriously) and I wonder if we might spend some time here together. I'm sure he would love the mountains as much as I do.

Everywhere here and in Boulder there are hundreds of books with titles like *Mountain Mysticism and Energy*, and I had previously snickered at them. Then I wished I'd written one too, so I could cash in on the gazillions of rich pseudo-hippie suburbanites who buy them, trying to find meaning in exclusive geography. Something has shifted, because now I pick these books up like old friends, turning the pages reverentially and nodding, 'It's so true, that's how I feel.' Maybe it's just grounding to be reminded that we are small and scurrying creatures. Being surrounded by natural landmarks so massive and timeless forces you to slow down and see what's in front of you. It's about the space and clean air. It's about perspective.

The ocean does a similar thing for me in Sydney, I suppose, but it's always moving, and, short of being out in a boat, unfathomable. I love the Blue Mountains just outside Sydney, and the Snowy Mountains down south (under which I was born) but Australia's ancient landmass means that stability and erosion have tamed our peaks. They lack the sharp, earth-splitting, sky-reaching grandeur of the Rockies. The solid majesty of these mountains can't be argued with. Despite the obvious signs of acute political awareness and myriad cross-cultural influences in Santa Fe, it still feels like we are very far away from that other, crazy world. Santa Fe is in a new world, a fairytale place, a story book made three-dimensional. My first reaction was that it's not American, but now I can see it's also the epitome of America. The Native American, Spanish and pioneer history colliding constantly with the past 100 years of diverse immigration, as well as with the money, drive, ideas and eccentricity that are found in such abundance in this nation.

I feel an odd sense of homecoming in this place so different from my own home. The mountains, sun, air, adobe and bright blue sky quite overwhelm me. It's more than the physical beauty. It feels so false and predictable to be drawn to the 'energy' of a place where the energy is as touted and commercialised as this, but I am. Maybe it's just the lack of oxygen.

Altitude is enough to provide this euphoria. Standing up too fast will give you the sinking stomach of roller-coaster drops and I've already had more than a few sudden nosebleeds. At least they dry up quickly. I'm lightheaded all the time too – mentally buzzed but physically fatigued from the lack of oxygen. I decide on a beer with lunch and my waiter smirks when he sees my tubercular tissue. 'You'd be surprised what two or three beers will do to you up here,' he warns, and insists on serving me coffee with each one. I'm not sure what he expects this combination to do, but two rounds of this beverage-highball later, I'm charging and completely overcome. My nose sprouts anew and I consider Tampax, but find myself unable to crawl as far as the bathroom. High as a cosmonaut in Manolos, I rant wildly at my cuticles before writing a small manifesto on my bar napkin.

Do I want America? I write, underlined in speckled blood and biro blobs. Yes, I decide. I really do now. I want to keep her. I'm moved to unexpected, drunken tears that people overseas and at home have such resentment and hatred toward a country I now know to be vast and beautiful (underlined) and much more intricate and complex (underlined repeatedly) than I might ever have imagined. This is a huge chunk of the planet populated by a huge chunk of the planet's peoples. There are mountains, deserts and forests, artists, innovators, poets and visionaries. Then there are ugly miles of strip malls and commercial monstrosities, soulless acres of junk-food, Kmarts, obesity and cultural waste-land, shocking disparities in education, lazy thinking, jingoism and ignorance. This is a country two and a half times the size of Western Europe, filled with 300 million individual souls. When we generalise about America we do the whole world (under-lined) a great disservice because the whole world (underlined) lives here and has helped create it.

America needs to be more transparent, I scribble, more accessible, more involved in the world outside its shores, not less. Less breeds the cultural pomposity of its leaders, who are dangerously out of touch. Americans need to travel. Their country is so big and culturally diverse that visiting each state is an experience for them, but they need to go overseas, earlier and for longer, and not stay in big hotels on package deals. No, Cancun doesn't count and neither does Club Med. American youth need to travel. And people coming to the US need to stop just going to LA because it can be a disappointing hole com-pared to different US cities and the national parks.

The world also needs to understand that for every big government mistake, for every Dubya comment that is crass and stupid and inflammatory, for every misguided Dubya who takes money away from birth control in developing nations, there are a hundred unseen philanthropists in the USA who raise money and use their country's staggering wealth for the benefit of countries who will always burn their flag anyway. There are Americans who fight tirelessly for the impoverished people of nations whose own governments embezzle money meant for their citizens and don't give a rat's arse about them. There are people who are aware of their providence and prosperity and work to give some back and pass it on, even though the world will continue to despise them.

There are real thinkers here, dreamers and activists, and American culture supports them. Michael Moore's books and films are bestsellers because millions of people in the country he is criticising agree with him and also want debate. Then there are self-righteous, ignorant assholes, school-shooters, abortion-clinic bombers, white supremacists and freaky evangelists. It's a nation of extremes precisely because so much is possible here, so much is permitted here that isn't elsewhere. Actually, not just permitted but promoted (underlined three times).

America is a nation of extremists, and the all or nothing stakes can produce the best and worst that global citizens have to offer. Let's reclaim her (rallying cry). Her communities are vast and inclusive. Everyone can find room. There is a one-way permeation of American culture. We only receive what we buy and what we buy are the stereotypes we're comfy with. Go and look for America, Walt Whitman's America of brotherhood, nature, community, possibility . . . (then, mercifully, my forehead slumps to the table and I peter out).

Getting drunk by yourself at high altitude is a silly thing to do in a strange town. I spend the rest of the afternoon stumbling around the charming adobe neighbourhoods, pausing every now and then to puke behind interesting pots and plants, and shivering my way through the impressive galleries. Seeking refuge back at the hostel, I hide out with some dry toast at the long kitchen table, feeling very silly and sorry for myself. When two guys come in wearing saffron robes and talking about the Zen of chickpeas, I decide that I'm too fragile for all this hippie shit and try to make an exit.

'Stay, friend,' the Zen guy implores me, 'I'm just about to make some tea.' Tea is a rare offering in America, unless it's served tall and cold in the South, and in my current condition I accept it gratefully. The guys are in town to do workshops on a Japanese healing technique similar to Reiki. They are big, blond, friendly Minnesotans, who have travelled all over the world. I want to show them my manifesto, but I'm too shy. They tell me they felt 'called' to come here, and their huge, genuine smiles get the better of me. A few hours later, I find myself eating organic hummus and drinking chai, saying, 'I feel like the adobe houses are like, *talking* to me, you know?' Did I really just say that? What's more, I think I might mean it. I pack myself off to bed immediately. It's been a very long day.

The second morning in Santa Fe I feel the same beautiful longing for the place rising like a lump in my throat. The hostel, in keeping with its commune-like atmosphere, requires each guest to complete a small chore in order to keep the room rates cheaper for everyone. I like this idea, until I realise that because all the other guests are up at the crack of dawn for their various courses, I have now got the bum-end of the chore choice cards. I skip swabbing out the disabled toilet and sweeping the acres of drive, and select weeding the rock garden in the back yard. I actually love to garden and fiddle about inexpertly with plants, and pulling weeds turns out to be therapeutic in the clear, sunny morning. I could really get used to the idea of working at something like this. Maybe I'll become a celebrity adobe gardener and move to Santa Fe.

Post weeding, I try to get a brush through my hair, and am forced to take stock. My crowning glory is long and listless and matted with bus detritus. It's now at the length where it can drag and dip into substances and places I wouldn't put my fingers on Greyhound, and then it has the habit of blowing across my mouth. Yeech. The top has gone nearly white blonde from the weeks of beating sun and so my fur now has a skunk-striped appearance to match its odour. I set off to look for a hairdresser.

I approach the counter of the first salon I see, wearing my backpack, sneakers and dirty denim, and ask politely for an appointment. The guy cutting hair can't see me, but can hear my sweet little voice behind his back and says, 'Sure! How 'bout in half an –' but he is cut off by an assistant who has all but leapt to the counter to head me off at the pass. The assistant is wearing more lip-gloss than I would ever dare even if it was viva-glam-Studio-54-in-tights, the off-off-Broadway production, and gets all openmouthed and snippy, overriding his boss's invitation with a terse '*No*'.

I can't believe this. 'Screw you.' I say. 'Don't try your cool-profiling on me! I'm pretty cute when I'm not riding mass transit with mouldy fruit and smelly crack whores.' Actually, I am much too chicken for that and try to beg an appointment for tomorrow or next year. 'No,' the assistant says again, with a tone announcing him to be a Soup Nazi under that Tinkerbell disguise he's wearing, 'No cut for you!'

Somehow I end up in a salon owned by the celebrity hairdresser responsible for the early Beatles and Rolling Stones hair; the man who invented the shag cut on the *Laugh-In* show in LA in '69. Of course, I don't know this, so when I walk in and boldly demand 'rock-star hair' the patrons are all a-twitter. The master-hairdresser himself smiles, obviously amused, and agrees to take my skunk on. He looks set to hack and I wave an imperious hand. 'Leave some length,' I tell him. He stands back, considers my head and delivers his verdict. 'Sorry. You can't.' It hangs between us. We are both staring at me in the mirror. 'It's my hair,' I point out. He nods in brief consideration. 'Not anymore,' he says and just shears.

One hour later there is much hugging and kissing and it's all become a bit *My Fair Lady* in Santa Fe. I can't quite breathe properly and I don't know if it's hairspray, altitude, lightheadedness from the missing weight of my hair, or the shock of handing over $200 Australian dollars for my new head. The latter is going to put me on a celebrity diet to match the hair. Walking back to the hostel, it soon becomes apparent that whereas once I was too cool for my tired hair, my hair is now much too cool for me. I'm looking in every reflective window on the street, pretending to read the specials on American Indian key-chains, when I'm really trying to get used to the idea that this Dixie Chick is me. My attitudinal blonde shag feels like false advertising and I'm in a panic. It's kind of Billy Idol meets Poochie and I can't stop touching it. People are going to ask *me* for drugs at the bus station now.

Post-haircut is a fragile time for a woman. It's best not to sign any important documents, change your last will and testament, or wander aimlessly through Santa Fe, New Mexico.

But here I am. Clouds have gathered over the mountains, and it soon starts to dump with rain. I take refuge in a closed-down Texaco station on Cerillos Road. I can still see the hostel in the distance, but have no chance of getting there through the howling storm. It blows in from all sides and I'm soon wet to the bone, freezing now with only a small tuft of hair to keep me warm. The cracked glass behind me reflects a shrunken, bobble-headed stranger. I don't look like me anymore. I look like some other girl. An American girl. It suddenly occurs to me that I have what my girlfriends like to call break-up hair. Definite break-up hair. Actually, caught-my-husband-in-bed-with-the-underage-babysitter-divorce-type hair. The hair of reinvention. I have had long hair since before I can remember, and this is big for me.

I ponder the implications for the Boy. Nope. He's still a keeper all right, which leads me to the startling realisation that who I've really dumped is me. Old me. Pre-Red-Rock-Canyon me. Pre-Maine-and-Minneapolis me. Pre-Greyhound me. People go to Africa for months and get malaria, or they disappear into Eastern Europe for a season, and when they return it's assumed they will never be the same again. It's accelerated change, travel. I know this, and I've had it happen to me before, I just never expected to feel so transformed after forty days across a big, Western, English-speaking nation filled with conveniences.

But I have been. It has happened. Each new state feels like a new country, each new city was a lifetime ago, each person I meet has a story as fresh as my last thought and as old as my atoms. My senses are fried. My circuits are tired out from all the input. Santa Fe itself is overwhelming me and I'm starting to really see the enormity of what it means that this vast land, this giant hunk of the planet, could be my country too.

I feel alone and terribly small, scrabbling around for my old ideas, my old hair, my old me. In the thundering rain, cowering at an abandoned petrol station, I cry a big, giant, girly cry with only the lightning and mountains as my witness. When it's over, I'm sobbed out and shaken, but I feel like a million bucks. I feel like I won the Green Card lottery.

Chapter 18

Accidental Albuquerque

At the Santa Fe Greyhound stop, I see people from the real world again. Well, kind of the real world – as real as it can get in these desert states. The men are all wearing string ties fastened with elaborate shell and turquoise ornaments, huge belt buckles and ten-gallon hats. Cowboy boots everywhere too, spit-shined or dusty, and long-sleeved shirts are on everyone's backs, despite the 100-degree weather. They must know something I don't, because the clouds gather again with indecent haste and it begins to pour and then to pelt down hail at the tiny bus shelter. I struggle across a muddy vacant lot to Blake's Lottaburger, the only place close enough with something to eat.

The dismal outskirts of Santa Fe look like any other town in this area and I hope the bus isn't too far away. I keep craning my neck to see out of the grimy windows at Lottaburger, where it takes me 20 minutes to get fries and a kiddy burger, even though I'm one of five customers to six staff. The reason I have decided to try a burger (apart from the fact that there's nothing else to eat) is that it promises 100 per cent premium grade Angus beef, known, allegedly, for its superior quality and taste. When the burger arrives it is as thick as a nickel or an Australian five-cent piece, dried to an Everest-expedition rations consistency and utterly without taste. Despite my growling belly, I'm unable to manufacture enough saliva to make this beef-wafer edible and so I make a meal from the tasty little gherkins, picking them out to make a gherkin-tomato sandwich, squashed between layers of fries.

The bus rolls up half full already. I struggle to push the tomato-pack into the overhead bin and everyone looks on as I pummel it into place, wedging it completely into the small space. I have to travel an hour or two to Albuquerque, then this bus continues on to Truth or Consequences, New Mexico, a town which ingeniously named itself after a game show in the fifties. These days, it's apparently just referred to as 'T or C'. I've called the hostel there and they have promised to wait up for me, telling me that Greyhound always gets in quite late. They sound like friendly people and the hostel has a reputation as being one of the most interesting in the US. It sounds a bit like a drop-in centre for the Santa Fe leftovers, but the owners have some progressive ideas about the environment and communal living that I'm interested to see in action. I can't wait to get there. I feel like I've been heading to Truth or Consequences ever since it jumped out at me from the map that day in Savannah.

A young grandmother is sitting behind me, with her three identical daughters and a grandson. God knows where these pale, grub-like people are from or where they're headed, but I just hope it's nowhere near me.

'Whaddyou want a goddamn hammser for?' Grandma asks the boy.

'Dunno,' the poor kid replies. 'Jes' do.'

'Your daddah had a rat once. But he got out and your Grandpaw had to kill it when we couldn't ketch it.' The women all guffaw mightily.

'Smashed his head in with a skillet, hey Maw!'

'Sure did!'

'I had a mouse once,' one of the women says, 'shit every-where. Then Bradley stuffed it down Darleen's bra and it suffocated in her tits!'

More guffaws.

The little boy looks ill. 'I gotta go,' he says and points to the toilet.

'All right, but you be gotta be quick, hon,' his Grandma warns. 'No crappin' in thar. You ken crap when we get to the nice potties in Albuquerque, uh huh? No *crappin*'!'

'Yes, Grandmaw.'

The little boy struggles into the toilet by himself, leaving the womenfolk of his family to weigh in on the issue at hand.

'You sure can crap in thar, they got bigger seats than they used to.'

'Yeah huh!'

'Well, I can't go anymore anyway. Not quick. Takes me about an hour. Muh doctor said I got to eat some fresh food and vege-tables, but I'm fussy I guess. Takes too long for that shit to cook.'

'Yeah huh,' they all agree. The rest of the bus looks sickened.

At Albuquerque, the driver announces a quick stop before we'll re-board this bus to T or C. 'Take your wallets with ya, folks,' he says, 'but you ken leave your luggage stowed. Be back in about 20 minutes.' It's funny to think of Albuquerque as a real place. It has always existed for me from a formative media diet of *Looney Tunes*, where I learned to shout along with Bugs, 'Dang! I shoulda toined left at Alba-koi-key!' It was some reference to Mr B. Bunny's wrong-headed tunnelling which left him too close to that rifle-happy Yosemite Sam and I never suspected it had a real geographic position outside of a colourful, 2-D landscape. I'm one of the last people off the bus and into the station, heading to the toilet for a quick pee before T or C. I'm finally on my way! Whistling a jaunty tune, shaking my hands to dry, I take the bus stairs two at a time.

There's a moment when everything goes sour. I'm not sure if there's a word in English that quite covers it; you'd probably have to look to one of the more guttural Slavic languages to find something that harsh and singular. It's the moment when your brain throws the red lever up like a hammer and your thoughts, just rolling along like water, freeze solid with panic. BAG. GONE. WHERE? is all I can manage, standing at the junction of what is and what could be. Option 1, tomato-pack is briefly moved and missing, can be recovered, and off we go to Truth or Consequences. Option 2: I'm fucked.

This time, the travel gods have chosen to smite me. Perhaps it's just Albuquerque, where I already used up my good fortune on its outskirts, but all that is left of my mute and faithful travelling companions are my cheap umbrella and my poor pillow, sitting alone in the middle of the aisle. The tomato-pack and all my clothes and possessions are very, very gone.

There are 20 or so witnesses who saw me disembark next to last while the driver was left alone on the bus, but there might as well be none. At least ten of these passengers would never pass the most basic cognition and reliable witnesses tests because they are insane, three are intoxicated, one is currently unconscious and blocking the south-west departure gate, and the others are Greyhound employees, who are honour-bound to total inaction in every circumstance involving the grievances of paying customers. It takes roughly eight minutes for all the euphoric epiphanies of my time in Santa Fe to evaporate – precisely the same amount of time it takes for Greyhound to devolve themselves of all responsibility and bid me a nice life – somewhere else. Clutching my pillow, I watch the bus to Truth or Consequences rattle off without me.

I storm to the counter and demand to speak to the station supervisor. The attendant stops clacking at her gum long enough to dial a number and hand me the receiver without looking up. Two teenage girls keep pointing at me, whispering and giggling. I turn my back to them as I begin my rant to the supervisor, demanding attempts be made to locate my bag, or at least the compensation of a hundred smackers that my ticket entitles me to. With my free hand, I fill out an incident report for the tomato-pack, shocked and still unable to believe that everything has really gone. The Greyhound incident report form has space for race, height and weight, and little else. It looks like a rap-sheet. The teenage girls draw closer. 'It's not my problem,' I tell the supervisor, 'that you're home in bed. But it's going to be a big problem when my –' The girls tap me on the shoulder and I whirl around, with one hand on the receiver. 'Excuse me,' one says, 'Could you all say that again?'

'I'm sorry?' I say, hope sprouting that perhaps these girls have knowledge of the missing pack. 'Do you know where my bag is?' I ask. The girls fall about giggling. 'Say it again! Say it again!'

'Say WHAT?' I scream, while the supervisor babbles on about how I have no proof of any luggage.

'Your voice,' they say, pointing at me, 'it's so cute! Say stuff again! Have you all seen *Grease*?'

'Look, I've just had everything I own stolen,' I tell them, 'and I'm really quite –' they cut me off with their giggles and hoots again, one shouting for her other friend to come over and listen to me 'speak cute like *Grease*'. The supervisor hangs up on me. Armed with a phone cord and my bare hands I'm easily capable of double homicide at this moment, and the only reason the giggle-twits escape is that I'm pretty sure I'd have to fill out another Greyhound incident report form destined for the shredder.

Many hours later, sitting alone in the orange plastic seats at 2 am, I am overcome with woe. I remember the smiling hippies waiting for tickets at Red Rock and Steamboat Springs, one arm raised in the air, the Grateful Dead signal for 'Can I get a miracle?'. Because no help can be found and no one is looking, I raise my own arm in the air and hold it there, waiting. All that comes is the smell of my own funky armpit, reminding me that all my clean clothes and underwear really are lost for good, I don't have soap or deodorant anymore and I'm somehow alone in Albuquerque. The armpit forces me to face my essential, animal state. No matter how upset I am, I still have to get out of here to feed and wash.

A Greyhound security guard, after assisting me on a fruitless search of dumpsters surrounding the station, offers to drive me into town to the motel I have just called, waking the Indian owner up at 2.30. I had started to make a reservation when he said, 'Just be coming in, okay?' and slammed the phone down in my ear. The security guard takes me out to his car, a brand-new, bright red Cadillac, which no doubt has been purchased with the money from stolen backpacks in special agreement with the cleaning guy and the driver, all of whom were the last to see my precious and only belongings.

I'm still asking questions of the 'So, if my bag turns up and I'm not here, where will it go?' variety, but the security guard is willfully ignoring me. He is, in fact, acting like this is our first date. 'So,' he says, hand on the radio dial just grazing my knee, 'what kind of music do you listen to?'

'Christian rock opera,' I reply, buzzing the window down. 'So, if my bag turns up around the station . . .'

He has slipped in a CD, which now blasts, 'It's getting hot in here, so take off all your clothes, I am get-ting too hot, I'm gonna take my clooooothes off!' at high thumping volume. Is he kidding me? I'm still madder than rabies and feeling a mother's anguish for tomato-pack out there in the dark with its kid-nappers. 'Yup,' he tells me, as we crawl though featureless streets, 'Albuquerque is a real bad place to get stuck. I hate it here. It's so boring and ugly. I'm from Canada, though, and I'll go back there some day.'

'Oh,' I say, pretending to be interested so we can get back to tomato-pack discussion, 'so what brought you here then?'

'My parents moved here when I was two weeks old,' he says, 'but I'm fixin' to go back real soon.'

'Great!' I say. 'So the police station, if they –'

'Hey,' he says, 'say that again!'

'Say what?' I ask.

'Have you all seen the movie called *Grease*?'

When he finally drops me at the utterly charmless University Lodge motel, he turns the music to something slower, one of those crooning-fakey R&B songs like my personal ironic schmaltz favourite 'Will you be my wifey', and fixes me with a meaningful look.

'So . . .' he says, 'what do you think you'll be doing later on?'

'Oh,' I say, 'probably washing out my only pair of undies, brushing my teeth with motel-soap and my index finger.'

'Yeah,' he laughs, unsure, 'but so, like, now you're in town, you wanna go out sometime this week?'

'Actually,' I say, struck dumb by this level of delusion and trying to figure out how to open the door, 'I wanted to get back on the road sometime *this morning* so . . .'

'So you wouldn't wanna go dancing Saturday night? Or maybe have a couple of beers, get a video? Something with Meg Ryan if you want,' he rolls his eyes. 'I know you girls dig that stuff. Gets y'all in the mood . . .'

Now that I'm free of any luggage, I can get out faster than an extremely pissed-off woman and slam the door shut without worrying about trapping my bag straps. I pay for the room with the credit card in my sagging back pocket and go inside. Having lost my favourite jammies of all time, I choose to sleep naked rather than filthy, but the sheets are badly bobbled and itchy. There's no AC either, so when I finally close my eyes at about 3.30, I have a hot, horrible half-sleep filled with bad dreams.

The morning brings with it little more than a slight lightening of the grey sky, and the realisation that I have no cosmetics, shampoo, razor, deodorant, toothbrush, toothpaste or any other items of comfort, and only my filthy, sweaty, grimy clothes and underwear to crawl back into. If only I'd done some laundry in Santa Fe, if only I'd . . . if only. Upon discovering the lack of even a sliver of soap in the tiled cave near my bed, I rub at my teeth with cheap and musty toilet paper, and get dressed. Good thing those bastards left my umbrella because it is already raining in Albuquerque.

I'm not sure whether to make my way back to the Greyhound station and travel due east and then south for as long as it takes to get home, or whether to re-provision myself from the ground up and continue on my mission. I get out my grubby bus pass, which is thankfully (or not, depending on how I want to look at things) still in my possession. I don't have enough days left for Truth or Consequences now, but there's still Austin, in Texas, and New Orleans to go. There's Disney World too. I sigh, knowing that the decision has been made to continue on. What little girl gives up Disney World?

I set off with an empty tummy and an empty heart. I'm forced to carry my ratty pillow on my back in a plastic supermarket bag I find drifting along the ground, using the stretched out handles as straps for an improv backpack. Carrying my jumper in my arms, I pass lots of people who point me helpfully in the direction of the big laundromat at the top of the hill. I must look like I'm dragging stuff somewhere to wash I guess, why else would a normal-looking person carry a stripy pillow on her back in a placcy bag? But I can't kid myself that I'm even a normal looking person anymore – I look like what I am, a Greyhound refugee. My now-missing John Frieda hair product had promised to make my new haircut look 'disarmingly disheveled'. Last night the combined efforts of Greyhound and University Lodge motel did it for free, so that's at least one less thing I have to replace today.

At the local bus stop I see a small, bright flower sticking up between the cracks of ugly footpath on the main road. I walk over and squash it flat before kicking a rock out into the street. I really shoulda toined left at Alba-koi-key. I sit on the Sun Tran bus as heavy as the clouds outside it, mourning my special American purchases: the cowgirl T-shirt from the café in Santa Fe, the antique leather cowboy belt with crossed Smith and Wessons over the silver buckle. A small tear slides over my well-greased cheek. Some things are priceless. The level of cool I attained with that belt holding up my pants will never be matched by another.

A Walgreen's super-pharmacy looms on the interstate, next to a Target and a large Ross Dress For Less discount-clothing store. I hit the bell. At Walgreen's I buy basic toiletries, still tantalised by the variety of available goodies in American stores, but miserable at the loss of my careful collection begun in Minneapolis and Vegas. Dad's travel hairdryer is also no more. I can only hope whoever is using it experiences a dangerous level of negative ions building up in their hair. All those cunning locks we bought are gone too, as well as my precious bits and bobs from the Mall of America.

At least the horrid little travel towel is gone. I allow myself a grim smile of satisfaction at the thought that the thief may have to touch it. I'm burning with hatred for whoever stole it, pleased to remember that the half-orange socks are still sweltering inside my bag somewhere too, and I hope they're being worn right now. I only wish I hadn't hurled my Hawaiian Tropic 30-plus sunscreen so the thief could be treated to a nasty, nasty sunburn as well. Heh heh heh.

Over the freeway at Ross, I buy some sneakers, flip-flops, a denim skirt (so I have something to cover my knickers while the jeans I'm still wearing are in the washing machine) two basic tops and a backpack to put them all in. At Target I buy some undies and a key chain that chirps out 'Hey, good-lookin'!' when you press it. My haul comes to a grand total of about 50 bucks. I thought bargain shopping would make me feel better – it always makes me feel better – but instead it makes me blisteringly angry about the lovely things I've lost. All those little trinkets and pretty clothes were the irreplaceable trophies of my trip around the US and it's not likely I'm going to reverse my route just to buy them all again.

I stomp along clutching my pillow in a little cloud of hatred and fury, my stiff new backpack on my back. Everyone in Albuquerque appears to me to be a potential bag-stealer; thieves and scoundrels all. Further along the freeway, struggling over muddy pipes and around chain link fences, I come to a food chain called Teriyaki Bowl. Inside, there's no music and no customers, just a big airconditioned restaurant soon filled with wolfish noises as I fall into my bowl of food. My poor wet feet are freezing in here, maybe that's why it's so abandoned.

With nothing else to do and nowhere else to be, I head back towards the Greyhound terminal. I can't wait to be shot of this whole sorry event. The SunTran bus takes me close enough to the station, and I walk along in the grey mud made from concrete dust, past tumbledown walls and graffitied warehouses, while rusted-out Caddys keep time beside me, dragging their chassis along the sodden bitumen. The station is less intimidating in the light of the afternoon and I approach somewhat emboldened by the thick straps of my new bag on my shoulders. I'm still in the game.

Inside, I ask the counter staff when the next bus in the direction of Texas is. 'Where in Texas?' they ask.

'How 'bout just the first bus going anywhere at least a mile from this particular station?' I growl, but they don't care. With four hours to wait, I figure I should make a final attempt on behalf of the tomato-pack.

I call the police station closest to Greyhound in the futile imagining that someone has handed it in from a dumpster. When I explain my sorry tale to the officer, he asks me what I expected, riding Greyhound and all. I sigh, and ask if I can at least leave my address in case it turns up. As I give it to him, I take his silence for concentration until he says, 'I'm sorry, could you say that again? It's just that you . . . Have you ever seen *Grease*?'

I call Nick. It's always handy to have an American friend to rag on when you get really pissed off with the nation. He's a Republican, too, so whenever I'm bored, I can make him try and defend his dribbling President.

'Nick. Hi. It's me.'

'Hey –'

'Ever been to Albuquerque?

'Yeah! Sure, once I –'

'Yeah? Did you like it?'

'It's a nice enough –'

'WRONG!' I shout, 'Wrong!'

'Okay,' he says, 'it's been a while but –'

'It's wretched,' I accuse. 'It is a town without so much as a cockroach fart to recommend itself.' I yell at him for some time and eventually feel a bit better. While I'm on the phone, the shift changes over, and a big fat Greyhound lady from last night comes up to me.

'Did you ever get your bag back, sugar?' she asks.

'Nope.' I reply, my lips as tight as I can get them, and I look away. Suddenly big meaty arms envelop me and she's saying, 'I'm just so sorry, I could barely sleep last night thinkin' of you all lawst by yerself. I just hope you don't go home hatin' America, there's good people here too.'

I'm really touched. Someone at Greyhound finally gives a damn. I promise Nick to work on my manners before my next call, and hang up the phone.

'Nya, it's okay,' I tell the roly-poly Greyhound woman, 'I guess it's only . . . stuff. I'll replace it.' My tone suggests I'm a long way from convincing myself of this yet.

She giggles. 'Oh, I'm sorry,' she says, 'but that was just so *cute*! Can you say that again? Your accent is just like . . . Have y'all seen *Grease*?'

A bus has been cut somewhere up the line and the usual delays ensue. It's now 4.30 and my bus won't be here till nine. I occupy myself by cataloguing everything in my stolen bag and calling Dad to have a bit of a cry. I've convinced him and Caroline to meet me in Orlando this coming weekend and experience Disney

World to round out my tour of the US. After Greyhound, my brain will need a soothing fantasy injection and my body needs the type of hotel room only parental units can provide – the crick in my neck is fast becoming a hump.

I watch the human traffic dejectedly for the next few hours. Beside me sits a big truckie on his way to a wedding. He tells me that driving his rig there would be too expensive with all the fuel it takes. He's singing along loudly to Bowie's 'Golden Years' on a crappy pink portable tape player from the eighties, talking to me quite unsolicited, and periodically ordering his terrifyingly ugly girlfriend around.

'Yessir, I love truckin',' he tells me, and I just keep nodding along.

'I don't pick up hitchhikers, though,' he says, 'nuh uh. No one rides in my truck but my woman.' He looks over at her affectionately. 'She's my pride and joy. Hey, honey,' he yells, 'this girl here is from Os-tray-yuh.' She looks up. 'Where my cig-ar-ettes at?' she demands. He tosses them to her and she misses. 'Fuck you!' she screams. 'Dumb bitch,' he mumbles back. They continue in this vein for as long as I'm there. They have eight hours until their bus arrives.

I go to investigate what's on offer in the Albuquerque Travellers' Grill. There are no instant noodles. Of course. My 'grilled' dining choices are limited to Doritos and Coke, or ancient-looking chilli boiling away like grey glue in a big bucket. Also for sale are miniature Greyhound buses, logo-ed backpacks and T-shirts. I'm aghast. Who would buy such a thing? A Greyhound-branded anything? I'm filled with a woeful shame for the company and all my fellow bus travellers, that we have fallen so far for merchandise to be a cringing embarrassment.

I realise I have to get out of Albuquerque and off the Greyhound. I've had enough of the groaning filth and grinding poverty. I've seen enough to know that this isn't the only real America, and there are only so many more hard-luck stories I can bear witness too. It's unbalanced. I burst out the doors and stride across the parking lot in the direction of downtown. Twenty minutes later I reverse course and head in the real direction of downtown.

Just around the corner from the station is a nice big movie theatre and a surprisingly good café. It's too late for me to see a movie before my bus rattles away, but I drink some hot chocolate and eat a big, squishy cookie with M and Ms in it. I feel so much better, lighter, to be surrounded by this lovely space, friendly smiles and the sugary nourishment of my snacks, which are much cheaper than what was on offer at the Travellers' Grill. Anyone trapped in that station, I think, my trucker friend or the others, they could catch a new movie and eat a good snack in here for what they're spending on rancid chilli, thin coffee and half a pack of cigs looking at the sides of Greyhound buses. I guess after a while on the Greyhound rung of life, it becomes a matter of where you believe yourself to belong, and what you expect you deserve. It's not just that I have folding money in my wallet and straight teeth – I realise what counts most of all is a sense of entitlement to a better life.

Back at the bus station, a charismatic young college student from Oklahoma is telling the herd a story, his thick black dreadlocks flicking around with enthusiasm. I take a bucket seat while he tells of the bus driver on the way here who openly relished the punishment of his passengers, especially in leaving slowpokes behind at rest stops. Apparently, the bus just in from LA lost four ticket holders on the way to Albuquerque. The last guy, left behind at a Burger King, had jumped in a cab that ran alongside the bus on the freeway. 'Everyone was lookin' out,' the student tells us, 'just rootin' for the guy, y'know, c'mon man, *c'mon*, and he's lookin' in, y'know, all panicked. The bus driver just motored on ahead and was laughin' like a maniac, he *loved* it! We stopped at some lights at the city limits and the guy takes his chance. Jumps outta the cab and runs to the bus, but the lights change, and so he's just standin' there, hair blown back by the acceleration. The cab follows us all the way to some pissant stop and he gets back on. Cost him 75 bucks!'

'Hoo-eee,' says the lady next to me. 'My goddamn ticket only cost that much!'

We each begin to tell Greyhound tales, which are similar in embroidery and emotion to fishing tales and war stories, and the crowd grows to two rows of the ugly orange chairs. The truckie eventually tells a story of a guy who drove his rig right into some federal building, immolating himself in protest at his working conditions, and we all agree that it's only a matter of time before a Greyhound driver does the same thing.

'Man!' the young college guy sighs, and there is a lull where we all just shake our heads, grateful to have spoken our dissatisfaction aloud for first time. We feel like a union. 'We all got these horror stories about the damn Dawg,' he says, 'so why the hell we all still ridin' it?'

'You afford to fly?' asks an old lady.

Pause.

'Nah.'

'Nope.'

'Nu-uh.'

'Me neither.'

'Muh Lexus is gettin' upgraded right now.'

Amongst chuckles and head-shaking, we slowly disperse.

Chapter 19

Don't mess with Texas

On the way to Amarillo, Texas, I'm stuck behind a Mexican family of 11 who kick wildly at each other and the back of my seat, shouting in a steady stream of Spanish. With six children singing 'la la la la LA!' in competition to see whose voice can get the loudest, the bus driver eventually intervenes, but the two parents continue to sit stony-faced – or stoned – through the whole thing. Each of the kids is wearing nappies, even though the eldest must be at least seven. I think it's a nifty idea, actually, and am considering investing in some Depends for the rest of this trip. Depends and a morphine/glucose drip, then I'll never have to leave my seat again.

I befriend a lovely young mum with a kid called Maximum Jones. Proving my sense-of-entitlement theory, she has turned the ponky bus into a grand adventure for young Maximum and it's nice to watch them colour-in together and discuss the possible size of rainbows. For me, though, the appalling pace of the bus provides for little more than slack-jawed meditation inter-mittently studded with drooling half-sleep. Oh, make it *over*.

It's 2 am when we reach Amarillo to discover that our bus won't be leaving again until 4.30. A collective groan goes up from the worn-out crowd. I mingle with the rest of the re-boarders – always an elite club because we get back on first and

have assured seating. The hot topic of discussion is the abomin-
able toilet situation on our bus – a sloshing, stinking nightmare
that we pray will be cleaned during this interim.

'Damn, they need to fix that shit!' a back-seat passenger
howls. 'When the AC catches it – whoo-eee!'

'You speakin' the truth if I ever heard it,' a big Jamaican
woman agrees, 'and the fa-cil-it-ees in dis station, if you can call
dem dat, is too few and too bad.'

'Too few is right!' a marine growls. 'It's like the dang military
in here – the seat's always warm! Ah want a cold seat. Ah at
least want to *feel* like I'm the only one, know what I'm saying?'

The terminal here is a mess, and bus problems mean lots of
people are now crying about lost luggage and missed connections. Nothing is open for people to get change and I find myself
giving away all my laundry quarters to people needing to call
home to tell them 'one more day'.

Despite our exhaustion leaving Amarillo, it's very hard to
sleep on the bus, all lumps and bumps and edges seem to be
greatly magnified. It's hard not to focus on my immediate
discomfort, especially now that all my travel drugs have been
stolen. Why I re-supplied myself with three flavours of lip-balm
but no Kwells is now emerging as one of the great mysteries of
my short lifetime. A few seats behind me, a man with outrageous
conspiracy theories keeps up a steady and impassioned lecture,
which the driver periodically interrupts with loud shushing.

Mr Conspiracy is quite beyond crazy, but he's also articulate
and interesting, and we all end up over-shushing the shushing
driver, because it helps our cause to keep this man on in the
background, like dodgy late-night TV. 'Why do you think the
government subsidises *corn* in America?' he whispers urgently.
'Why do you think they put high fructose *corn syrup* in everything we eat, huh? That's where they test the *vaccines*, man, in
the *corn*. When the Russians re-group and join Iran, the USA
will be the only nation able to withstand the bio-bombs, and it's
all down to the *corn*, see? Crop circles? All in *cornfields* . . .'
Eventually, the entire bus is soothed into slumber by the ranting
of this madman – the perfect Greyhound lullaby.

*

We make Wichita Falls, Texas, at nine o'clock. Having used a polyester airline eye-patch against the Texan sun, I wake to find my hair crimped tightly with a crooked line, my eyelashes disturbingly baked upwards and plastered with eyelid sweat. Did you know eyelids can sweat independently? Mine must have, because the rest of me is snap-frozen. I flatter myself that I'm at least in better shape than some of my travelling companions. The woman beside me is wearing a giant messy wig, which now looks like a small animal has crawled up there and died wretchedly during the night.

We have stopped near a Carl's Jr. Burger and a Burger King, and are ordered off the bus to sort out some breakfast. Outside, the humidity hits me in the face like a hot, wet, doggy kiss and my new haircut slicks to my cheeks, where it collapses, wetly, never to recover. Note to self: don't get haircut in zero humidity unless it's your natural environment. The smell of this muggy air makes me homesick for Florida and Sydney summers. In the distance, on the other side of a massive freeway, I spy Macca's and at the thought of a McMuffin my tummy growls to life.

The golden arches hang there in the distance, an invitation to early morning adventure, and before I know it I'm hurtling half-blind across the interstate, arms outstretched and feet thumping wildly. I order a balanced breakfast to enjoy on the bus, including both food groups, fats and lipids. Processed sausage, eggs processed into a thin yellow crepe of 'omelet', a biscuit (scone) of flour and hot salty lard, potato starch crisped in beef tallow and some coffee to wash it all down. If you eat it quick, it's dee-lishous, but if you wait four minutes longer – the length of time it takes to get back across six lanes of traffic and re-board a Greyhound at top speed – it congeals to form an inedible mess, thickly pasting your fingers and the roof of your mouth.

My breakfast isn't much assisted by the fact that I'm eating it next to a rural Wal-Mart, with acres of cheap manure piled high in the car park, and I'm pleased to set off again. Sitting up straight and stretching myself out, I try to stay alert and interested in the miles of abandoned buildings and gas stations. These are poorer areas of the state of Texas, the places where the Clampetts didn't find no black gold, Texas tea. The town of Bowie is largely empty, with only a few storefronts still hanging in, but a plethora of religious activity. In general, I have learnt that the poorer the state or the city in America, the more they gots religion.

Throughout this area, all the passengers we pick up are adorned with the popular WWJD merchandise (What Would Jesus Do?) including T-shirts, bracelets, key-chains and neckties printed with the thought-provoking acronym. A T-shirt with 'Pray Hard' written on it features a picture of basketball-sneakered legs with holes worn into the knees of baggy jeans. Another has a shirt that simply shouts 'REPENT'! But my personal favourite is a T-shirt that says, 'Jesus died for your sins! And rose from the Dead!' with the word 'dead' drawn two hands high in wiggly, horror film writing. Hmm. *Jesus, Easter of the Living Dead III The Revenge* – This time, it's *personal*. A large woman has a T-shirt with I ♥ Jesus hand-printed on it in puffy paint that looks like something girlish carved on a school desk. Who knows? Maybe she just has a Mexican boyfriend.

We pass roads with names like Wagonseller and Bootscoot, and bumper stickers the polar opposite of Oregon's, stickers like 'My wife said she'd go if the guns didn't. I sure do miss her.' We pass the Kickapoo Catfish Restaurant and pick up a black man outside a lonely building called the Cowboy Church, who keeps scratching at a poor-man's home-made tattoo, featuring a skull and crossbones over the Confederate flag. Still hungry, I look sadly at the parking lot for 'Eat at Joe's Crab Shack'. It is filled with emergency vehicles, including fire rescue, and I know from friends in the emergency services that if they're parked out the front, the food will be good, hearty and reasonably priced. That or someone's choking to death, but it's a pretty safe call.

Our skanky bus wheezes in to some two-coyote town called Scab Butt, Texas, and picks up a snaggle-toothed maniac and her seven bags of crap. Snaggletooth is well over the luggage limit, but the driver relents in order to get the bus moving again, and because he can make little sense of this woman's increasingly violent ramblings. Snaggletooth has matted orange hair to her waist and oozing sores crusted into a dense layer of grime on her uncovered arms. She is filthy and wretched and, unfortunately for us, well-ticketed. She screeches her way to the back of the bus and sets up camp in the row of empty seats beside our putrid toilet door.

I hear someone up the front wail to the driver, 'You're not *serious*, man! Jeezum!' I feel miserable for Snaggletooth then, and have a conversation with my seatmate about how hard it must be to be mentally ill, destitute and lacking basic dentition. Feeling very much like the late Princess Diana (but with cooler jeans) I pinch my nose internally and go to offer the mumbling woman some assistance with her fetid luggage. 'Ma'am,' I start, 'do you need any . . .'

'FUCK YOU, you skinny little CUNT!' she screams, before giving me the (scabby) finger. 'FuckyoufuckyouFUCKYOU!' Well. I feel that she has made her feelings clear, and her breath alone causes a hasty retreat. The bus is incensed on my behalf. I bask briefly in the glory of being that-nice-girl-who-tried, affecting a beatific smile of resignation and delivering half-waves like the Pope.

The back of the bus begins to smell like nothing else on earth. It hit us in rolling waves, causing much swooning and moaning and covering of nostrils. Snaggletooth begins a low diatribe of insults and nonsense that slowly grow to a fever pitch. She produces a rusted butterknife and begins to saw clumsily at her forearms, breaking old wounds and producing sluggish trickles of blood. Eventually, a giant black man sitting across from me shakes his head and laughs a little. 'Man,' he says, 'I know the Greyhound is hell, but shit, it's VIET-naaaaam back there. I BIN to Vietnam, man, an' I ain't going back for no one. I know bug-ass crazy when I sees it.'

Apparently, there is nothing wrong with Snaggletooth's hearing and she zeroes in on our conversation despite her steady stream of babble. There is silence for a moment, and then, distinctly, 'Nigger.' A collective gasp goes up. Snaggletooth loves it. 'NiggerniggerniggerblackniggardlyniggerNIGGER!' At least half the bus is black. I shrink in my seat, predicting a riot, predicting *Rodney King The Rematch: Justice Is Served*. Snaggletooth hoots with laughter and racist slurs, brandishing her butterknife. At precisely this moment the bus swerves off the road and into Dank Stream, a one-coyote town, and we clang to a halt at a lonely level crossing. A general bus mutiny has been declared and this creates an impromptu ventilation break. We spend the next hour eating jalapeño-flavoured sandwich crackers, the only fare on offer, inside a rotten little gas station in the Texan heat. By the time we get back on, Snaggletooth has mercifully fallen asleep (or bled out, who could tell) and the odour has dissipated somewhat through the open door.

This brief adventure into stench, depravity and green-coloured, chilli-hot, belly-ache carbohydrates, reminds me just how the bubble of the bus can become a world of its own. It has its own heroes and villains, torments and oases. It is cut off almost completely from the status or amenities of the outside world and I start daydreaming about a possible *Survivor – Greyhound*. Maybe I should call Mark Burnett. I while away most of Texas with open-mouthed imaginings of increasingly complicated scenarios in which passengers and drivers get voted off and lose or gain their pathetic privileges.

At our next stop, the bus fills completely and I gain a new seatmate. A young guy with dreadlocks and bolts through both ears, as well as numerous bags filled with eco-friendly urban-camping materials. When I get out my new copy of the hostels guidebook, he leans over to comment and we start talking. He is half-mad and quite beautiful, but very stinky. He snacks on waxy-looking carob chocolate while I tell him about my theft, and how I had wanted to go to Truth or Consequences. 'Oh, man, lucky escape!' he says, 'Truth or Consequences has, like, this total vortex of energy that won't let you out. Dude, seriously. I went to visit a friend who was chillin' there at the hostel. I went for like, two days, and I ended up staying for two months! There's weird shit in that town, man, a lot of heavy drugs too; heroin, crack. No one seems to live there, but I was just camping and suddenly there were two, then three, then four people and none of us could leave, man. We like, tried, but we just couldn't get out. The hostel is real nice though, really chilled, great people . . .'

Wow, I think, maybe it wasn't vengeance from the travel gods after all, but evil-vortex protection. It sure would be crap to be stuck in spittin' distance from Albuquerque for the rest of my life. My seatmate has just bought land in Belize with a local government grant and wants to start a commune there and disseminate truth. On the outskirts of Austin, he gives me a crystal, a raw emerald, and tells me not to be afraid to use it if I get into trouble again – how, I'm not sure, but I am grateful for the gesture.

Texas is dead flat and extraordinarily boring to traverse. It runs on endlessly and by the time we arrive in Austin proper, I have no idea what day it is or why I wanted to stop in this town. I consult the hostel book again, and take the local number 7 bus in the direction of Lakeshore Boulevard. After much consultation, the good driver still forgets to alert me to my stop and so, an hour into our trip, I discover I have to travel back on the bus for another half an hour. I'm doubly furious because, for once, it's not my own stupid fault. The hostel, when I can finally see it, is attractively situated next to a large, tranquil lake, but it's well outside the downtown area. My guidebook has really fallen down here, because I suddenly remember the point of Austin, live music capital of the world, and would much rather be down where the action is on Sixth Avenue, than stuck in quiet, suburban Texas.

It's been many long, itchy hours since my cat-wash without any detergent-based products in the Albuquerque motel and I've been living – and sleeping – in the same pair of filthy jeans for over three days. The shower is large and institutional, in a large tiled room without privacy, which is very un-American. Despite what Islamic fundamentalists, the Hooters restaurant chain and Hollywood's adult movie industry might suggest, most Americans are actually modest to the point of prudishness. Topless sunbathing may be de rigueur in Europe, but it will get you arrested almost everywhere in the US. Americans don't blink at fake breasts (or rather, they do blink, quite a bit, which is why there are approximately 4280 per cent more breast enlargements in the US than any other nation) but so much as hint at a nipple, and you'd better get a lawyer. I turn on all four shower prongs in the middle of the room and run around for an hour or so in the steam and bubbles, getting very, very clean, before putting on fresh clothes.

My new backpack is crammed with undies and T-shirts still on little plastic hangers, with tags and all. Who knew there could be such comfort found in a few shapes of cotton? I have a nearly religious moment of Nirvana as I dress my raw, peachy skin and hurl my other stuff (the three pieces of apparel Greyhound left me with) into the hostel washing machine. I set it to Chernobyl and sigh deeply, relaxing for the first time in days. It feels very good.

At 9 pm, I set off downtown to find something to eat, but I don't get very far. I am informed by a traveller on the steps that the bus I need to catch is in a dicey neighbourhood after dark and that a taxi will cost a small fortune. I wander back inside. I last ate at 9 am when I had breakfast on the bus. The hostel kitchen reveals a loaf of green bread, half a Pop Tart and what may or may not be textured soy protein. Eventually I use the vending machine to prepare a small meal for myself out of Cool Ranch Doritos, microwave popcorn and Mango Snapple to wash it down. I eat it crouched under my bunk because there is a girl in the foyer singing tortured songs and playing guitar, and the crowd are too cool for my popcorn-snacking noises to interrupt their reverie. With no PJs and limited clothing, I fall asleep topless in my new Target Superman Y-fronts ($3.82 for pack of four) and pray there won't be a fire.

The next morning I figure out what day it is, recalibrate my McDonald's napkin charts, and remember to call my mother for her fiftith birthday. It's winter night-time tomorrow in Australia, where we like to be a good day and a season ahead of everyone else, and Mum sounds very far away. I prattle on about Greyhound and my odd little adventures, trying not to sniffle when she asks me how the Boy is, who I haven't seen for nearly nine months now. 'What about your lotto prize, Neeni?' she asks me. 'Do you know if you're going to hang on to it yet?' I don't know what to tell her. Each day that passes I'm growing more homesick, but more and more entranced by this massive land. There doesn't seem to be a simple solution.

Mum puts my brother, Simon, on the phone. He laughs at my wild bus stories and then says, 'Hey, Sa, just head on back to

Dad's house. The bus sounds like shit. Doesn't Dad still have a pool and an ice-making fridge? Why are you missioning it around the US anyway? You're still coming home, right?'

'Yes, but I can always come *home*. With a Green Card, I could live and work anywhere in the USA!'

Silence. I rattle the sticky Verizon payphone. 'I said, I can live and –'

'Heard you the first time, Sa,' he says, 'just wondering why you'd want to move.'

I guess I've vented too heavily on my disenchantment with Greyhound bus travel. I tell him this, adding that America is larger, more unusual, more complex and more beautiful than I could ever have possibly imagined. I take his non-committal sounds for envy.

'Don't worry, Si,' I say, 'maybe Dad can sponsor you somehow. Hey! You could go to uni here! You don't need a Green Card for that.'

'Thanks, sweets,' Simon says, yawning, 'but I'm doin' okay over here.'

'But it's America!'

'Mmm,' he says.

'You love American music!' I accuse, 'and animation and sneakers and brands of cunning outerwear!'

With a sibling's insight, he asks me who I'm trying to convince.

I miss my brother. A big Billy bad-time bunch (this seems to be a Texas-style quantity), and my mother, too. Do I really want to move to the US? What happens when you move somewhere for a year or two at 24? If you start to make an adult life somewhere, does that slide on in to being your future faster than you can say 'they've taken me off the electoral role'? Will I be unwittingly starting a life of flying home once a year for six days of a prawn-filled Australian Christmas? Am I signing up for a broken heart from the Boy and a match with a nice American like Guilia suggested? Will my future self be taking kids called Molly and Tyler to school in Minneapolis if I'm not careful? Is that really such a bad thing anyway?

And I decide that it is a bad thing, yes, a very bad thing if my widgets can't see their cool Uncle Si often enough to learn how to cheat at Xbox and or spend Wednesday afternoons at Grandma Lynneeta's house making fairy bread. But I'm so unwilling to relinquish my prize too. This country is feeling more like a great treasure with every new state, despite the rough edges I'm always pressing my unwashed face against. I dread the bus but I dread the end of the journey even more, when there will be no more surprises, nasty or otherwise, just the semi-predictable sameness of the end of the line.

I call the Boy. He's with friends, ordering a chicken sandwich to take away, and I listen with a growing sense of disconnection to the following conversation:
    'Mate, mayo?'
    'Sorry, mate?'
    'Mayo on your sanga, mate?'
    'Oh, cheers, mate, yep, thanks, mate.'
    'Here ya go, mate.'
    'Ta, mate.'
    'Thanks, mate.'
    'Cheers, mate.'
    'Mate?'
    'Yeah, coming, mate, just a sec,'
    'Oh, you're on the phone, mate,'
    'Yeah, mate, it's Sa,'
    'Oh, G'DAY, SA!'
    'Sorry, babe,' he says, 'Texas did you say?'
And Texas feels a very long way away indeed.
    Now that my handbag and day-pack are gone, I put my wallet in a little plastic bag from Walgreen's and set out to get me some Texas. Downtown buses only cost 50 cents, and they are big old-fashioned tram-style cars called 'Dillos, for the actual armadillos seen waddling everywhere around these parts. The primary-coloured armadillos featured on bus signs are so cute and I'm easily charmed by the Wiggles-world public trans-portation announcements 'transfer here to the 1, the 5, and the red and yellow 'Dillo!' They must have a problem with flooding in Texas, because the 'Dillos are wall-papered inside with advertisements shouting 'Gone in a flash!' beside pictures of

submerged houses. I'd always thought of Texas as perpetually arid and dusty, but yet another public service announcement warns, 'Don't drive into *any* water!' showing a tsunami and a submerged car.

I take the 26 bus to another Guadalupe Street, this one near the University of Texas. Home to some 50,000 students, the U of T is one of the biggest schools in the country. College kids are everywhere here, beautiful and vibrant, and the street is loaded with interesting eateries and clothing stores to cater for their dollars and taste. I walk along enjoying the atmosphere – despite the literal atmosphere being extremely humid, so that my plastic bag begins to stick and slap and slide against my sweaty legs. The weather forces me in to the air conditioning at an Einstein Bros. Bagel chain, where I make the welcome discovery that they have bottomless coffee. I remain here through the heat of midday, writing letters home in between fixing litres of different coffee roasts at the beverage station like a science experiment – half a beaker of cream, half of skinny milk, dash of butterscotch syrup, sprinkle vanilla sugar, hold the cinnamon. Hmm, let's go again with the choc and hazelnut, hold the half and half.

Two girls sit behind me having a conversation that goes, 'So, like, he, like, totally weirded out, and I was all, like, totally, you know, and he just was all, oh-kayyy, and I was all, *whatever*, and he's, like, c'mon, and I'm, like, totally just, and we just, I mean, I guess that's how these things happen.' Her nodding friend seems to have translated nicely, but I eavesdrop for half an hour and never figure out quite what is at issue. I gulp coffee until I get the mean jitters and have to leave, grinding my teeth and twitching through the aisles at another Walgreen's. Products are my weakness.

I cut across a campus park with my new purchases, passing a young woman with a broken leg stretched out in the sun, scratching at the cast absentmindedly. Now there's something to think about. I've never been very sick or injured in this country, but the thought terrifies me. Healthcare in America is either very expensive or simply not available. Those are your options. Unless you're a bit of a money-bags, people put off going to the doctor here until they're half-past dead. After a week of shocking cluster headaches in Sanibel, it cost me US$200 to see a regular GP, only to be told that I would need a CAT scan before she would prescribe me a migraine medication regularly dispensed at home. I didn't even want to ask what the CAT scan cost, so I left and bought a case of medicinal beer instead. Beer is very cheap in America.

At university in Mississippi I saw firsthand what an emergency without easy-access healthcare looks like, and it was ugly. After a night of international cultural exchange at a couple of bars near the college, a phone call woke me at an unreasonable hour to pass on news of a fallen comrade. Our friend Danny, a crazy, cattle-branded Texan, had come undone over a girl. Or rather, his ear had come undone when her boyfriend made an untimely return to her apartment and bit it off. All Danny had left was a small piece of buckled cartilage like a broken snail shell at the top of his aural cavity.

Horrified and hungover, both of which greatly magnified the other, I ran off to find him on his way to the hospital. It was indeed a ghastly wound. 'Hey, darlin'!' he said, dizzy and green, 'looks like ol' Danny have ta grow his hair long again.' They make 'em tough in Texas. Danny had been taken to the hospital earlier that night, but, unable to provide immediate proof of insurance, he was sent away after his wound was flooded with salty water to the tune of 100 bucks up front. In case you missed it, this was an amputated body part. Salty water is for shaving cuts. Or storing fetta.

Returning hours later with his Blue Cross insurance card and a credit card with a higher limit, the hospital became instantly more understanding of the fact that Danny's oozing space-formerly-known-as-ear might indeed be causing him some pain and trauma. Plastic surgeons were immediately summoned. Pain medication was drawn up; cards of heavily initialled counsellors were pressed into his shaky hand. Suddenly everyone wanted to come to the party at Danny's head, and I was shocked at the turnaround.

For some reason I found myself sitting in during surgery, trying to distract my pal from his incredible pain and the dawning realisation that, without the aid of double-sided tape, he would never wear sunglasses again. The doctor informed us gravely that the ear should have been seen to much earlier, as the skin surrounding this cartilage had already begun to die and shrink away. This meant that much more of Danny's poor ear would now have to be cut away in order to draw the thin skin over and close the wound. I remember being furious then; apoplectic with scorn as only a citizen with Medicare can be.

'He was here *eight hours* ago and you guys sent him home!' I said, thumping my little fist into the kind of cushy chair that all this money will get you. The doctor explained that his services and the medication used were all going to be very expensive, and if you can't prove payment in the US, well, you just get whatever you can afford at the time. A top-of-the-line fibre-optic camera in your rectum, or just a hamster with a tiny miner's helmet and some dental floss tied to one foot. One of the most valuable lessons I learnt from this experience was to never get your ear bitten off in the first place. Ever. Don't even allow anyone a nibble unless you're very sure of their intent.

Hospitals at home in Australia often resemble cinder-block airports in regional Mongolia, but the high level of subsidised health care inside was something I had always taken for granted. Being sick or hurt is frightening enough without worrying that it will burden your family to bankruptcy or that you just can't afford the treatment you need. I think about this in the park until a big knot appears between my eyes and I realise I've chewed a dent into the corner of my mouth. What's the point of living and working in America if an emergency appendectomy will bankrupt me, screw my credit rating and I lose everything I've worked for? There are things you can never plan for, things that Qantas won't agree to babysit for 16 hours across an ocean so that I can get home to Medicare. What about having a family? Kids get sick if they look sideways at something and it costs as much as a mid-sized car to give birth to one here. This is probably a much bigger issue than 'Can I get a laksa in this city?' and I start to think I've been going about this Green Card thing all wrong.

I catch a slow bus back to the hostel, still wired from coffee and complicated wonderings. Hot, bothered and feeling lonely after my too-short calls home, I decide to move myself on to New Orleans. Packing to leave takes minutes now that I have so few possessions and I set off to catch up with Señor Greyhound again after only the briefest of intervals. It's still very muggy outside and now that I'm back on this part of the map, my new haircut seems destined to look like ass forever more.

It might not be good for the hair, but Texas, Loozianne, Mizzhippy – these states all share some very sexy weather. The humidity makes the air hazy, like vaseline on the lens, and your skin turns moist and dewy. Steamy and languid, it's the antithesis of the invigorating Rocky Mountain air. It's kissin' weather. BBQ weather, with a cold beer on the back of your neck and your damp hair held up in the other hand. The sun in the afternoon is very soft, lighting everything up in gold, purple and deep, lush green. Mardi Gras colours. Suddenly I'm so excited to see Noo Awlins again that the last few days of theft and rain and grubbiness evaporate. New Orleans. The Spanish moss hanging from the trees, the Gothic houses, the rich stink of the cobbled streets, the glorious, wheezing streetcars, the deep voices, heavy and drawn-out like spooning molasses, the spicy food and the spicy music. Tomorrow night I'll be there again, I promise myself, and I'll finally be old enough to have a drink in the French Quarter.

I find my way back to the Greyhound station, heading for the land of gumbo and good times. Leaving Austin, the driver is having trouble with our cantankerous old bus. He bunny-hops a bit and then throws the bus into reverse. We back out with a jiggling reverberation – *dadadadadadadadada* – until we are all bouncing up and down, teeth chattering, cheeks wobbling. The kids in the back just lose it with giggles and us grown-ups are having a hard time trying not to smile. The bus stops. We lurch forward. Then stop. Then *dadadadadada* for a few metres until the whole bus is giggling. Suddenly two wheels go up on the median strip and burn rubber through a carefully planted flowerbed and we laugh until we are clutching our sides. 'Lemme drive her, Captain!' come shouts from the back. 'Hey, buddy, need a copilot?' Each bad crack is greeted with howls so contagious that pretty soon even the hapless driver is laughing.

He starts doing tricks now, pulling up sharply to one side and then the other, dancing the big old ugly Trailways bus around for his audience. We come to a screaming halt at the first red light and everyone slides forward in the tiny seats, looking over the laps of the person in front. By this time we are jelly-limbed with mirth and the tiniest thing sets off giggles that last for half an hour.

As the sun begins to set and the bus has set a bump-free pace (hell, it could be hands-free, Texas is such a straight shot) the kids on the bus begin singing 'This Land is Your Land'. This Woody Guthrie classic can be translated into a fairly childish and tuneless ditty, which is why American kids take to it with such gusto, belting it out at every occasion parents are invited to watch them in costume at school. As a slightly confused student in Mrs Apfel's second grade class in Los Angeles, I once sang the song loudly myself. 'This land is your land, this land is myyyyyyyyy land, this land was made for you and me.' I like this song now. In the same way I am a huge (secret) fan of 'We Are Australian', another inclusive composition. 'We are one, but we are many,' it starts, 'and from all the lands on earth we come. We share a dream, and sing with one voice, I am, you are, we are, Australian.' That could be America's song too. It's much better than our actual Australian anthem, of course, which includes the word 'girt'. Yeech. I love 'The Star-spangled Banner' though. It's a stirring, beautiful poem and a ripper of an anthem. Still, it's a song of war and of defiance, and bland though ours may be, I'd rather rejoice to a yawning melody that Australians are young and free with lots to share than exclaim 'Up yours, we're still the best', which is the essence of 'The Banner'. Will that get me an FBI file, I wonder?

Another oddment recently remembered from my stint at Paradise Canyon Elementary was the daily pledge of allegiance. With my hat off and one little hand covering my heart, like every other school-age child in this country, I had started each morning with 'I pledge allegiance to the flag of the United States of America and to the Republic for which it stands.' Heavy stuff, eh? How can a six-year-old pledge allegiance to anything, let alone a Republic? I couldn't reliably spell my mum's name at

that stage. This bizarre ritual came back to me a few weeks ago
when I read that there is some hoo-ha at the moment about
removing part of it. The rest of the Pledge goes on to finish 'One
Nation, under God, indivisible, with liberty and justice for all.'
About a month ago, a federal appeals court ruled that the Pledge
is unconstitutional because it contains an endorsement of
religion by the phrase 'under God', which, by the way, was
added over half a century after it was written, during the
McCarthy era. I'm inclined to agree. President Bush, however,
calls this 'ridiculous'.

Whichever way you say it, the Pledge doesn't seem to fit, to
me, with the great freedoms enjoyed by the people of this
country. The liberty part is great, and I'm sure it's all intended to
be sweet and patriotic, but I find it unsettling and vaguely fascist
to have to grow up publicly pledging allegiance to a Nation-State
each day. American life can be so contradictory in this way, and I
can't just blame Dubya, or his government, or the one before
that, or the fifties or the NRA. With great freedoms come great
conflicts and in every aspect of life here – from snacks and cars
to religion and politics – things can easily spiral out towards the
extremes. I might think the Pledge is weird, but I also think the
court's response to it is a fine example of the American justice
system looking out for its citizens, and I wonder if other
countries are as conscientious about examining freedom.

Still humming nationalistic songs, I lumber off the bus in
Houston and make my way to the sleepy line for New Orleans.
I will have from 6 am to midnight to rediscover the city before a
long trip to Florida; to Disney World and home. I can't believe
the end is in sight. I know I had a life before Greyhound, but I
can't seem to conjure up what it was like and the Boy just looks
like a payphone to me now. My wandering days are nearly over.
I only wish the poor tomato-pack could have made it this far.

Chapter 20

The Big Easy

'Okay, everyone, here we are. The Biiiiiiig Eeeeee-SAY, here she is. Mmm mm. What a town.' I wake up and rub my eyes as the bus creeps into the Greyhound station at dawn. I remember it being in a bad part of town (when is it otherwise?) and set off quickly, looking determined. New Orleans you don't want to mess around with. In the same way people demonised New York City in the late eighties for crack and crime, N'Awlins can be huge trouble in the wrong places. It was the FBI murder capital of the world in '94 and again in '01, and its dodgy neighbourhoods are still pretty damn dodgy. All the memories come flooding back as I walk past the Holiday Inn with the huge clarinet painted the entire height of the building in front of me. The magic names are leaping out at me: Pontchartrain, Rampart, St Charles. I catch a cab around the corner to a downtown hostel, dumping my bags in a hurry before fleeing with a bursting heart.

On the beautiful streetcar the dreadlocked attendant has thrown the old wooden windows in front of him down and the early morning miasma washes over us in gentle, rolling waves. It is so humid in New Orleans – a town officially *below* sea level – that it seems to rain upwards. The scenic aboveground cemeteries here aren't just grand and gracious, they're a public service. You actually can't bury the dead in New Orleans without them floating back to the surface. It seems like no one wants to leave. I don't blame them. I lean back in my seat and gaze out the windows. I remember that it's illegal here to touch or take the atmospheric Spanish moss dangling down from the huge trees along these streets because the unusual plant, so tied to this town's image, takes such a long time to grow. These ancient trees and plants match the beautiful antique houses all around us and even the ghettos in New Orleans appear to consist of crumbling mansions and dilapidated turn-of-the-century neighbourhoods that must have been lovely once.

I hop off on Canal Street, the big tourist centre, and start walking instinctively. Four years later it all comes rushing back, like toppling dominos, with each corner I turn. There's the Popeye's Chicken where I had my first fix and the chain is even better here in its home town of N'Awlins where they serve up shrimp étouffée and pecan pie. Here's Decatur Street, which, like most French names in New Orleans, is pronounced phonetically. Don't go trying to turn Candolet into 'Cando-lay' in this town. Now I'm standing on the street corner that was the first image I ever saw of New Orleans; watching the blaxploitation Bond film where the American agent gets done in at a jazz funeral right here in the French Quarter.

I'm passing all the places I once couldn't drink with new relish, looking at the yard-glasses and mixers full of tasty, alcoholic ice. This is the state with drive-through daiquiri bars. There's our meeting place for Mardi Gras and there's the lamppost I cracked my head on due to the excitement of seeing Harry Connick Jr. aboard a float in the parade. These familiarities make me long for my old Southern Miss friends like a real, physical pain. I sit on the kerb and tear up, overwhelmed. I need caffeine and sugar, fast.

I stumble along to Café Du Monde, an old-world eatery I have the fondest memories of; memories of mountains of powdered sugar hiding dumplings of fried dough called beignets. The service is not sugary and Southern though; my half-asleep Chinese waitress doesn't even look at me, just barks back my order and she's off. It's a lovely old inside/outside kind of place, and you pay for the food on delivery to avoid confusion. When she brings my coffee and beignets I have the temerity to ask for more milk after I have already paid. 'You wan' milk,' she says, 'one dolla thirty-seven!'

'No, sorry, not a glass of milk, just a splash more in my coffee.' She grabs my mug, swearing unintelligibly, and it comes back cold and almost white. She cannot be corralled for twenty minutes and I'm truly dying for a piping hot cup. I'm exhausted from being up all night bouncing on the ponky bus. It's like I've been jetlagged for a week now. I walk my slosh up to the front and smile my sweetest powdery-moustache smile. 'Hi!' I say to the cashier, 'I can't seem to get a hold of my waitress, and my coffee is pretty well undrinkable.' She yawns. 'You'll have to take it up with her.' Wow, is this still America? Usually your waiter tries to force-feed you everything on the menu and then offers to suck your toes and drive your Granny to bingo.

Finally I go looking out the back for my waitress. All the waitresses are together in a clump on some hidden chairs while their Midwestern-tourist patrons frantically scan the crowd for them. It's 8.45, after all, peak Java-injection time. I find them reading newspapers and magazines in Cantonese, one frantic with a toothpick, the other actually flossing, and one asleep with a bowl of rice in her lap. It looks like a Kowloon alley back here, not next to the mighty Mississippi in the oldest restaurant in New Orleans. Café Du Monde is open 24 hours a day, though, and as a veteran of the late shift, I forgive them. Sort of. After all, the only things on the 140-year-old menu here are coffee, OJ and beignets.

I'm in the touristy part of New Orleans, which, at Mardi Gras, becomes one of the biggest tourist centres in the world. Standard-issue tourist-wear is hilarious. Sneakers and khakis and 'fanny packs' and an expression that reads 'I'll not be partin' with my wallet, ya Cajun crooks!'. I slurp on my coffee, watching these travellers buy bendy-balloons from the same rough, boozy-looking clown who's been here for years, embarrassed to remember that I was also flattered into thinking that I was the only 'cool' tourist, and that it really was fascinating that I was from Australia – which is now being substituted for Jersey or Oklahoma City. This French Market coffee haunt is still as beautiful as I remember, but the coffee is crummy and covering tourists in powdered sugar now seems like a cruel, snickering joke. Hmm. Sounds like more caffeine is essential.

Jazz starts up for our tips and early morning pleasure. The buskers are so damn good that I even consider ordering another bad coffee, but I remember that this town is positively bursting with good music and I have a limited amount of hours. I set off down the darling little streets, admiring flower boxes and ornate iron balconies, ending up at the Central Grocery on Decatur Street. I purchase another New Orleans specialty, the Muffuletta sandwich. Olive salad, ham, salami and provolone cheese on fat, fluffy white bread. Deelish. Afterwards, I buy a bag of fresh pralines from the nearby French Market, one of America's oldest marketplaces. I take my treats for a walk along the river, watching the great paddleboats steam in and out and soaking up the accents of passers-by. It's a lovely sound, often described as Brooklyn meets the Deep South, and a New Orleans city accent is a real favourite in America (although New Orleanians always complain that Yankee actors get it wrong, so you'll never know it unless you visit).

The day is cloudy, with bursts of rain and a gathering darkness. This rules out a trip to the spooky and beautiful Audubon Park. As the heavens open, I realise it might rule out a lot of things. After years of waiting to get back here, I find I'm too tired to function properly and am I overcome by the rain and humidity. I go into the big Riverwalk shopping centre beside the Mississippi and call Mike, my old N'Awlins beau. He's been waiting to hear from me and tells me that he's getting off work early and driving down from Baton Rouge, the Louisiana state capital, so we can hang out. Jeezum, as he would say, I'll need a nap before then or I'll fall asleep in my beer.

I'll need a clean-up too. The last time I saw Mike he had broken my heart – caught making out with a girl from the college volleyball team on the hood of his vintage Mustang outside her sorority house. Nothing is subtle in America, I guess. Up until that point, it had been a great deal of fun to 'date' a Southern gentleman, on a campus where boys fling themselves down halls and across lawns to make sure they get to open the door for you, and girls are treated as though they might expire if made to do anything strenuous, like pay for their own drinks. I went to parties at Mike's fraternity house where the boys lined up in freshly pressed shirts to take our coats at the door and serve us sugary cocktails. We went to the pictures and necked in cars. I wore his class ring for a couple of days and generally felt like I had stumbled into a fifties love song after the cynical, feminist, postmodern intellectualism of my Australian university life. It was a strangely wonderful time, but quite alien.

We had made an unlikely pairing. Each fascinated with the other's accent, I was nevertheless horrified by his preppy clothes (no self-respecting Aussie boy dresses like his dad at uni) and he was equally horrified by my flared jeans and 'hippy shit'. Not since I was 12 had I worn a skirt, but the South had me in ribbons and curls before you could say 'sorority princess'. I never quite joined the ranks of twin-sets and matching lipstick, nor did I go to the hairdresser every other day, but I learned a great deal about different beauty ideals across America. My petite breasts are treated like crooked teeth in America – 'You know, you can get that fixed now, they even do lay-away.' The South is unusual, though, I know that, and I still maintain that the most beautiful women in the Western world are bred here as a result.

It begins to pound down with rain and I'm swamped in. Trapped at the creaking hostel I have a shower and a nap, waking to a dark and thundering sky. '*Laissez les bon temps rouler*,' they say here, let the good times roll, and I hope to find me some when I'm rescued. Mike turns up looking exactly as I remember him, and it's great to hear his *Streetcar-Named-Desire* growl of a voice. He is incredulous about the neighbourhood I have landed myself in. 'Have you walked through any of the streets next to this one?' he asks. 'Actually, no, 'course you haven't or we wouldn't be havin' this conversation!' he laughs. His wonderful old Mustang is no longer with us (the girls in my dorm used to hear the engine rumble coming from Frat Row for long enough for me to do my hair and read a magazine) but his new car has a red velvet interior, which still passes my kitsch test.

Mike takes me to Madigan's, a local establishment where we drink the finest beer in the US: Abita, pride of New Orleans. They do a variety called Purple Haze, which tastes miraculously of raspberry in there somewhere, with no sweetness, just a refreshing bite. Over the next few hours we get gloriously drunk, much too drunk for him to drive me to the Quarter, where it's still pouring anyway. We start drinking at five and by midnight we have worn a distinct groove into the bar. Driving at four miles an hour and navigating using the giant Holiday Inn clarinet as my only guiding landmark, we struggle to deliver me back to the Greyhound station. After exploring several radii out from the clarinet, we eventually find it. I forget that Mike is the only person I've ever met with the same poor sense of direction as me. Maybe it's a blonde thing after all.

The bus is delayed and I roll drunkenly through the terminal for the next two hours, checking out the grey meat in the still-open Subway sandwich concession. I take handfuls of vitamins, gulp gallons of water and run around smiling foolishly at the worst collection of uglies and nutters so far because I don't care, because it's my last trip, because it's the last leg on this crazy bus, because I'm going to Disney World in 24 hours and because I'm off my dial. I boogie by myself to the rock 'n' roll soundtrack of the 'Born to be Wild' song coming from a video poker booth ('Strictly 21!'), drawing shaking heads from two cops in black uniforms with shiny badges. The city's abbreviation leads to some funny observances, like 'NO PD', which some locals use to denigrate the police force in this town.

When I hop on the bus, one of the smelly old chillers, I vow for the millionth time to have Lasik eye surgery. My contacts freeze and adhere to my suffocating eyeballs, while I claw at them wretchedly with dirty fingers. The temperatures on this bus are so frigid that my lukewarm bottled water is growing thick and slushy with ice, and I find myself tied in a knot with my sheet, wheezing and coughing along with the rest of the passengers, our noses covered with all manner of improv balaclavas.

I wake just outside Tallahassee, Florida's capital, with a dry mouth and a bitter hangover. The bus is a terrible place for a hangover. No wonder Greyhound never let you drink – it's a community service. I'm a little sorry now that I drank away much of my longed for re-visit to New Orleans, but I blame the weather, my bus-lag and the chance to relive my memories of that town with an old friend. I vow that next time I go back, I'm taking someone with me. I don't want to be the only witness to these cities anymore. I want to share my delight with adobe out loud and rediscover my favourite places through someone else's eyes.

Coming in to the station, my hangover spies a Popeye's Chicken about a ten-minute walk away, but the cranky driver threatens that he's leaving in fifteen minutes, with or without us re-boarders. Inside, the station is crowded and horrible and I line up instead at one of the worst Travellers' Grills yet. Okay, the worst. I'm making the call. Sorry, Tallahassee. The choice is severely limited, but my hangover is insatiable and only an offering of hot grease will calm Onepinttoomany, one of the lesser gods of excess. There are chicken wings that are actually phosphorescent green at their tips and the burger patties slapped in a pan for cheeseburgers are thin and yellow. It's dark and gloomy under the greasy, splattered glass that I'm pressing my nose to, playing guess-that-substance. How are people ordering this stuff? I pick a ham and cheese Hot Pocket, because it's prepackaged and microwaveable. How bad can it be? So bad. So, so bad. With one hand and my forehead pressed against a wall, I munch joylessly through the rubbery mulch, mourning the Popeye's that almost was, as our bus is again an hour late.

At the next stop, we pick up some transfers from a broken-down Greyhound. A Texan college student gets on and we share a moment of instant recognition as the only normal people adrift in a transport sea of horrors. Well, calling a Texan 'normal' is relative, of course (this is a compliment: Texans abhor normality). Her name is actually Texas, Tex for short, and she is on her way to spend the summer working at a camp for disabled kids run by one of her sisters. She has three sisters, who are all Christian ministers like her parents. Tex tells me she's done quite a bit of travelling, especially enjoying a recent church-sponsored mission to Scotland (to help the poor backward *Scots*?) and we soon begin swapping stories and giggling, each glad to have a proper confederate at last.

The bus is taking forever now that I know it's the home stretch. We have a break for an hour and a half outside a train station for no apparent reason and now, 40 minutes later, we are pulling off the freeway again for another meal break. I groan, but lo, the travel gods have issued me a final blessing. Our rest stop includes Popeye's and Krispy Kreme. In the same place. Together. I'm in heaven and order double servings. Tex is horrified. 'But you're sooo skinny!' she exclaims, and I am. I look down, munching. I am terribly thin.

Apart from Pillow, food has often been my only friend and constant companion on this trip, so I'm beginning to think I must have malnutrition. 'Nuh uh,' Tex says, 'your gut sticks out with malnutrition, hon.' In between my sixth donut and my second buttery biscuit dipped in the mushy, smoky red beans and rice, we hypothesise about what great reversal in the order of life as we know it has caused me to ingest a steady diet of the fattiest comfort food and yet rapidly lose weight as a result. 'I know!' she exclaims, 'You accidentally did some kinda Atkins diet! With all the fried chicken!' Yes! No. Pizza, pancakes, biscuits, donuts, pie, rice and fries have made up the bulk of my snacking.

Bored and half-delirious with sleep deprivation, we consider taking me to a hospital to draw blood and test for some unique compound. We decide I will make millions of dollars and I sit up excitedly, prodding my tummy which, even after two buckets of chicken, a tray of donuts, biscuits, sides and half a litre of Cherry Coke, looks like it belongs to a 12-year-old gymnast. It's astounding. I am the missing link. 'Wait,' says Tex, 'How long you been travelling for?' About a month and a half, I tell her. 'Just sittin' on your ass on the bus?' Yep. 'What'd y'all do when you got somewhere?' Found a hostel, saw the sights. 'Y'all hire a car?' Good heavens, no, I walked. Now Tex sits up. 'So, basically, you been walkin' around this big-ass country every single day. For weeks. Just walkin', like, full-time.' I'm crushed. Exercise, my nemesis. Turns out it really works. I've practically been in training all this time without knowing it. My metabolism must be powering through the roof. Tex looks at my abdomen and snickers. 'Y'all about to go sit on your ass again for a while, huh?' I nod. 'I'd lay offa the Popeye's when you get home, hon.' She giggles and lies back down on the two seats across from me.

Tex and I have cabin fever. We have our heads opposite each other on the arm rest, our sneakered feet up on our own windows. She has a brightly coloured blanket she bought while she had dysentery on a mission in Mexico. I have my yellow striped sheet and the trusty pillow. We have bad eyebrow re-growth, dull and spotty bus-skin, freezing cold noses and we loll unattractively in a food coma. We are having some fun out of our misery though, behaving like we are bundled up at a frozen ski lodge and chatting like kids at camp. The bus goes on and on, taking hours to travel the increasingly tiny distance between me and Disney World. Three little girls up the front are performing spelling bees out of their names and, occasionally, those of their dogs, cats, grandmas and teachers. To no one in particular, their mother says, 'Mommy's so tired of being on the bus.'

'I'm in Mommy's club,' I pipe up, and there is a chorus of agreement. We doze.

At the back of the bus, two big black guys are talking gangsta crap and posturing. Every few seconds one of them says, 'Know what I'm sayin'?' and waves his arms around all Snoop Dogg-edy. This stream of BS has infiltrated our light sleep for some time now, incorporating itself into uncomfortable dreams, before waking us completely. From my hidden place of bunked-down safety, I shush them loudly. I am going home. I don't care anymore. Tex giggles nervously. 'They were talkin' about jay-al!' she whispers, and my skinny chest swells. She thought I was a badass, I could tell. 'I sure hope I don't have to sit next to someone scary like that on mah way home,' Tex says. 'Texas is just so far away, I have to go overnight all the time . . .' She sounds worried. I sigh heavily, propping myself up on a shaky elbow. 'Look,' I say, 'you gotta know the tricks, girl,' and proceed to hand down knowledge from on high. 'Twitch,' I say. 'Scratch. Mess up your hair and then drag it over your face. When pretending to be asleep, do not close your eyes peacefully, open your mouth wide and make phlegmy, sucking noises,' I demonstrate, and she follows my lead. 'Good work,' I tell her. 'Moving along. Food-wrappers: these are your friends. *Never* throw them away. Combined with empty chip bags and water bottles, your reeking burger wrapper will be the centrepiece in your on-seat collection of filth. Get these items out and lay them around before each stop. What we're aiming for is a look that says to the new passenger, 'Hello, I've been here for a week. I am filthy and now so is this seat.' Establish squatters rights early in the game.'

I go through a list that lasts a considerable amount of time, until both of us have long stopped giggling, sobered by the depth of my observations. 'This sure is a crazy way to travel,' Tex says finally. 'I hope you don't think we're all like this,' she flutters a hand around our can of nutters, 'in the States. Everyone's real different in this country, y'know? These people are just really down on their luck. It's beautiful here too. There's lots of everything, not just Greyhound, y'know?' I assure her that I do know. Because now I do.

We drive through a town called Ocala, a name that reminds me of Ogallala, Nebraska, and recalling that place feels like last year. I think about what I've seen of America while riding Greyhound. Mountains and deserts, squalid filth and civic pride, grass and rubble. Sunflowers growing riot in old tin mines. Small, rainbow-coloured children in Union Square Park; children with running noses and gummy eyes; pregnant women eating fois gras in sparkling sun by depthless lakes; pregnant women wearing tie-dye, spinning in slow circles in Red Rocks; pregnant women with broken bones and flat, hard eyes; pregnant women who can't read; a pregnant woman on her way to Tanzania to teach other women to read. Mexican, Indian, Asian, Russian, Irish, Czech, British, Dutch, Nigerian, Nepalese, Iranian and Somali people, and on and on and on, living everywhere, standing on every corner, buying, fighting, loving, eating, walking. And riding the bus. On and off and on and off in LA, Denver, San Fran, New York, New Haven, New England, New Mexico, always riding the bus with me.

I'm nearly home. I've lost my hair, my body, and most of my clothes and possessions along the way. Secrets are being revealed to me, riddles are unravelling. My back brain has finally caught up with the scatter of my consciousness and hidden kernels are blooming. Monstro. The name of Pinocchio's whale, the beast that carried him dumbly to redemption, carried him onwards to life as a real boy. The driver was right. There is no story without the whale, but no one really concentrates on how they are travelling, only where they started and how they hope to arrive. I wonder how many more years of asking that question it will be before someone answers him 'Monstro', and if the moment comes, I wonder what he'll ask next. Hurtling through this giant country on never-ending roads, I have begun to understand what a tiny speck on earth I am, just one amongst so many people moving forward in our little tin contraptions, so many stories rushing on into the next town, a new city, the future. It has made me feel insignificant in the best possible way, reminding me how small our individual footprint on the world actually is, reducing all my problems and concerns to those of a very immediate nature. It's forced me to relax at a deep and fundamental level. But it's also lit a small fire inside me. I have seen the evidence of so many other people's lives, dreams and desires. So many of us on and off the bus, into mountain towns or gleaming cities, desert slums and barren suburbs. I finally understand just how many opportunities lie before me and I've woken up so hungry for it all, so anxious not to take for granted the ways I've been lucky in comparison to most of my fellow Greyhound riders.

The rain is coming in driving sheets as we pull into Leesburg, into a petrol station doubling as a bus stop. A fat girl is struggling up the stairs, smiling with tombstone teeth and hefting a massive great teddy bear. She scopes the bus and heads straight for me. The ideal seatmate. 'Lord send us strength!' Tex breathes, 'incoming.' I give the giant girl the window seat to avoid asphyxiation and she thanks me. 'Now I can see Leesburg by the bus!' she says. 'I never seen it by the bus before.' She turns slightly and knocks me to the ground with her same-size teddy bear.

'Whoa,' I say, 'does he have a ticket?'

'Him?' she says, clutching it grimly. 'Nope. Will they make me buy one? I don't have no more money, all I got is five bucks . . .'

'No,' I say, 'sorry, it's okay. Does he have a name?'

'Nope,' she says, looking at him tenderly, 'he doan got no ticket and no name either. Just Bear, I guess. Hey!' she says, pointing down some little street, 'my dad used to work there!'

I nod, closing my eyes. My kindness has expired. 'My dad,' she continues, 'is one of them people which moves around a lot. Right now he sells bait. For fishin'? And my mom, she's gonna be grill manager at McDonald's. But she's gotta wait till summer's over and the right-now grill manager goes back to high school.' I nod again. She starts to cry. 'I miss my mom already,' she blubbers, and I groan, but Tex is moved to sympathetic eye-watering. 'What's your name, hon?' she asks, even though I'm shooting her looks of the what-did-we-just-talk-about variety.

Her name is Dawn and she's travelling on to Minnesota from the next big stop. She met this guy on the Internet and they've been 'phone datin'' for six months now. As soon as she finished tenth grade she got a job stuffing envelopes to pay for her Greyhound ticket to the other side of the country, where he's asked her to come and live with him. Her Momma has talked to him and made him send a photocopy of his driver's licence in the mail. Good thinking, mum. 'Y'all know what he looks like, right?' says Tex.

'Uh huh,' says Dawn. 'He had a big operation on his mouth, but he's still real cute. He sent me three pictures.'

'And did you,' Tex asks, delicately, 'send him a picture of you, hon?'

'Uh huh. He's seen a picture from when I was in choir.'

'When was that?' we ask together.

'When I was eleven, no, um, twaulv. But it kinda looks like me still. I don't know no one with a camera now. My teacher took the choir one.'

Tex and I are horrified. 'I'm real excited,' says Dawn, 'but I'm scared too. If he don't like me off the phone, I ain't got a return ticket. And I only have five bucks, but Dwayne's gonna pay my way for a time when I get there. And I still don't have a coat. Did you know it snows in Minnesota?' she says wonderingly.

I snap to attention. 'Dawn,' I say, 'do you know how far away it is?'

'Uh huh,' she says, 'gonna take about four days on the bus.'

'Did you bring any food?' I ask. She pulls out a plastic bag for us to inspect. One packet of Hostess cakes, one of Twinkies.

There's enough for one meal, if a meal can be had from processed sponge-cake. She offers us a cake and unwraps the other one. 'Hon,' says Tex, 'you're gonna get real hungry, you pace out those cakes now.'

'It's okay,' Dawn says through a mouthful of fake cream, 'I didn't eat for two weeks once. Just because I didn't want to anymore.' She is incredibly heavy, poor girl, and I very much doubt this. How will Dawn eat across the US on five bucks? She is appallingly naive. My hours in all the terminals around America have paid off for something. On a piece of paper I write out the Greyhound number and a set of instructions. All the bus stations have posters advertising a charity service for teenage runaways, with a 'When you're ready to go home, we'll get you there' kind of message.

'Dawn,' I tell her, 'if things don't work out with Dwayne, you call that number and just tell those people your story like you told us. They'll send you right back to your mum and dad. For free.'

'For free?' she gasps.

'Yep.'

Orlando is fast approaching, and each of us is leaving the bus – Tex and Dawn for new buses and me for good. We relieve Dawn of her fiver and her ticket, which have so far been clutched in one big pale hand, and tuck them into a little vinyl and velcro wallet that Tex got as a freebie about three hours ago with a women's magazine, along with the Greyhound number. We each add ten bucks of our own and Dawn looks like all her Christmases have come at once. 'Thank you, guys,' she whispers. 'You're the best friends I ever had. Bear too.' Tex and I get teary then, Tex looking at the ceiling and waving her hand quickly at the corners of her eyes. The bus wheezes in and Tex clutches me in a brief stinky hug. 'Forget what I said,' she says as she jumps off. 'Even Greyhound can be a beautiful place! God bless, hon!' and she's gone.

I pack up my camp slowly, gathering all my bits and pieces. I can throw the wrappers and chicken buckets away now. I'm pretty sure no one's going to steal my seat in the Jeep Cherokee. Out the window I can see the top of Dad's head, and his inimitable moustache. I grin to the bottom of my toes. Suddenly I'm off the bus and strangled in a big hug, chattering at top pitch while Dad tells me I'm so skinny and wipes a few stray Dad-tears away. 'And, Dad,' I tell him, 'so this girl, Dawn, she was going to live in Minnesota with this guy she only knew from the net? And she's, well, only sixteen, and really naive, and I met this other girl, and we . . . we ate at Popeye's together, and hung out, and . . . and stuff.'

My Greyhound life has somehow lost its meaning in the transition between the bus and leather seats of Dad's car. My faithful pillow and sheet, tossed in the back without a second glance, will never be resurrected. They are stripped of their importance forever. It is a kind of betrayal and I feel it, even now, even through my excitement. The Greyhound girl is dead. My hair will grow, I will fatten up and these jeans will never, ever be worn again. It's over.

But of course, there's still Disney World. The Happiest Place On Earth™.

Chapter 21

The Happiest Place on Earth™

I blame Saturday morning television. I don't know if it's a global phenomenon or not, but I do know that nothing will stop the Australian under-ten set from getting into Mum and Dad's room at 6 am on the weekend demanding permission to call a 1-800 number for the chance to win a 'Disney Family Vacation!'. The glowing Grail of kid's TV prize packages, I grew up thinking of Disneyland (Anaheim, California) and Disney World (Orlando, Florida) as little suburbs of heaven existing on earth. Places where everything you wish to be possible is made possible, where fairies might in fact be found and every sweet concoction you wish to ingest is available with a smile. Kind of like Amsterdam, but for kids.

In our current era of progression and tolerance, children are probably the last group of humans it's still perfectly acceptable to admit a dislike for or deny entry to. Fancy hotels, fancy swimming pools, fancy restaurants, fancy clubs, most movies, romantic bed and breakfasts, tour groups – and it's not just the places that directly exclude them either. How many times do we tell children 'Shh! This *isn't* a place for kids,' meaning 'Just try to be less like what you are, and then disappear for a bit'? But Disneyland, Disneyland hangs on the horizon, whispered down the chain-gang that somewhere is a place for us, somewhere, the crazy are-you-getting-enough-calcium adults have to relinquish their powers and caramel popcorn becomes a legitimate food group.

Disney World is the mega-realisation of that dream. Beyond a theme park, it has become a self-contained city, with its own power supply (complete with a giant metal transformer in the shape of Mickey-ears), zip code and police force. It has over 22 hotels servicing four huge 'worlds' – Magic Kingdom, Animal Kingdom, Epcot Center, and Disney-MGM Studios – as well as hundreds of shops, restaurants, a metro-transport service, a couple of lakes and huge entertainment complexes. My guide-book tells me that it's twice as big as Manhattan, employs over 20,000 people and attracts 20 million visitors a year, which is the population of Australia. It's astounding.

I imagine Disney World to be a quintessentially American experience. After all, only American culture would allow, encourage and facilitate dreams and mythmaking on this grand a scale. Look at Hollywood. The rest of the world? We either don't try hard enough or care as much as we should about the need for plastic castles in the sky and grown-ups dressed as Cinderella. We don't think it's necessary that for all the people who are never going to make it to Africa? Hey, it might be fun to just fake it for a few square metres out in Lake Buena Vista, with a couple of giraffes to wander outside your Animal Kingdom hotel window. We need to know why this is important, but America just asks, why not? Why not indeed, I say, as the huge gates swing open and I am admitted into a magical, wondrous realm of fakery.

It is already dark when we roll up to Disney's Wilderness Lodge, seemingly constructed from huge tree-trunks (of the *giantus concretus falsii* family) and decorated with a vague Rocky Mountains theme. It's surprisingly tasteful for a theme-park resort and quite authentic-looking. At over $200 a night, it would want to be. Without wasting time investigating the rooms, we park the car in something like Eagle-Moose p9##13, and hop a Disney transit shuttle 'downtown'.

Having missed out on the real thing in New Orleans, I'm thrilled to discover a House of Blues club and restaurant (in America, if it's good there's just one question left: can we franchise that?) where I'm promptly treated to the best and most expensive jambalaya I've ever had. I also order the étouffée and smoked salmon carpaccio, after inhaling my beer in one gulp. Dad, Caroline and the other diners are casual and laughing, ordering big and enjoying the tunes in this dark and ambient joint. I am so astonishingly aware of the ease, the comfort, the cleanliness of this place, the sheer normality of the interactions. I'm sitting stiff-backed, eyes darting, eating quickly. I look like an ex-con. After the second beer, when I can physically feel myself start to unwind, I know for certain that I have been slumming it too long to get an accurate picture of life in these 50 states. There are thousands of people from all walks of life at Disney World, and they're all living very differently from my fellow Greyhound passengers. I feel so lucky to be here, safe in this other reality, that it overwhelms me. I make Dad order more beer.

When I wake the next morning, my heart is still full. I rush to the balcony of my room to find that it overlooks the serenity of a pine-filled Colorado mountain retreat, in what I know to be reclaimed Florida swampland. A rushing waterfall tumbles to an icy-looking pond, surrounded by boulders and spruce trees. Ha ha! What tomfoolery is this? I'm so excited that I begin to sing along with Jiminy Cricket on the TV, flapping one thonged foot and letting everyone know exactly what happens when you wish upon a star. There's something else rattling around in my head, like the tail end of a thought I can't shake. Sticking my head out into the corridor I realise that I'm not dreaming – 'Zippity Doo Dah' is indeed being pumped everywhere from invisible sources, and this is good news for my mental health self-check. It is also playing in a loop on the in-room entertainment, which, like a kind of kiddy-Vegas, is set up to tell us how best to spend our time and money outside of the room. With Dad and Caroline in tow, I educate myself on the use of the 'smart-pass' accelerated ride-queuing system, before running off to find breakfast.

Outside as inside, everything in Disney World is controlled; the noise, temperature, smiles, scenery and mood. A light, atmospheric sheen is visible around us, and I think it could be molecular Prozac. Mickey is everywhere here, king of this nation, benevolent dictator, his face and ears adorning everything. In the rest of the country, I've found that there isn't much people feel can't be improved by adding an American flag. In here, it's Mickey's head.

Arriving at the entry gates, the false impression that entry to all four Disney theme parks can be had for $52 each is rudely shattered when we are asked to select a specific kingdom or hand over $600 for the three of us. As the youngest person in the party and honorary child, I get picking rights and choose the Magic Kingdom, the traditional, original park with all the things I loved at Disneyland as a kid: Space Mountain, Pirates of the Caribbean, Big Thunder Railroad and the magical parade.

Caroline hasn't yet warmed to the idea that we are in Disney World by choice and I think my selection makes it worse. An hour later, we are sitting in the Tiki Room singing 'In theee Tiki *tiki tiki tiki tiki* Rooom,' with a bunch of six-year-olds and some stuffed mechanical birds (in my defence, she does own a parrot) and I catch a distinct eye-roll. Outside, a kid tugs on his mother's jeans, 'Mo-om, can we go and buy some more stuff now?'

'What stuff, honey?'

'Just more stuff!' Caroline lifts her brow. 'This is the Magic Kingdom, Caz,' I tell her, grabbing an elbow. '*Anything* could happen. Look! What's that over there! It's Snow White!' We rush over – okay, I rush over – to where the Disney parade has just started. Snow White herself is standing beside her handsome, kiss-me-quick prince in a big glass bubble aboard an ornate float. Her smile is magic and so is Cinderella's, who laughs and waves, dainty as a fairy princess beside her own prince. These girls are immaculate, divine, utterly convincing and the tiny pixie in me waves back to them. 'Over here!' I call. 'I've read all your Golden Books! Seen every film! I have your dolls,' I cry. 'Over here! Hi! It's me!' I forget my dodgy Santa-Fe hair and grown-up self, and give myself over to wide-eyed worship. Real! Princesses! Here! My heart thumps as the parade continues underneath the delicate spires of the Magic Kingdom Castle.

Call me a sentimental, gullible, buy-anything twit, but I love all this and just want more. I suppose I never grew out of the longing for a place where things are done purely for fun. I just love the attempt. That's why I like Vegas too. Of course it's fake, but that's the *point*. After all, you wouldn't go to a fancy dress party and say, 'Oh my God, you are so not Cleopatra. I can see you under there, don't be ridiculous,' and that's what Disney is: one massive fancy-dress parade. If you don't like fancy dress then bugger off, you'll hate it. Otherwise, please smile, hold on tight, suspend disbelief and enjoy the ride. I try explaining this to Caroline, who so far, as the only American on our sojourn, is frankly embarrassed that I should be lauding Disney World as a cultural high point of her country.

After a jaw-dropping show at Disney's purpose-built Cirque du Soleil arena, we dine on exquisite sushi at Wolfgang Puck's, another high-end restaurant-turned-chain, and enjoy cocktails (grown-up magic) at Jimmy Buffet's Margaritaville. The casual wealth, the effervescent smiles, the huge meals, the abundance of entertainment; Disney World is a very American experience all right. But typically American? Quintessentially American? I'm embarrassed to have thought that. This the America of Saturday morning telly, after all. The sanitised America of sitcoms and big-toothed infomercials, of the Globo-cop movies and starlet-filled press we get at home.

Unlike the controlled America of the Disney Corporation, of canned laughter and white people and a commitment to predict-ability, the America I've been wandering through is a bawdy house of surprises. My America, the America I've been sitting next to and looking out at and sleeping under for the last 45 days, bears no resemblance to this watered-down, artificially sweetened America of sameness. My America is a hog-wild, untamed, sprawling masterpiece of nature and construct, and her truth, however elusive, will always be stranger than her fiction. My America is the definition of 'Amusement Park' and 'Wonderland', and poor old Disney suffers from the comparison. I'm glad I had the chance to make it.

In the morning, we drive back across the state of Florida; out from the middle and down to the south-west corner kissed by the Gulf of Mexico. From the climate-controlled comfort of the Dad-mobile, we listen to erudite discussion on America's excellent

National Public Radio service, stopping only for a leisurely breakfast, where we drink fresh Florida orange juice with our buttermilk pancakes, or to buy tropical fruit from roadside stands. He has made a nice life here, my dad. When we cross back over the long Sanibel causeway, pelicans are flying at eye-level over the Caribbean-coloured water, which gives way to white sand and luxurious palm fronds. Sanibel looks glorious and my heart leaps unexpectedly to be back.

In three short days I'll be home in Oz; home to my friends, the rest of my family and my Boy, after nine long months away. Nine months. 'What do you want me to get you?' the Boy has asked. 'Laksa soups? Turkish bread? Vegemite scrolls? Passion-fruit pav?' But as quickly as I'm making lists of all the Aussie treats I've longed for, I'm nervously stockpiling all the new favourites I'll have to take back with me. After months of being a winner, I'm about to lose again, and it's not just America I'll lose, either. In a strange way, I can see that my Australian self will fade a little as well. I am always 'the Australian' here, always introduced and remembered as part of my country, that one nation, under the Sun, a very long way from Here. I have never felt my nationality more than I do in the USA, and I've never been more thoroughly Australian than when I'm not there.

An accented workmate of mine once rolled his eyes when I described him as South African. 'Don't worry,' he said, 'everyone does it. I've had an Australian passport for fifteen ficking years, but I won't stop being South African unless I have the good fortune to be in some international airline disaster and get counted among the Australian dead.' In America, I get to be Australian every day. It's like a grand costume. Each trip to the supermarket here, each public holiday and social event; all are adventures into the jungle of a new culture, with surprising pitfalls and rewards, and the potential for occasional hilarity between my hosts and me.

Except they're not just my hosts anymore. I am now a legal, permanent resident of the United States of America. In the sweating leather of my wallet there lives a Florida State Driver's Licence, a Social Security number, a Bank of the Islands debit card, a Bank of America credit card and a Green Card bearing my name and image. Oh, and a tipping chart too, on account of gratuity and my previously-mentioned mathematical skills. I pull these items out, stack them together and put my American alias into the little white envelope my 'Welcome!' letter arrived in, which I place inside an empty drawer. For the rest of my life, every calendar year, I must return to this envelope unless I want to lose this place.

It's very quiet now, off the bus. Sitting on the edge of my big white bed, the Florida dusk lazing tendrils of light through the windows, I contemplate the lightened wallet. Only the Australian plastic remains. After 17,000 kilometres, I don't know how much closer I am to understanding my prize. After so many months and oceans away from the people and places in my heart's neighbourhood, I don't know when I'll be back here, either, but somewhere deep down I'm beginning to suspect that I will be. I'm not sure if I've found something to say yes to, but I think there might just be too much out there for me to say no to. My next ticket though, is for home.

Chapter 22

Home is where they have to let you in

I've always had great empathy for Bilbo Baggins. After all, we are both small creatures, fond of tea and snacks, and I must say that after Santa Fe I am really warming to the idea of living under an earthen hill. Reckless adventuring makes us panicky and comically fearless in turns and, like Mr Baggins, I also agree that it's a dangerous business, stepping out your front door, but not just because the road may sweep you off somewhere unexpected. Sometimes I think the world might actually shift sideways behind you, and if you get too far away before you turn back, your home might not be where you thought you left it.

Mine is now distinctly missing.

This sudden surety is exacerbated by the fact that I've just woken up next to a strange man in an equally strange hotel room. The man is the Boy, of course (the Greyhound has taught me how many ways loose morals can get you into trouble), but he is also not the Boy I remember. Still, it is entirely possible that waking up with any boy after nine months of solitude and 24 hours of jet lag would be unusual. They are very large and rather wild-looking.

Scrabbling for the remote control, I am further dismayed by the desperate slowness of Australian television. The ads seem to last for eight minutes apiece and I can't tell if people are talking or having a Valium and a good lie-down. SBS is throwing up a test screen, and with four and a half stations to flick through, this primitive black box makes me feel like I've returned home to Kazakhstan by mistake. 'Hey,' I say, suddenly ecstatic at the remembrance of real bacon and coffee, 'let's get breakfast!'

Outside, my beloved Sydney is cold and grey and distinctly unwelcoming. In shops and restaurants the prices seem ridiculous, the portion sizes tiny, and my cheerful greetings, questions and praise are met with bemused indifference. I can hear my own words ringing in my ears and I know that something's wrong with them. They're out of place, but I can't override the syrup now pouring naturally from my mouth. The Boy has to physically restrain me from tipping everyone an automatic 20 per cent. 'Thanks,' I beam reflexively at a cashier, 'have a great weekend!' She gives me a smile reserved for drunks. 'Wow,' the Boy says as we leave, 'was I like you when we got back from New York?' What does he mean? Americans find me quiet and sarcastic. Don't they? Aren't I? A knot is slowly twisting in my stomach and I spend the rest of the month searching high and low for evidence of my sunny, friendly Sydney.

The seasons change and so does my mood. I secure a good job that lets the muscles in my napkin-folding arm atrophy and my American life begins to recede. I drop 'a whole bunch of' as a collective and begin to delight in the comforts of home. My city's streets are wide and clean and barely covered with people. Asian spices tickle my nose and an ocean surrounds me on all sides. Down by the harbour the air is sharp and clear, and the water is squid ink covered by dark blue and silver peaks. People are slender and pedestrian, and instantly, faultlessly, effortlessly familiar.

I share hangovers with my brother as we stroll Glebe markets. I submit cheerfully to hour-long teasing from the friends close and dear enough to remember the horror of past boyfriends and formal dresses. During amateur weeknight pedicures we discuss celebrity outfits, economics, Islam, white chocolate and our secret dreams. I travel to Melbourne to enjoy six-latte breakfasts with

Mum and watch Friday Night Crime on the ABC. I spend week-ends playing backyard chasings with the Boy and his dog at his family home, while his Mum cooks lamb roasts and his sisters make tea. Hot tea. I am home and it is beautiful. It should be enough.

But it's very hard to get rid of an extra country once someone has given it to you. Oh, you can push it out of the living room, stuff it into the hall cupboard and lean back against the door, but even though you can't see it, you know it's there. After a few months something will remind you of it and you'll smile – a smell perhaps, a picture, or (more likely) devilishly indulgent television and a packet of Doritos – and you'll go back to the cupboard for a quick peek. Before you know it, it's out again and you'll itch to use and enjoy it until it begins to take up too much room and then you'll have to figure out how to pack it away. But you can never throw it out. It would be a mistake to think that, despite what you might have promised yourself when it arrived.

I have come to see the Green Card as a wild card, a party favour from the gods (those travel gods, most likely) thrown into my life at precisely the junction where it would be the most bewildering of gifts. It multiplied my options to a seemingly infinite degree just at the time when those options were already feeling like excess baggage. But the Greyhound made me stronger. I gots rights. I won't give up my prize unless I am forced to vacate the seat. My decisions are getting easier. Australia can never be taken away from me. Barring catastrophic action, my passport is safe. Sure, America is mine too, but she is my *discretionary* country; my lover not my mother. As much as I might come to love my American life and its possibilities, it will always be a cautious love.

My love for the Boy is much simpler. I want to be where he is and until we find a way for him to share my prize, my Green Card is not worth nearly as much as it purports to be. The Boy is also a wandering Hobbit at heart and it upsets him that I might be giving up on any American adventures on his account. Having accepted that I don't want to be somewhere he can't live, he asks me where I'd go if he was hit by a bus (or, more likely, if he's choked into the afterlife by a Babybell cheese). I used to admit to myself that if he weren't in the equation I would probably move. Head off to the great unknown with my magic ticket. I would pack my bag and head for Alaska, Puerto Rico or Hawaii.

But the problem with the unknown is its stubborn disposition to becoming the *known* in a very short period of time. As soon as that inevitable transformation occurred, I can see myself missing Oz badly. Missing the wonderful surety of living where I fit perfectly just by being myself. I would miss my family, my old friends and our common cultural background. I would miss the beauty of my country, its people, its animals, its humour. I would miss it all like oxygen. Then I would return home and begin to get sick of it again, sick of the predictability and numbing comfort, and I'd move myself back to the chaos and novelty of the USA. And then back again.

Annoyed at myself for harbouring such an extreme case of grass-is-greener, I finally just accept that I will do this until my hand is forced and my documents are snatched up. On a smelly bus through the Carolinas, I was once counselled not to give myself over to confusion, but having done it, I feel great. Who knows what will happen in a year? In six? I thought I had too many options once, thought my choices were crippling. Greyhound cured me of that. It showed me how lucky I am and how ungrateful I have been. In one short life there can never be too many choices. I will do what I can to hold on to America.

After two years, the decision about what to do with my life post-Green Card win has evolved quietly to become my life; small decisions made on a daily basis that have little to do with what career I'll choose, when I'll have children, who I'll have them with, where I'll raise them and whether I might just prefer a brace of kittens instead, but I can see now that simply putting one foot in front of the other will determine my journey's end regardless.

Much and little has changed since the bus. As Virginia predicted, I am still moving forward into the future at a pace that races and slows and plays tricks on me, with stretches of the unremarkable punctuated by short bursts of wild beauty and stressful activity. The seat isn't always comfortable by any means, but it really beats the only other option, which is waiting at the purgatory of Greyhound stations as the buses drive away, dithering over which bus might be better. Sure, I can go ahead and put a bold pin on Truth or Consequences, but that doesn't mean I'm really headed there. Life can take me to Albuquerque if it wants to, and that will be determined by where I put my bag down after a few minutes of idle thought just as much as by the map and mission statement I've drawn up for myself in my pocket.

Now it's Green Card time again and so I've come back once more through the customs line that says 'US Citizens' with the small cardboard addition reading '& Residents'. Legal Aliens. My own personal – vaguely extraterrestrial – minority group. In a few weeks' time the Boy will arrive to join me on holiday, so I have another big map out on the floor now, posted with ambitious plans for the rediscovery of Santa Fe and a gluttonous detour to Las Vegas, and littered with a sheaf of literature from all the big national parks. I have a travelling vehicle at last, as well as instructions on how to manually re-gas a broken air conditioner.

'Are you sure we don't want to get Greyhound passes instead?' the Boy asks long-distance. 'This crazy girl I used to know said they were really good value.' I silently minus one donut from the tray of Krispy Kremes I've promised him. This year, the Boy is also entering the Green Card lottery. He tells me he still dreams of himself as that wide-eyed Aussie boy in the shining canyons of New York and, after all, you never know your luck in the big city.

My own American dreams are still with me. I have yet to move into that loft apartment or create my fortune in cookie making, but I am thinking of writing *Chicken Soup for the Greyhound Soul* and adding it to the series. I wonder if they'd go for that. I'm working on the pitch right now. After all, I'll tell them – and quite sincerely, too – there's not much you can't learn from 45 days on a big ugly bus, coast to coast and counterclockwise.

Acknowledgements

Confession – I am a serial peruser of acknowledgements. Sometimes I read them first, even if they appear at the end of the book. Especially long thank-yous are often flicked to several times during the course of my reading. I like the names. I check for relatives. Make sure their mum gets a mention; love it when there's a Mr. Whiskers or Pingo the ferret. Ferrets must be a great help. I should get one.

In memoirs it's more fun. I enjoy sleuthing for the real identities of 'Jimbo', the jerk, or 'Tamsin', the closet alcoholic. In most novels I have no real excuse. I don't know why I do it. It's not even that interesting. Some people (who are these people?) seem to get away with 'For Patty'. Did no one fix their hard drive at 2 am? Or remind them that Micronesia is not a country for the purposes of a punch line? Are they self-published perhaps, or else in the middle of familial trauma?

Too long is also a problem, as is alphabetical – spare me alphabetical, I only scan them then. Fergus Williams might have been there through the hard times, but no one gets much past Judy Abbey, even if she is only a hafta-thank, the one who kept Kinkos open for an extra five minutes. It's not fair. It's not weighty enough, the alphabetical thank you.

Mine will start at the top. Mum and Dad. Lynneeta and John.

The money, the hours, the tears, the sacrifice. And that was just kindergarten. This book is for them. All books will be for them. The Boy. There is no story without him. He is exceptional in every way, I wish the world could meet him. Okay, it's for him too. For Simon Darmody and Renee Thompson, who keep me sane and are still the funniest people I know. For Special Agent Fran Moore, my lovely friend and fairy godmother, without whom my books would be exercise books, tucked alone in a drawer. For Fiona Henderson, Kim Swivel and Jessica Dettmann; kind, clever, brilliant as microchips, if only they could run the world.

For Caroline Hoisington, Peter Tremewen, and the Buchanan family, whose support is boundless and arrives in delightful ways when it is most needed. For all my friends in America who have opened their hearts and homes to me over the years; Erin Whitlock, Merideth Finn, Ann Phillippe, Nick Hodgdon, Mike Riches, Sara Gilliland, Tom Mullinix, Kevin and Brian Cogbill, Pam and Fred Brodersen, Sharon Michie, Cinnette Wilder and Kim Gremoud.

For my dear friends Kaila Mikkelsen, Sian David and Andrew Edwards, who helped me discover America, Greyhound, Southern cooking, and my happy-self. For Michelle Chambers, Zoe Benjamin, Amber Byrnes and Natalie Laharnar, who helped me more than they know. This book is also for the Darmodys, Watersons, and Sandalciyans who assisted through their many kindnesses. A special thank-you to everyone at the New South Wales Fire Brigades (NSWFB) for reminding me just how great it is to be Australian.

God, this was so fun, I'm going to write another one.